Governing
The American
States

Governing The American States

A Handbook for New Governors

National Governors' Association
Center for Policy Research
Hall of the States   Washington, D.C.

Andrew S. Thomas Memorial Library
MORRIS HARVEY COLLEGE, CHARLESTON, W. VA.
99823

353.91
N213g

The National Governors' Association, founded in 1908 as the National Governors' Conference, is the instrument through which the Governors of the fifty states and the Commonwealth of Puerto Rico, the Virgin Islands, Guam, American Samoa, and the Northern Mariana Islands collectively influence the development and implementation of national policy and apply creative leadership to state problems. The Association works closely with the Administration and the Congress on state-federal policy issues from its offices in the Hall of the States in Washington, D.C. Through its Center for Policy Research, the Association also serves as a vehicle for sharing knowledge of innovative programs among the states and provides technical assistance to Governors on a wide range of issues.

The development of the material in this publication was made possible in part with the assistance of grants from the U.S. Civil Service Commission under the Intergovernmental Personnel Act (PL 91-648), the Defense Civil Preparedness Agency, and the National Science Foundation (ISP-78-15531 and 78-25325). Any opinions, findings, conclusions or recommendations expressed herein are those of the authors and do not necessarily reflect the views of these agencies.

November 1978

Library of Congress Catalog Card No. 78-65728

© 1978 by the National Governors' Association, Washington, D.C. Permission to quote from or reproduce materials in this publication is granted when due acknowledgement is made.

Printed in the United States of America

Contents

Foreword xi

Acknowledgements xiii

1. The Experience of Being Governor 1
    Problems of the Office 4
        Working with the Legislature 5
        Demands on Time 5
        Interference with Family Life and Invasion of Privacy 6
        Tough Decisions 6
        Working with the Federal Government 7
        Intramural Government Squabbles 7
        Building and Keeping Staff 8
        Working with the Press 8
        Day-to-Day Management of State Government 8
        Other Problems 9
        Least Difficult Tasks 9
    A Day in the Life of a Governor 10
    What Goes on Around the Governor 18

2. An Overview of Transition 21
    The Importance of a Smooth Transition 24
        Benefits of a Good Transition 24
        Contributors to a Smooth Transition 25
    Financing the Transition 26
    Sources of Transition Assistance 28
    Improving the Next Transition 29
    Other Aspects of Transition 30

3. Organizing the New Governor's Office 31
    Decisions on Major Office Functions 34
    The Governor's Executive Assistant 35

      Should There Be an Executive Assistant?   36
      What Executive Assistants Do   37
      Executive Assistant's Influence   38
  The Press Secretary   39
      Selecting the Press Secretary   39
      Press Secretary or Communications Director?   39
      The Governor and His Press Secretary   39
      Functions of the Press Office   41
      Size of the Press Office   41
  The Governor's Political Advisor   42
  The Legislative Assistant   43
  The Governor's Personal Secretary   45
  The Scheduling Assistant   45
  The Governor's Legal Advisor   46
  State-Federal Relations Coordinator   47
  Special Assistant for Appointments   48
  Assistant for Liaison with State Agencies   48
      Arguments for Agency Liaison Assistants   49
      Arguments against Agency Liaison Assistants   49
  Staff for Handling Public Contacts   50
  Staff for Contact with Special Groups   51
  Perspective Keeper   52
  State Emergency Management Coordinator   52
  Office Manager   53
  Directors of Outlying Offices   54
  Clerical Support   54
  Special Project Personnel   54

4. Staff Support for the Governor   57
  The Immediate Office   59
      The Need for Early Staff Work   59
      Qualities of a Good Staff Member   60
      Sources of Potential Staff Members   62
  The "Extended" Office of the Governor   66
      Competence in Central Staff Agencies   66
      Finding Competence in Existing Staffs   68
      Organizing Staff Support Agencies   68

5. Selecting the Cabinet and Other State Officials   69
  Categories of Appointments   71
  Making Key Appointments   72
      Appointment and Resignation Procedures   74
      Finding the Bad Apple   75
  Where to Find Good Appointees   75
      Incumbents   76
      State Senators and Representatives   77
      Campaign Staff   77
      The Federal Government   77
      Recruiting Other Candidates   77
  Compensation   78
  Agency Head Independence   79

      The Governor's Ground Rules   79
          Deputies and Others in Agencies   81
  The Patronage Decision   82
      "Exempt" Positions   82
      What Patrons?   83
      Is Patronage Obsolete?   84

6. Policy Development   85
  Choosing a Leadership Role   88
      Governors as Managers   88
      Staff Support for the Policy Process   89
  Broad-Scale Planning Activities   90
      Futures Projects   90
      Goal Processes   91
      Comprehensive Plans   91
      Development Plans   91
      Land Use   92
  Planning State Government Activities   92
      State Investment Planning   93
      Budget Planning   93
      Program Evaluation   93
  Policy in the Budget Process   94
  Management by Objectives   95
  Formal Policy Statements   95

7. An Approach to Management   97
  Cabinet Government   100
  The Governor and His Staff   100
  Staff-Line Relationships   101
      Staff, Line and Support Functions   101
      A Management Model for Line Relationships   103
      Staff Roles in Management   104
      Interaction of Staff and Line Agencies   105
      Avoiding Staff-Line Conflicts   106
  Day-to-Day Management   111
      The In-Box   112
      Files and Records   113
  Emergency Preparedness   115
  Survival in the Sunshine   117

8. The Governor's Schedule   119
  Allocation of Time   121
  The Scheduling Activity   122
      Authority to Commit Time   122
      Dealing with Scheduling Requests   124
      Meetings with Staff Members and Agency Heads   125
      Scheduling Ground Rules   126
      Active and Passive Scheduling   128
      Breaking Scheduled Appointments   128

9. Dealing with the Mail and Public Contacts   129

　　　　Handling the Mail　　132
　　　　　　Types of Mail and Routing　　132
　　　　　　Acknowledgements　　134
　　　　　　Response Times　　135
　　　　　　Review Procedures　　135
　　　　　　Guarding the Governor's Signature　　136
　　　　　　The Mail Problem during Transition　　137
　　　　Phone Contact Procedure　　137
　　　　Conserving Time　　138
　　　　Proclamations and Endorsements　　139

10. **Dealing with the Press and Media**　　141
　　　　An Approach to Media Relations　　143
　　　　　　Attitude Toward the Press　　144
　　　　　　Press Access to the Governor　　145
　　　　　　Reaching Local Media　　146
　　　　The Press Secretary: Advocate and Advisor　　147
　　　　　　Access to the Governor　　148
　　　　　　Trying to Serve Two Masters　　148

11. **The Budget: A Spending Plan and Policy Tool**　　151
　　　　The Fiscal Plan　　153
　　　　Dealing with the First Budget　　156
　　　　　　Getting an Early Start　　156
　　　　　　Delegating Budget Responsibilities　　157
　　　　The Budget Process　　158
　　　　　　The Governor's Decisions on Budget Guidelines　　160
　　　　　　What Documents Should the Governor See?　　164
　　　　　　Multiyear Format　　165
　　　　　　Exempt Agencies　　165
　　　　　　Exempt Funds　　166
　　　　　　The Format of Review Meetings　　167
　　　　　　When Governors and Agencies Can't Agree　　168
　　　　　　Management Relationships and the Budget　　170
　　　　Capital Budgeting and Bonding　　172
　　　　When Forecasts Miss the Mark　　173
　　　　Fiscal Impact Statements　　174

12. **Approaches to Legislation**　　175
　　　　Three Major Speeches　　177
　　　　　　The Inaugural　　177
　　　　　　The State of the State　　178
　　　　　　The Budget Message　　178
　　　　Developing the Legislative Program　　179
　　　　Presenting the Legislative Program　　181
　　　　Getting Legislation Passed　　182
　　　　　　Early Decisions　　182
　　　　　　The Veto Power　　183
　　　　The Legislative Appropriations Process　　185
　　　　Special Sessions　　185
　　　　The Governor and Legislative Elections　　186

      Primaries in the Governor's Party   186
      General Elections   186
  Leadership Selection   187
  Legal Aspects of Legislative-Executive Relations   188

13. State-Federal Relations   189
  The New Governor's State-Federal Agenda   191
      Designations for Federal Programs   192
      Grant Applications and State Plans   192
      Federal Legislation and Regulations   193
      Compliance Issues and Audits   193
  State-Federal Mechanisms   194
      The National Governors' Association   194
      The Washington Office   195
      The State-Federal Relations Staff   196
      Planning, Budget and Line Agencies   198
      Other Groupings of Governors   199
      The Congressional Delegation   200
  Power Points in State-Federal Relations   200
  Level of Involvement   201

14. Approaches to Reorganization   203
  The Reorganization Decision   205
      Authority for Reorganization   205
      Early Steps to Consider   206
      A Caution on Reorganization   207
  Strengthening Executive Control   207
  Reorganization of Line Agencies   208
  Organizational Options for Staff Support   210
      Alternative Central Staff Locations   211
      The Impact of Personnel   214
  Combined Planning and Budgeting Agencies   214
  Separate Planning and Budgeting Offices   217
  Other Coordinating Mechanisms   217

15. Ethics and Standards of Conduct   219
      Unethical Purchasing Practices   221
      Corruption in Regulatory Functions   223
      Taking Unfair Advantage of Employees   223
      Using Inside Information   224
      Stealing State Property   224
      Unique Problems for the Governor   224

16. The Governor and His Family   227
  Time and Privacy   229
  Security   229
      The Office   230
      Personal Security   230
      Government Operations   230
      The First Family   231
  Some Household Notes   231

    Managing the Mansion   232
    Social Functions   233
    Guest Lists   234
The Governor's Spouse   234

Appendixes   237

1. A Transition Timetable   239
2. Critical Dates in Gubernatorial Transition   242
3. State Provisions for Gubernatorial Transition   246
4. Model Gubernatorial Transition Act   248
5. How Executive Assistants View Their Roles   252
6. How Agency Liaison Officers View Their Roles   253
7. Gubernatorial Staff Support by Planning and Budget Offices   254
8. Policy Development   255
    Memorandum on Policy Review Process   255
    Memorandum on Cabinet Subgroups   257
    Sample Decision Memorandum   260
    Example of Issue Analysis Paper   264
9. How State Planning Offices Spend Their Time   268
10. State Agencies Designated to Handle Federal Planning Programs   270
11. Sample Policy Statement   271
12. Administrative Organization   274
    State Cabinet Systems   274
    Kentucky Executive Branch Organization Chart   275
    South Dakota Executive Branch Organization Chart   276
13. Scheduling   277
    How Governors Spend Their Time   277
    Governors' Responses to Typical Scheduling Requests   278
    Memorandum on Proposed Scheduling Procedures   279
    Sample Scheduling Request Forms   284
14. Managing the Mail   289
    Memorandum on Proposed Mail Control System   289
    Sample Mail Control Forms   292
15. Budget Agency Functions   293
16. Alternative Planning and Budget Office Locations   297
17. The Governor and the Legislature   300
    The Governor's Legislative Program   300
    The Governor and the Veto   301
    The Governor and Lobbying   302
18. Legislative Program and Procedures   303
    Memorandum on Legislative Issue Development   303
    Memorandum on Legislative Analysis and Procedures   306
    Sample Legislative Forms   309

Selected Bibliography   311

Foreword

Few positions of leadership in the United States offer the challenges that await the newly elected Governor. It is for those who are to assume these challenges that this handbook is written.

A new Governor often has devoted extensive time, energy and resources to establishing a firm understanding of the needs of his constituents with an eye toward the opportunities of a new administration. In many instances, however, the complexity of state government management may be an overwhelming obstacle during the first critical days of the administration. The National Governors' Association has addressed this problem in recent years through biennial seminars for newly elected Governors and resource materials including *The Critical Hundred Days: A Handbook for the New Governor* (1974) and *The Governor's Office Series* (1976).

This handbook is a comprehensive reference document designed to assist the new Governor with the many key decisions and actions of the first year of the administration. It combines portions of earlier materials with extensive new information to address the major tasks facing the new Governor—transition, appointing a staff and cabinet, preparing a budget and legislative program, dealing with state-federal issues, and many more.

It is the hope of the National Governors' Association that this handbook will be of great value to gubernatorial staff members and state agency officials, as well as to those for whom it is intended—the Governors of the American states, who bear some of the nation's most demanding responsibilities for political and managerial leadership.

> Julian M. Carroll
> *Governor of Kentucky*
> *Chairman, National Governors' Association*

Acknowledgements

Many persons participated extensively in the production of this handbook. Among the most thoughtful and stimulating contributions were those made by the many former Governors who were eager to assist new Governors by reflecting candidly on their own experiences.

Jack Brizius, Director of Policy Research for the National Governors' Association, coordinated both the research and the writing process. Harold Hovey and Kenneth Olson played a major role in the writing and research effort, as did Timothy Knaus of the NGA Center for Policy Research.

A number of top-level officials in past and present state administrations provided important editorial assistance through their review of the draft manuscript. They include Thad Beyle, Kent Briggs, Gordon Duke, Dan Garry, Brad Leonard, Lynn Muchmore, Gary Passmore, Allen Pease, Dan Reese and Terry Smith.

Equally helpful were the executive assistants, planning directors and budget directors from the 50 states whose responses to survey materials provided much of the useful information contained in the handbook. The comments of Robert Wise, Staff Director of the Council of State Planning Agencies, and Raymond Long, Executive Director of the National Association of State Budget Officers, were particularly helpful.

In addition, the manuscript benefited greatly from review by several members of the National Governors' Association staff, including Scott Bunton, Bonnie Davis, John Lagomarcino, James Martin, Joseph McLaughlin and Hilary Whittaker.

Dwight Jensen, Pat Jensen and Beverly Bailey provided expert editorial and production assistance. Ellen Field and Ellen Demboski of the NGA Center for Policy Research also were extremely helpful in facilitating the development of the handbook.

Stephen B. Farber, *Director*
National Governors' Association

CHAPTER ONE

The Experience of Being Governor

I'd have to say that being Governor was one of the most rewarding times of my life. The challenges were unending, and it seemed as though time was at a constant premium. Yet, I survived the Governorship—I hope the Governorship survived me. I personally received tremendous satisfaction from leading our state through difficult times.

— a former Governor

SUMMARY

As first citizen of his state, the Governor is at the center of American political life. He fulfills many roles: head of the executive branch, legislative leader, head of his political party, national figure, ceremonial chief and family member. More than any other public figure, it seems, the Governor is perceived by his constituents as the one who can solve their individual problems and respond to their concerns.

A 1976 National Governors' Association survey of former Governors found that most recalled their years in office as having been both challenging and rewarding. Asked to identify which demands of the office they considered most difficult, the former Governors ranked the following major problems in descending order:

- Working with the legislature;
- Interference with family life;
- Ceremonial demands on their time;
- Invasion of privacy;
- Long hours;
- Tough decisions;
- Working with the federal government;
- Intramural government squabbles;
- Day-to-day management of state government;
- Working with the press; and
- Building and keeping staff.

Clearly, management problems, policy and program development and implementation, legislative strategy, and ceremonial and political functions, as well as the demands of the press and public, make long hours inescapable and cannot help but interfere with family life. The new Governor will be beset with tough problems that require tough decisions. But former chief executives were emphatic that problems awaiting decision must not be allowed to pile up, that Governors should organize themselves to deal with each problem promptly and then move on to the next.

On the other hand, the former Governors cited as one of their most satisfying challenges the recruitment of competent staff and effective agency heads who would help make difficult tasks manageable and the solution of complex problems possible.

They also agreed that the management of time is of crucial importance. The Governor's most precious resource is time; it must be tightly budgeted and coordinated to match the Governor's schedule with the administration's objectives.

Those who have been Governors report that the experience of being Governor can lead to isolation and poor judgment if the new Governor fails to keep his perspective. Typical advice from seasoned Governors includes the need to stay accessible, be decisive, and communicate a clear sense of direction to subordinates and the public.

A typical day in the life of a Governor is highly pressured and complex. The number and diversity of people and problems with which the Governor must deal each day make the effective management of time even more important. Conserving time should be uppermost on the new Governor's agenda, beginning the day after election.

In designing his office structure, the new Governor would be wise to remember the complexity and competitiveness that will characterize the interaction of his staff and agency heads. While a multitude of transition tasks will clamor for his attention in the period between the election and inauguration, the new Governor will want to move quickly to establish a system in his office and in state government to manage his time effectively, make clear decisions, and focus on the agenda he has set for his term of office.

The Experience of Being Governor

The American Governor is chief executive of a large and complex organization. In his capacity as head of the state government he has a number of different roles, including:

HEAD OF THE EXECUTIVE BRANCH. The Governor is one of the largest employers in his state. Altogether, states employ many more people than the federal government. States spent $153 billion last year, and gross receipts in many states are as large as those of most companies in the Fortune 500. As manager of the executive branch, the Governor recruits and appoints people to hundreds of positions each year, is expected to supervise them in some fashion, and must adjudicate differences of viewpoint among aides, cabinet officers, interest groups and various coalitions of each.

LEGISLATIVE LEADER. The Governor is, ex officio, probably the single most powerful legislative leader in the state. He must worry about both the substance of legislative programs and legislative strategies, in order to get favored programs passed and prevent passage of measures he opposes.

HEAD OF PARTY. The Governor is the leader of his state political party. He is expected to play a role in determining who fills party leadership positions, raising funds, formulating and articulating positions, selecting candidates, and participating in national party affairs.

NATIONAL FIGURE. He is also expected to be concerned with federal government actions which affect his state and the entire country. The Governor is, in effect, the chief program officer for many of the federal programs administered through his state government. He must approve plans, set policies and see that programs are carried out.

FAMILY MEMBER. While family responsibilities do not begin with assuming the Governor's chair, neither do they disappear with election to high office.

CEREMONIAL CHIEF. Governors have a number of ceremonial duties. They may include such diverse functions as receiving foreign dignitaries, receiving petitions, announcing national dill pickle week, crowning the queen of the gooseberry festival, shooting film extolling the virtues of his state or its products, presiding over the opening of the state fair or the graduation at the state police academy, and having his picture taken with the state's oldest veteran.

The Governor serves as first citizen of the state and symbolizes it to a vast number of people. Of all the public figures in his state—United States Senators and Representatives included—the Governor's name is usually the most recognized. Often, more than 90 percent of the people know who he is. When something goes wrong—or right—in a state, the Governor takes the blame or credit in the public mind.

The political significance of the office of the Governor is immense. It is the highest elected office in the state government and is often sought by those who have previously been elected to state and local office. Congressmen frequently come back to run for Governor. After their terms in the statehouse, Governors often become United States Senators or accept major federal appointments.* On occasion, a Governor becomes President of the United States.

PROBLEMS OF THE OFFICE

The office of the Governor is clearly both satisfying and demanding. Former Governors were surveyed by the National Governors' Association in 1976 on the most difficult and demanding elements of the job. The list they were given to choose from and their choices are shown below:

Most Difficult and Demanding Aspects	*Former Governors' Choices***
Working with the legislature	23
Interference with family life	20
Ceremonial demands on time	16
Invasion of privacy	14
The hours	13
Tough decisions	11
Working with the federal government	11
Intramural government squabbles	11
Day-to-day management of state government	10
Working with the press	8
Building and keeping staff	7

**Total of 52 responses. Former Governors could indicate more than one if they chose.

Many of the former Governors provided an explanation of why they characterized certain aspects of their former job as difficult.

---

*In 1978, 16 former Governors were serving in the U.S. Senate, and four Governors sought election to the Senate. Increasingly, however, Governors faced with a choice between seeking election to the Senate and reelection as Governor are choosing the latter, citing a preference for the executive responsibilities of the office.

Working with the Legislature

"Working with the legislature," commented one former Governor, "involves being available to see each member of the legislature about problems which are generally of little significance or importance, but a Governor can rarely refuse to see a member of the legislature, and with [more than 100] . . . members it is apparent that considerable time is involved in this activity." Another chose this problem "because there seems to be an undercurrent in all legislatures of jealousy for public attention and a defensive attitude concerning their own powers. They do not want it to appear they are being pushed around by the Governor." Another commented: "It is very difficult to reason with legislators who may be politically antagonistic or ambitious in their future desires for higher office, including that of Governor." One former Governor suggested that his problem might be explained by the fact that his party held only one-third of the seats in each house, while another suggested that it is sometimes impossible for the legislature and the Governor to agree, "whether the legislature is or is not controlled partly or completely by the Governor's party."

Chapter 12 of this handbook is devoted to the Governor's legislative program and legislative relations.

Demands on Time

Many of the former Governors commented on the heavy time demands of the office. Some typical views:

> Ceremonial demands on time make it impossible for a chief executive to accomplish much during normal working hours; picture-taking sessions for one function or another along with scheduled appointments simply take most of each working day. Then speaking engagements away from the Capitol take so much time for travel that a Governor's work time is severely restricted. Ceremonial demands are too frequent and too much is expected.

> The public expects you to be their servant and attend every old settlers reunion and annual town picnic in addition to serving as chief executive of the state.

> Governors are working stiffs. The constant demands of the press and public can produce a condition of mental and emotional exhaustion.

> Long hours are inescapable but tough.

> The pressure and irregularity of ceremonial demands on time make family life almost impossible unless one takes a very rigid stance with regard to denial of public appearances when they interfere with long-range domestic plans.

> The Governorship makes more inroads on personal and family life than any other public office.

> It's a 20-hour day.

One former midwestern Governor indicated that he made it a practice to avoid ceremonial occasions and that he cut only one ribbon in four years as Governor. In retrospect, he feels that he should have participated in more ceremonial activities because they provide an "easy way to meet people without stress and obligation" and because event sponsors often react negatively when their request for the Governor's time is rejected. However, a former eastern Governor said that "a Governor should limit ceremonial appearances despite criticism from some groups." He added: "It wasn't too many years ago that the job of a Governor was largely ceremonial—but no longer."

Just as the perceptions of former Governors about the office dwell heavily on the use of time, the new Governor will be faced almost immediately with critical decisions about how to ration his limited time as the many things he seeks to accomplish begin to compete with each other. The problems of scheduling and use of time are dealt with in detail in chapter 8.

Interference with Family Life and Invasion of Privacy

Many former Governors commented on the extent to which the job interfered with their family lives and made them such public figures that they could not have private lives. Some of their comments:

> Interference with family life and invasion of privacy is obvious and a part of the Governor's position.
>
> Perhaps the most difficult part of being Governor is trying to allocate the attention that should be given to one's immediate family. Children vary in their ability to absorb political shock. Some youngsters are permanently scarred from having to live in a fishbowl.
>
> I had a family of five children, all preteens and early teens. This was a crucial time in their lives, and I felt keenly about not giving them much time.
>
> To a person not completely accustomed to public life, the total lack of privacy can be stultifying. Being "on stage" every moment, even among closest friends and advisors, tends to create an artificial and distorted personality.
>
> There is no privacy—you can't even enjoy a football game.

A substantial number of former Governors, however, did not cite either interference with family life or loss of privacy as problems, and one, from a heavily populated state, commented that he "had no great interference with family life or invasion of privacy."

Dealing with the impact of the office on the Governor and his family is discussed in detail in the final chapter of this handbook.

Tough Decisions

The former Governors who identified making tough decisions as one of the most demanding aspects of their jobs made comments like these:

> Always two sides to a question. Political connotations and impact on economy, particularly relating to taxes, cause much anguish in making decisions. A Governor must feel an internal satisfaction that the decision is right.

Unlike the legislative branch, where decisions can be deferred, a Governor must make a decision every 15 minutes or so throughout the day. If decisions are allowed to backlog, they can become a millstone around one's neck.

Anyone seeking the office of chief executive automatically invites and should expect tough decisions. However, events and timing significantly affect the harshness of such decisions. Critical state financial problems existed when the office was assumed, and a series of natural disasters . . . combined to form a series of hard "no win" decisions.

Tough decisions require hours of consultation and examination and soul searching.

As the saying goes, "the buck stops here." It seems as though every major decision in government has to be determined at the executive level. There are always all types of decisions to be made with the equities pretty evenly balanced in many instances; each time you make a decision you're probably alienating a lot of people. Hopefully, over a period of your term of office your decisions have been approved by a majority of the people.

Decisions are tough. After making one, move on to the next one. Don't worry about it. That's what you are elected for.

Working with the Federal Government

Although problems with the federal government were mentioned by only one-fourth of the former Governors, they were clearly of great importance for some, as indicated by these comments:

> Working with the federal government requires patience to alleviate frustrations of difficulty in getting things done in a timely way.

> The fact that a Governor must depend upon his legislature and upon the federal government for much of what he hopes to accomplish adds another dimension to the problem that has no parallel in, for instance, the private sector.

Many states now require that most federal funds received by the state—which may account for a quarter of total state expenditures—must be appropriated by the legislature before they can be spent. This requirement can further complicate the Governor's role in dealing with the federal government. State-federal relationships are the subject of chapter 13.

Intramural Government Squabbles

Eight former Governors indicated that infighting among state officials was a major problem for them. Two elaborated as follows:

> Intramural government squabbles represent "kingdom building" by the various state departments with the jealousies of each over its own domain and the resulting quagmire of red tape, fragmentation and duplication. Much of my time was spent in refereeing these disputes.

> Inbred bureaucracy, certain it will outlast a Governor, reluctant to change, resistant to accommodate merger or abolition, is frustrating because a Governor seldom can will his way. It takes forever to make personnel changes, and it takes time and anguish to persuade, convince and cajole the civil service.

Dealing with the state agencies and career employees will take a great deal of the Governor's energy. Much of this volume will be devoted to methods of getting the most out of the state bureaucracy.

Building and Keeping Staff

Fewer than 20 percent of the former Governors listed staffing as a major problem, and several commented that they did not experience significant difficulties in this aspect of their work. One who singled out staffing problems noted that "the initial liaisons are made fresh from the campaign, and there is a strong tendency to work with campaign staff, which may not be suited."

Another former Governor cited salary limitations and the lack of longevity in jobs as major problems. Several former Governors cited staffing as a demanding aspect of their work, but did not indicate that they had particular difficulties in handling it. Among their comments were:

> The success or failure of an administration is largely determined by the character of the Governor's staff and advisors.

> The time spent in procuring exceptional talent will be rewarding. This applies to cabinet posts, judicial appointments, regulatory commissions, in fact all appointive positions. Once they are appointed they should be supported and supporting.

Chapters 3 and 4 of this handbook deal with the problems of organizing and staffing the Governor's office.

Working with the Press

Problems with the press did not rank high among those cited by the former Governors. One former midwestern Governor indicated that the "press forms biases and opinions and then endeavors to prove their views by the use of 'informed sources' which in most cases are each other." The same former Governor offered this comment on the difficulty in refuting rumors about scandals: "If you respond to every word-of-mouth story, you will be constantly on the defensive." A former western Governor indicated that the poor quality of the largest morning newspaper in his state greatly complicated his job. Several former Governors noted the demands made on their time by the press. See chapter 10 for a full discussion of press and media relations.

Day-to-Day Management of State Government

State government management also did not rank high among the problems cited by the former Governors. Those who mentioned management problems made comments such as these:

> The demands of time, invasion of privacy, rough decisions, etc., are not any more onerous for a Governor than for any other full-time public elected official, but the management of a very large and complex service organization is quite difficult and demanding and quite unlike any other job.

The Governor must see that the machinery of the state is running right. It is his responsibility and not delegable. If proper attention is not paid to management, a variety of other tough problems are created. They do not arise under proper management.

Good knowledgeable people are hard to find. You can get a lot of political types who can't run a good shop.

Management of state government is discussed extensively in chapter 7.

Other Problems

Former Governors were given the opportunity to cite problems other than those listed in the questionnaire. One from a southern state mentioned "weeding out the unimportant" and commented: "A study I remember concerning former Governor (Richard) Ogilvie of Illinois showed that although he worked very hard, only 19 percent of his time was spent in supervising a huge state government. I think that is typical." Another former Governor cited security as a major problem and asked: "How do you avoid appearing to be a big shot in the eyes of those who cannot fathom the need for security, and how do you remain close to the people with it? This is the dilemma: Avoid the nut and make the real folks comfortable and at ease."

Least Difficult Tasks

That the Governor's job is not always plagued with problems was indicated by a substantial number of former Governors who volunteered comments on particular problem areas that they did not find to be difficult. The former Governors were asked: "Based upon your experience, which aspects of the job should we advise new Governors that they will find the easiest to handle?" Among those who responded, ceremonial duties, dealing with visitors, and media events were the overwhelming favorites as the least difficult aspects of the job. Several mentioned day-to-day management of state government and building and keeping staff, while several others indicated that it would be difficult to generalize for a new Governor's benefit. These were some of the other comments on the easier functions:

> With a good staff, new Governors will find it easiest to handle the more difficult and serious problems, those which require planning and implementation. These are problems which by their nature will require attention and study and thus will not be sacrificed by the time and demands of more routine activities.

> Nothing will be easy except that for which the Governor has a real interest and inspiration.

> Perhaps the easiest part of the Governor's work is the day-to-day management of state government. This is true particularly if the Governor has been able to attract top-flight managers into his administration.

> Ceremonial demands and public appearances, if they enjoy people and recognize that this is an obligation of an individual who is in the public limelight.

Perhaps none of it is easy. However, there should not be undue concern about continuity of government. The system has enough momentum—or inertia—that the new Governor has time to get his feet on the ground.

Acknowledging the congratulations of those who said they voted for you.

If you have a good and loyal staff, many other problems are solved. This is most important because the staff determines to a great extent who and what the Governor sees. Also, I feel that anyone who survives a campaign can make tough decisions.

This will depend on previous experience. Anyone without some previous state government experience will have the most difficult time.

A DAY IN THE LIFE OF A GOVERNOR

It is difficult to convey to a new Governor the importance of maintaining control over his time. One approach is to present a typical day of a Governor who has been in office for some time and is no longer concerned with transition problems. This section hypothetically portrays such a day—assuming that there is anything like a typical day (which there isn't) of a typical Governor (which there isn't). It is presented here to point out the importance of managing time well, and of developing time-management ideas during the transition period.

8:00-9:00 a.m.

Scheduled office time; no staff or calls allowed. The Governor instituted this practice after realizing that if he wanted to work alone for as much as an hour, he would have to demand it.

Reads newspaper stories on state government; dictates short congratulatory notes to juvenile delinquency director for fine press coverage on opening of new facility, and to editorial staff of major newspaper for editorial commending his support of the facility. Writes note to mental health director on press story about beating of retarded child in state facility.

Notes local controversy about highway location in southern part of state; makes mental note to discuss it with highway commissioner. Notes editorial and news comment that next legislative session is likely to be a rough one. Notes speculation that he is about to appoint Jones as new bank commissioner; tells press secretary to get speculation killed; he hasn't decided, but knows it won't be Jones.

Starts working on screened morning mail (a small part of mail actually received). Mayor of large city wants to be moved up on sewer project priority list; refers mayor's letter to the department. Official of smaller city complains that mass transportation money is unfairly going to larger cities; refers letter to department. National party chairman requests Governor's cooperation in upcoming congressional campaign financing; Governor writes a reminder to discuss with political advisor. Major contributor comments that branch banking law changes being considered by the staff would seriously threaten savings and loan institutions; Governor dictates letter indicating he is aware of problems and is concerned.

Reviews telegrams from environmental groups requesting that he reverse his decision to support Corps of Engineers water supply project; other telegrams from local mayor and county leaders and builders ask him to reaffirm support of project. Decides to stay with earlier decision.

9:00 a.m.

Receives delegation of legislators and mayor of suburban community seeking superhighway. Highway department briefing materials say that the road shouldn't be built at all; and if it is, it couldn't be started for 10 years, unless, of course, the Governor wants to propose new gasoline taxes to fund commitments to other areas. Governor tells delegation he is working on the problem and is sympathetic, but has other pressures for use of funds.

Asks friendly legislator to stay after the meeting, and finds out that the county chairman is wavering from support of his candidate for state senate and is unhappy with the way state party headquarters is run.

10:00 a.m.

Kicks off National Cancer Week campaign with pictures and awards plus handshaking with county chairmen. One person catches him at end of meeting and asks that he solve problem of son who is in trouble with the Army. Governor pleads inability to handle problem, but offers to try. Calls federal relations aide aside to explain, and asks if aide can work something out to get friendly Congressman to check on the case.

10:30 a.m.

Checks secretary for phone calls: has calls from two cabinet officers, one board chairman, his wife, two legislators, one local business leader, plus three aides who "must" see him.

Starts to return phone calls, but gets interrupted by press secretary who says major local issue is developing over announced layoff of 20 employees in state TB hospital; department says it's true; press secretary recommends saying Governor is looking into it and to tell the department to hold off. Governor tells press secretary to hold off comment until he has talked to department.

Now makes calls, postponing 11 a.m. meeting with transportation secretary and budget director on additional matching money for highway construction until 11:30 a.m., and 11:30 meeting with insurance commissioner until noon.

Mental health director advises that he is having some success with local mental health directors in meetings Governor had asked him to hold. Notes in passing (obviously real reason for call) that he is having some trouble with Governor's political advisor on staffing the department and is convinced that the professionalism of the department must remain inviolate.

Arts board chairman says he's getting lots of pressure from legislators for local interest arts projects and has decided to emphasize these projects almost solely in this year's fund allocation. Reports considerable sentiment in the business community that administration spending is getting out of hand and warns against proposing any tax increases.

Wife reminds him to do something about getting some state agency to support a statewide program to put art and music in state institutions for mentally retarded. Governor calls budget director and asks for prospects of doing it. Budget director believes the art board has no new statewide projects this year—concentrating on local concerns instead. Does Governor want it changed? Governor is not sure, and budget director offers a memo later in the week explaining the choices; Governor decides to wait for the memo.

Expecting the first of the legislators on the telephone, Governor gets his legislative aide instead—his secretary explaining that he had asked that Governor talk to him before the legislator. Legislative aide says legislator is extremely upset because Governor's budget bureau and perhaps higher education coordinating council are apparently not going to approve a community college for which locals have already raised money. Legislative aide feels it is absolutely essential that the project be approved before the fall election and asks the Governor to pry the issue out of whatever agency it is in.

Legislator says just what legislative aide said he would. Governor agrees to look into it and call him back.

The other legislator whose call Governor returns is concerned about a rumor that Governor is firing employees in TB hospital and planning to close it; says he understands problem but hopes that Governor will understand his, and that he'll have to issue a press release this afternoon criticizing lack of concern with TB patients and local community if Governor goes through with it. The local business leader is also concerned about the TB issue.

12:00 noon

Secretary says transportation secretary, budget director, and transportation aide are waiting; also insurance commissioner. Meeting at 12:15 p.m. with major newspaper reporter pending, and more phone calls.

Governor has brief meeting on transportation funding. Budget director argues for passing up federal money for new highway construction on grounds of Governor's austerity program. Transportation secretary notes that funds are 80 percent federal and argues for a go-ahead. Governor says he'll read both memoranda and decide after checking with executive assistant.

Governor is scheduled to leave at 1 p.m. for a ribbon-cutting highway opening about an hour away. Asks secretary to see if he can scrub highway opening and to hold calls, and says he will see the reporter after press secretary has a minute to brief him. Press secretary says press is all over him on TB thing—what has the Governor decided? Governor asks secretary to get health director on phone, finds he is addressing public health association lunch right now—does the Governor want to interrupt. No, have him call just as soon as he is through speaking.

Reporter comes in to begin interview on whether Governor is taking position in key party leadership fight over mayoral nomination in eastern part of the state; Governor sets ground rules as background and begins to expound on his preferences.

Secretary buzzes on intercom and reports that top aides (all of whom are now waiting to see him) advise OK to cancel highway opening, highway commissioner will handle but Governor should call mayor and apologize because there may be a big crowd which the mayor gathered. Governor tells her to call mayor on his behalf and explain situation, and that he will call the mayor himself later in the day.

Interview concluded, secretary brings in lunch that he was originally scheduled to have during trip to ribbon cutting.

1:15 p.m.

Health director on the phone reminds Governor that there are no more TB patients to be cared for, that most of the people in TB sanitorium are alcoholics who can be readily cared for elsewhere, that firings are part of his budget plan, and that he has no funds to continue employees. Governor finds employees were offered jobs elsewhere, but many of them don't want to leave the community. Director says he can keep the facility open as long as the Governor provides the money. Governor asks press secretary to tell press of meeting on subject at 2 p.m.

Asks secretary to tell legislator to please hold off the press conference criticizing the TB closing for another day. She says she has had three calls from union leaders and a couple of legislative calls protesting the closing and that his political advisor wants to talk about them as well as other things. Governor sets up meeting for 2 p.m. with health director, budget director, press secretary and political advisor.

Secretary provides messages from other calls: . . . Three different people with candidates other than Jones called to express hope that the press story on Jones was not true. One wanted to talk to Governor before an appointment is made so he could tell him some confidential information about Jones . . . Jones called, said he didn't know he was being considered, but would be happy to talk about the job . . . Chairman of the commission on higher education said please make no commitment on the community college matter without talking to him. Budget director called with the same message . . . Federal relations aide called, wants a decision this afternoon on what to ask Senator Smith to do on strip-mine control amendments affecting state regulation. Senate votes tomorrow, and the Senator wants to go with Governor's position. Memo in in-box (which has been resting untouched on desk since 10 a.m.).

1:45 p.m.

Governor tries to call federal relations aide while reading memorandum. Can't reach, he is on the way back from Washington. Governor asks secretary to find out whether he has talked to head of state environmental protection agency on subject . . . no one knows, he'll call in about an hour.

Governor tells secretary to tell insurance commissioner he is sorry to keep him waiting and for him to get lunch and check back about 3 p.m. Secretary says aides are still waiting, some of their business is pretty urgent, plus remember the 4 p.m. meeting on office space, and that he has an engagement this evening.

2:12 p.m.

Meeting with health director and others (now including legislative, personnel and legal advisors) on TB matter. Political and legislative advisors say they don't care how we got where we are, it is imperative that the state not be laying off employees right before election, and with key labor negotiations going on in other departments. Personnel advisor tends to agree, but notes that employees had some prior knowledge of likely layoffs. Budget director and health director are adamant on merits of closing the facility; health director says he will keep it open if budget is increased; budget director says no chance, the legislature cut the overall health budget last year. Legal advisor proposes compromise to keep the facility open until after election, funds to come from health budget, but administration would have to seek some supplemental appropriation to reimburse health budget. Health director is dubious, budget director opposed, personnel advisor says that where he comes from, if you are going to bite a bullet you do it all at once, not in stages. Meeting drags on. Obvious that these layoffs are just the beginning if Governor stays with health director's plan.

Meeting continues while Governor takes call from federal relations aide. Yes, he has talked to the environmental protection agency, and the position he recommends on strip mining is concurred in by them. Governor returns to TB meeting. Finds potential solution is to have mental health department take over part of facility instead of closing it. Unknown if mental health director will agree; health director is on phone to him now.

Governor leaves TB meeting with legal advisor to discuss status of suit by welfare rights organization to require higher welfare payments.

3:20 p.m.

Returns to TB meeting, which now includes mental health director. Mental health director says he can't make a final decision now, needs to review the facility and prospects for transferring some patients and doctors from another of his facilities. Press secretary proposes to tell media the administration is looking into new possibility and layoffs are deferred. All agree, except budget director, who argues for closing, and political advisor, who urges a solution that will hold for a few months, not a few weeks. Governor accepts the solution anyhow. Instructs press secretary to inform media and legislative advisor to inform local legislators.

3:35 p.m.

Secretary advises that insurance commissioner is back, other advisors are waiting, and Governor hasn't done anything about in-box. Plus more messages: . . . Neighboring Governor called and wants to discuss developing a common regional position on safety rules for zinc mining. Governor has secretary call federal relations aide to get in touch with neighboring Governor's staff to see what can be worked out . . . Press secretary calls with information that p.m. papers are breaking a story that a legislative leader of the Governor's party is suspected of selling real estate to the highway department, using inside information on new highway location . . . Highway commissioner is back from ribbon cutting and needs to talk . . . President of largest state university would like to chat briefly about prospects of a new law school . . . Speaker of the house wants to talk, important and personal . . . Secretary has arranged the scheduling meeting at 5 p.m., after the office space meeting.

Insurance commissioner is still waiting, has staff with him and two hours worth of visual aids. Governor calls the commissioner in alone—commissioner is prepared to talk about the new insurance consumer protection program he was asked to prepare; meeting was rescheduled twice already. Governor tells him he's sorry about the scheduling problem, asks him to leave the written material and promises to try to read it tonight and to make apologies to his staff.

Calls political advisor in. Asks about speaker's call; finds that speaker wants to be reassured that Governor would not back rival for speakership even if party wins handily in fall election. Political advisor says leave him hanging for awhile; call tomorrow and say that Governor doesn't control the membership but appreciates his support in the past, etc.

Political advisor discusses bank commissioner appointment and recommends someone other than Jones; Governor agrees and asks him to prepare press release. Political advisor stops at door to remind him that he had agreed to spend more time away from the office and with the people; says he must schedule more local events like the ribbon cutting today and then keep to the schedule; asks if mayor who arranged it has been called yet.

4:30 p.m.

Governor calls the mayor and has a 15-minute conversation in which the mayor says pretty much what the political advisor did. Agrees to check a bridge situation within city limits and instructs secretary to check the point with the highway commissioner.

4:45 p.m.

Governor begins the 4 p.m. office space meeting, knowing he still has the scheduling meeting and a couple of calls to go and that he should be receiving guests at the mansion at 6:30. The meeting requires his presence because the public works department, which allocates office space, is at loggerheads with the agencies. The agencies want more space—whether they have to lease it, get private companies to build it, or whatever—while public works wants to hold them off and build a new office building which would require the Governor's approval. The meeting is incredibly dull, with charts and graphs about office space, so at 5 p.m. the Governor leaves, indicating he has another meeting and leaving two or three agency heads, budget director and one aide with instructions to work out a recommendation for him that they can agree on.

5:00 p.m.

Handles more messages. Has secretary get the facts on the law school from budget bureau and commissioner of higher education before calling president of university back tomorrow. Reminds secretary to call the speaker tomorrow. Calls the highway commissioner to find out what the mayor has already told him.

Has secretary tell aide who is waiting to talk about a project for cooperation between university students and law enforcement department to wait until tomorrow. Has consumer protection advisor do likewise.

Reviews brief remarks prepared for dinner session with group of business leaders. Remembers that one of the leaders is board chairman of the community college that all the fuss was about earlier in the day. Asks an aide to quickly collect the views of the higher education commissioner and the budget director and give him a briefing before he leaves the office.

5:30 p.m.

Governor enters scheduling meeting. His secretary asks if he wants the aide left in the office space meeting or brought into the meeting; he answers "both." The scheduling meeting is no different from the last one, not likely to be different from the next.

The political advisor wants Governor to make fund-raising appearances at five geographically diverse places in the next week, appear at supermarkets with two legislative candidates, and attend two rallies for legislative candidates. In addition, advisor suggests strongly that Governor drop in at the Chinese-American society dinner next Saturday night and appear at a teacher's convention the following day.

Secretary says wife wants to hold Saturday all day at home and prefers to spend that evening with friends. Wife does not want to travel on Sunday, secretary says, reminding Governor that one of his children is making his debut as a high school football player on Friday. Governor's scheduler ticks off the remaining demands for time the following week:

- One state trade association meeting (already accepted) and two more which request his presence and will schedule for a major address if he can make it;
- One statewide labor meeting;
- Three requests for local political functions, beyond the ones the political advisor knows the Governor had;
- A request from the federal relations aide to visit the congressional delegation in Washington next week and deliver testimony for the National Governors' Association before a Senate subcommittee;
- A request from two key agency directors to accompany them to Washington to resolve problems with federal agencies;
- A request from the press aide for a news conference announcing the new bank commissioner, a backgrounder with a representative of a national magazine, and at least one additional general-purpose news conference during the week;
- Six cabinet officers and three board or commission chairmen wanting to discuss one subject or another; and
- Three county chairmen, four legislators, five major contributors, six local delegations seeking highways or other state construction, and the usual flow of private citizens wanting to see their Governor.

In addition, the schedulers report back on various events the Governor requests be scheduled, which have not been scheduled yet, including a visit to a mental hospital for inspection and employee relations, a meeting with educational advisors on potential for improving the state aid formula, a meeting with the planning director and several cabinet officers on land-use planning, and the remainder of the meetings on the consumer protection program similar to that with the insurance commissioner today.

Secretary reports Governor should take one complete day off just to concentrate on the paperwork in the in-box.

The scheduling meeting goes on to 6 p.m., at which time the Governor expresses preferences, delegates the exact schedule to the group, and receives a delegation from the office space meeting seeking to resolve a couple of questions. Indicating that he has to shower and change to be ready at the mansion by 6:30, Governor asks them either to write it up or talk to him in the morning (not remembering that tomorrow's schedule is worse than today's).

His secretary shouts out a couple of other phone calls; he says "tomorrow" and leaves office accompanied by aide trying to brief him on the community college situation, matching him pace for pace as he walks out. The community college situation is complicated indeed, so Governor decides not to decide yet and to finesse the question if it comes up in the evening.

After a quick shower and change accompanied by as much recitation of family affairs as time permits, Governor finds himself in the receiving line not quite promptly at 6:40, facing the ordeal of trying to remember 40 people whom he knows he should know. Cocktail conversation centers on bank regulation issues, exhortations to avoid tax increases, discussion of the business climate, costs of workers' compensation, and some general discussion of national politics. After dinner Governor talks briefly about some of his major programs and the need for good business climate in the state and retires to family quarters about 9:45 p.m.

In these moments of potential relaxation, Governor retrieves in-box correspondence from his briefcase. First, the "information only" items consisting of magazine articles, FYI memos from staff, and the like; these he scans briefly, primarily to see if there is any action he need take. A memo from the welfare secretary which indicates negotiations may break down with hospitals over Medicaid reimbursement rates is sent to his political advisor with a question, "Can we handle this if negotiations fail?"

Now the "action" items. Some 20 letters to sign prepared by staff; 16 are OK, two require rewrite instructions to someone, and two more the Governor rewrites himself. Now it is 10:15 p.m., his definite cutoff time for relaxation and talking to his family, even though he has five or six complicated problems, including the community college issue, left hanging.

* * *

This example is obviously atypical for some, while typical for other Governors, only because it happens to cover a quiet time without a major crisis (prison riot, natural disaster), or having the legislature in session. It suggests the Governor's constant need to make choices in the use of his own time and, more important, to avoid becoming a captive of the pressures on him. In a day such as the one described, it is hard to imagine the Governor contemplating, much less doing much about, his broad strategies for government leadership and party affairs.

When the moment of reflection does come, a Governor may find that his campaign did not result in his capturing the office, but in the office capturing him. He will see that many aspects of his predecessor's style that he wanted to change are things he is unable to change.

There is no obvious solution to these problems. There are ways to make it manageable only if the Governor designs his administration's priorities during transition—and avoids being totally "captured."

WHAT GOES ON AROUND THE GOVERNOR

While the Governor goes through these frenetic paces, his staff attempts to stay one step behind—or at least only a few steps behind—anticipating his needs and following up commitments made on this typical day. Since a Governor is often judged by the quality and thoroughness of his staff's work, it is worth considering who did what around the Governor in connection with just a part of this "typical" day.

Consider, for example, the 15 minutes at midday encompassing the highway-funding meeting and a few of the staff involved.

- Three weeks previously, the Governor's scheduler had addressed some hard decisions. Should the Governor attend the highway ribbon cutting, or should he turn it down and send a representative? How many people would be annoyed or slighted? As the "typical" day approached, the scheduler had perhaps 20 or so similar decisions to make before making final the public portion of the Governor's day. And, even then, the schedule was changed.

- Sitting with the Governor and the suburban legislators early in the day, the executive assistant to the Governor worried about his phone messages, large numbers of which mounted up in little pink piles on his desk. He usually kept two secretaries busy sorting correspondence, responding to requests, and placing calls. The suburban group's request for a new superhighway reminded him that the Governor was going to meet later in the morning with the budget director and transportation secretary on highway funding in general. The two men disagree and each will come well prepared with opposing arguments; he knows the Governor will ask him to help resolve the problem, but when will he have time to study it?

  As the Governor's day unfolded, he reminded himself that his symbol of power—the office next door to the Governor's—was also a millstone around his neck. Much of his life, he realized, was taken up in "hand holding" and being a "sounding board." If only he could get caught up, he thought, he would be able to work on that new tax-reform initiative which the revenue department had failed to deliver in adequate form. But Senator Brown had called, and he had to get back to him before noon because the Governor might run into him at the ribbon cutting that afternoon. Perhaps this evening he could stop to think about the Governor's tax program.

- "Why is the executive assistant allowing the transportation meeting to be delayed?" the budget director wondered at five minutes until noon as he waited to see the Governor. After all, the budget office's work on this issue had been going on—in fits and spurts—for six months. In fact, last night he and his unit chiefs were up until 3 a.m. completing the memorandum which would be devastating to the department of transportation's case for more highway construction. But if the Governor ran out of time this morning, the decision could be delayed again. The budget director had called the executive assistant to urge him to hurry the Governor along, but his call was somewhere at the bottom of the pink pile in the inner office.

- The secretary of transportation didn't enjoy the budget director's dry personality, so he had passed the time waiting for the Governor's meeting by drifting across the hall to chat with the Governor's personal secretary. Besides the fact that he was a gregarious soul, he knew that staying on the good side of the Governor's secretary never hurt.

Sometimes he absolutely had to talk to the Governor, and she would always put him through.

He was nervous about the Governor's reaction to his request for more highway money, in light of the Governor's austerity campaign. Just for insurance, he had let the Governor's political advisor know that many of the campaign pledges made in the politically critical rural areas of the state could not be met without the road funds. And then, of course, there were 75 campaign workers from key areas of the state whom he had hired at the political advisor's request—they might have to be laid off if the new money was not found in the budget somewhere. He hoped that the advisor had mentioned these problems to the Governor. If it seemed that the decision was not going his way, he planned to ask for more study—a delaying tactic to ensure that the Governor would make the final decision only after being apprised of all the financial and political ramifications of the decision.

- The planning director sat in his office working on the "Rural Development Plan" which the Governor had promised during the campaign, and which was now six months and scores of public hearings in the making. He was worried because he feared that the Governor's meeting on road money was going to preempt consideration of the section on farm-to-market road repair, a centerpiece in the rural development program he was about to unveil. If the road funds were put into the budget, he might still have time to influence the pattern of expenditures. "If we don't rebuild the small bridges on our rural roads," he thought, "five years from now the farm economy will be in deep trouble." He knew that the budget director had been working on a memorandum to convince the Governor that the department of transportation's spending plan was premature, but the planner was unsure of the outcome. Until the issue was clearly resolved, he could not move forward on his development plans.

Others worked, watched, and waited on the outcome of the short meeting with the Governor.

The press secretary was concerned; the Washington office director wanted to be able to credit her office with getting the federal dollars; the environmental protection liaison was quietly lobbying against more highways.

In this "typical" day, these developments were only a small sample of the detailed staff work and intra-staff competition that are inevitable in the Governor's office.

CHAPTER TWO

An Overview of Transition

> In campaigning you seek people—in governing they seek you. The demands for access and jobs, and adjustment in relationships with political supporters, need a discriminating hand.
>
> — *a former Governor*

SUMMARY

During the transition period between election and inauguration, the Governor-elect will assemble a new administration to implement objectives of both substance and style. As the state government is being reshaped during the transition period, the new Governor's ability to manage difficult initial tasks will be watched carefully. A smooth, productive transition process will supply the new administration with political momentum in the eyes of the media, the legislature and the public.

A coordinated transition is also important to the outgoing Governor, who should wish to ensure that efficient operation of state government will continue without interruption. The outgoing Governor and his staff should allow ample time to consult with the new administration, and they should make resources such as planning and budgeting staff and office records available to the Governor-elect in a timely fashion.

The Governor-elect first must determine how the transition is to be financed and staffed. Expenses during the transition will result from preparing for the inauguration, winding up the campaign, and running the transition office. Three-fourths of the states provide some kind of financing for the transition office.

The first step is to prepare a transition office budget which does not include campaign-related costs. In addition to state appropriations, sources of support for transition work include leftover campaign funds, special solicitations, volunteers, contributed services and state agencies.

The transition office will have a substantial agenda, including:

- Recruiting staff;
- Selecting appointees to key positions;
- Managing transition task forces;
- Planning the Governor's move into the executive residence;
- Identifying an initial policy agenda; and
- Preparing the inaugural address.

Sources of substantive transition assistance include state and campaign staff task forces. Task forces may obtain comprehensive briefing materials from state departments on functions and key issues. An overly formalized task force structure, however, may lead to disillusionment over slow implementation of recommendations, expectations by task force members that they will be appointed to agency jobs, and extra administrative burdens. It may be preferable to appoint task forces selectively to deal with problem areas identified during the campaign.

The Seminar for New Governors conducted by the National Governors' Association (NGA) and publications produced by NGA are other sources of transition aid. Concentrated and specific transition assistance on structure and operation of the Governor's office, planning, budgeting and identifying potential appointees to key positions is available from the state services office of NGA's Center for Policy Research. Current and former Governors and staff members can be valuable sources of informal assistance.

To enhance the effectiveness of subsequent transitions, the new Governor should consider early legislative action to improve transition procedures and funding. Legislation might be introduced which ensures a transition appropriation, office space for the Governor-elect, designation of a transition liaison by the outgoing Governor, and systematic disposition of files and records.

An Overview of Transition

Emerging victorious after a long campaign, a Governor-elect may view himself as about to embark on a grand crusade. That crusade might include such noble objectives as the following:

- Honest and competent people will be drawn to state government and, with the leadership of the Governor, will revitalize the state bureaucracy and "get the government moving again."
- Situations which have lacked effective government action for too long will be redressed through aggressive legislative programs and administrative action by the new "do something" government.
- Pockets of waste and inefficiency will be eliminated through a better budget process to ensure that the taxpayer gets his money's worth from every dollar that he puts into state government.
- Corruption and petty bureaucratic nit-picking will be reduced, if not eliminated entirely.
- The Governor, and perhaps his spouse, will set a new tone for leadership, and their example will influence citizen action in many fields, not just state government.
- The state party will be revitalized, and stronger candidates will be fielded for state legislative and congressional seats and in local elections.
- The state will, by the Governor's strong leadership, make its mark on the national government, and the Governor's own political acumen will help improve national decisions and perhaps even propel him into the national spotlight.

Equally important, and perhaps more pressing, will be such substantive goals as equalizing support of education, fighting crime, developing a more progressive tax policy, and improving air and water quality or human services. In some cases they will be achieved; in others they will not. Whether, when and how well these and other objectives are achieved will depend to a major degree on what happens between the election and the inauguration.

THE IMPORTANCE OF A SMOOTH TRANSITION

Transitions are inherently difficult. The new Governor has all the problems of someone assuming a demanding new job. In addition, he is expected to recruit many people to state service in a short period of time and weld them into a smoothly functioning team capable of producing a budget (or amending one) and a legislative program, working with the legislature and the press, and answering an enormous volume of mail. (See suggested transition timetable in appendix 1.) At the same time, in states with a Governor's mansion, the Governor must worry about moving his family into a new house. As one former Governor described the transition situation:

> No corporation, even in a hostile takeover situation, would ever handle transition the way we do in the states. It's as though you fired the president of a company, plus all the heads of operating divisions and the staff of the corporation central office all at once.

For the new Governor the transition is of critical importance. A good transition can help him manage the necessary office details between election and inauguration more smoothly, improve his capacity to develop a budget and legislative program almost immediately after taking office, help him learn his job better and faster, and provide his staff with systems and procedures that will at least see them through the period before they have decided upon their own procedures. Most important, a good transition can give the new administration momentum in the eyes of the press, public and legislature—momentum that can feed upon itself as further successes develop.

A good transition also is important to the outgoing Governor, who usually will want to do as much as possible to guarantee continued good and efficient government in his state. It is also likely that the outgoing Governor will want to be personally helpful to his successor—in some cases from personal friendship and from having had a hand in choosing him, in other cases from common political party affiliation, and in still other cases from a concern for the government of the state. He may want the new Governor to take into account the personal needs and problems of the existing staff, perhaps even to retain individuals in certain positions. And, a cooperative transition atmosphere may encourage the new Governor to provide the outgoing Governor with the clerical support and office supplies he will need to handle correspondence regarding his term as Governor.

The combination of an outgoing Governor who recognizes no responsibility for transition whatever and an incoming Governor who does not plan properly for transition and/or does not implement well whatever plan he has can mean disaster for both the old and new administrations.

Benefits of a Good Transition

These are likely to be among the benefits of a good transition:

- The new Governor's transition office is not usually tied up with the campaign "clean up" role of thank-you notes and paying bills; it establishes a schedule of dates in preparing to assume office and adheres to those dates.

- A budget director-designate is named, and extensive liaison takes place with the current state budget staff so that the new Governor is not forced to live with his predecessor's policies and priorities as reflected in the budget, but instead places his own distinctive mark on the budget.

- A budget coordinator assures that the outgoing Governor will not spend the Governor's office budget during the first part of the fiscal year at a rate above what is sustainable for the whole year.

- The new Governor designates appointees to key agency positions and/or assures existing agency directors or deputies that they can remain on an "acting" status, maintaining senior personnel in all key agencies.

- Mail received in the transition office is efficiently answered, and mail the new Governor receives after assuming office is properly responded to, leaving writers with a favorable impression of the new Governor.

- The press praises the new Governor because of his initial display of leadership and management ability, and there is similar praise for the outgoing Governor's help in transition.

- The day after inauguration, the Governor's office phones ring incessantly, but receptionists, facing their first actual day on the job, have been trained to handle requests for appointments with the Governor, citizen calls on policy, requests for positions in the new administration, and policy problems by referring them to a staff that has clear assignments on who is responsible for what.

- The new Governor, who promised to reshape state government, has developed a good working knowledge of state government issues and comes up with a well-designed program. He also gains significant momentum with the legislative leadership.

It is easy to see by these examples that a good transition effort between election day and inauguration can produce a long-lasting favorable political and administrative impact. A successful transition makes it possible for the new Governor to have a successful and productive first 100 days, establish a "honeymoon" relationship with the legislature and the public, and develop substantial momentum for the budget and legislative program.

Contributors to a Smooth Transition

The outgoing Governor's primary contribution to a smooth transition is to communicate throughout his administration the policy that, regardless of what may have happened in the campaign, the transition will be a cooperative one. The outgoing Governor should make available a reasonable amount of time for discussion with his successor on the duties of the office, and he should require his subordinates to do the same with the new Governor's staff or their designated successors in office. He should avoid decisions that he would not make were he succeeding himself, such as spending the Governor's office budget at a rate that could not be sustained for the entire year or last-minute reclassification of state positions. Problems of the Governor-elect may be eased by making available to him resources, such as planning and budgeting staffs, that will be underutilized during transition, and by encouraging those staffs to prepare briefings for the incoming Governor. He may also make sure that he leaves for the new Governor the documents and records essential for efficient operation of the Governor's office.

Often the new Governor begins with transition tasks that the campaign staff considers most important, such as eliminating campaign debts, writing thank-you letters, and closing campaign offices. It is critical to an effective transition, however, that these functions be delegated as much as possible to junior staff members and volunteers, while the senior staff focuses immediately on key transition problems.

Of course, the new Governor must quickly assess, and meet, the various constitutional and statutory deadlines for transition. (See appendix 2.) In addition, the new Governor and his staff need to avoid attitudes that tend to make transition cooperation less palatable for the outgoing administration. As one former Governor, who was defeated by his successor, commented:

> The incoming and outgoing Governors can make transition work smoothly and relatively painlessly if they want to. Each must eat a bit of humble pie and see to it that staffers do likewise. In our state, it worked well once the incoming Governor was reminded that the campaign was over . . . and that sarcastic statements to the press afterwards were not helpful to orderly and cooperative transition.

Some of the responsibility for smooth transition falls on civil servants whose protection from political turnover is justified in part by the need for continuity. Transition imposes a special obligation on those professional staffs who contribute to the decision making of the Governor, such as state planning and budgeting staffs. New Governors and their staffs can profitably focus on the potential of such agencies to help them both before and after inauguration. These staffs are in an especially good position to provide useful information on state government to the new Governor and his staff in such areas as government organization, budgeting and major issues which affect more than one department.

FINANCING THE TRANSITION

An orderly transition is impossible without some kind of funding. New Governors are provided some form of transition financing in 39 states. (See appendix 3.) Statutes in many of these states require the incumbent to designate a staff contact for transition and make available office space and support services. However, because some states do not have these arrangements and others do not cover all costs, the new Governor must normally consider other ways to finance the transition office operation.

Costs during the transition period fall into three categories: (1) preparing for the inauguration; (2) winding up the campaign; and (3) running the transition office. Inauguration costs usually are (and should be) handled separately by an office or committee responsible for inauguration arrangements. Post-election campaign costs (e.g., closing down campaign offices, paying bills for prior service to the campaign, thank-yous to workers and contributors, and filing necessary financial reports) should also be separated from transition costs, particularly in those cases where state funds will be used to finance the transition office.

The transition office rapidly becomes a busy operation. The transition staff has to identify, recruit and interview potential appointees to key positions. This activity alone will consume the Governor-elect's time for many days and can easily tie up several full-time staff members. And it will generate a substantial volume of mail that should, at a minimum, be read and acknowledged. In addition, the transition office may be appointing and managing transition task forces, planning for the occupancy of the Governor's office, beginning to look at the major state issues that will be faced at inauguration, and preparing the inaugural address.

An immediate post-election priority for the new Governor or his chief of staff is to prepare a transition office budget. This budget, which should separate out campaign-related costs, will give him a reasonable idea of the financing problem which he faces. The budget can be financed in one or more of these ways: (1) transition funds from the state; (2) leftover campaign funds; (3) additional fund solicitation as an extension of the campaign; (4) a special solicitation for transition support, which unlike campaign expenses can be deductible for tax purposes; (5) use of volunteers; (6) use of contributed services, such as office space and copy machines, from private organizations or the state; and (7) indirect state support along the lines discussed below. Because state laws differ, the new Governor's staff should examine their state's pertinent statutes before pursuing these alternatives.

In addition to the transition appropriation in the states that have one, there are numerous ways that an incumbent Governor can use state resources to assist in meeting transition costs, whether or not a specific transition statute exists. These include:

• Encouraging state department directors to hire the new Governor's designees as consultants during the period between their availability for full-time work and inauguration;

• Making available state office facilities for all or part of the transition staff and task forces;

• Providing state office supplies and equipment to the transition office;

  • Detailing state clerical help to the transition office; and

  • Utilizing the Governor's office budget or those of the planning and budgeting agencies to purchase the services of transition staff members working on matters closely related to the mission of those agencies.

SOURCES OF TRANSITION ASSISTANCE

In most cases, the major sources of staff work for the transition will be the Governor's campaign staff and those existing state staff members the outgoing Governor will (or can) make available to his successor. The specific tasks that can be assigned to these groups are discussed in detail in the chapters of this handbook that deal with such matters as mail, scheduling, appointments to positions, office organization, and policy development.

In addition to state and campaign staffs, Governors have some other potential sources of assistance during transition. A number of Governors-elect have established task forces to assist in the formulation and resolution of transition issues.

The most elaborate approach is to assign one or more individuals to every major department or function of state government for transition purposes. The objective of such task forces is to obtain, on a department-by-department basis, briefing material that could come from central staff agencies and individual departments, such as listings of major functions, key current issues, and policy proposals. Task forces may also share in the responsibility for identifying persons who would be suitable for key positions. These task forces could be concerned with the mechanical aspects of transition or with broad policy issues such as welfare reform, or both.

Task forces may provide some insights for the new agency director, but most of their findings will not result in any action until the new director is selected. One problem with such an approach is that the public or state agency officials may become disillusioned if the task force recommendations are not acted upon early in the new administration because the Governor is preoccupied with the selection of personnel and development of a budget and legislative program.

Perhaps a preferable approach is to appoint transition task forces on a more selective basis. This approach has much to commend it because it requires much less effort in recruiting and supervising task forces and can be tied directly to the campaign commitments of the new Governor. Some task forces, formal or informal, may have developed around particular issues during the campaign and can be continued. Others can be put together on a temporary basis to deal with particular issues where the new Governor has a position that needs to be developed into specific legislation, administrative rules or budget proposals early in his term.

Such task forces are particularly suitable in complex areas where a number of detailed decisions need to be made and where the proposals need to be in final form quickly. Examples are tax reform, election law reform, sunshine legislation, school aid formula revision and government reorganization.

A note of caution for the new Governor about transition task forces: some members of such groups may feel that their work is tantamount to appointment as an agency director or at least a major position in state government. A Governor is wise to clarify the limits of a task force's mandate—before appointing its members. In addition, part-time volunteers may not do as thorough a job on assigned issues as the new Governor might desire.

For the outgoing administration, an array of task forces can be treated as an extension of the staff of the new Governor. However, the outgoing administration should avoid deferring excessively to the views of members of such task forces. There may be situations in which the outgoing administration will wish to be influenced by the views of the incoming one, as expressed by the new Governor and his immediate staff. However, it does not follow that either the outgoing Governor or the incoming Governor would like individual cabinet members to make decisions reflecting the views of task force members who may have only occasional contact with the new Governor and his staff.

In addition to whatever help is provided by the outgoing Governor, the new Governor may find former Governors of his state to be useful advisors on subjects ranging from organizing the office to major policies. Governors of other states provide transition assistance through the Seminar for New Governors and publications of the National Governors' Association (NGA).

Additional assistance is available from the NGA Center for Policy Research. Through the Center's office of state services, NGA makes available staff members with top-level experience in Governors' offices, as well as persons experienced in state planning and budgeting. In addition, members of current Governors' staffs, schedules permitting, can come to state capitols for short periods to consult with new Governors and their aides. Besides this organized effort, current Governors are often pleased to render advice to their new colleagues on an informal basis. On occasion, current Governors have loaned key staff members, such as budget or planning directors, to new Governors for brief periods.

IMPROVING THE NEXT TRANSITION

When the new Governor is occupied with the problems of taking office, concern about the transition that will occur when he leaves office will clearly not be uppermost in his mind. However, his first year in office, when the next transition is a distant event, is probably the best time to achieve legislative action on transition matters.

New Governors in states that do not have transition statutes should consider recommending legislation to cover such matters as providing funds to the new Governor during transition, the use of state office space by the new Governor, the designation of someone responsible for transition liaison by the outgoing Governor, and perhaps the disposition of files and records. Consideration should also be given to authorizing later dates for the submission of the Governor's budget and legislative program during the new Governor's first year.

There also should be consideration of plans to provide the outgoing Governor with certain staff services and office space to ease his transition out of office. Much of what former Governors do during their initial months out of office is essentially state business—answering correspondence and reviewing files and papers for archives.

OTHER ASPECTS OF TRANSITION

Many activities of new Governors that begin during transition will continue through the critical first 100 days of the new administration. The extent of such activities will vary a great deal from state to state. Before inauguration, some new Governors will have made a good start on such subjects as the detailed development of legislative programs and will have completed the task of finding persons to be appointed to key positions. Others will make less progress during the transition period.

Because of these differences, most of the substantive aspects of transition are considered along with the activities of the first 100 days in office in the chapters which follow. The suggested timetable in appendix 1 of this handbook provides a detailed check list of matters to be undertaken during transition.

CHAPTER THREE

Organizing the New Governor's Office

The choice and structure of the Governor's staff is clearly a decision critical to the success of his administration. If the staff is organized in such a way as to fairly reflect and represent the Governor's outlook and desires, many, if not most, of the details of the administration—both from functional and policy viewpoints—will run without the day-to-day personal supervision of the Chief Executive. The Governor's time is too limited and the calls upon that time too demanding to permit more than a general overview of most of the actions of his administration.

— *a former Governor*

SUMMARY

Although the size of the Governor's immediate office staff tends to vary with the state's population, many basic tasks must be performed by the Governor's office in all states. The size and structure of the staff will be determined by the Governor's initial decisions on how to handle liaison with state agencies, staff-line roles, support agencies, regional and Washington, D.C., offices, and constituent services, as well as by budget constraints.

The Governor's executive assistant manages the Governor's time and work load as well as the operation of the immediate office. The executive assistant often oversees the interaction between staff members and the Governor, supervises responses to nonroutine mail, participates in all policy or program decisions, and serves as an alternate policy contact for agency heads. The extent to which the executive assistant may control staff and agency access to the Governor is a sensitive issue that requires early and careful resolution.

Other common staff positions in the Governor's office which are described in detail in this chapter include the following:

• *The press secretary* has one of the few jobs in the Governor's office that is similar to its counterpart in the campaign. Some Governors have expanded the role of the press secretary into that of a communications director, who may pursue an aggressive program of public information on behalf of the Governor. Press secretaries usually have direct access to the Governor and often participate actively in development of new policies. Press offices range in size from one part-time person to about 15 people.

• *The legislative assistant* sometimes has a combination of functions, particularly in those states with brief legislative sessions. Duties include assisting in preparation of the legislative program, scheduling regular meetings between the Governor and legislators, serving as the administrative contact for legislators, evaluating bills for the Governor's signature or veto, assessing legislative reaction to administration proposals, and exercising supervision over agency lobbying.

• *The Governor's personal secretary* often is responsible not only for correspondence and paperwork management, but also for controlling access to the immediate office and supervising clerical personnel. Sometimes the personal secretary also manages the Governor's scheduling.

• *The scheduling assistant*, in offices where the personal secretary does not handle scheduling, develops the Governor's itinerary and receives, and sometimes creates, invitations for appearances by the Governor. Since the Governor's time requires careful management, the scheduling assistant is usually responsible for the weekly schedule, while the personal secretary manages last-minute changes during the day.

• *The legal advisor* is the liaison between the Governor and the attorney general. He provides legal advice to the Governor and his staff in addition to supervising clemency and extradition procedures. The extent to which the legal advisor monitors agency requests to the attorney general for legal opinions varies from state to state.

• *The state-federal relations coordinator* is usually found in medium-size and larger offices. The state-federal relations function is sometimes undertaken by the executive assistant; it also may be shared with a Washington office or other state agencies.

• *The special assistant for appointments* does the staff work for hundreds of appointments that the Governor must make each year to boards, commissions, regulatory agencies and judicial positions.

• *The assistant for agency liaison* frequently is appointed to be the Governor's representative to and coordinator of state agencies. The liaison assistant is often responsible for directing interagency activities and monitoring specific programs of interest to the Governor.

Dealing with the mail, casework and telephone calls from the public will require a great deal of staff time. Some Governors also designate staff members to solicit suggestions, advice and support from special ethnic, regional and professional groups whose interests transcend agency jurisdictions.

Most Governors' offices have someone who functions informally as the principal political advisor in addition to other specified duties. There also is usually a "perspective keeper," a person (often outside the administration) who ensures that the Governor is not insulated from constructive criticism and public reaction.

Organizing the New Governor's Office

In considering the appropriate size for their staff, new Governors may find the experience of their colleagues in other states to be as helpful as the experience of their predecessors.

To obtain this information, the National Governors' Association conducted a survey of the states' practices regarding staffing of the immediate office of the Governor. The immediate office staff was defined as persons who:

> . . . are located in physical proximity to the Governor, report to him or a member of his immediate staff, and function primarily in the capacity of rendering advice and assistance to the Governor in such areas as office management, clerical work, legal advice, press relations, appointments and personnel matters, state-federal relations, speech writing, etc.

On the basis of returns from a representative group of 34 states, the average Governor's office in 1976 had a staff of 38 people (clerical and professional). The distribution of offices by size is shown below:

Staff Size	Number of States Reporting
Under 10	2
10-20	7
21-30	13
31-50	6
Over 50	6

As would be expected, the size of the Governor's office tends to vary directly with the population of the state being served. However, in proportion to population, Governors' staffs tend to be larger in the less populous states. This result is not surprising because certain tasks, such as those associated with developing a legislative program and budget, are the same in certain respects for a Governor's office in a large state and a small one.

The size of the Governor's immediate staff does not necessarily indicate the degree of activity. Rather, it may reflect differences in the allocation of tasks to the Governor's immediate staff. For example, the state planning office—although generally located outside the Governor's office—is used for many functions performed in Governors' offices in some states.

As the size of the Governor's office increases, more specialization in staff functions tends to occur. Analysis of data furnished by Governors' offices in 1976 suggests that larger staffs are more likely to provide for:

- Functional area liaison dealing with subjects like transportation, education, environmental quality, etc.;
- State-federal relations;
- Separation of legal and legislative responsibilities; and
- Policy or planning coordination.

However, factors other than aggregate staff size also influence decisions on staffing, and no hard and fast conclusions can be drawn from these data.

The question of how large a staff to have interacts with the budget available for the new Governor's staff. Other factors, such as salary levels necessary to attract good people, interact with budget size. However, there is not always a direct relationship between staffing and budget; state practices vary regarding which staff members and costs are carried in the Governor's office budget and which are in the budgets of other agencies. These questions are considered at the end of this chapter.

DECISIONS ON MAJOR OFFICE FUNCTIONS

From a functional standpoint, there are a few major decisions which must be addressed in deciding the overall framework for the Governor's staff. (Note that each of these functions is discussed in greater detail in subsequent chapters.) These decisions include:

Liaison with state agencies—Governors in many states have their agency heads deal directly with the Governor's press secretary, legislative assistant and other staff members and, when appropriate, with the Governor. Governors in other states have aides with functional specialties (e.g., health, transportation) who are assigned liaison responsibility for particular agencies. Offices with formal agency liaison functions generally have a significantly larger staff than those without them.

Staff-line roles—The new Governor's choice of management models, as discussed in chapter 7, will have a major impact on staff size. If the Governor plans to rely heavily on line agencies (the major state departments with program functions) and to accomplish coordination primarily through lead agencies and coordinating groups of agency personnel, the need for staff in the immediate office of the Governor will be less than if the Governor contemplates a stronger coordinating role for his personal staff.

Use of staff agencies—Agencies such as those charged with planning and budgeting responsibilities can provide considerable staff support to the Governor. (See appendix 7.) The more the Governor decides to rely upon these agencies for staff support, the smaller his immediate staff can be.

Other offices—Some Governors choose to maintain offices outside of the state capitol that they consider to be a part of their immediate office. These include: (1) offices in Washington, D.C., to deal with state-federal relations; (2) offices in the state's largest city when it is not the state capital, such as the New York office in New York City and the Illinois office in Chicago; and (3) decentralized Governor's offices around the state to receive and act on citizen concerns, as in Kentucky. Decisions to have such offices can substantially increase the Governor's staffing needs.

Dealing with mail and citizen complaints—The size of a Governor's staff will obviously be affected by the volume of citizen relations activities. The Governor's decisions on how to deal with phone calls and mail from the general public will also affect staff size. At one extreme, some Governors assign much of this activity to line agencies, thus minimizing demands on the immediate office staff. Other Governors prefer a strong staff role in responses and follow-up action.

The decisions made on major office functions such as these will help determine staff size. But whatever decisions are made on these functions, any Governor's staff will reflect most, if not all, of the staff roles that are discussed in the following sections.

THE GOVERNOR'S EXECUTIVE ASSISTANT

State constitutions and statutes are generally silent on the composition of the Governor's staff, unless the Lieutenant Governor is considered to be a part of that staff.

Because of the differences in states' historical patterns and in personal preferences and operating styles among Governors, and because of the varied interests and skills of the persons who work for them, there is no single typical organization for a Governor's office.

However, the position of executive assistant or principal aide is a common one among the states. Although perceptions of the role vary from state to state, it typically involves someone on the immediate staff of the Governor who is considered the senior or top-ranking aide, or the "first among equals" of the aides to the Governor. In some states this position has a long history, and it is simply assumed that a new Governor will appoint someone to this role. In other states the role has differed from administration to administration.

The title executive assistant is used in 21 states. Other titles used for the position, in order of frequency of use, are: executive secretary, administrative assistant, administrative director, senior executive assistant, executive assistant-chief of staff, chief executive assistant to the Governor, chief secretary, chief executive officer, counsel to the Governor, executive administrator, executive coordinator, and administrative assistant-legislative and legal affairs.

Should There Be an Executive Assistant?

One of the most important—and sometimes one of the most difficult—questions facing a Governor-elect is whether to have an executive assistant. As noted above, most Governors do.

Asked whether they would "advise new Governors to have an executive assistant or chief of staff through whom most of the agencies and immediate staff would report on most occasions," three-fourths of the former Governors responding said yes. The comments in support of this conclusion focused primarily on utilization of the Governor's time. Some examples of comments supporting affirmative answers are:

> In my state there are over 200 agencies and departments, and if each reported to the Governor (as each would like to do), the Governor would not have time to do anything else. It is essential that someone screen agency reports, not to keep them from the Governor but simply to condense them into manageable size. Each agency would like to make a presentation of several hours to each Governor, and this is obviously impossible.

> This (yes) answer is valid only if the Governor keeps up thoroughly with what is going on. There can be no "deputy Governor."

> There is a necessity for clearance through a staff member of management matters in order to better utilize the Governor's time. Many matters can be disposed of without directly going to the Governor when the assistant knows the policy and attitudes of the Governor. However, never preclude an agency or staff member from having access to the Governor if the situation requires. Keep an open-door policy.

> It is not practical for a Governor to divide his time between decision making and maintaining a system of orderly procedure for receiving requests for decisions and then transmitting these decisions back to their source. An administrative assistant must be that special person who fully understands the administrative and economic views of the Governor, as minor decisions and options must be reflected by that person from time to time. That assistant should know by instinct when to render an opinion and when to merely log the request and refer it to his Governor.

> This is almost an absolute necessity if the Governor is to have enough time to do constructive thinking.

Many of the former Governors who support the concept of an executive assistant were careful to warn that the executive assistant should not be allowed to cut off the access of agency heads and/or staff to the Governor personally on at least some occasions and subjects. The former Governors opposed to the concept of an executive assistant also stressed the point of access:

> Department heads want to deal with the boss. Only the Governor has the authority and moral leadership to coordinate and solve small problems before they become big ones.

> The major concern I had was to be sure I was fully and accurately informed. Therefore, I wanted all department heads to have direct access to me at all times. They were given the responsibility, and I wanted no layer of staff between us.

> A Governor is an administrator. There should not be a barrier between the Governor and agencies reporting to the chief executive.

Especially immediate staff (should report directly to Governor). The inflow of ideas, solutions, opportunities must be varied and diverse. The filter principle is inevitable, but if a Governor can't accommodate the direct reporting of administrative/financial/legal/press/political (aides) and at least his party chairman, he is becoming the alter ego of his own subordinate.

It is better to have several and perhaps as many as a half dozen who have access to the Governor as well as areas of responsibility.

I believe that state government is not so large as to prevent a Governor from meeting with the heads of agencies. He cannot delegate that responsibility.

Access, of course, is more than a matter of titles. The comments of former Governors suggest that some of them with strong views about maintaining access did so while having a single executive assistant. Even in states having no formally designated executive assistant, a single dominant staff member may emerge.

What Executive Assistants Do

In considering the role of executive assistant, it is important to distinguish between states with relatively large Governors' staffs and those with smaller ones. In those with larger staffs, such functions as legislative liaison, office management, schedule coordination and legal counsel tend to be handled by specific individuals who perform only one such function. In such states, the executive assistant has greater responsibility for internal staff coordination than in states with smaller staffs where the executive assistant performs one or more of these other functions.

In the 1976 survey, when asked if others on the Governor's staff "routinely clear with you before interacting with the Governor," only six executive assistants said no. Sixty-nine percent responded with an unambiguous yes, and the remainder indicated that this is generally the practice in their states. Nearly all executive assistants reported that they receive nonroutine mail and are responsible for answering it, although responses may initially be drafted elsewhere in the office or in the agencies.

Only 14 percent of the executive assistants reported that they do not routinely sit in on all meetings where policy or program decisions are being considered by the Governor. The remainder perform this function generally or with a few exceptions. Twenty percent reported that they are not the prime point of contact for agency heads who want to discuss policy or programs with the Governor. The remaining 80 percent do act as the point of contact, but many reported some exceptions regarding agency heads who are particularly close to the Governor.

Executive assistants also generally review, monitor or screen the Governor's office staff paperwork before the Governor sees it. Among their other duties, most executive assistants also act as a contact point for people outside the state government structure, review proposed form letters of response to the Governor's mail, and clear press releases. More details on how executive assistants view their roles are contained in the table in appendix 5.

From this discussion it can be seen that the executive assistant is often the person who stays "back home" and keeps things going when the Governor travels out of state.

Yet no combination of data from the various states can capture the subtle interpersonal working relationships that develop in even the smallest of Governor's offices and the changes in those relationships over time. For example, a new Governor may have designated an executive assistant early in his administration with the intent of creating a strong role, almost a deputy Governor role. As his term progresses, the Governor may find himself relying more on the advice and assistance of someone else on his staff and/or one or more members of the cabinet, such as a secretary of finance or administration. These types of shifts are more likely to affect informal views of working relationships than formal roles as seen from the outside. Thus, when an executive assistant reports that staff members routinely clear with him before interacting with the Governor, as nearly seven in 10 did in responding to NGA's survey, he may be referring to a relatively pro forma interaction in one state and a clear supervisory relationship in another.

Executive Assistant's Influence

As a practical matter, organizational charts of the Governor's office normally do not fully portray the impact of the executive assistant. In some, the executive assistant is positioned between the Governor and the rest of the staff of the immediate office, signaling that everyone on the staff reports to the executive assistant. In others, the staff is divided between those who report to the executive assistant and those (typically including the press secretary and legislative liaison) who do not.

Whatever his location on the organizational chart, an executive assistant often has as much influence on the activities of agency heads as on the staff in the immediate office of the Governor. Over time, the power of his office depends on such factors as:

- The accessibility of the Governor;
- The accessibility of the executive assistant;
- The extent to which the executive assistant is perceived as a correct predictor of the Governor's views;
- The "clout" of other staff members in the Governor's office;
- The extent to which the Governor will accept "clearance with the executive assistant" as an adequate defense for any agency head whose actions are criticized; and
- The extent to which the executive assistant has hiring and firing authority over other members of the Governor's staff.

The consensus among former Governors' staff members is that, regardless of the role envisioned, one person nearly always assumes the role of cabinet coordinator and staff director. He or she is usually the executive assistant.

THE PRESS SECRETARY

All Governors' offices have someone responsible for contacts with the media. In about half the states, this person is called the Governor's press secretary. Other states use such titles as news secretary, public information officer and director of public affairs.

Selecting the Press Secretary

The function of press secretary is one of the few functions of the Governor's office that bears strong resemblance to the same activity in the campaign. For that reason, many Governors have as their first press secretary the person who held that job during the campaign. In 1976, about 40 percent of the press secretaries had served on their Governor's campaign staff. Press secretaries generally have had some experience working for the news media. About 68 percent of the press secretaries active in 1976 had previously worked for print media, 45 percent in public relations, and 39 percent for electronic media. Twenty-three percent had worked outside of these fields, primarily as teachers. A number of press secretaries had had experience in more than one field, with print media and public relations the most frequent combination.

Press Secretary or Communications Director?

Some states, as well as the White House, have experimented with the position of director of communications. The thought behind this title is that there is much more to the job than dealing with the press. Advocates of the concept argue that Governors should adopt an overall approach to communications, including both activities normally performed by press secretaries and activities, such as mail and public contacts, that are often performed by others. They urge an aggressive approach to scheduling, for example, with the Governor's staff seeking out events rather than selecting among an array of invitations that happen to have been received.

This approach can, of course, be adopted without a communications director. In one state, the Governor's news secretary took on the task of redesigning the state's graphics (e.g., letterheads, news release forms, and certificates). Others in press secretary positions have become concerned with the readability of departmental annual reports and brochures. These are but two of many instances where press secretaries have adopted a broader view of their communications functions.

The Governor and His Press Secretary

The relationship between press secretaries and Governors tends to be quite close. Press secretaries are frequently given the authority to interrupt meetings and to see the Governor without going through any kind of scheduling process, sometimes even without checking with the Governor's personal secretary. While this flexibility can disturb an otherwise orderly schedule, it does permit the administration to react quickly to media problems. Press secretaries also frequently accompany their Governors on out-of-town trips. In 1976, 55 percent reported that they normally travel with the Governor, and only seven percent reported that they seldom, if ever, do.

One press secretary summed up the significance of his role to the Governor:

> It is important for the Governor to understand and appreciate that good press relations can make or break an administration. It is imperative that the press secretary and Governor have a good rapport and that the press secretary be assured of ready access to the Governor and to policy decisions and other activities within the administration.

Press secretaries tend to value highly their direct access to the Governor, no doubt reflecting the frustrations of the job when the Governor is unavailable and the statehouse press corps is demanding an immediate answer to a question that the press secretary cannot answer without consulting him. As one press secretary put it:

> If I had to single out the most important tool of a press secretary, it would be that the press secretary must be fully informed of both the policy and work of the Governor's staff and the policy and work of the agencies under the Governor's control. It is imperative that the press secretary attend all meetings where policy decisions are made or where background is presented in advance of those policy decisions. One cannot react to media inquiries or help shape the public image of the Governor without this kind of information. The lack of it is dangerous and detrimental to the media and ultimately the public conception of the Governor.

Obtaining and maintaining this access, however, can be made more difficult if the press secretary abuses it. Other staff members who have access problems of their own tend to resent the use of access for matters which they consider less important. There is, of course, no solution to this problem except the Governor's own judgment. From the perspective of a press secretary who is trying to maintain good relations with the press and a reputation for quick response to press questions, confirming or denying the rumor that the Governor is considering a particular person for some minor appointment is important. From the perspective of a Governor and his executive assistant who are busy putting the finishing touches on an important speech due to be delivered in 20 minutes, it may seem less important.

A comparison of the responses of Governors' executive assistants and press secretaries suggests that actual working relationships vary substantially among the states. In states where tradition and the personalities involved have combined to give the executive assistant a very strong role, the press secretary probably gets much of his substantive guidance from the executive assistant rather than from the Governor directly, although the press secretary and the Governor might have considerable direct contact. In other states with a somewhat less powerful executive assistant, the press secretary not only has ready access but can be a powerful force in the making of policy.

A new Governor needs to consider which role he would like his press secretary to play. One approach is for the press secretary to serve as one of the senior members of the Governor's group of advisors who is invited to all major meetings, who is listened to on many subjects which may or may not have press relations aspects, and who feels free to discuss with the Governor such matters as overall administration strategy. This approach is feasible only when the Governor values highly the advice of the press secretary on a wide range of subjects.

A second approach is to have the press secretary participate in the deliberations leading up to major policy decisions, but to limit his role to commenting on such questions as how the press is likely to react to the alternatives being considered. Where potential press reaction is not a factor in the decision, the press secretary would not attend meetings with the Governor.

There are arguments for each approach. On the one hand, having been in on the decision-making process, the press secretary will be in a better position to explain the decision and why various alternatives were rejected. His participation will also facilitate the preparation of press releases and statements announcing decisions.

On the other hand, such participation can be viewed as not fully necessary. Fifteen percent of the press secretaries reported that they do not normally sit in on meetings where policy and program decisions are being considered. One of these press secretaries noted: "It is not the role of a press secretary to formulate policy. Rather, his role is to report policy."

Functions of the Press Office

Essentially all state press offices serve as a point of contact for media personnel seeking to schedule time with the Governor. Press offices arrange news conferences, prepare news releases, and advise the Governor and his top staff on potential media reaction to proposed policies. Most press secretaries also are responsible for preparing news summaries or clippings for the Governor. The Governor's media relations are discussed in greater detail in chapter 10.

Almost all press offices do some speechwriting. In 1976, 86 percent of Governors' press secretaries reported that they prepare speeches and messages. When the writing is done elsewhere, press secretaries normally review drafts for potential impact on the public.

Size of the Press Office

The appropriate size for a press office will depend upon such questions as the number of reporters to be dealt with, the extent to which the press secretary will also serve as a policy advisor, and the involvement of the office in the preparation of speeches and proclamations. Of the 45 states reporting their staffing patterns in 1976 (clerical and professional combined), four handled the press functions with one person working less than full time; four used a single person; 13 ranged between one and one-half and two and one-half full-time persons; eight had an office of three persons; and the remaining 16 had staffs ranging upward to 15 persons.

Whether or not there is a speechwriter on the staff depends on the Governor's need for speech material. A number of Governors are comfortable without prepared texts for most speeches and have major speeches—such as state-of-the-state addresses and budget messages—written as a major effort by many different staff members. Other Governors prefer to operate from prepared texts or detailed notes and like to have others collect for them such diverse materials as humorous stories and "local color" information on the places where they speak. In the latter case, a speechwriter may be part of the Governor's office staff.

The speechwriting function includes:
- Collecting substantive materials and recommendations from the agencies and staff members who are the Governor's advisors on a particular subject;
- Obtaining information about the audience before which a speech is being given;
- Developing and circulating draft speeches; and
- Working with the Governor and others (e.g., the press secretary) to put speeches in final form.

THE GOVERNOR'S POLITICAL ADVISOR

Most Governors' offices do not have a position called "political advisor." Political concerns affect all functions in a Governor's office, from press relations to personnel selection, and from legislative liaison to policy and budget allocations. All of the Governor's advisors are political advisors in the sense that they assess the possible repercussions of alternative courses of action on legislative relations, subsequent elections, and the Governor's standing with the general public and with interest groups.

However, most Governors' offices informally designate some staff person as the principal political contact, while others evolve some specialization in matters considered political. This specialization can help to cover any weaknesses in political experience in other staff positions.

In some cases, the role of political advisor is an "elder statesman" role. In others, specific duties are involved, such as advising the legislative staff on ways to persuade individual legislators on priority issues, handling patronage, dealing with state party headquarters, serving as contact person for candidate selection and recruitment, and overseeing political polling.

THE LEGISLATIVE ASSISTANT

Governors generally have one or more staff members who are responsible for dealing with the state legislature.

There is no uniformity in the titles of those who perform the legislative liaison function. Some of the titles in use include legislative liaison, legislative counsel to the Governor, legislative assistant, legislative coordinator, legislative secretary and deputy assistant for legislation. In many states, the legislative liaison and counsel functions are handled by the Governor's counsel or legal advisor.

Whether the legislative liaison job is full time or is combined with other staff functions in the Governor's office depends on the extent to which the legislature itself is full time. In some states, the legislative assistant develops the legislative program in the fall, works with a legislature that is in session from January to June, reviews bills that have been passed and sent to the Governor for signature or veto, handles special committees and special sessions in the late summer, and then begins the cycle all over again. In other states, the legislative session is restricted to shorter periods (60 days in some states) in which all legislative activities tend to be concentrated. In such states, combining the legislative function with other activities is both feasible and practical.

The normal duties of the legislative assistant include:

• Supervising the preparation of the Governor's legislative recommendations, except in states where there is a separate legal counsel who has this function;

• Working with the Governor's scheduler to arrange meetings between the Governor and legislators and providing staff support for such meetings;

• Helping with the Governor's social functions that involve legislators by advising on guest lists and scheduling;

• Serving as the point of contact within the administration for legislators who seek action by the Governor;

• Advising the Governor and other members of the administration, including agency directors, on probable legislative reactions to the administration's proposals and on how best to deal with individual legislators;

• Working with legislators and interest groups to secure acceptance of the Governor's legislative program; and

• Administering the procedure used by the Governor to determine whether to sign or veto bills that have been passed.

In those states where the Governor becomes involved in state legislative races, the legislative assistant is normally involved in providing staff work to support this activity.

In states with large legislative liaison offices, various approaches to division of labor are used, such as assigning separate staff members to the house and senate.

The legislative assistant will need to participate directly in the policy development processes which determine legislative needs. He will typically participate in discussions in the Governor's office dealing with issues ranging from budget priorities and tax policy to institution closings and judicial appointments. Normally, the legislative aide would not be expected to develop the policy or recommend a specific appointment. However, in states where the legislature meets less frequently and for shorter periods, legislative liaison duties may be assigned to staff members who are part of the Governor's policy development process, such as the executive assistant, the policy coordinator for particular functions such as human services, the planning director, the legal advisor and others.

The legislative assistant also has another key role—exercising control over agency lobbying. This control is exercised through the clearance of proposed legislation, as well as through informal checking with legislative assistants about the position the Governor would like the agency officials to take. In most states, agency officials are expected to contact legislators, work with interest groups, and perform the other activities necessary to obtain the passage of legislation in which they have an interest and for which they have the support or acquiescence of the Governor.

Several states have adopted laws to control lobbying that are applicable to agency officials as well as to private interests. In these states, agency officials must register and report expenses in much the same way as private groups. One state reported that lobbying is done by legislative assistants only. A number of states reported that they have policies that generally discourage agency officials from attending legislative sessions unless their presence has been requested by a legislator. In several other states, the primary burden of lobbying is borne by the Governor's immediate staff and a few key agency directors, such as the director of administration. Chapter 12 deals extensively with furtherance of the Governor's legislative program.

Legislative assistants have expressed their view of the unique role they play as follows:

> We (the Governor and I) feel that our greatest accomplishment was establishing a good working relationship with each legislator. We went out of our way to help them with their problems, dealt with them openly, and displayed our understanding that at times issues arise that require individual legislators to take a position opposing ours. When we requested their help on matters of special interest to us, they generally responded.
>
> The two most important factors in establishing an effective legislative liaison are (1) the ability to provide a full, factual set of arguments or explanations for executive policies, and (2) the ability to develop good personal working relationships with legislative leaders and legislators. Sometimes legislators will go along with you without question, but you

should never depend on it. Know your facts. It is also very important to understand the legislative power system and hierarchy and the rules under which the legislature operates. You have to know who to talk to, when he should be approached, and how.

THE GOVERNOR'S PERSONAL SECRETARY

The job of the personal secretary to a Governor is comparable to that of personal secretary to the head of any large organization. However, in some administrations the personal secretary's job is divided into several components, including scheduling, correspondence, and sometimes a separate clerical function to handle the Governor's dictation and much of his typing. Activities associated with the personal secretary include controlling access to the immediate office, receiving and relaying messages to and from the Governor, placing phone calls and screening incoming calls, making personal arrangements, and providing a source of information for the Governor.

The personal secretary, in some combination with the executive assistant, would normally handle all paperwork that has not been channeled elsewhere. This would include correspondence marked personal or confidential for the Governor, letters from other Governors and key federal officials, mail from the Governor's close associates, and letters or memoranda from key staff and agency heads.

A highly competent personal secretary—who has the Governor's confidence and is unswervingly loyal to him, knows the Governor's personal and political friends, recognizes important people and problems quickly, and can deal pleasantly and surely with difficult situations—can be one of the Governor's greatest assets.

THE SCHEDULING ASSISTANT

The scheduling and appointments function involves receiving (and sometimes creating) requests for the Governor to appear at events, give speeches or hold meetings; corresponding with requestors; helping the Governor to decide which requests to accept; and arranging the details of the Governor's itinerary. Chapter 8 and appendix 13 are devoted entirely to the problem of scheduling.

In small offices, this function is often handled by the Governor's personal secretary. In larger offices, an individual is usually designated to handle the schedule on a full-time basis.

There are a variety of ways to divide responsibilities between the Governor's personal secretary and the scheduling office. One common arrangement is for the scheduling office to handle all scheduling of meetings and events that require any kind of advance planning and preparation, while the secretary administers the schedule during the day. The secretary in this arrangement deals with delays and same-day rescheduling and polices the movement in and out of the Governor's office by staff members, such as the executive assistant and press secretary, whose meetings with the Governor are not formally scheduled.

When a Governor uses the concept of "advancing," the function is generally handled by the scheduling office. State practices in advance work vary considerably. In some states, personal advance work is not done at all; the scheduler arranges for someone to meet the Governor on his arrival at the event, which he attends alone or accompanied only by his security personnel. Other states have more elaborate arrangements, with someone from the Governor's staff expected to arrive at the site of the event well ahead of the Governor to check out all details, down to a minute-by-minute itinerary and all physical arrangements for the event, in order to avoid confusion or mistakes.

The advance person may also be called upon to encourage good attendance at the event, gauge the crowd, introduce the Governor to key people, and handle any last-minute requests the Governor may have.

THE GOVERNOR'S LEGAL ADVISOR

The attorney general is the Governor's legal counsel under the constitution and/or statutes of practically all states. However, in many states, the relationship between the Governor and the attorney general is not a comfortable one.

Most attorneys general are elected and are frequently not of the same party (or wing of the party) as the Governor. In addition to whatever political differences there may be between them, there are several operational areas of potential conflict. These include differences over the extent to which the lawyers employed by state agencies should report to the attorney general or to the agencies, concern that the attorney general normally provides "yes-no" answers rather than discussions of the legal risk of various options, and the potential frictions inherent in any attorney-client relationship.

As a result, most Governors' staffs include a legal advisor, who is responsible for the Governor's dealings with the attorney general's office and may oversee relations between the attorney general and agencies reporting to the Governor. He also provides legal advice to the Governor and his staff and often handles clemency and extradition decisions for the Governor. In many states the legal advisor position is not full time and is often combined with the legislative liaison position.

The extent to which the Governor's office oversees the relationship between the attorney general and state agencies reporting to the Governor differs from state to state.* Nine of the legal advisors who responded to the 1976 NGA survey reported that they review requests by

---

*Persons whose responsibilities include dealing with the attorney general are encouraged to see National Association of Attorneys General, Committee on the Office of Attorney General, *Powers, Duties and Operations of State Attorneys General* (Raleigh, 1977), which provides excellent material on such subjects as the common law powers of the attorney general and case citations involving the representation of state agencies.

state agencies for formal legal opinions before they go to the attorney general; 15 reported that they do not; and one reported that he reviews such requests sometimes. Four-fifths of the legal advisors reported that they had discussed the adequacy of representation of state agencies in specific cases with the attorney general or someone on his staff.

Legal advisors were asked to pass along any advice they may have for their counterparts in other states and for new legal advisors and new Governors as well. Some of this advice deals with the role and operating style of the legal advisor:

> The only advice I can give would be based upon my experience with my Governor, who does not stand on formality and resists excessive memoranda and paperwork generally. I can only suggest that a Governor's legal advisor try as best he can to adapt to the style of the Governor. I also recommend that extradition and clemency responsibilities be delegated to a deputy in the Governor's office. In a [large] state like [ours] . . . this is a full-time job for an attorney (who has two clerk assistants) who reports to me.

> My very first advice to a newly elected Governor would be to select a legal advisor who had a minimum of 10 years in the private practice of law. He should not be chosen from the ranks of attorneys employed in any governmental entity. Secondly, the legal advisor should, as quickly as possible, meet with the Governor and all of the administrative staff of the Governor's office to impress upon them the significance and importance of the state constitution and laws governing gubernatorial actions. . . . Also, he should zealously protect the Governor with respect to his signing documents, letters, or taking other actions requested of him by his arch supporters and campaigners who are frequently unaware of the legal implications of their honest requests. This is a constant vigil. It is also of utmost importance for a new legal advisor to establish a professional, as well as quasi-political, relationship with attorneys holding public positions throughout the state. Many times problems can be averted based solely on the quality of this credibility.

> Work with the attorney general if you can, even if he's of a different political persuasion. Most times, politics will not make a difference in legal counsel. Don't try to supplant the attorney general. Have the departments go to the attorney general for counsel if they do not have their own. Remember, your opinion is just the opinion of one more lawyer. If you have the attorney general's opinion, the Governor or department head can safely rely on it.

STATE-FEDERAL RELATIONS COORDINATOR

States usually have someone in the Governor's office dealing with state-federal relations, although this person is sometimes also the executive assistant. Many states maintain Washington offices, some of which are attached to the Governor's office, while others are attached to state agencies. Because the state planning office generally has some responsibility for federal programs and policies affecting the state, state-federal relations functions are often delegated to that office.

In the larger offices, someone working full time on state-federal relations is common. The size of the staff, if any, supporting such a person depends on the distribution of state-federal relations responsibility among the immediate office of the Governor, line agencies, and planning and budget offices.

State-federal relations is the subject of chapter 13.

SPECIAL ASSISTANT FOR APPOINTMENTS

Most Governors are responsible for making literally hundreds of appointments each year beyond the initial selection of agency heads. These appointments include university boards of trustees in some states, professional licensing boards, policy boards, state regulatory commissions, advisory commissions and special task forces.

Governors generally assign a specific staff person to handle this appointments work load, which generally includes:

- Maintaining a log of all positions filled by the Governor;

- Creating a system that triggers preliminary work on vacancies well before they are due to be filled (these two functions can be easily handled by a computer program, which greatly simplifies the work load);

- Receiving communications from agency heads, interested groups and individuals with recommendations as to who should be appointed to particular positions;

- Seeking out potential appointees to broaden the Governor's choices;

- Considering individual appointments in light of overall criteria for appointments, such as representation of political parties, sex, race, and geographic areas of the state;

- Making recommendations to the Governor and the other staff members whom the Governor consults about appointments; and

- Working with appointees on paperwork, confirmation procedures and conflict of interest questions.

While certain aspects of this position require an ability to deal with potential appointees and persons making recommendations, much of the work can be performed by persons upgraded from clerical positions. In some smaller offices it is combined with certain semiclerical functions, while in larger offices it can be the major preoccupation of a relatively senior professional staff member. In most states, recommendations for appointments are reviewed by the political advisor to the Governor.

The process of selecting persons for major state appointments is discussed in detail in chapter 5.

ASSISTANT FOR LIAISON WITH STATE AGENCIES

Many Governors have assistants who are responsible for dealing with particular state agencies or groups of agencies. These staff members may handle correspondence addressed to the Governor that relates to their agencies, coordinate the work of agency directors who are dealing with common problems, track the progress of programs that are of particular interest to the Governor, and alert the Governor to matters he may wish to discuss with the agency directors. (See appendix 6.)

In about two-thirds of the states, there are agency liaison personnel in the Governor's office. Among the remaining one-third, some have other personnel—such as "super cabinet secretaries" in Massachusetts and Virginia and the central planning staff in Utah—who serve much the same purpose. Agency liaison assistants are found more often in larger states than in smaller ones, but no absolute pattern prevails. Governors who do not have such assistants deal directly with agency directors or have their executive assistants do so.

Arguments for Agency Liaison Assistants

In some states, there are as many as 200 separate state agencies, more than the Governor can reasonably be expected to manage on a day-to-day basis. Each agency has its own set of constituents and problems. Many persons affected by the agency want to be able to discuss agency problems with someone in the Governor's office. The Governor wants to ensure that appointments to agency positions are sensitively made, to communicate his policies to the agency director, and to determine whether his policies are being followed. It is difficult for staff members engaged in such activities as press relations or legislative liaison to perform agency liaison functions because they, like the Governor, have responsibilities that extend to all agencies. They cannot effectively specialize in the problems of any particular agency or set of agencies.

Even in those states that have reorganized state government into roughly 12 to 20 agencies reporting to the Governor, assistants for agency liaison are often used to coordinate programs among agencies, handle mail, ensure that the rest of the Governor's staff understands the problems of the agency, and make certain that agency personnel understand the Governor's priorities.

Arguments against Agency Liaison Assistants

Governors in some states do not have assistants for agency liaison because they wish to keep the staff relatively small or because they lack funds. Some Governors also believe that agency directors, if properly selected, do not need help or interference from the Governor's office. In fact, some Governors feel that assistants for agency liaison might weaken the reporting relationship between them and their agency directors and thereby reduce, rather than increase, agency accountability to them.

In some states, liaison positions are designated only for agencies where the Governor has a strong personal interest or lacks the power to appoint the director, as is frequently the case in state education agencies.

According to the results of NGA's 1976 survey of agency liaison personnel, most states have a relatively small group (four to six professionals) involved in the liaison function. The most common broad functional groupings are education, transportation, labor regulation and economic development, natural resources and environment, public safety, and health and social services. These groupings often overlap those found in state budget offices and provide the Governor with another, more politically sensitive source of advice.

STAFF FOR HANDLING PUBLIC CONTACTS

Public contacts of the Governor—mail, phone calls and persons dropping by the office—will consume a considerable quantity of staff time in any Governor's office (see chapter 9). Many Governors feel that it is essential that these contacts be handled well. As one former Governor put it:

> No area is more sensitive to maintenance of good public relations for a Governor, and conversely to creating unneeded ill will, than the responses made to written and telephonic communications addressed to the chief executive's office.
>
> Accordingly, perhaps more personnel and more staff hours were devoted, in my administration, to creating and maintaining such a system than to any other single function of the office.

An average Governor's office can expect to receive at least 500 pieces of mail each day and at least half as many phone calls. Although the Governor will reach more people through the media and his speeches and travels around the state, this inflow of mail and calls represents one of his major opportunities for serving or disappointing the public. For the citizen involved, the impression he receives of the Governor and his office from responses to mail and calls will be much more "real" than images gained from media exposure.

The decision on how to organize the staff that works with the mail depends upon a number of factors—including the volume of mail, whether casework mail (mail involving an individual situation such as a person seeking payments under a particular program) will be handled totally or largely by departments, and how the Governor's staff is organized for other purposes, such as liaison with departments and agencies.

In states with a low volume of mail and a relatively small Governor's staff it is possible to combine responsibility for the mail with other staff functions.

Many Governors have established an office, such as an ombudsman or constituent service office, to handle complaints and concerns of individual citizens. Where these offices exist, they normally handle the casework mail.

When there are staff members for agency liaison, it is common for the mail to be routed to them for a decision on how it should be handled. In some states most kinds of mail are handled this way, but casework mail is handled by an ombudsman or transmitted directly to the departments by the person handling all mail.

Unless the new Governor has plans to stimulate more mail than his predecessor (e.g., by "write the Governor" campaigns), the size of his predecessor's staff for mail and public phone contacts should be indicative of the level of activity that will be required. Generally, in a state with one million or more inhabitants, filing of mail and answers will be close to a full-time job, and at least one person will be needed simply to operate automatic typewriters to issue routine responses.

The critical variable in determining the size of the staff that handles contacts with the public is the extent to which the Governor's staff—as distinct from agency staff—will do casework. If a person with a complex social problem is referred to the state social services agency, not much time will be spent on casework. If, however, someone in the Governor's office "keeps the case" and tries to line up agency services for the person, the staffing demands in the Governor's office will be substantial.

STAFF FOR CONTACT WITH SPECIAL GROUPS

Most state agencies are organized around the delivery of services (e.g., social services, education, transportation) rather than the kinds of persons to whom services are being provided (e.g., residents of central cities, farm laborers, Spanish-speaking persons, other minorities). Agencies which are organized to deal with a particular clientele, such as departments of aging or veterans affairs, frequently do not encompass many of the major state programs that reach those groups. To the extent that such groups are organized, they seek improvements from state government in areas spanning a number of different agencies. Many Governors deal with these groups through the designation of a staff member in the Governor's office to handle their special concerns. In addition, for political and/or policy reasons, Governors frequently wish to reach out to these groups for suggestions, advice and support.

In larger states, some liaison jobs of this type are considered full time. In other cases, however, the task of maintaining relations with a group will be combined with other related responsibilities. For example, the person in the Governor's office who is responsible for dealing with the agencies administering unemployment compensation, or manpower training, may also be assigned the responsibility for maintaining contact between the Governor's office and organized labor.

Decisions on whether to have liaison assistants for special groups and whom to select for such roles are difficult. In general, Governors tend to select persons who are members of the group involved (e.g., a Spanish-speaking person to serve as assistant for liaison with the Spanish-speaking community) and who have developed credibility with leading organizations representing that particular constituency. In some cases, the Governor's contact person is chosen from the leadership ranks of one of the key groups involved.

However, when selections from such groups are made, the person occupying the liaison role may have a conflict between the interests of the Governor and the interests of the group. On the one hand, persons in such positions are being asked to represent the Governor's policies and convince the outside group of their merits. On the other hand, they serve a useful purpose in keeping the Governor informed of their group's thinking. But if they let the group's norms influence their own conduct too much, they will cease being a part of the Governor's staff and become paid advocates of their group's interests within the office of the Governor.

PERSPECTIVE KEEPER

The Governor's office is an easy place in which to lose perspective. The public life of the Governor usually differs a great deal from his previously private one, with the addition of security personnel, service personnel in the mansion, and a large staff. Practically all contacts, in social as well as office settings, have governmental and political overtones. Governors seldom hear criticism, except from those on whose toes they happen to be stepping at the moment. The staff may be insulating the Governor in some fashion from the realities of public opinion or governmental administration.

Governor's office organization charts do not normally have boxes for a "perspective keeper." Someone assigned full time to keeping perspective would probably be the first to lose it. Frequently, persons with this role tend to be outside of the immediate staff—old friends, business associates and spouses. Some Governors have found cabinet officers to be useful in this regard. Staff members who have constant contact with particular groups, such as the press and legislative relations personnel, also generally play a role in trying to retain perspective.

STATE EMERGENCY MANAGEMENT COORDINATOR

Emergencies can strike at any time and have monumental human, economic and political consequences. While state agencies—such as emergency services or civil defense, energy, national guard, health, transportation and natural resources—will have roles in emergencies, the Governor should have an immediate staff member who coordinates all emergency-related activities on his behalf. In some states, this person is a special assistant who coordinates with the emergency services office and other related agencies; in others, the emergency management director is in the office of the Governor; in still others, the Governor deals directly with a trusted agency or division director.

Through his emergency manager, the Governor must be prepared to exercise a number of emergency-related options:

- Establish and maintain a comprehensive emergency management program—not only for preparedness and response, but for mitigation and recovery activities—a program based on continually updated vulnerability analyses for all risks and carried out in the context of overall state development plans;
- Coordinate a special alignment of state offices, including planning, budget and emergency services, the legislature, and substate and federal agencies to ensure comprehensive emergency management of all hazards, whether attack, man-made, or natural;
- Issue state or area emergency declarations and invoke appropriate state response actions;
- Activate emergency contingency funds and/or reallocations of state agency budgets for emergency work;
- Apply for and monitor federal disaster and emergency assistance; and
- Encourage orientation and training as needed for all state emergency program personnel.

Governors should plan in advance for an emergency management staff to carry out the role of the state in accelerating current services and providing new state and/or federal services to local governments when their resources are inadequate to mitigate, prepare for, respond to and/or recover from emergencies.

The Governor and his emergency manager may want to refer to *Comprehensive Emergency Management: A Governor's Guide*, a December 1978 publication of the National Governors' Association Center for Policy Research.

OFFICE MANAGER

The office manager is responsible for the day-to-day administration of the office. Responsibilities typically include preparing and implementing the office budget, processing fiscal paperwork, handling travel arrangements, overseeing purchasing, providing supplies, arranging for modifications of office space and telephones, and scheduling and supervising those secretaries and receptionists not assigned to particular staff members.

In some offices, responsibilities for budgeting and fiscal clerk functions are handled by another agency (such as department of finance or administration) as a service to the Governor's staff, with the executive assistant maintaining control of major decisions.

Office manager is a civil service position in some states. The skills required are comparable to those of fiscal/personnel positions in state agencies, along with the capacity to manage clerical personnel. In small offices, this function is handled as a sideline by a competent secretary, usually under the supervision of the executive assistant. In larger states, the position of office manager tends to be full time. The staff member holding the position may be called administrative assistant, office manager, special assistant to the Governor, or administrative officer, among other titles. Many persons performing this function report directly to the Governor, but in the larger states they generally report to the executive assistant.

DIRECTORS OF OUTLYING OFFICES

In states which have Governor's offices outside the capital city, the Governor must determine the reporting relationship of the directors of those offices to him and various members of his staff. With the exception of large-city offices frequently used by the Governor personally (e.g., New York City), such offices are normally quite small and are sometimes headed by a part-time person. Generally, they are staffed by relatively junior professionals who do not report directly to the Governor.

CLERICAL SUPPORT

The need for clerical personnel must also be considered in the staffing plan for the new Governor's office. Besides clerical support for professional staff members, the work associated with the mail as described above, and the keeping of any official records that the Governor is required to maintain, Governor's offices generally have at least one person who serves as receptionist and answers phone calls placed to the public number for the Governor's office. It is important for this staff member to be both competent and courteous.

SPECIAL PROJECT PERSONNEL

Some Governors expand the staff roles discussed in this chapter by temporary, and sometimes permanent, assignment of special project personnel in the Governor's office. This is one way to staff a program personally initiated by the Governor that covers responsibilities of several agencies. In other instances, Governors have created posts such as science advisor or economic advisor to produce cross-cutting advice to the Governor, his staff and agencies. Unless such staff members are clearly assigned to a tightly defined area of responsibility, jurisdictional problems may develop. Some states handle this problem by placing special projects personnel in staff support areas such as planning, budgeting or administration.

As noted earlier, the new Governor's early decisions on staff size, major functions to be handled within the office, and positions to be filled will determine to a great extent the overall organization of the office. This chapter has reviewed the principal positions found on typical Governors' staffs. Throughout this handbook, the functions of these staff members will be addressed in the context of the Governor's day-to-day management, policy-making and political duties.

CHAPTER FOUR

Staff Support for the Governor

> Without any question the most crucial aspect of an effective administration is the selection of staff. Exceptional talent and loyalty are the most important considerations. Watch out that arrogance doesn't creep into staffers' manner when dealing with state agencies. Effective campaign workers often do not prove to be the best staffers. By way of warning, any Governor in any state can drown in the details of state government and end up accomplishing nothing. He should select talented people to head agencies, give them broad responsibilities, back them up and save himself for major decisions.
>
> — *a former Governor*

SUMMARY

A new Governor must act quickly to identify his immediate staff and to utilize existing staff support to complete crucial tasks, such as budget reviews.

The demands of working in a Governor's office require more than competence alone. The Governor will require a staff with a rare blend of confidence, humility, loyalty and accessibility. An important guideline in recruiting staff is to broaden the Governor's political base by hiring individuals beyond those with personal or partisan commitments to the Governor.

One obvious source of personnel for the immediate office is the campaign staff. Recruiting from the campaign staff has the advantages of availability, shared objectives and existing working relationships. Disadvantages, in the case of some members of the campaign staff, include a lack of interest in administering state government and unfamiliarity with program operations. Sometimes it is preferable to recruit campaign staff for departmental positions rather than for the Governor's immediate staff. Other sources of personnel include the former Governor's staff, existing state agency staff, loaned executives, university personnel, officials recruited from other states, and individuals identified through the Talent Resource Exchange of the National Governors' Association.

Sources of staff support beyond the immediate office must be developed to avoid work bottlenecks, especially during the early months of the administration. The new Governor should identify valuable staff resources and expertise among state agencies. Particularly useful agencies for this purpose are the budget and planning offices, the community affairs agency and, in the case of state-federal issues, the Washington office.

- *The budget office* usually is either an independent agency reporting directly to the Governor or a division within a department of finance and administration. The budget director frequently is a political appointee or reports to an appointee of the Governor. The budget staff normally is organized along functional lines. The type of support that the budget staff will provide the Governor depends on whether the office considers its primary function to be policy development or strictly budget formulation. This orientation usually will determine whether the staff will be generalists with policy analysis skills or finance specialists seeking permanent careers in budgeting. Both can offer important staff support to the Governor.

- *The planning office* varies in size and function. Because the planning staff will not be preoccupied with completing a new budget at the time the Governor assumes office, the planning office is a valuable source of assistance for the new Governor. Staff assistance provided by the planning agency may include review of federal regulations and legislation, development of management options, response to gubernatorial correspondence, troubleshooting, development of the legislative program, and lobbying for the program. The planning staff will often perform the key analysis of major policy choices for the budget and legislative programs. Some planning offices also have legislative liaison and management responsibilities.

- *The department of community affairs* also may provide important early staff work for the Governor, particularly in designing programs of local assistance.

- *The Washington office* can be an excellent source of information and guidance on federal programs and can provide immediate advice on decisions regarding federal relations which are placed before the new Governor by aggressive agency directors.

In addition, the Governor may want to request briefing books from state agencies to obtain information on key agency issues and programs and to determine how great a contribution the agencies' staffs are able to make. Following this initial experience with staff work from different sources, the Governor can consider ways of reorganizing his staff support to accommodate the needs and direction of the new administration.

Staff Support for the Governor

The selection of staff is key to the success of any administration. This is particularly true for the immediate staff of the Governor—the executive assistant, press secretary and other persons who will work directly with the Governor.

THE IMMEDIATE OFFICE

The immediate staff will be the eyes and ears through which the Governor will gather information to help him formulate opinions on the substance of issues and the performance of state and federal agencies. The staff will be of major importance in determining whether the Governor can anticipate problems and head them off before they become serious. The press and the legislature, as well as state workers, will evaluate the Governor in part on the basis of their impression of the caliber of the immediate staff.

Errors in staff selection can result in situations that are personally and politically painful. If a Governor has little confidence in or has to remove a member of his personal staff, he is admitting, in effect, that he made an error in judgment in his initial staffing decision. Correcting errors in staff selection becomes even more painful when the person involved has close personal ties to the Governor or gave considerable personal time to the Governor's campaign. Moreover, some staff members have ties to particular constituencies and may be seen as symbols of the Governor's attitude toward the area of the state, wing of the party, or ethnic group of which they are a part.

The Need for Early Staff Work

During the first 100 days of his term, the new Governor will be making a number of important policy decisions. Some of those decisions will be based upon work done primarily by his immediate staff. Examples are:

- Recruitment and selection of department heads and other key administration personnel;

- Overall strategy and image questions—the major issues to be emphasized and the pace at which the Governor will press to implement his campaign commitments;
- Press relations; and
- The administration's relationship with the legislature and the Governor's political party.

A number of other issues involve quite different types of staff work that generally will be available from staff agencies, such as planning offices, budget offices and personnel offices, and those line agencies that have some staff functions, such as community affairs agencies. These agencies will provide early staff work in budget preparation, development of the legislative program and consideration of pending state-federal issues.

Qualities of a Good Staff Member

The criteria for selection of persons to work in a Governor's office will be similar to criteria for other important positions. The staff should have strong capacity to analyze problems, express themselves well on paper and in person, work with others, know the subject matter with which they will be dealing, and follow the leadership of the Governor. However, work in a Governor's office demands additional skills.

Self-Confidence. Higher-level employees in the immediate office should have a solid base of self-confidence. In the positions they hold, they are potentially the subject of considerable criticism and should expect to take criticism that is deflected from the Governor to them. In addition, they will often find themselves in situations where it is important to the Governor that they act on imperfect information, rather than delay. A high degree of self-confidence is required to deal with such situations, but arrogance must be avoided. This is often a fine line to walk, but it is critical to the successful operation of the Governor's office.

A Governor can pay a high price for staff members who lack self-confidence. Such persons often worry about their status in the organization and are reluctant to see others take charge of work they cannot complete. This approach causes a "hoarding" of problems and resulting bottlenecks, lack of accessibility and inaction.

Humility. Working in a Governor's office is heady business, particularly for younger persons. Staff members who five years ago were trying to figure out how to pay $25 speeding tickets may now find the head of the highway patrol waiting to see them. Heads of corporations and labor unions can be reached without delay. Paperwork flows from agencies at the hint of a request. Staff members are lobbied by many different groups, some of which may consider even an appointment to be an act of grace.

The attention received by staff members can easily lead to problems:

• Staff members may get sloppy in checking facts and in considering other opinions;

• They may appear arrogant to political supporters, legislators, agency heads and the press, all of whom may impute the apparent arrogance to the Governor personally; and

• They may develop habits—such as making people wait, delaying the return of phone calls, and cutting off comments—that will waste the time of other persons (generally other staff members and agency personnel) and alienate them.

Only a staff person with the combination of self-confidence and humility to see the attention he receives in proper perspective and place the Governor's interests first in every instance can be a true asset to the Governor.

Accessibility. How accessible the Governor and his staff can be is determined largely by their work loads. They will want to be accessible. They should want to learn the views of the average citizen, of agency middle-management personnel, of legislators, of interest group representatives. Even when other pressures on them are most severe and their time is most limited, it is important that members of the Governor's staff deal with such groups and individuals in a manner that conveys the impression that the state's highest office is interested in and accessible to them.

For example, early in an administration, groups with specific pressing problems of less-than-statewide significance (e.g., problems with a particular road) will seek to bring a delegation to see the Governor or one of his staff members. The choices available to a staff member in this situation are to agree to see the delegation or to schedule something else. Too often, staff members will agree to see such a delegation and then keep them waiting, not see them at all because of other pressing priorities that day, or rush them in and out of the office without giving them what they feel is an adequate opportunity to be heard. The result frequently is that the person who organized the delegation (often a legislator) "loses face" with the rest of the delegation and the problem doesn't get resolved.

Another approach is for the staff member to call the leader of the delegation, indicating that (1) he wants to see the delegation but will have difficulty scheduling a meeting of proper length soon because of budget preparation or other urgent problems; (2) he wants to try to solve the problem, if possible, without putting the delegation through the inconvenience of coming to the capitol at this point, and perhaps a meeting might be held later to explain the solution; and (3) he would like the leader to explain over the phone what solution the group is seeking. If there is a good backup staff, it is sometimes satisfactory for a busy

Governor's assistant to have a more junior staff member or competent secretary make the call for him.

Assuming that the staff person actually does something about the problem within a reasonable time, the second approach conveys the sense of a more accessible administration. The new Governor, in picking and instructing top-level staff, will want to consider seriously the question of accessibility.

Political sensitivity. By their nature, campaigns for office are oriented toward a specific individual and his immediate supporters. While support comes in varying degrees from other elected officials and one's political party, the candidate and his staff usually are the primary actors in raising money, making arrangements, taking positions on issues and winning voter support. This phenomenon is easily understood in an election context; it also is easily carried over as a philosophy into the immediate office of the Governor, where it is dangerous.

The accomplishments of the Governor in the campaign depend largely on persons who have committed time, money and effort. The accomplishments of the Governor in office will often depend on persons who did not make such commitments, including:

- Legislators of the opposite political party;
- Legislators, secure in their own political base, who choose to support the Governor on particular issues;
- Interest groups, acting in their own interest; and
- Bureaucrats, just doing their jobs.

Many staff members coming into a Governor's office from a campaign do not perceive the importance of these nonaligned parties. In a campaign it is essentially true that those "who are not with us are against us." This is not true in office. The mayor who is most vociferous in opposing the Governor's ethics bill for state and local government may be the strongest supporter available for a bond issue for roads. The legislator who strongly opposes the Governor's tax plan may be willing to sponsor the ethics bill.

It is a rare Governor who has a political base that provides secure majorities in both the electorate and in the legislature. Thus, a Governor needs to make sure that staff members are careful to recognize the necessity to work with many individuals and groups beyond those previously committed to the Governor.

Sources of Potential Staff Members

Persons who have worked with the Governor before and in whom the Governor has confidence are the most obvious and common source of staff for new Governors. In many cases, the Governor has had jobs (e.g., lawyer, academic, member of a state or local legislative body) with few or no employees. In such circumstances, the major source of staff members is the individuals who have worked for the Governor in the campaign.

Campaign staff. The use of the former campaign staff as the nucleus of the Governor's immediate office staff has a number of advantages, including:

1. Availability. The campaign staff is usually readily available, the election having terminated their major activity.

2. Reward. In some cases, staff members will have accepted the long hours and low (or no) pay associated with campaigning with the expectation of finding a job in state government after the election. In other cases, the Governor will simply want to do something helpful to assist former campaign workers in finding a job.

3. Loyalty. The campaign staff is an obvious place to look for persons who are loyal to the Governor.

4. Shared objectives. Members of the campaign staff would not normally have been there unless they knew and shared the major policy objectives of the Governor.

5. Existing working relationships. Campaign staff members have a history of working together and can presumably carry these working relationships from the campaign through transition and into the new Governor's office.

These advantages are normally accompanied by some disadvantages, including:

1. Lack of interest. It is a fact of life that some people like campaigning and do not like administering governments, and vice versa. For example, someone who has become very adept at recruiting and using volunteers in a campaign may be more comfortable in a state position that deals with volunteers than in a Governor's office. Key campaign personnel may feel more comfortable in other campaigns than in the Governor's office.

2. Lack of requisite attitudes and characteristics. While the attitudes and characteristics discussed above (self-confidence, humility, accessibility, appreciation of the need to broaden the political base) may be helpful in a campaign, many persons who can operate successfully in campaign situations lack one or more of them. Such persons may be perfectly well suited for some positions in state government, but not necessarily in the Governor's office.

3. Lack of specific knowledge. It is very common in the first year of a new administration for the staff (and chief executive) to be criticized by older hands—such as the press corps, senior bureaucrats, interest group leadership and legislators—for "not knowing their way around." These criticisms are often valid. To some extent, they can be avoided by hiring

staff members who will bring to the new administration valuable background and knowledge, such as:

- Understanding of programs of state government and how they operate;
- Experience in dealing with the legislative process and the sensitivities of legislators;
- Knowledge of public or business administration and management principles;
- Understanding of local government problems and operations;
- Acquaintance with federal government programs and operations; and
- Familiarity with the key people in state government.

Another reason for not bringing some campaign staff members into the Governor's office may be that the Governor needs to use them elsewhere. In a few states, the Governor's appointment powers are limited, at least in the early days of the administration, to the immediate staff. Departmental positions are controlled by civil service personnel or members of boards and commissions whose terms of appointment have not expired. In those states, the Governor will have to face the problem of complete accountability with limited power. However, in most states, the Governor has the authority to appoint new department heads and a limited number of staff members within departments. Where this power exists, the best use of some of the former campaign staff members may be in individual departments as deputies or aides to the new cabinet official. (See chapter 5 for a discussion of appointing subordinates in agencies.)

The former Governor's staff. Whether a new Governor will be comfortable with any of the staff members of the former Governor will obviously vary with the circumstances. On the one hand, the new Governor may have unseated the previous one, and the old staff will not want to stay. The new Governor, having campaigned against decisions participated in by these same staff members, would probably not be willing to retain them anyway. On the other hand, some new Governors have run on the same ticket as the previous Governor and have taken over with his support. In such cases, the new Governor may be quite comfortable with some of the previous staff members.

Existing state staffs. In recent years, there has been a substantial increase in the use of generalists to staff state government agencies, such as planning and budgeting and particularly legislative services. These generalists, who are comfortable operating in a political environment, are a natural source of experienced and knowledgeable personnel for a Governor's office.

The potential difficulty with such staff members is divided loyalties. Many of these persons will have established close working relationships with individual legislators, the press corps and representatives of interest groups. These relationships, while of considerable value for a Governor if used for him, can present great risk if used against him.

Loaned executives. A Governor looking for experienced staff will often find that they cannot be lured away from their existing employment because they are in a career pattern that does not permit them to terminate employment and then return later. Such individuals are understandably reluctant to sacrifice their careers for a job of inherently limited duration, subject to the ebb and flow of politics. Individuals in this situation will be found in the academic world, in not-for-profit organizations, and particularly, in businesses such as utilities and larger corporations.

These organizations and businesses are often willing, and sometimes eager, to allow employees to interrupt their careers for several years to work in the public sector. Frequently, they will continue fringe benefit coverage (note, however, the conflict-of-interest possibilities) and sometimes will cover part of the salary involved.

University personnel. New Governors have had mixed experience with using university personnel during, and after, the transition period. In some instances, a state university school of public administration or bureau of business research has individuals with a long history of close contact with state government. In such cases, there have been some good examples of close consulting relationships with Governors. Other Governors, however, have found their university resources to be simply too academic in their approach to be of much help in solving the problems of the first 100 days.

Unsolicited applications. Governors will find that their mail system is overwhelmed with job seekers during the transition and early days of the administration. This mail should not be overlooked, as it is likely to contain letters from individuals who have worked as volunteers in the campaign, who are committed to the objectives of the administration, and who are currently holding jobs they are willing to leave. Some very highly qualified individuals may be found in this group.

Personnel from other states. The pattern of support from incumbent Governors for new Governors that begins with NGA's Seminar for New Governors sometimes leads to a loan of key staff members for short periods of time. Such loans have the advantage of bringing experienced personnel who know how to work in a state government quickly to the assistance of new Governors. However, such arrangements are, by their nature, temporary ones and cannot be substituted for the development of permanent staff competence necessary for the new Governor.

The National Governors' Association. The National Governors' Association Center for Policy Research has provided extensive assistance to new Governors. Such assistance can be useful in identifying and recruiting staff, organizing the Governor's office, establishing procedures for policy formulation and office operations, and addressing major budget and policy problems. In addition, the National Governors' Association operates a Talent Resource Exchange which provides a listing of experienced Governors' staff members recommended by outgoing Governors across the nation.

THE "EXTENDED" OFFICE OF THE GOVERNOR

As the previous section indicated, the Governor may pick a number of individuals from his campaign staff for roles in the administration. This group may include the press secretary, advance persons, secretaries, persons who answered the mail and speechwriters, and possibly an executive assistant. People who do work of this type, plus office managers and public liaison personnel, will constitute a majority of the staff of the immediate office of the Governor in many states. Their roles and what the Governor can expect from their functions are discussed in other chapters of this book.

It is a common error for new Governors and, particularly, their immediate staffs to assume that most of the staff work done for the Governor will be done in the Governor's immediate office. When this assumption is made by the staff, there are two undesirable consequences: (1) work bottlenecks develop in the Governor's office in the early months of the administration, and (2) substantive and political mistakes are made because knowledge that lies within state agencies is not used properly. These problems can be avoided through a recognition early in the administration of alternative sources of staff support.

Competence in Central Staff Agencies

Although it may not be obvious initially to the new Governor and his staff, a substantial number of persons in state government are being paid to be responsive to the Governor's policies, priorities and needs for staff work. The first step in obtaining control of the major machinery of state government (besides appointing people in whom one has confidence as agency heads) is to get these central staff persons working for the new Governor. This is often not difficult because both the professional orientation of many of these staff persons and the logic of their continued tenure and success depends upon how useful they can make themselves to the new Governor and his staff. Because of differences in organization and philosophy in different states, there can be no single road map for finding and using all these sources of competence. The following discussion will fit situations in most states.

The budget staff. The budget staff is usually housed organizationally in an independent budget (or budget and planning) agency reporting directly to the Governor, or as a division within a department of administration or finance that also has responsibility for central management services. A new Governor will normally have access to the budget staff through a new director he has appointed. However, where a budget director reports through a secretary of administration or comparable official, he may be a career professional.

Budget staffs are normally organized along functional lines. Individual examiners or analysts are assigned to an agency or a group of agencies. The budget staff will also include staff persons responsible for putting together summary tables, writing budget procedures, and keeping score on appropriations actions, allotments and other governmentwide activities. Depending on which other functions are in the budget agency, this staff may also include such persons as revenue estimators and bonding experts.

There is a range of roles played by budget staffs. Some see themselves primarily as policy staff to the Governor whose handle on the policy process comes through the budget. Such staffs, which are modeled on the federal Office of Management and Budget, tend to be generalists who have a variety of educational backgrounds. Typically, the staff at the budget examiner level is composed of younger persons who want to gain experience for a relatively short time before moving into other positions, such as middle-management positions in the line agencies.

At the other extreme is the budget staff that tends to see budget formulation as its only role, as distinct from being a general source of policy advice to the Governor. These budget agencies tend to be staffed by persons who have greater experience, more detailed analytic ability and a greater orientation to a permanent career in budgeting. Obviously each type of staff has its unique advantages from a Governor's perspective. (See appendixes 7 and 15.)

The planning staff. State planning staffs vary greatly from state to state in size, background, agency contacts and interests. Because the planning office represents a pool of resources that is responsive to the Governor's office and not totally tied up by the budget process, early contacts with the planning staff can provide ready staff assistance for the new Governor. (See appendixes 7, 9 and 10.)

State planning agencies are, therefore, an important source of staff support for the Governor during the first 100 days and beyond. A 1978 survey of Governors' offices conducted by the National Governors' Association indicates that many planning agencies fulfill a variety of staff support roles, usually reporting directly to the Governor or the executive assistant. These services include development of executive policy options and response to gubernatorial correspondence, review of federal legislation, development of management options, "trouble shooting," development of the Governor's legislative program, and lobbying. (See appendix 7.)

Some planning staffs are likely to be personally interested in playing a major role in the policy-formulation process. Such staffs are like the policy-oriented budget staffs described earlier in the types of competence they offer. Governors often use members of these staffs in such roles as: (1) staff analysis of major policy choices for the budget and legislative program; (2) taking leadership (sometimes as a team with a member of the new Governor's immediate staff) in priority projects of the Governor; (3) developing new management systems; (4) coordinating interagency committees and task forces on particular subjects; and (5) dealing with intergovernmental relations issues.

Departments of community/local affairs. Almost all states have departments or divisions of community development or local government affairs. Some of these are combined with the agency handling economic development. Such departments commonly administer some programs, such as the state's housing and community action programs, but also have functions which cut across the functions of the line departments. In such cases, the community affairs agency staff may also be a source of early staff support for the Governor—particularly when the Governor is trying to put together programs of assistance to local government or to alter the overall relationship between the state and its local governments.

Washington offices. State Washington offices also represent a ready source of staff work for a new Governor. The transition period is likely to be difficult for such offices unless the new Governor quickly appoints someone either to head the office or to serve as liaison for him to the office, or affirms an earlier appointment. Once this organizational tie is made, the Washington office staff (and the counterpart state-federal relations staff in the state capitol) can become an excellent source of information on federal programs and emerging federal policies affecting states. (See chapter 13.)

Finding Competence in Existing Staffs

As part of the overall transition, the new Governor will have contacts with a number of state agencies. In a cooperative transition, it will be possible to use these contacts well before inauguration to determine the ability of staff agencies to contribute during transition and the early period of the administration.

One approach is to ask for some specific products, such as briefing books on issues facing the agencies involved and important to the new Governor. The resulting documents are likely to provide the Governor and his staff with an indication of the areas in which the agency staff is competent and insight into whether the approach the staff is taking is consistent with that of the Governor. In some cases, the Governor or his staff may want to assign drafts of speeches to these agencies.

Organizing Staff Support Agencies

After identifying the potential support activities that central staff offices may provide, the new Governor might consider reorganizing these functions to better accommodate his operations. For instance, if the Governor intends to invest more policy analysis in the budget process, he may want to place the planning and budget offices in a new combined agency. Because of the importance of staff support from these key central agencies, it is useful for the new Governor to consider alternative approaches to organizing these staff functions before making changes. A comprehensive discussion of these options is included in chapter 14.

CHAPTER FIVE

Selecting the Cabinet and Other State Officials

> The time spent in securing exceptional talent will be rewarding. This applies to cabinet posts, judicial appointments, regulatory commissions, in fact all appointive positions. Once officials are appointed they should be supported and supporting.
>
> *— a former Governor*

SUMMARY

Perhaps the most challenging task facing the new Governor is the appointment of individuals to hundreds of state government positions in the administration. The recruitment and selection of the Governor's cabinet, in particular, will require many crucial and politically sensitive personnel decisions. Few other early decisions will have such a long-term effect on the success of the administration. The selection process must ensure that competence, broad experience, affirmative action and political loyalty are taken into account. Since appointments generally require legislative confirmation, acceptability of candidates to the legislature will also be a strong factor in cabinet selection.

New Governors should develop a systematic process for selecting appointees and making critical appointments on a timely basis. Both immediately and throughout the term, the Governor will be required to appoint directors of agencies and members of professional boards, regulatory commissions, advisory boards, boards of trustees and state agency commissions, and to make appointments to numerous other positions. A computerized search capability can quickly retrieve information on the position, incumbent and term, statutory requirements and a description of duties.

There are a variety of sources from which the Governor can recruit professional staff and appointees:

• *Incumbent agency heads* are frequently interested in remaining with the new administration especially if the same political party is in power. Retaining agency heads can promote continuity and maintain needed expertise. By offering temporary appointments to these individuals, the Governor has the option to take more time in making his final selections. There may be problems with this arrangement, however, if the loyalty of the holdover and the top agency staff is divided between the new Governor and his predecessor.

• *Promoting from within* presents many of the same advantages and disadvantages as retaining incumbents, except that the individuals may not have a proven track record of top-level management.

• *State legislators* are a valuable source of personnel because they frequently have expertise in specific fields and capacity to enhance legislative relations for the new administration. Legislators sometimes tend to lack managerial experience, however, and may be of more assistance to the Governor and the department's legislative program by remaining in the legislature.

• *Appointing campaign workers* to top positions ensures loyalty, a familiarity with the Governor's policies and a clear commitment to the Governor's positions, but lack of relevant experience and qualifications are possible drawbacks.

• *Appointing federal employees* to top positions is particularly useful in fields actively involved in intergovernmental relations, such as social services, environmental protection and budgeting.

Simple criteria for a good appointment unfortunately do not exist. Because the Governor is ultimately responsible for the successes and failures of his appointees, safeguards should be implemented to identify potential problems for the administration. Thorough personal and professional reference checks on potential appointees should be conducted. Financial disclosure requirements are also desirable. To avoid future problems, the appointee and the Governor should agree on resignation procedures should they ever be necessary.

Gubernatorial appointment of key agency subordinates may be desirable but can cause serious management problems. Alternatively, the Governor can recommend candidates, but leave the final choice to the agency head. Governors often will be able to fill a number of non–civil service positions at a lower level. An early inquiry should be made to identify those jobs, establish who may recommend hiring, and determine the advantages and disadvantages of patronage.

Selecting the Cabinet
and Other State Officials

The newly elected Governor faces a task that could make or break his administration: the selection of the directors of major state agencies. This task should be done as promptly as the state's laws and constitution permit, or the administration will be unnecessarily slow in gaining momentum. Yet it must be done right the first time, for a Governor does not get many second chances in selecting agency heads. Frequently an agency director will assume office with personal standing in the state and gain popularity with interest groups and individuals in the administration. The natural reluctance to fire people and the statutory terms of office that exist in many states combine to make it very difficult for a Governor to reverse bad personnel decisions.

CATEGORIES OF APPOINTMENTS

Most states give the Governor the power to appoint people to what seems to be an incredible number of positions. Many of these are not traditionally considered a part of the cabinet but are, nonetheless, of substantial importance to the management of state government, and of considerable interest to special interest groups. The nature of the Governor's appointments and whether they are paid or unpaid differ substantially from state to state, but they tend to fall into seven major categories.

Heads of agencies. Although comparatively few in number, the Governor's appointments to head state agencies will be among his most critical early decisions. They may include such key administration officials as the commissioner of social services, director of revenue, director of administration, secretary of transportation and commissioner of corrections. These will usually be full-time, paid positions requiring appointees of personal stature and professional competence. Many of these appointments will be subjected to the scrutiny of legislative confirmation.

Members of professional boards. Barbers, beauticians and doctors are some of the typical professional groups governed by gubernatorially appointed boards. These positions are unpaid (but expenses are reimbursed) in most states and tend to be viewed by the professional societies involved as "their positions" in the sense that they expect to be consulted about appointments. Governors are appointing "consumer" members of these boards in increasing numbers.

Regulatory commissions. Railroads, intrastate trucking firms, telephone companies, gas and electric utilities, savings and loan associations, banks and credit unions are among the many industries subject to state government regulation. Positions as regulatory commissioners frequently are salaried and of substantial interest to the regulated industries and to consumers and environmentalists. There is similar interest in positions on state-level tax appeal and equalization boards.

Advisory boards. Usually established by state statute, federal laws, or the Governor's executive order, these boards generally reflect the efforts of one or more interest groups seeking to institutionalize their influence in a particular agency. As with regulatory commissions, interest groups frequently have particular concern for these positions.

Boards of trustees. In most states, the boards of trustees of educational institutions and state institutions, such as children's homes, state boards of education, and higher education coordinating boards are appointed, in whole or part, by the Governor. Many of these positions are unpaid, with the primary organized interest in the appointments coming from employee organizations, such as teacher representatives in the case of an appointed state board of education.

State agencies run by commissions. Frequently such functions as support of the arts, management of a state monopoly, or enforcement of civil rights legislation are supervised by commissions and their executive directors. In other cases, such as the administration of federally funded programs in traffic safety, law enforcement and manpower, federal legislation dictates the establishment of a commission with authority to pass on grants to local governments and state agencies. These commissions are normally unpaid and frequently include a substantial number of ex officio or designated members.

Subsidiary officers in agencies. In many states, the Governor rather than the cabinet officers appoints subsidiary officers within departments. These might include the heads of major operating units or persons of special political visibility, such as a fish and game commissioner within a department of conservation or natural resources. In other cases, the agency head makes appointments with varying degrees of consultation with and concurrence of the Governor.

MAKING KEY APPOINTMENTS

Governors in some states are in command of the machinery of the state personnel department. This department is equipped to fill state civil service positions, but frequently does not have the selection capability for higher-level positions not subject to civil service. Therefore, staff is needed to help a Governor make appointments to boards and commissions, fill cabinet and subcabinet positions, deal with mail and phone calls from potential higher-level appointees, and handle requests for jobs from legislators, county chairmen and friends. A Governor has a large personnel responsibility whether he wants it or not.

The question then becomes how to handle the task of filling key jobs. These are the alternatives:

- Assign it to the personnel director. This is probably the most efficient route, but it doesn't work when the person whom a Governor wants to perform his immediate office personnel functions is not the same person he wants as his personnel director.

- Assign it to another cabinet officer. This approach is used in some states where the Governor's top political aide traditionally assumes a cabinet position after inauguration.

- Keep it in his own office.

The size of this operation will depend on how many state employees there are and the extent to which they are hired outside the civil service system.

Early in the transition period, a new Governor should obtain a complete list of the positions to which he must make appointments. The prior administration may have such a list (perhaps computerized) and may be willing to share it. If not, states that have computerized statutory search capability can come up with a relatively complete list. Such lists can take a number of forms but are probably most useful when they indicate the following:

- Name of board, commission or position;

- Incumbents and dates terms expire;

- Special statutory restrictions on appointment, such as occupation or political party;

- Statutory reference; and

- Brief description of duties.

A file can be constructed from such a list showing, by date, when the Governor must make the various appointments.

In all appointments, understanding legal constraints is important. Care must be taken to avoid proposing an appointment that, for one reason or another, turns out to be legally invalid. The pitfalls vary from state to state. Among them are:

- Prohibitions affecting legislators, such as statutes against appointing a legislator to a position for which the salary was increased by legislative action while the prospective appointee was a member of the legislature;

- Prohibitions against appointing people who have held or will continue to hold party office to particular positions;
- Residency requirements; and
- Professional requirements, such as a specific number of years of experience in a particular field. In some states, appointment of acting directors is an accepted method of dealing with a professional requirement that appears unduly restrictive.

A new Governor may want to review some appointments not only with groups representing their professions, but also with consumer groups and other public-interest representatives.

Appointment and Resignation Procedures

Governors frequently differ from other managers in their exercise of personal power. Some Governors tend to favor administrative arrangements in which independent boards and commissions are largely responsible for certain issues, and they are not afraid to have subordinates who have their own political bases and long-standing reputations. Such cabinet officers may provide the Governor with less effective control over departmental activities, but correspondingly, public and legislative accountability shifts to some degree from the Governor to the cabinet officers. The Governor cannot, of course, avoid ultimate responsibility for state departments, but he can dilute that responsibility substantially. On the other hand, a Governor seeking to maximize his power and influence in a department will make sure that cabinet officers are "fireable." In this case, he would avoid appointing people who could not be fired without offending a major special interest group or faction of the Governor's political party.

Many Governors-elect reach an oral agreement with their appointees concerning how any subsequent "falling out" might be handled. Agreement can be reached that, in the absence of corruption, a cabinet officer wishing to resign for policy reasons will agree to do so without being critical of the Governor publicly. Similarly, the Governor, when he wishes to remove the cabinet officer, will permit him the opportunity to resign without public announcement that the resignation was involuntary. Such an agreement obviously depends for its enforcement solely upon the parties involved.

A new Governor should carefully review his options for reorganizing departments or agencies (see chapter 14) before appointing new cabinet and subcabinet personnel.

In the case of incumbents, some action is needed to bring the incumbent onto the new team. Some Governors advocate obtaining the resignation of an incumbent and then, in effect, reappointing him to the new administration based upon a face-to-face discussion with the new Governor similar to an interview with a potential new appointee. Others do not consider this step necessary but advocate mechanisms to bring the personnel of the new administration together by weekend retreats, social events or meetings.

Discussions between the Governor and/or his staff and potential appointees are normally undertaken on a confidential basis. In some instances, it may appear probable that a potential appointee will leak the Governor's interest to further his own candidacy, or the fact that he is under consideration will leak for other reasons. In such circumstances —particularly when it is possible that the candidate will reject the offer but publicize it—the Governor may wish to have a staff member approach the candidate rather than doing so personally. This indirect approach can be used to ensure before the actual offer is made that the candidate will take the job.

Finding the Bad Apple

In appointing the hundreds of people who are recruited by a Governor-elect and a very busy staff in a short period of time, the chances of making some bad choices are high. There is no proven way to avoid the "wrong person for the job," but a number of steps can be taken to ensure that a Governor is not embarrassed by his choices.

In addition to interviews and reference checks, it is possible to obtain credit ratings through normal channels. Arrest records can also be checked. Background or "field" checks can be conducted by state investigators, where such activity is authorized.

Individual state laws vary on disclosure of income and assets by public officials, but the Governor may wish to require such statements as a condition of employment. If this is done, potential cabinet officers should be informed that it will be a requirement.

Besides these protections, the Governor should consider asking the following question before making an appointment: "Is there anything in your background which might be a potential embarrassment to me or to you if it were to become public?"

Chapter 15 contains a detailed discussion of ethics and standards of conduct in public positions.

WHERE TO FIND GOOD APPOINTEES

Unfortunately there is no reliable way to predict the success of individuals in either national or state government. For example, a cabinet officer is responsible for supervising large numbers of employees, but many successful cabinet officers come from positions as university professors or lawyers without previous large-scale supervisory experience. Prior experience is desirable in many specialized areas such as corrections, transportation and mental health, but a number of success stories exist even in these areas when nonspecialists have been appointed.

A good cabinet officer must be willing to be a member of an administration team and strong enough to accept the press and public criticism that almost surely will come. He must be capable of getting along with the legislature and his administration colleagues and of contributing good management and policy leadership in his field.

In considering potential appointees, the new Governor and his staff should recognize that they are the ones who will suffer the results of incompetence. If the appointee cannot maintain effective and proper relationships with his constituency, it is the Governor and his immediate staff who will have to calm the troubled waters. If the appointee cannot operate his department economically and efficiently, the Governor will have to pay for that failure by having less money to spend on other programs. If the appointee causes press problems, it is the Governor and his press secretary who must try to solve them. These facts place a premium on acquiring and retaining competent appointees.

Incumbents

Shortly after election—and even before in the case of candidates not running against incumbents—the Governor and his assistants receive overtures from a number of existing agency heads who would like to stay in their positions. Some incumbent cabinet officers will not approach the Governor directly, but might be interested in staying if asked. Each incumbent should be judged on his merits, but some general observations can be made.

If the new Governor is of the same party and general philosophy as the outgoing Governor, retaining some incumbents may make sense. Incumbents with poor track records can be replaced, and the strong ones can be retained, thereby reducing the problems of transition. It is also possible to offer incumbents the opportunity to stay for less than the full term of the new administration, so that the Governor is not faced with recruiting a successor until he has had time to find a good candidate. Cabinet officers, in some cases, have fixed terms so that the Governor has no option but to replace them immediately.

Retaining the incumbent can present problems. Some Governors shift cabinet officers as a matter of principle, in the belief that someone who has been loyal to the previous Governor could not be loyal to his successor. Others retain incumbents selectively, particularly in smaller agencies. Generally speaking, retaining an incumbent will give the Governor the least control over a department, and make it most difficult for him to shift general policy in fields such as legislative and press relations, personnel and general management.

Appointing a cabinet officer from within the existing staff of an agency has many of the same advantages and disadvantages as appointing an incumbent. An additional disadvantage is that while the incumbent has a proven managerial track record, the performance of other staff members is more of an unknown. A further advantage is that the new appointee will presumably owe his loyalty to the new Governor.

State Senators and Representatives

State legislatures provide a fertile recruiting ground for administration posts. Aside from personal capabilities, legislators have the advantage of bringing experience which can be used to enhance legislative relations. They have their own political bases, which, as with incumbents, can cut both ways. Some legislators who have specialized in a particular field or issue in the legislature may bring considerable technical knowledge to a job.

In considering the appointment of legislators, a Governor should take into account the fact that the legislators whom he might select are probably those who can provide him with the strongest support if they remain in the legislature. If they have limited administrative experience, legislators who are appointed to state positions should be encouraged to bring in deputies with strong administrative backgrounds.

Campaign Staff

As in building the Governor's office staff, the campaign staff is a desirable recruiting ground for other state appointments even if those on it do not seek a commitment for a position in state government. The obvious advantages of a campaign staff are loyalty to the Governor, a willingness to work for his positions, and familiarity with his policies. Campaign staff members also know and have worked with the people who will become some of the top staff members in the Governor's office.

Individual campaign workers will clearly have the training and experience required for some positions and not for others.

The Federal Government

Under the Intergovernmental Personnel Act, the federal government can "lend" personnel to state governments. A federal agency may continue an employee's full salary or may agree to some combination of state and federal payments to provide the employee with the same salary and fringe benefits he would receive in federal service. Many states have had good experience with appointing federal personnel to cabinet-level or other jobs with or without this mechanism, particularly in areas where federal functions parallel those of the states, such as tax administration, environmental protection and budgeting.

Recruiting Other Candidates

The groups listed above are all obvious sources for personnel, and no special effort is required by a Governor to find them. It becomes more difficult when candidates from these groups are not acceptable and some additional recruiting is needed. There are many ways to find names of potential candidates in business, labor unions, universities, other states and elsewhere, but all involve putting out the word. Various approaches include:

- Making public announcements, which has the advantage of reaching candidates who could not be found in any other way and the disadvantage of producing mail from many ambitious but underqualified people;

- Asking an inner circle of supporters and staff to recommend people and giving them authority to contact others;

- Reaching out to a broader group for recommendations, including top business and labor leaders, university presidents, legislators and local officials;

- Checking with outgoing Governors in other states for people who might be available and qualified; and

- Turning to professional "head hunting" organizations. There are a number of firms in the recruiting business that accept public assignments. Many management consulting and accounting firms will also perform this service.

COMPENSATION

A Governor's ability to attract subordinates depends to a significant degree on what he can pay them. In many states, cabinet salaries are set by statute and are, in the short term, unchangeable. Salaries of the Governor's immediate staff are generally more flexible. Even when salaries are statutory, however, recruiting can proceed on the basis of the Governor's plans to recommend salary increases for the positions. If potential cabinet officers are to be approached on this basis, the Governor should have his legal advisor make sure that the state constitution and statutes do not prohibit an increase in salary after a cabinet officer has assumed office.

An early question facing the new Governor is whether salaries should be changed. In considering this question, he will want to look at salaries of comparable positions in other states. This can be done by consulting tables found in *The Book of the States,* published biennially by the Council of State Governments, and adjusting for inflation.

If the new Governor does not wish to promise that he will recommend specific salary increases to particular cabinet officers, he may wish to enhance his recruiting prospects by at least offering the possibility of such increases in the future. One mechanism to review salary structures is an outside compensation study. Such a study can provide an objective basis for salary recommendations that reduces the heat a Governor must take from his own officials for salary disparities among them, and from the legislature and the public for raising salaries. The disadvantage of such a study is that, having requested it, a Governor may find it hard not to follow its recommendations. The study can be done by management consultants, a blue-ribbon commission of businessmen appointed by the Governor, or a committee of the chamber of commerce or similar group.

A new Governor must also decide the question of salary supplements in specific cases. These questions arise when cabinet officers are offered salary supplements and fringe benefits while they are on leave from their regular employment, when a cabinet member wants to accept a teaching appointment to supplement his income, or in other situations where state officials have opportunities for outside income. Laws in some states prohibit such practices. The advantages to a Governor stem from obtaining a person who would otherwise be unavailable; the disadvantages include legislative and press criticism of exceeding the statutory salaries by special arrangements and any real or apparent conflict of interest that may be involved.

AGENCY HEAD INDEPENDENCE

A major consideration in deciding how to fill agency positions is the extent to which the Governor wants to maintain control over the appointees. In some cases, of course, the responsibilities of line officials are established by state statutes. In most states, for example, the Governor does not have the authority to appoint or remove the chief state education officer. Appointments may be for a fixed term, and the Governor's ability to remove may be limited to cases of malfeasance or misfeasance in office, or the equivalent. The differences between an "independent" agency and a cabinet agency headed by an officer subject to removal without cause are shown in the table on the following page.

The Governor's Ground Rules

To the extent that the Governor has flexibility in establishing ground rules on agency independence, he may wish to tailor the degree of agency control exercised. For example, a Governor may wish to have no power over cases or controversies heard by a quasi-judicial agency such as a regulatory commission, but at the same time he may wish to exercise central budget and press controls over the same body. Conversely, he may feel strongly that he should be consulted on such major decisions as a telephone rate increase, but not really care whether he has the automatic support of the rate-setting commission on budget matters. The freedom allowed an independent agency can be a constant source of friction in an administration in which the Governor desires to exercise some degree of control.

The key questions in determining the extent to which Governors wish to encourage independence in their cabinets must be decided before appointments are made. If the Governor wants an agency head to behave like a cabinet officer, agreement should be reached before the appointment is made. Conversely, if the Governor wants him to operate independently of the Governor's press, legislative, budget and other operations, that too should be made clear.

Conduct of Independent and Cabinet Agencies in a Strong Executive System

Function	Independent Agency Practice	Cabinet Agency Practice
GUBERNATORIAL SUPPORT	No presumption of political support of Governor	Agency head expected to support Governor's policies in all fields, in speeches, etc.
PERSONNEL	No appointments for Governor and no clearance of appointments	Agency head follows any appointments procedures in effect—will clear nominees to top echelon positions with Governor if Governor wants
BUDGET	Budget procedures followed (usually a statutory requirement) but agency head may argue publicly against Governor's decision	Agency follows Governor's budget procedures and agency head supports budget decisions which the Governor makes
FEDERAL RELATIONS	Agency may work with Governor's staff but may take positions different from Governor, and may work through associations of state agencies rather than Governor	Agency works with Governor's federal relations staff in formulating state positions
POLICY CONTROL	Agency head considers Governor's interest as meddling in agency business and has no duty to respect decision	Agency head recognizes authority of Governor to direct agency head to make decisions
LEGISLATIVE RELATIONS	Legislation not subject to prior clearance. No need to take legislative positions consistent with Governor's	Agency head submits proposed legislation to Governor for clearance prior to submission to legislature; does not take positions on legislation different from that of the Governor
PRESS RELATIONS	Independent of Governor's press operation	Agency subject to general press procedures established by Governor. Will provide news for Governor to announce, etc.
PLANNING	No need to follow planning guidelines on economic or demographic assumptions or to follow procedures	Agency follows Governor's planning procedures and uses guidelines developed by planning agency

Deputies and Others in Agencies

Organizational doctrine in both public and private administration suggests that the scope of the chief executive officer in personnel selection and management should extend downward only one level. That is, when a Governor appoints a commissioner of welfare, he is holding that official and that official alone responsible for the conduct of the department. This logic suggests that subordinate personnel in the department are serving at the pleasure of the director or commissioner, not the Governor, and that they should be chosen by their immediate superiors.

For a variety of reasons, these principles frequently are abandoned in state government. Sometimes a good candidate for a subordinate position is found before the cabinet officer is selected, and a newly appointed cabinet officer may find that the Governor has already selected one or more of his subordinates. A Governor may also have strong preferences for a particular individual in a subordinate position, and may simply tell the cabinet officer to accept him. Or the Governor may have strong preferences for getting certain types of people into top-level positions, and ignore all but the most strenuous objections on the part of the cabinet officer involved.

The interest of the Governor in top-level subordinates generally is exceeded by the enthusiasm of his top aides for becoming involved in the appointment process, and for influencing some aspects of the internal organization of departments. The press secretary wants departmental press relations officers changed in favor of people more acceptable to him. The political advisor will advocate major changes in personnel to satisfy his need to make appointments, and to make sure that there is someone at the top to listen to his problems. Similar interests are displayed by other members of a Governor's staff, such as the budget director, legislative liaison, and legal and personnel aides. Staff members with agency liaison responsibilities often attempt to screen subcabinet appointments.

However he gets there, the presence of a subordinate in the top level of a department who owes his allegiance only to the Governor or his staff creates a difficult situation in the management of the agency. The department head will seek to obtain the personal loyalty of the employee. If that fails, he will frequently find ways to keep the individual at a distance from the major policy-making process in the agency. The individual employee will face constant loyalty conflicts, such as whether to go to the Governor or the Governor's top staff with his side of the story on a high-level decision with which he disagrees.

Fewer of these problems arise when a Governor consults with the agency head in advance of an appointment. At a minimum, the Governor may receive at least tacit support for his appointment. If the Governor wants to strengthen agency head control, he will have his immediate staff make their recommendations to the agency head and let him decide.

The interests of the agency head and those of the Governor are not necessarily divergent on many of these staffing issues. An agency head should want a deputy who is acceptable to the Governor. Similarly, he is better served when his public relations person, for example, is acceptable to the press secretary, his personnel aide to the personnel director, etc.

The single-deputy situation, as distinct from a group of coequal deputies reporting to the agency head, can also be a source of organizational friction within a department. Where a deputy has everyone in the agency reporting to him as well as to the agency head, there is no logical basis for deciding where the deputy's authority ends. If a single-deputy arrangement is to be used, the deputy and the director should have different personal characteristics and interests so that they will each assume different facets of the responsibility. One common division of labor is for one to do "outside" work (legislative liaison, speeches, etc.) while the other concentrates on "inside" work such as day-to-day administration.

THE PATRONAGE DECISION

"Patronage" is one of those words in the American political vocabulary which, like the word "politician," sometimes carries adverse connotations. Political leaders who use a patronage system frequently find some other name for it. Those who claim not to use it often speak the word as if it were synonymous with "murder" or "corruption."

Nevertheless, patronage is a fact of life in most governmental systems and in many private ones, and it must be dealt with early in any Governor's administration. Patronage simply derives from the word "patron," or "sponsor." In the broadest and most useful sense, a patronage system is simply an organized way of dealing with people who wish to sponsor the employment of others. Not all patronage is political. Suppliers have been known to hire the children of their customers; private employers have a way of hiring nephews; many people hire consistently upon referrals of friends; and even college professors develop mechanisms for placing their students. A Governor must decide whether to have patronage, in what positions, and who the acceptable patrons will be.

"Exempt" Positions

All states have some form of civil service or merit system covering at least some—and in many states, most—of their employees. At the same time, all states also have some positions that are exempt from this system for one reason or another.

Exemptions are normally accorded to high-level positions of substantial policy-making responsibility, or positions with a confidential relationship to top officials. These normally include directors of major agencies, frequently deputy directors and other top-echelon officials, and executive secretaries. These are the same kinds of positions that are expected to turn over in private organizations when leadership changes.

Many believe that one of the reasons state government is allegedly "unresponsive" is that no matter what mandate a new Governor gets from the electorate, he may still find himself wed to many key policy makers merely because they were appointed through civil service. Governors who perceive this problem seek some additional authority to exempt top positions or, alternatively, demand to be convinced that the civil service "can produce." These and related issues are at the heart of civil service reform initiatives in both the states and the federal government.

Top-level exempt positions are normally filled without involving "patrons" at all, except to the degree that most candidates for key positions will have one or more groups advocating their appointment. A variety of other positions are exempt from civil service in many states, including:

- Positions, such as some highway maintenance workers, which were not included in civil service when some states moved to a civil service system;

- Jobs, such as those in the building trades, that are often filled by union-related procedures;

- Part-time and provisional employees; and

- Persons viewed as independent contractors rather than employees.

What Patrons?

Clearly, a Governor needs some sort of central recruiting mechanism for the positions he must fill personally. Unless he delegates this function completely to a civil service commission, personnel department or state party headquarters, he will have to rely on his central recruiting staff.

This staff will soon encounter what might be called VIP patrons, who may not be political in a partisan sense at all. Old friends of the Governor and his top staff, heads of major corporations and universities, campaign contributors, cabinet officers and others will have a variety of recommendations.

The central staff will also encounter campaign workers, many unpaid or underpaid. Some will seek state jobs as the best they can find, and others will expect to enter state service to further the crusade they began in the campaign.

In addition to local party leaders, Governors must also contend with the varying patronage preferences of legislators. These may stem from the Governor's own party and from the opposite party. Alienation of key legislative leaders by ignoring their patronage preferences may result in subsequent weak support for legislation of interest to the Governor. Legislators also are involved frequently in clearing appointments, even when patronage is not involved. In some states, the name of a potential appointee is customarily presented to the political leaders of his area. In other states, Governors find it desirable to consult with leaders of key committees in the legislature before appointing agency heads whose programs fall under their jurisdiction.

Is Patronage Obsolete?

Substantial arguments can be made against any form of political patronage. Conventional wisdom of good government argues that downplaying merit to reward a "patron" inherently leads to the selection of less-qualified candidates and that patronage is viewed by the public with increasing negativism.

The argument on the other side of the question begins with the notion that a strong political party structure is essential if democracy is to function and that ideology or personal appeal offers insufficient motivation for enough citizen participation to sustain party structures. It can also be argued that patronage most commonly occurs in situations where qualified candidates are virtually indistinguishable in competence, and it really matters little whether they are selected by patronage or by some other system.

Whichever approach is taken, the Governor is best served by making the patronage ground rules clear and sticking to them.

CHAPTER SIX

Policy Development

Decide early what two or three things you want to accomplish; develop a sound public information program to let the people know; and devise and constantly revise methods for evaluating your own performance, using outside sources.

— a former Governor

SUMMARY

Early in the administration, a new Governor must make some highly visible decisions. Through his budget or amendments to his predecessor's budget, and through major policy addresses and the legislative program, he articulates decisions which the public, press and governmental officials view as expressing his policy.

Over time, the Governor may choose to establish a more coherent and systematic method of setting administration policy. Among the processes that have been used are issuance of a formal Governor's policy document, incorporation of policy messages in the budget materials, and the formulation of state plans.

New Governors who view their roles as both active managers of government and leaders of the people will be concerned with all issues that affect state residents. The adoption of a broad set of policy pronouncements expresses this concept of the Governor's role.

Other Governors may want to define their roles more narrowly to focus on the management of state government. Governors adopting this style may set specific policy goals for agency directors and actively participate with them to attain results.

By contrast, other Governors may set broad policy goals for department directors and allow them to develop their own objectives. With this approach, the Governor would focus only on issues of major interest to the administration.

A number of tools are available to the Governor and his staff to aid in formulating policy. The National Governors' Association, the Council of State Planning Agencies and the National Association of State Budget Officers are sources of technical assistance to help consider implementation of the following techniques:

• *Goal processes,* like futures activities, involve active citizen participation and are oriented toward identifying state goals and objectives. Questionnaires and public hearings are heavily used to identify goals, but the development of programs for attaining goals is left to the normal procedures of state government.

• *Comprehensive plans* have lost appeal among those Governors who consider them either unwieldy or too difficult to implement. Many Governors support broad-based planning processes, although a formal "state plan" is usually not produced.

• *Development plans* have been the focus of planning activities in a number of states concerned with economic growth in depressed rural or urban areas. Such plans usually identify economic problems and prescribe detailed economic development strategies.

• *State investment planning* is designed to produce a more systematic allocation of the state's capital budget for facilities such as highways, schools and local construction.

• *Advance budget planning* may be used to project expenditures and revenues over a multiyear period to ensure that the Governor and agencies consider long-term policy implications of state expenditures.

• *Program evaluation* must be geared toward ensuring that the evaluation is completed in a timely fashion and is useful for budget or program development. During the first year, new agency directors will want to conduct their own evaluation of programs; later, the planning and budget staffs are more useful as evaluators.

With planning-programming-budgeting systems, and more recently with zero-base budgeting, many states have systems which make the budget process a primary element in policy development and evaluation. Segments of state government are divided into programs and subprograms with distinct purposes and objectives. These objectives can also be used as management tools by agency directors. Similarly, the Governor and the agency head may agree on a management-by-objectives approach where an agreement is reached on the agency's objectives for a given time period.

Policy Development

The pressures of events in the first 100 days force the new Governor into a number of decisions, yet these are not usually organized into coherent sets of policies. A state-of-the-state message must be delivered and is expected to have some discussion of policy, if no more than reiteration of campaign statements. A budget, or amendments to a predecessor's budget, must be decided upon. A legislative program, or at least a few pieces of legislation supported by the Governor, must be developed. Bills will appear on the Governor's desk for signature or veto. Mail is received asking the Governor to take positions on issues. Typically, policy making during this period is ad hoc. Relatively detailed positions may be taken on issues of particular interest to the Governor, while other issues may not be addressed at all.

Whether the Governor likes it or not, the public and the press will tend to sum up these ad hoc actions into a notion of the Governor's "policy," both in judging the success or failure of the new administration and in evaluating actions on specific items. This chapter explores a range of options which Governors have used in combining the many isolated decisions of the chief executive into more coherent policies. Examples of typical policy-development procedures and techniques are presented in appendix 8.

The new Governor has a variety of choices for formats for the articulation of policy choices. The key decision he must make is the extent to which he perceives himself as the "leader of the people," as well as manager of state government. Given this choice, there are a variety of tested mechanisms available for articulating policy for the public. These vary in length of time considered for achievement of objectives, in public participation, and in integration with the budget process.

The development of these policy-making and program-monitoring systems in recent years, as well as the growth of state planning and budgeting offices, reflects Governors' recognition of the complexity of state government. Governors have found that, regardless of whether they wanted to or not, they have been increasingly thrust into the role of state government manager. This is because a Governor, as the most visible political figure in the state, is viewed by the public as ultimately responsible for the state government's successes or failures.

CHOOSING A LEADERSHIP ROLE

Generally, the reactive mode of decision making that tends to evolve early in the transition can be continued throughout the Governor's term of office, and it is in many states. A reactive Governor does not seek to develop broad policies, except where it is necessary to do so in the context of making specific decisions. Policies are made as each year's legislative program is reviewed, in the periodic review of the budget, in decisions on whether to sign or veto legislative bills, and in meetings with department heads, legislators, federal officials, local officials and interest groups that are structured around specific issues to be resolved.

When a state is governed in this fashion, someone seeking to determine the Governor's policy or the "state's policy" on a particular subject will have to depend upon a combination of (1) the budget message and text of budget documents, (2) speeches, (3) recommended legislation, and (4) responses to the Governor's mail.

An alternative approach used increasingly by Governors is to adopt a process that results in general policy statements covering all major activities of state government. Different Governors have experimented with various ways to do this, including the issuance of a general policy document, putting policy material into the budget process and documents, and various forms of state plans or "futures" processes.

Whether the Governor wishes to become involved in one or more of these policy-formulation processes depends upon his conception of his own role, as well as his appraisal of the effectiveness of the various approaches.

Governors as Managers

Most Governors view themselves as active managers of state government and leaders of the state's people. The Governor in his "leader of the people" capacity is presumed to be concerned with all of the programs of the citizens of the state, whether or not those problems can be addressed very effectively by state government. He is concerned with a broad range of federal policies, from agricultural subsidies and welfare to decisions on whether military bases are closed or expanded. In this role, the Governor is also concerned with the conduct of local officials and with activities in the private sector.

Such a concept of the role of the Governor makes it logical that he sponsor and, indeed, lead efforts to plan for improvements in economic activity, government service and the quality of life in his state, whether or not state action is to be involved.

Other Governors focus their leadership more narrowly on the management of state government but take quite different approaches to that management. Some see themselves as relating to state government much as the president and chairman of the board would relate to the employees of a private corporation. This concept has the Governor responsible for actively leading state government, including setting goals for his individual subordinates and leading them to the achievement of those goals through interaction with them.

Other Governors either do not accept this leadership role in theory, or they accept it in theory but do not follow it in day-to-day practice. Those Governors may be much more comfortable with department heads who set their own objectives in their areas of activity or with a cabinet that operates relatively independently. They may opt not to intervene in situations where, for example, independent boards and commissions deal directly with the legislature in policy formulation. Also, if they have experienced some early failures, most Governors are wary about taking on too many problems and issues. While some Governors will point with pride to policy statements of hundreds of pages with positions on all major issues, others will emphasize a half dozen major issues and leave the remainder to be covered by others.

The policy machinery which a Governor adopts should be related directly to his own concept of his role. The new Governor will not want to fall into a decision-making style which deemphasizes formal policy development and then attempt to impose a new system later. If he contemplates setting forth coherent goals and policy guidelines for state government, the Governor should make an effort to set up decision-making processes early in the game which will be adaptable to large-scale policy development. The process of policy development need not be in place during the first 100 days, but the Governor should be aware of his long-term goals and take them into consideration, not precluding those goals, for example, by delegating power in an area of special interest. Once delegated, power is difficult to recapture without severely damaging agency morale or the Governor's political base.

Staff Support for the Policy Process

If the Governor perceives himself as a leader of the state's people as well as their government, problems will develop if his policy process is not strong enough to support this role. This type of Governor is likely to prefer some form of public deliberative process. In addition, he is likely to want staff support to allow him to be "on top of" such major issues as the state's economic development, problems of the cities, and the success or lack of success of public education. If the state's policy machinery, particularly the planning and budget processes, has not emphasized this broad view, the Governor will have to lead these staffs in new directions to get the information he wants.

Problems arise when the staff is oriented toward the broad role of the Governor as the leader of the people and the Governor is not. Such a staff will tend to put problems, issues and plans on the Governor's desk that deal with subjects on which the Governor may not wish to take any action at all. This can embarrass the Governor and frustrate the staff. A new Governor with a narrower view of his role than his predecessor would be well advised to check on any broad-scale planning efforts in progress and determine early whether he wants them narrowed in scope or directed toward other problems.

A Governor oriented toward managing state government as a company president would manage his business will probably not feel comfortable without a fairly rigorous policy-formulation and management process. Such a Governor will feel that he is being denied the capability to manage unless the system ensures that major issues covering all aspects of state government will reach his desk.

However, these processes (such as comprehensive budgeting systems, management by objectives, or an overall state planning system) will simply serve as a source of frustration for a Governor who does not choose the corporate management model for his decision making. They will bring to the Governor's desk issues that he does not want to decide, and his inattention to the process will trigger its deterioration in the eyes of the agency heads who have to live with it. Decisions won't get made and problems will multiply.

Thus, the Governor needs to decide early in the term what kind of policy-development process he is comfortable with.

BROAD-SCALE PLANNING ACTIVITIES

Those Governors who have harnessed state government to give leadership to local and private efforts have chosen an interesting array of devices for planning. Some alternatives are discussed below. The models for gubernatorial policy making are not mutually exclusive; elements of one may be combined with elements of some of the others. A thorough analysis of these activities can be found in the 16-volume *State Planning Series,* published in 1977 by the Council of State Planning Agencies.

In addition, a wide variety of funds—federal, state and, in some cases, private—can be put together to accomplish these tasks. Technical assistance is available to Governors from groups such as the National Governors' Association, Council of State Planning Agencies, or National Association of State Budget Officers to help set up one or a combination of these processes and find the funds necessary to do the job.

Futures Projects

Some states have initiated projects involving systematic looks at the possible future condition of the state, its business and its people. Such projects usually involve specialized groups looking at particular functional areas (e.g., education, pollution control) or planning in geographic subareas that culminates in an overall state approach.

Conceptually, futures projects involve one of two approaches:

- Projecting economic, demographic and other trends in the absence of policy change, appraising whether the predicted result is satisfactory, identifying improvements in the outcomes, and reasoning backward to the policy changes required to reach the desired outcome; or more simply

  - Developing desired outcomes for future periods and then

examining alternative policies for reaching those outcomes.

Futures projects, such as those implemented in recent years in Minnesota and Washington, involve a high level of public involvement and usually have commissions directing the activities. These commissions are often created legislatively and include top leadership of the state legislature.

In some states, futures projects have been restricted to broad policy making, such as more emphasis on environmental protection and less on growth. In general, however, detailed and quantitative goals have been set up for state government.

Goal Processes

Goal processes are conceptually similar to futures projects and traditionally also include considerable public involvement through such means as questionnaires and hearings. The purpose of these projects is to identify a specific set of outcomes (e.g., a low unemployment rate or stopping migration out of rural areas) that are desired by the state's citizens and, sometimes, statements about the policies that would be required to reach those outcomes.

In both goal and futures projects, the process of developing goals and studying futures is often considered as important as the resulting statements about goals and/or futures. The process provides the opportunity for citizens of varying backgrounds, interests and aspirations to discuss future state and local government actions together. The process can also put the Governor at the center of these deliberations.

Comprehensive Plans

Particularly in the 1960s, a number of state governments sought to write comprehensive plans for private and public-sector activities. In many cases, the initial impetus for these plans came from the federal government. These plans, which had many parallels to plans prepared by individual city governments, were designed to be "comprehensive," covering all geographic areas of the state and many aspects of economic activity.

Developing comprehensive plans at the state level has often proven difficult. In some cases, the plans involve highly sensitive issues. In other cases, the process of consensus building becomes unwieldy, and final plans may never be developed. Nonetheless, some Governors continue to support planning processes that are relatively comprehensive, although the objective is usually not a final document that could be referred to as "the state plan."

Development Plans

Some states have focused their planning and policy efforts on development—generally economic development of the state or particular areas within the state and the development of rural areas or central cities. Typically, these policy-development efforts include an attempt to describe the magnitude and causes of economic problems in particular areas and "strategies" for state action to deal with the problems involved. The resulting recommendations can become the basis for state economic or community development policies. Massachusetts, Michigan and California have recently completed such development plans.

Development plans are typically oriented toward economic objectives, such as jobs and income, rather than toward land use. They often include a very specific project orientation, grounding them in the political reality of visible improvements, such as the revitalized downtown of a particular city or town, or a plant opening in a rural area.

It should be noted that the Governor has the opportunity to direct many of the planning and policy-making activities of state agencies in much the same way that the heads of corporations use their corporate planning processes to drive the activities of various divisions. The central planning staff can be used to provide assumptions (e.g., population change, economic growth) that are to be used by various state agencies in policy-making activities.

Certain of these assumptions can be extremely important in decisions by state agencies that have major implications for the future development of the state. Those driven by population projections are good examples. Centrally formulated population assumptions can affect the size of water lines and sewage treatment plants and indicate whether a particular highway should be two lanes or four. Individual communities may, not surprisingly, contest such central estimates as being less optimistic than their own.

Land Use

All states are involved in some form of land-use planning. Land-use plans are required as a condition for receiving federal planning funds under the Section 701 program of the Department of Housing and Urban Development, the Coastal Zone Management Program of the Department of Commerce, and a number of others. Most of the states which have pressed forward with detailed planning processes tied to action programs have been facing difficult issues caused by competition for scarce land. Hawaii and Florida are examples of states that have moved intensively into planning for land use.

In many states, the land-use patterns and the shape of growth are determined more through "back door" land planning, such as using air quality regulations, setting transportation corridors and regulating utility siting, than through publicly unveiled plans. Increasingly, environmental protection regulations are playing an important role in guiding land use.

PLANNING STATE GOVERNMENT ACTIVITIES

Although planning models often include many activities outside the scope of state government, most Governors' policy-making processes concentrate on what state government can do to solve problems. It is difficult to draw hard and fast distinctions among the state planning and management activities that are related to the corporate president model of the operations of a Governor, but the following approaches are common.

State Investment Planning

With the aid of federal funds, states make major investments in such facilities as highways, airports, sewage treatment plants, higher educational institutions, parks, and correctional and mental health facilities. In addition, many states support local government programs for construction of correctional facilities, mental health centers, vocational schools, elementary and secondary schools, and other capital improvements. The location of these investments has substantial influence on which substate areas grow economically and how job opportunities are distributed between central cities and suburbs.

A strong case can be made for systematically planning these investments in advance. In some cases, such as transportation, advance planning is essential so that activities such as engineering and land acquisition can take place well in advance of actual construction. In the case of programs such as mental health and higher education, current activities must tie closely to planned locations of future facilities. In addition to these arguments for planning within individual functions, planning can reflect the interrelationships among these state investments. The most obvious case arises in those investments (e.g., highways and parks on a given site) that are potentially conflicting. However, coplanning of complementary investments (e.g., a community college and the transportation investments that make it accessible) is also desirable.

Investment planning also interacts with (and is sometimes the same as) budget planning. For example, in state governments that pay for capital investment programs by borrowing, only an investment plan can give an idea of future borrowing needs. The borrowing requirements of an investment plan can be matched with estimates of the capacity of the bond markets to absorb additional state borrowing at reasonable interest rates.

Budget Planning

Many state governments seek to provide overviews of future revenues and expenditures beyond the year(s) for which budgets are being formulated. The development of these plans is discussed in chapter 11. This kind of advance budgeting, whether released to the public or not, can give agency heads an idea of the resources to expect in future years and can provide a basis for decisions on such projects as the construction of new office space.

Program Evaluation

Many Governors have promised in the campaign to look closely at state government programs to determine how they may be improved and whether they should be dropped. Translating this general objective into specific action in the policy context of the Governor's office is not easy. Two elements are involved: (1) making sure that the evaluation gets done, and (2) making sure that it is used to affect decisions.

In many cases early in the administration, a newly appointed cabinet officer may be the best person to evaluate a program in a particular department. After the administration has been in office for some time, the programs being evaluated will generally be strongly supported by the responsible cabinet officer, so the central budgeting and/or planning staffs would be more appropriate evaluators.

It is important to remember that evaluations can get lost in state government unless they are considered when key decisions about programs are being made. Normally, it will be appropriate to time their submission to coincide with the budget cycle and to make sure that the budget director raises the evaluation questions (and findings) along with other materials relevant to the budget decision.

POLICY IN THE BUDGET PROCESS

Many states retain a budgeting system that resembles closely the planning-programming-budgeting systems (PPB or PPBS) developed in the 1960s and early 1970s as the predecessors to zero-base budgeting. In such systems, as well as some zero-based systems, the budget process is used as the main policy-development instrument and the budget document as the main document containing the articulation of that policy.

The general approach is to combine activities of state agencies into related and mutually exclusive groupings called programs. For example, highway safety might be designated as a program. The program can be divided into subprograms; for example, traffic signals and traffic law enforcement in highway safety. Each program (or subprogram) is given a general statement of purpose or objective, such as reducing the loss of life associated with traffic accidents. Time-specific goals are sometimes also associated with programs; for example, reducing the number of lives lost in traffic accidents from 135 in 1978 to 111 in 1979. The results of this process provide an overall indication of the policies of state government.

Some states also use work-load statistics that are related to the goals. An example is to write 20,000 speeding citations in 1979, an increase of 10 percent from 1978. These work-load goals are sufficiently specific to provide a basis for determining agency performance relative to earlier promises. When work-load measures are used, they are generally applied to an activity that is under the management control of the agency (e.g., speeding citations), rather than to activities influenced by other factors for which the agency can't be held responsible (e.g., the number of lives lost in traffic accidents).

The state governments that use this kind of system generally combine management uses of the information after the budget is passed with the uses that arise during the budgeting process itself. Agency heads are often asked to report accomplishments in relation to the stated goals.

While processes of this type do provide a large group of gubernatorially approved policy statements, the statements basically cover only actions of state government that have significant budgetary implications. Such documents would not normally indicate policies on such subjects as fixed sentencing of offenders, abortion or the Equal Rights Amendment.

MANAGEMENT BY OBJECTIVES

Some Governors have experimented with systems of "management by objectives." The underlying premise of such a system is that the Governor and department head should come into agreement on the subordinate's objectives for a particular time period (often a year, with quarterly progress milestones). This way the Governor will know what the department head is promising to accomplish, and the department head will know what is expected of him.

Systems of management by objectives resemble the work-load reporting systems described above with these differences:

• They include only statements of objectives that are sufficiently specific so that progress against them can be measured.

• They are oriented toward work load that is controlled by the agency, as distinct from work load (e.g., number of requests for transit of hazardous cargo processed) that is controlled by outside forces. Generally, the motivation for adopting a management-by-objectives (MBO) system is internal management of state government rather than the articulation of policy to the outside world. However, such a system can provide a basis for public statements of a Governor's policy.

Budget analysts or members of the Governor's personal staff are usually assigned to monitor MBOs, and regular "Governor's review" sessions are held. In opting for a fairly extensive management system such as an MBO process, the Governor must be prepared to chide and push agency heads who fail to live up to their stated targets.

FORMAL POLICY STATEMENTS

Some state laws require that fairly formal statements of policy be made by the Governor. For example, in Georgia the Governor is required to issue an annual policy statement. A sample section from that statement can be found in appendix 11.

Even where not formally required to do so, some Governors issue annual policy statements. A good example is the Governor of Michigan's practice of making his state-of-the-state message a written document of several hundred pages. The more common practice is to have no single policy document, but to issue ad hoc messages to the public or the legislature on issues of particular importance.

CHAPTER SEVEN

An Approach to Management

At first do not view events as immediate crises. Realize that sometimes events are more clear with the passage of time. . . .

Beware of advice that tells you "this must be done this way now." Haste can sometimes cause errors in judgment that are difficult to correct. . . .

Take the time to make up your mind. Get as many facts and opinions as possible before you do. But then stick to your decision. . . .

— former Governors

SUMMARY

The new Governor's management approach will evolve early in the administration as day-to-day problems and crises occur.

The way the Governor chooses to delegate work and utilize his cabinet will help define the new administration's management style. Some Governors use their cabinets as formal mechanisms to set policy and coordinate the management of state government. Others use their cabinets less formally and ask agency heads to serve as public spokesmen, participate in cabinet task forces to develop legislative proposals, or maintain liaison with interest groups.

One of the most difficult aspects of managing state government is the development of workable relationships among the Governor's staff; line agencies, such as transportation and mental health departments, which provide direct services to the public; and the other agencies, such as administration and central services, which support them.

A frequently used management technique limits a top manager's activities to establishing general objectives and constraints for his subordinates. Under this model, the Governor would set broad goals for his cabinet officials but would allow them wide latitude to determine agency organization, hire staff and allocate resources. While the Governor's staff should never assert powers over line agencies that he would not assert, it should be responsible for gathering information for decision making on policy issues and budgets, and the agencies should respond to reasonable requests for program data.

It is important for the Governor to set clear ground rules for staff-line interaction. The staff must ensure reasonable access to the Governor for line agency officials, and line agencies must keep sources of information open to the staff. Problems in interaction may well arise, however, and a third party, such as an executive assistant, should be given authority to resolve disputes.

To avoid disputes wherever possible, the Governor must attempt to ensure "due process" in decision making. The decision mechanism used by the Governor should allow all line and staff participants to express their positions. The decision-making process also should require complete staff work, in which interested parties attempt to resolve questions of fact and have concise positions ready for the Governor's review. Once the decision is made, those involved should be informed directly, not by a third party, whenever possible.

In order to handle the enormous amounts of reading required of a chief executive, a new Governor also will need to set clear guidelines for the types of issue papers, briefing materials and decision memoranda he will read.

Similar guidelines must be set for the management of files and records. The predecessor's staff will negotiate with the new Governor's staff over which files will remain. Files on legal matters, interstate agreements and continuing task forces are particularly important. The new Governor's filing system should include subject or chronological files to ensure efficient retrieval of information; tickler, follow-up or suspense files to ensure that staff work does not become bottlenecked; and reading files to keep staff members and other key officials informed of the Governor's policy positions.

Because it is the Governor who must manage the response in the event of a natural disaster or emergency, early thought should be given to the state's likely response. Development of a plan for comprehensive emergency management and the early appointment of a director to coordinate the state's activities in such situations are two steps which the new Governor should consider seriously and promptly.

An Approach to Management

Making and monitoring policy will consume far less of the Governor's and his staff's time than day-to-day management. From the first day, the Governor will face what appears to be crisis after crisis. How he handles day-to-day crises will determine the Governor's management style. This style will permeate his relations with staff and line agencies and will in many cases set the ground rules for the internal workings of his entire administration. Because the initial management style is so difficult to change, a new Governor may be especially interested in what former Governors have said about management.

In the 1976 National Governors' Association survey of former Governors, one piece of advice appeared frequently as the former Governors looked back at their performance in office. Avoid a panic or crisis mentality, they advised.

The former Governors also offered considerable advice on the way a Governor should view his own management style.

Be yourself; don't try to prove you are something you are not. You won't succeed, and you'll be frustrated. . . . Be in command.

Keep your sense of humor.

Maintain the same attitude and life-style as before the election.

Remember you can't make everyone happy.

Don't worry about what the press says about you—sleep nights.

Set the example by being it yourself. Remember that you can't please all the people. Do the best you can. The rest will follow.

Always make the decisions that you believe are right, regardless of what the editorial writers, critics or the opposition think.

Take command decisively and immediately.

The Governor should not take himself too seriously. He and his staff should see the humorous side of their lives and work together and profit from the change of pace and diversion which good humor brings. It can be like a fresh cooling breeze to many hot, tense and inexplicable situations.

Be firm. The public expects it and supports it.

Don't worry about reelection; it will take care of itself if you do a good job.

My advice is to make the tough decisions—not waffle—then have no later regrets.

CABINET GOVERNMENT

Establishing clear staff and line roles is critical not only to policy development, but also to day-to-day management. A Governor's "cabinet" may range from 15 to over 100, depending on the state. (See appendix 12.) Governors have dealt with the problems and potentials of using agency heads in a number of ways.

Some Governors use the cabinet as a formally constituted advisory body. With the enactment of "sunshine" legislation in many states, however, some Governors have been reluctant to submit issues to cabinet meetings, since free discussion and dissent is difficult with members of the press in attendance. Others use formal cabinet meetings as forums at which to announce policies, overall budget targets or work-load goals.

Even if a formal cabinet system is not used, the Governor may choose to use groups of cabinet members for various purposes. In some situations, an agency head may coordinate certain assignments which are broader than his agency mandate. For example, a director of economic development may also have functions equivalent to those of a special assistant to the Governor for relations with business groups. Similar liaison roles may go to the head of the labor department, head of a community affairs agency, and heads of such agencies as veterans affairs and aging. One approach for using members of the cabinet in policy development is illustrated in the Cabinet Subgroups section of appendix 8.

Agency heads in small groups can also be part of advisory structures. For example, some Governors hold periodic meetings with a group consisting of both top members of the immediate staff and selected heads of state agencies, generally those who are viewed as both perceptive and as politically close to the Governor.

If a reasonable attempt is made to keep them informed of overall administration positions, agency heads can also be quite effective ambassadors for an administration. They normally devote considerable time to making presentations before their own constituencies and are generally in demand for speaking engagements for broader audiences.

THE GOVERNOR AND HIS STAFF

As the transition unfolds, Governors recognize that their greatest single need is a first-rate staff. To be first rate, the staff must be highly intelligent and moral. Their energies and loyalties must be devoted unflinchingly to the achievement of the Governor's success. They must know the Governor—his hopes, his ideals, his standards and the direction he wishes to go. Then they must be willing to accept these as their own. There must be clear, forthright communications between the staff and the Governor. The Governor is primarily responsible for establishing and protecting these communications channels. However, he should not encourage his staff to indulge in constant praise and adulation. He must deal frankly with them and insist that they in turn deal frankly with him.

It is not unusual for members of a Governor's staff to feel that the Governor is not treating them correctly. Many former members of the campaign staff will feel more isolated from the Governor because they will not enjoy the same easy access that they had before. Other staff members will find their recommendations apparently swallowed up in the small bureaucracy of the Governor's office without getting decisions that they want or decisions at all, and without having the Governor explain to them what happened.

Obviously, the staff exists to serve the Governor and not the other way around. However, the extent to which the Governor will get good service out of his staff depends on how well he can motivate them to do good work and to work hard.

One factor that is very important to staff members is not being left in the dark. For personal reasons if for no other, they hate to be the last ones to know what is going on. Of more importance to the Governor, however, are the dealings that staff members have with the outside world in which they represent him. To make those dealings serve the Governor's purposes, it is important that the staff know what his policies are and the reasons for various decisions. This is also important when the Governor has decided *not* to adopt a policy or position on a given issue. Otherwise, the staff may think that there was some kind of failure in the decision-making process.

Particularly in large office situations, staff meetings chaired by either the Governor or the executive assistant can be a way of communicating with the staff and a format in which some staff members are comfortable in communicating with their superiors.

STAFF-LINE RELATIONSHIPS

One of the most difficult decisions that a Governor must make, and one which, unfortunately, must be reinforced over and over again, concerns the appropriate relationship between the Governor's immediate staff and state agencies.

Staff, Line and Support Functions

The field of public administration has developed some terminology that should be useful to Governors in dealing day to day with various persons in state government.

The first concept is that of a "line agency" or a person in the "chain of command." This concept derives from an organizational hierarchy such as the one below:

Governor
▲ ▼
Director of Law Enforcement
▲ ▼
Chief, Highway Patrol
▲ ▼
Division Supervisor, Highway Patrol
▲ ▼
Area Three Supervisor
▲ ▼
Patrolman

The diagram shows the reporting relationship for a single highway patrolman. Everyone on a line following the chain of command to the one who actually renders a service to the public (e.g., a patrolman) is performing a "line function." The agencies in which such functions are performed are "line agencies." Other examples include mental health and transportation departments.

Some state employees are not on a line traced through the chain of command between the Governor and those serving the public. Many such personnel are in "support" functions. Support agencies usually provide support to line agencies so that the latter can perform their functions. An example is a central services agency that provides and maintains office space for state employees and runs a motor pool.

"Staff" personnel, such as the immediate staff of the Governor and planning and budgeting agencies, exist to support the decision making of the person to whom they report.

The remaining departments are basically line agencies. Boards and commissions and semi-independent agencies may share all three qualities.

However, there are some ambiguities in most state organizations. For example:

• Community affairs or local government departments sometimes administer programs (line) and are responsible for overall policy toward local governments (staff), including policy affecting other departments.

• Some economic development and community development agencies (which have some line functions, like industrial development and community action administrations) also contain the state planning agency (staff).

- Personnel departments are responsible for recruitment and classification (support) as well as for making recommendations on pay policy (staff).

In most competently managed organizations, quite different types of conduct are expected of managers performing in these different roles. Giving clear guidance early on the relationships between staff and line functions is one of the most important things a Governor can do to make sure that his staff operates efficiently and fairly.

A Management Model for Line Relationships

Generally accepted public and business administration doctrine provides a prescription for the relationship between any two managers in a heirarchical relationship to each other (e.g., a foreman and a member of his crew or a Governor and a cabinet officer). The superior is expected to perform these functions:

- Setting objectives, such as a five-percent return on sales or cutting the rate of welfare fraud;
- Setting constraints, such as a requirement that 20 percent of all new employees hired be members of minorities or that no mental hospitals be closed;
- Establishing the level of resources to be made available and providing those resources; and
- Providing necessary support services, including (1) obvious forms of support services such as motor pools and building maintenance, and (2) less obvious but important support such as using the power of the Governor's office to mobilize public opinion when necessary for the achievement of agency objectives.

Not only should supervisors be doing what is on the above list, but they presumably should not be doing what is not on the list. Unless such matters are covered in the constraints that are developed initially by the supervisor and the person being supervised, the supervisor would be expected to avoid getting into the details of operations.

In this style of management:

- Agency heads have wide latitude in determining the internal organization of their agencies. The chief executive is involved in the question of what functions should be given to or taken away from the agency vis-à-vis other agencies, but not in internal agency reorganization.
- Agency heads control the hiring and firing of all of the employees of the agency. The Governor or his staff can suggest names (sometimes strongly), but the agency head can opt to avoid hiring specific individuals.
- Agency heads control most of the decisions about the allocation of resources within totals prescribed by the chief executive.

With this management approach carried to its extreme, the Governor would also leave to the agency head much of the responsibility for formulation of a legislative program and dealing with the legislative body. However, some controls are always built in so that agencies do not take contradictory positions or support legislation that would cause costs to rise above the approved budget.

While this management model fits the private sector extremely well, most Governors recognize the need to modify it to some degree. Because the Governor is publicly accountable not only for the resources, constraints and production of a line agency, but also for the general conduct of state employees, he will no doubt be required to become more personally involved than accepted private-sector management theory would advise. Nevertheless, distinguishing between staff and line relationships and enforcing that distinction among staff and agency heads are important steps in getting ahold of the reins of state government.

Regardless of the level of personal control over agency operations, the Governor will want to develop a management system which treats agency directors consistently and fairly.

Staff Roles in Management

Under this management model, the Governor's staff obviously is limited to using only those powers that the Governor personally would assert.

For example, if the Governor gives agency heads management assistant but would not force the removal unless there were serious grounds for doing so. If the Governor were exercising this degree of restraint, it would follow that the most the staff could do would be to encourage—but not order—the cabinet officer to remove the individual. Conversely, it would follow that where a Governor involves himself in personnel decisions within an agency, his staff could at least acquire information with which to advise him in such matters.

This is but one example of the potential conflicts between staff members and agency heads.

In such a management model, the functions of the Governor's staff include:

- Administering decision-making processes that produce advice to the Governor in particular formats and on a particular schedule. The function of the budget staff in prescribing forms and schedules is an example of this, as are guidelines for submission of recommended items for the Governor's legislative program and capital planning documents.

- Providing advice to the Governor on subjects that cut across agency lines. Some examples are relationships with the press, legislative relations, and dealing with federal programs, members of the state's congressional delegation and local officials.

- Providing common assumptions or planning guides to be used by all elements of state government. An example is the common population projections that many state planning offices provide for the use of planners in various state agencies.

- Gathering information from various agencies and handling crises in conjunction with the Governor and the agency director.

Interaction of Staff and Line Agencies

In many cases, the ground rules for the interaction of staff and line agencies can easily be set by the Governor. In the standard management model, the staff either cannot *direct* line personnel at all or can do so only in cases where the Governor has delegated to the staff the authority to perform a function that involves many agencies.

The line agency head is obligated to cooperate with the Governor's staff to make sure that the Governor has all the options before him on any decision affecting the agency. If, for example, the legislative assistant is putting together a potential legislative program for the Governor to consider as a whole, an agency head should not refuse to provide his recommendations for the purpose of having them collected and analyzed together. The agency head can ask for assurances that the legislative assistant will not cut off his communication with the Governor by suppressing legislative recommendations, but he should not be allowed to take the position that he will only send such recommendations directly to the Governor.

Likewise, it is the obligation of the agency head to allow staff members who are working on a problem to have reasonable access to the information held by the agency. For example, budget agencies often conduct far-ranging reviews within agencies, which may or may not result in recommendations to the Governor. The Governor presumably wants recommendations, but only after budget staff members have dug out facts, decided whether recommendations should be made, and convinced their superiors to make them. A substantial number of recommendations get weeded out in this process. But if an agency head tries to prevent a budget examiner from acquiring information about an issue, the budget director will probably take the issue to the Governor. And the Governor who permits such interference may soon find more controversies on his desk than he needs to deal with.

Staff members, too, have an obligation not to withhold potentially useful information from line agencies. For example, an agency head working on a legislative program that would include changes in procedures for citizen participation in a program should be told if the Governor has previously taken a position on another agency's procedures.

In the general management model forming the basis for this chapter, the staff can never cut off access of line agency heads to the Governor, and the line agency heads cannot cut off access to information.

Obviously, any Governor wanting time to sleep and see his family will hope that this access privilege is not used too often. It will not be if the staff and line agencies are willing to work together.

Whatever the model, there will be circumstances where, as a practical matter, the Governor cannot decide an issue, and it is unclear whether a staff person or a line agency should decide. A typical case finds the head of the agency and the legislative assistant at a legislative session late at night. A key amendment is introduced without warning, and the administration needs to come up with a position quickly. If the Governor is not available or the two decide that the issue isn't big enough for the Governor, the question becomes: what is the administration position if the line agency head and the legislative assistant disagree? Unless some third party, usually an executive assistant, is available to adjudicate, this question will never be resolved. The Governor will not want to give either the general power to overrule the other.

Avoiding Staff-Line Conflicts

The relationships between line agency heads (and their staffs) and the Governor's staff will have some competitive aspects. This is as it should be in those many cases where the Governor values two conflicting goals.

When the mental health director battles for more funding for better mental health and the budget director tries to control total spending, both may be reflecting the Governor's position. Their disagreement serves to bring the issue to the Governor, where it should be. When the legislative staff wants a department to concede a point to a legislator in the name of better legislative relations and the department doesn't want to concede because of inconsistency with departmental priorities, both may be reflecting the Governor's priorities. When the state planning agency wants to release population projections to improve planning but the figures will cause a political problem, the planning director can reflect the Governor's desire to have more rational planning and the political advisor the Governor's desire to minimize political problems.

These types of conflicts are healthy ones. Any Governor who, for example, tells one person to go out and take charge of cleaning up the environment quickly and another to make sure that no industry leaves the state should expect, sooner or later, to see both individuals in his office asking him to resolve a situation in which the two sets of objectives seem contradictory.

Unfortunately, not all of the conflicts are this clear-cut, nor do they all involve situations in which the Governor should want to make a decision. Line agency heads and the Governor's staff on occasion exhibit a tendency to want to make all of the decisions that they can get their hands on. There are a number of ways that the Governor can avoid losing his power to ambitious subordinates and ensure that appropriate staff-line relationships are maintained.

Guidelines from the Governor. Generalities about staff-line relationships can be useful in understanding the Governor's management choices. However, in day-to-day operating situations, the staff-line relationship will vary from staff member to staff member and from agency head to agency head. No formal prescribed relationship will be followed in all cases. The Governor will, in each situation, have a perception of the competence of the individuals involved that will, and should, affect the relative roles of the individuals.

As a result, it is extremely important for a Governor to send clear, decisive signals to his staff about his preferences. These usually will include the following:

- Complete staff work must include all sides of an issue—fiscal, substantive and political.
- Meetings should normally be held to make decisions based on complete staff work. Meetings should not lead merely to more meetings.
- When made, decisions should be communicated clearly to all parties.
- Affected persons have the right of one, and only one, appeal to gubernatorial decisions.

These rules or similar arrangements and customs will reduce "gaming" and streamline the Governor's management of his office and his state government.

Joining all parties. Governors with a legal background will be aware of the approach in many legal proceedings of avoiding *ex parte* proceedings—that is, proceedings in which only one side of a case is represented. The logic for joining all parties in discussion is that the truth is more likely to be reached when an interested and adverse party is present to challenge facts that are asserted and to offer facts that are omitted, as well as to mention arguments that should be considered. Healthy working relationships between the Governor, his staff and agencies are more likely to be maintained if consistent "due process" is a central part of the decision-making process.

It is easy for a Governor to forget this logic in the press of daily business. The Governor's executive assistant may, for example, come rushing to the Governor for a decision on some matter. The Governor's first problem will be to make sure that those whose advice he values (e.g., the head of the agency involved with the problem and, say, the press secretary) have been consulted. The second problem is to ensure that the decision is made based upon a reasonable reflection of their views—both their recommendation and any arguments for and against other positions. In complex cases, a meeting that includes all relevant advisors will guarantee this much better than a decision based upon a single advisor's presentation of everyone's views.

Where meetings are not possible, a reasonable substitute would allow the unrepresented parties to put their arguments in their own words in the Governor's decision package through a memorandum or letter.

When Governors omit key advisors in making decisions, they sometimes find themselves changing those decisions later when the key advisor takes a position. Such deviations can give rise to criticism of the decision-making process as being controlled by "who saw the Governor last"—criticism that can be avoided if everyone sees the Governor at the same time.

Complete staff work. The military has a notion of "complete staff work" which has a certain bureaucratic ring to it, but which may quickly become a desirable concept for a new Governor. The concept is that when a problem comes to the Governor for decision, all background information necessary to that decision comes with it. This includes both factually relevant information and the positions of those whose advice the Governor seeks.

Take, for example, a complex situation typical of the many problems which reach a Governor's desk. The highway department is ready to acquire right-of-way which runs parallel to a scenic stretch of river that the conservation department hopes some day to turn into a park. Some local interests strongly want the highway where it is planned to go; others would give up the highway entirely to save the land; still others want the highway, but on a variety of different locations. Legislators have been badgering the Governor and his legislative advisors, and the conservation department has been pressing the budgeters for money to acquire the land. The county chairman has spoken to the Governor's political advisor on the subject.

Early in his administration, a Governor has probably not decided whom he would consult on an issue of this type, much less communicated that information to others. As a result, he is likely to receive communications such as:

- An urgent memorandum from the highway director stating that he must have approval to go ahead with the route along the river;
- An urgent letter from the conservation director stating that he must have the money to start acquiring the parkland and that his staff has discovered a good alternative route for the highway;
- A communication from the budget director indicating that a request from the conservation department for funds for the park is likely, recommending that approval of funds be withheld until the regular budget cycle, and suggesting that the Governor could keep the highway department from building the highway and not request funds for the park until later;
- A note from the legislative staff indicating the extent of legislative interest in the issue and pointing out the legislators who want to see the Governor about it;

- A series of memos from the scheduling aide which list all the people who want to meet with the Governor on the subject; and

- Questions from the press secretary and the mail-answering operation on how to handle the questions they are getting.

All of these people work for the Governor, and they all are piling up problems on the Governor's desk without providing solutions. Further, many of them are using the Governor as a mail-routing service. Discussions which should take place between the highway director and the conservation director are being routed through the Governor's office.

The reason for the confusion is that early in the administration the highway department is testing the Governor to see if it can get a decision affecting the department of conservation without having to consult conservation; conservation doesn't like the idea of having to consult with the budget bureau about money; and everybody considers himself an expert on working with the legislature and doesn't need any advice from the Governor's legislative advisor.

A Governor will never totally solve all these problems, but sending clear signals in the beginning that he will demand "complete staff work" will help. The likely response to the situation just described is to ask an aide to straighten it out, which he will probably do by consulting all these people and making a recommendation to the Governor.

Much of the unnecessary paperwork can be avoided by stressing the desire to eliminate communications which do not suggest conclusions and solutions, and by indicating clearly whose advice is wanted in what circumstances. Some Governors have found that structured decision memoranda are the best method to deal with problems such as these. A sample of this technique can be found in the Decision Memorandum section of appendix 8.

Avoiding messengers. A special communications problem arises when the Governor does not have the affected parties present when decisions are made. Having a staff person report the decision to the affected parties is not always the best approach because, if it is pursued consistently, the affected persons will feel that they are out of direct communication with the Governor.

When others deliver "The Governor told me to tell you . . ." messages, it becomes difficult to draw the line between the part of the instruction that comes from the Governor and the part that represents the thinking of the messenger, particularly when the recipient of the message wants to discuss details that the Governor may not have considered at all. Many times, simply picking up the phone and delivering a decision directly can save a great deal of time and misunderstanding later.

Problem meetings and solution meetings. In scheduling meetings, the appointments secretary will find that demands for time with the Governor most often grow out of problems that defy comfortable solution. Industry X is suffering and wants some concessions that the staff doesn't like, or a legislator wants a local project which isn't one of the administration's construction priorities. If a Governor is to have time for anything other than meetings, he will need to set a few ground rules. For example, he should:

- Never let meetings get bogged down in discussions about facts that can be determined independently. A general services department may be right that they could save money if they took over the printing operation of the mental health department, or the mental health director may be right that it would cost them more. In any case, a Governor is wise to have some neutral party on his staff make the factual finding on cost, and then use the information in making whatever policy decision is necessary.

- Do not let the office become a place for other people to talk to each other. After the Governor has decided to approve a project to build a new tollway, the press secretary and the highway director should not be permitted to hammer out the details of the press release in the Governor's office. One should be designated to come back with either an agreed text or a draft, along with a summary of objections to the draft.

- Try to keep meetings with outsiders to good news and handle the bad news some other way. When a Governor has requests from two chambers of commerce and local legislators to meet on projects, one of which he can support and one of which he can't, he should try to avoid the meeting on the project he can't undertake unless he really expects to get new information or a fresh perspective. If he holds such a meeting, he will spend 30 minutes in argument and, at best, end by promising to "consider it." It is easier for the Governor to call the legislator or community leader involved to explain why he cannot accede to the request so that local reputations will not be staked on what is bound to be an unsuccessful public appeal to the top.

Open communications links. The pressures for the Governor's time will cause him and his staff to erect barriers that prevent junior staff members and some heads of agencies from having an adequate opportunity to meet with him in an office setting. These procedures may also inhibit agency heads from seeing the Governor on any but the most important matters. While such procedures are often necessary, they will tend to cut off useful short comments from these astute observers on how the administration is going, procedural problems and possible future concerns.

The Governor will want to find informal ways to provide communication opportunities for individuals and topics that are not appropriate for formal meetings. Having a staff member linger a moment after formal meetings, conversations in the hall, taking a moment to visit staffers' offices, picnics and cocktail conversation can all provide such opportunities.

Dealing with independent officials. While the situation varies from state to state, the Governor and his staff in most states are confronted with the problem of dealing with a number of officials who are not directly responsive to the Governor. Usually they are people that he can neither hire nor fire:

• Elected officials such as the lieutenant governor, secretary of state, comptroller and/or auditor, treasurer and sometimes elected heads of such departments as highways and agriculture;

• Chairmen of regulatory agencies who are serving fixed terms or are selected by members serving fixed terms; and

• Agency directors who are selected by boards that the Governor does not control. Examples are state superintendents of public instruction, chancellors of boards of regents or boards of higher education, and university presidents.

Assuming that there are policy issues being dealt with by these agencies in which the Governor has an interest, the Governor and his staff have to search for ways in which the laws and political situation peculiar to their state will allow them to exercise an impact on the policies of the agencies and those who run them.

In general, the most powerful levers over these agencies are those provided to the Governor by statute. Most significant among them is the budget power, including the power to recommend budgets to the legislature, to appropriate funds, and in some cases impound them, and otherwise to control finances. Additional important powers are those involving personnel (including pay and classification), data processing, purchasing and service operations.

In addition to these formal powers, Governors will often have indirect power over supposedly independent boards because of the desire of some members to be reappointed. The appointed head of an agency run by a board will also want to survive after the composition of the board has been changed by the Governor's appointments. In the eyes of elected officials, the Governor may have a potential effect on either their reelection to the same office or their nomination and election to higher office. The Governor's superior access to the press and media can also be significant, as can whatever power he may exercise in the legislature.

DAY-TO-DAY MANAGEMENT

The Governor's first several months in office, in most cases, will be devoted largely to appointing personnel and settling upon legislative and budget initiatives. During this period, day-to-day management will probably not receive a great deal of attention. Sooner or later, by conscious decision or evolution, the Governor will develop a system for managing the continuing operations of state government.

The most passive and least time-consuming approach avoids any periodically scheduled meetings or reports. The Governor's involvement in policy making in any agency occurs at the agency's initiative or in response to news articles, citizen complaints and legislative interests. In addition, the Governor becomes involved to resolve differences between one agency and another, or between some staff members of a staff agency and the line agency, and with questions that the agency heads and staff members refer to him. Doing these things alone can keep a Governor busy. This work load can be reduced still further if the executive assistant is empowered to make certain types of decisions on the Governor's behalf.

Medium-range involvement in day-to-day administration can be developed around a more formal reporting system, using either oral reports, meetings with cabinet members and staff, or a system of periodic written reports from departments and staff. These reports provide an opportunity for the Governor to impose his policies on the activities of departments beyond the questions which his staff and cabinet members might otherwise raise with him.

Even greater involvement occurs when the Governor seeks to work with individual agency heads to formulate policy on the full range of their activities. This involvement may be relatively unstructured—such as weekly meetings to discuss policy, program and problems—or highly structured through subcabinet meetings, management by objectives or a similar system. Either way, the process presumes that major agency policies are initiated and reviewed by the Governor, and that progress toward objectives is monitored by him as well as the head of the department.

Whatever system is chosen, a Governor will find it desirable to focus upon one of these approaches early so that indecisiveness about what must be considered by him and what can be done without his input can be held to a minimum.

Governors are not generally involved in such office routines as reviewing sick leave and vacation requests, passing on vouchers for purchases, or approving requests for travel reimbursements. Top staff members don't have much interest in them either. However, a Governor should protect himself from irregularities in these matters. Unfortunately, the vulnerability to problems is great because many new staff aides are not familiar with state rules governing travel and what can be purchased with state funds under what circumstances. Further, they and their secretaries may attempt to evade finance and accounting regulations unless the Governor makes very clear that he does not want any privileges extended to his immediate staff, or to himself, which are not normally open to state employees. Governors would be especially wise to institute tight controls on staff travel and use of the telephone for long-distance calls.

The In-Box

A Governor soon finds that the correspondence, memoranda and reading materials provided him far exceed the capacity of any human being to absorb. Out of self-preservation, if for no other reason, he finds ways to delegate this work load. In the process of fighting to get out from under paperwork, a Governor should remember that the paperwork he gets is material other people think he needs to see. Unless he sets clear guidelines, he will find his reading time dominated by others' concepts of what he needs to see, rather than by his own. The Governor should decide at the outset whether he wants to receive information systematically from his staff which they may not volunteer. The following is a basic checklist of information for the Governor and, equally important, his secretary:

- Clippings of all significant state government coverage in major newspapers (excluding duplicate wire service stories);
- Clippings from special interest newsletters and mailings (chamber of commerce, state AFL-CIO, bankers' association);
- Any national magazines or nationally oriented newspaper considered relevant, either clipped articles or entire editions;
- Weekly summaries describing the volume, subject matter and complexion of incoming mail, with a cross-section of samples;
- A weekly or monthly report on how fast mail is being answered (90 percent acknowledged within 48 hours, 40 percent of all substantive replies mailed within a week of receipt, etc.);
- Periodic public opinion polls on issues of interest, such as the Governor's own popularity;
- Summaries of television news coverage of the Governor's activities and state issues;
- Weekly (or daily) reports from the legislative staff on the status of the legislative program;
- Weekly or monthly reports from department heads; and
- Monthly reports on the state's financial status and other timely items, such as changes in welfare case load, in mental health and correctional institutional populations, in the number of state employees, and progress in highway construction.

A Governor must exercise some care in demanding reports from his department heads. Unless he plans to read and act on all such reports, a Governor will be wise to keep them to a minimum. Department heads frequently use them as clearance devices and assume that the Governor concurs in an action or policy if it is included in their reports and elicits no comment to the contrary from the top.

Files and Records

A new Governor will find that no matter how friendly his transition into the office, there will be considerable reluctance on the part of the outgoing Governor and his top advisors to turn over all their files. Some of the reasons for their reluctance are sound, and the Governor-elect will discover much of the material he needs duplicated somewhere in the bureaucracy he inherits. Which files are to be left is normally negotiated between a member of the incoming staff and one of the outgoing Governor's top aides.

Preventing the indiscriminate destruction of all Governor's office files is an obvious objective. A few files and papers will be of no particular use to the new Governor but should be maintained for auditing and accounting purposes; these include property and payroll records and invoices. In other cases, personnel in the Governor's immediate office may have been involved in activities which were not politically sensitive and in which continuity of records is desirable; examples include representation on interstate compacts and task forces of agency personnel. In addition, the new Governor will need the files of legal actions such as pardons and extraditions.

The remaining files in most Governors' offices are more sensitive, and getting ahold of them may be difficult for the new staff. The more sensitive papers might include memoranda on why particular legislation was vetoed, political files, and files relating to personnel and budget matters. The outgoing Governor may have every good reason to remove these or to obtain a commitment that they will remain confidential.

If a Governor-elect or his staff get into arguments with the prior administration over files, it is well to remember that in many states the new administration is on solid legal ground. Files are the property of state government, and many states have laws against the removal of public property or its destruction. And, both the incumbent Governor and his successor should keep in mind the historical value of all gubernatorial records.

As a start in planning a filing system, it is reasonable to ask whether documents need to be kept at all. Much routine paperwork goes on in state government. If it is maintained in files in some state agency, there is no reason to duplicate it in the Governor's office. Similarly, it normally is not necessary to keep purely informational material in the Governor's immediate office. The monthly report on welfare case load or the state's revenues may be interesting, but it need not fatten the Governor's own files when the welfare department or budget office can replace it in minutes.

Kinds of filing systems include:

Subject and chronological files. The Governor does need to be able to retrieve anything bearing his signature quickly. This material can be filed by subject, in chronological order, or in a combination or duplication of the two. Some of it can be stored separately. For example, the mail staff may keep outgoing answers to routine mail and the press office may keep back press releases.

Tickler, follow-up or suspense files. For many reasons, some aides will not get things done when promised unless they know the Governor has an organized system for remembering what they promised to do, and when. There are a couple of simple systems to accomplish this. The first is simply a file, kept by a secretary, which includes everything the Governor wants followed up. The secretary makes sure that every assignment in it gets done and has the authority to prod people or refer the matter to the Governor.

The second approach is the tickler or suspense file, which can include reminders to the chief executive as well as follow-ups for others. In using a tickler file, a Governor simply designates a future date by which he wants certain paperwork to reappear on his desk, and his secretary arranges to give him that paperwork on or before the date he designates. A sophisticated tickler file also includes automatic follow-up based upon certain general rules, such as having the draft of a speech in hand at least 48 hours before the speech is scheduled.

Reading files. Many offices maintain files containing copies of major outgoing correspondence by the Governor and his top staff. In a Governor's office, much of the activity related to such functions as press, legislative and political matters does not result in file copies. However, many positions on programs and issues are first outlined by the Governor and his key staff in correspondence with constituents, interest groups and affected department heads. A reading file is useful in keeping staff members who do not have regular access to the Governor and his top aides—and some who do—informed on such matters.

Additional arrangements will be necessary, however, to keep cabinet and top staff members abreast of the positions the Governor is taking and his plans for the future. If he expects them to support his positions and not contradict him in their public statements, they need to know what he is saying. Approaches to keeping them informed should include making sure that the press office circulates all significant press releases (regardless of subject matter) to the cabinet and top staff, having major news stories about state government clipped and circulated to this same group, and circulating sample responses to issues in the Governor's mail.

EMERGENCY PREPAREDNESS

During his term, a Governor will undoubtedly have to deal with a number of different types of disasters. Many are situations where a key vote in the legislature has been lost or someone leaked a sensitive memo. While these may seem like disasters at the time, they usually pale next to the Governor's responsibilities for dealing with natural disasters and civil emergencies. More than one Governor's future political career has been made or broken on the basis of how the public perceived his handling of a public emergency situation.

The chances are great that a Governor will have to face one or more such problems, according to a recent survey conducted by the National

Governors' Association. The 52 states and territories responding indicated the following experience with disasters in the past five years:

DISASTER TYPE	NUMBER OF STATES
Flood	47
Wind	38
Drought	38
Snow and ice	34
Fire	28
Utility failures	26
Land movement	17
Pollution, epidemics	18
Radiation	11
Terrorism	4

Clearly the best way of dealing with disasters is to prevent them entirely or to take steps to make sure that damage is minimized. The responsibility for doing this is spread across state government—from those who control state building codes, to departments of transportation, to state planning offices and legislatures.

The Governor will have a number of agencies at his disposal for dealing with disasters when they occur. The National Guard exists in all states, as do civil defense or emergency services offices with state preparedness and response plans. In addition, depending upon the nature of the problem, the highway patrol, departments of transportation, and public health and welfare agencies are likely to be involved.

Long-term recovery issues are also important and need to be planned, implemented and coordinated in conjunction with overall state development plans.

To avoid inadequate or inept-appearing responses to emergency situations, the Governor should take steps before disaster strikes to make sure that state government functions smoothly in an emergency. Perhaps the most important of these steps is a public policy statement on comprehensive emergency management—not only for preparedness and response, but for mitigation and recovery—together with the appointment of a state emergency management director. The director would oversee the emergency services office and coordinate statewide emergency management on behalf of the Governor, as discussed in chapter 3.

While significant state and federal funds are used for planning responses to disasters, few states have adequate coordination of mitigation or recovery funding. A Governor's staff is often unfamiliar with the planning processes and the alternatives that are open to them in the event of a disaster, as well as the relationship of preparedness and response to mitigation and recovery activities. The new Governor may wish to assign a staff member to work with the comprehensive emergency management director, or may have the emergency manager report directly to him. Whichever is done, emergencies must be managed by someone with the Governor's direct support and confidence. Early on, this manager should ensure that the administration has answers to the following questions:

- What should happen if a general alert is issued that the President fears imminent enemy nuclear attack?
- What is the appropriate state response when warning is received of a major natural disaster?
- When a prison riot occurs, who has what authority and who reports to whom?
- How is a derailed train with hazardous cargo best handled?

Because the federal presence is so often publicized in the event of major natural disasters, it is easy to overlook the extent to which Governors need to be involved, not only in responses to natural disasters but to man-made emergencies. Federal assistance during and after such events is triggered by justified requests for assistance from Governors. The Governor and his employees are vital in coordinating local, state and federal resources for all phases of emergency management.

As noted in chapter 3, the new NGA manual, *Comprehensive Emergency Management: A Governor's Guide,* to be published in December 1978, will provide valuable guidance for the Governor and his emergency manager.

SURVIVAL IN THE SUNSHINE

In an increasing number of states, "sunshine" or "open meeting" laws have been passed. The intent of these laws is to move government out of "smoke-filled back rooms" and under public scrutiny. The theory is that decisions arrived at in open forums are likely to be better than decisions made in private, where erroneous assumptions can go unchallenged and improper motives unnoticed. These laws vary in their details, but they often require public notice of many meetings, including such activities as the Governor's meeting with his staff to decide on legislative recommendations and administrative actions.

These laws can present dilemmas for Governors who generally support the type of open decision making for which they call but who feel they must have confidentiality in discussions of policy. These Governors are willing to defend any decisions or recommendations that they might make but want their advisors to be able to speak freely about such matters as personalities and political factors.

It is the duty of a Governor, whether he likes the laws or not as they apply to his particular circumstances, to make a good faith attempt to comply with them while seeking any changes that he might consider to be necessary. However, some of the exceptions provisions can be used to avoid exposing all meetings to the press and public, particularly when policy decisions can be separated from the discussion of relevant facts.

CHAPTER EIGHT

The Governor's Schedule

Clearly the most important decisions made by a Governor have to do with the allocation of his time. There is no magical formula for this except that a Governor who thoroughly thinks through his schedule in terms of his objectives will fare much better than a Governor who allows his time to be allocated for him on the basis of pressures and events.

Overscheduling of a new Governor can create a very serious physical, emotional, and mental condition of exhaustion that is very difficult to cope with.

— a former Governor

SUMMARY

Managing the Governor's time effectively is extremely important—and difficult. The demands on the Governor's time are tremendous, and it should be viewed as a scarce resource that must be budgeted carefully. From managing state government as chief executive to attending a party function as political leader to cutting a ribbon as ceremonial chief, the Governor's diverse roles each demand their share of his time.

The first rule of scheduling, as defined by former Governors, is to make sure that the schedule is handled by only *one* person. In most cases, the power to commit the Governor's time should not rest entirely with the Governor himself. He should generally rely on his scheduling assistant to develop scheduling strategy and to protect against overlapping commitments.

Developing an effective system for scheduling is important because many people form their impression of the Governor through the way in which their request for his time is handled. Although time constraints require that most invitations be declined, an undiplomatic rejection can have serious ripple effects.

Most schedulers have a limit on how far in advance they will schedule the Governor, normally about two months. This can cause difficulties because many organizations like to schedule months in advance, while the Governor needs to retain some flexibility in his schedule. Arranging in advance for a substitute to attend an event is an effective method of making sure that, if the pressures of business force the Governor to cancel his appearance, he will still be represented.

In planning their requests for time with the Governor, his immediate office staff and agency heads should understand that Governors, by their own estimates, spend only one-quarter of their time on the management of state government, primarily in meetings at the state capitol. Only by careful scheduling and thorough staff preparation can the limited meeting time be used to the best advantage.

The scheduling process will function much more smoothly and will create fewer strains for all involved if both the Governor and his key staff members have a clear understanding as to the types of invitations he will be most likely to accept and the number of major appearances he normally will be willing to schedule in a given week.

Ground rules for scheduling should enable the Governor to attend as many engagements as possible, yet realistically reflect the chief executive's work habits. The scheduler should ensure that adequate provisions are made for:

- Office time and paperwork;
- The family, including vacations;
- Some out-of-state travel; and
- Evening and/or weekend rest.

Despite all their efforts, schedulers can expect the Governor to be—or at least to feel—overscheduled. Many Governors have regular scheduling meetings with key advisors, including the Governor's spouse, to determine a scheduling strategy for the upcoming week.

Some Governors urge their staffs to schedule aggressively, seeking out opportunities to present the administration's point of view, rather than waiting for invitations. A new Governor may want to decide early whether he will want to follow a policy of active rather than passive scheduling as a means of strengthening his political base and building support for his objectives and programs. However, aggressive scheduling has to be handled with great care because too heavy a schedule can result in excessive strain on the Governor. Exhaustion can lead to bad decisions that will have far more serious consequences than will the rejection of an invitation.

The Governor's Schedule

One of the most difficult problems faced by any new Governor is management of his time—who controls it, who can make demands on it, and how he plans to use it. With his time, a Governor signals priorities and establishes the basis for his administration's record.

Because the demands on a Governor's time are seemingly infinite, the scheduling dilemma will never be fully resolved. When former Governors were asked to select from a list of 11 items the aspects of the job they found the most difficult and demanding, the three items relating to schedule (interference with family life, ceremonial demands on time, and the hours) ranked second, third and fourth in number of times mentioned. (See chapter 1.)

ALLOCATION OF TIME

It is very easy for new Governors and their staffs to make scheduling mistakes early in an administration. The staff, or a major part of it, has become accustomed to the pace of the campaign and often has little feel for the pressures that will develop on the Governor's time. To provide assistance and standards of comparison for new Governors and their schedulers, current Governors and schedulers were asked to indicate the percentage of the Governor's work time devoted to various functions. A table summarizing their responses is included in appendix 13.

As a number of schedulers noted, the Governor's schedule varies appreciably during the year. In the early part of each year, when most states have legislatures in session, much more time tends to be devoted to working with the legislature than the averages would indicate. After the legislature has gone home, the schedule for other matters such as appearances outside the state capital is increased. As fall approaches, in most states more of the Governor's time tends to be demanded for the preparation of his budget and legislative program and messages describing both.

The allocation of time also varies somewhat from year to year. In the first year, appointing people to agency head positions and boards and commissions looms larger in the schedule than it will later when these positions are filled with people of the Governor's choosing. Political activity will also vary, depending on the years in which legislative and gubernatorial elections are being held and on the Governor's participation in the nominating process of his own party for national and local offices.

Two points emerge from an examination of this composite schedule. First, the ceremonial functions of the office are important and very time consuming. Second, because of the other great demands on their time, Governors do not have the same amount of time available for management as would, for example, the president of a major corporation.

Good scheduling can help the Governor claim back some of the time that he needs to pursue his interests, his program and his personal life. But whatever time the Governor can preserve for management must be extremely well used if he is to have a major impact on the workings of state government.

THE SCHEDULING ACTIVITY

Governors receive innumerable requests to speak at meetings, attend parties, participate in symposiums, cut ribbons, and join in everything from parades and celebrations to the crowning of queens and the launching of new products. In addition to those time demands, they are expected to manage state government on a day-to-day basis by meeting with agency heads and staff members, meeting frequently with the press and public, and maintaining good legislative relations—not to mention trying to maintain a modicum of personal life. As a result, the Governor's time needs to be viewed as a scarce resource that must be budgeted as carefully as money.

Although scheduling may appear to be a relatively routine job, it is easy to underestimate its importance. Many significant groups will form their impression of the Governor from the way in which his office handles their requests for his time. More significantly, the control over who can easily get to see the Governor and who can't will help determine how the power is distributed within an administration.

All states have some sort of scheduling system for receiving and evaluating requests for the Governor's time and deciding which requests will be accepted. The staff position for scheduling was discussed in chapter 3. A proposed scheduling procedure and samples of basic scheduling forms are included in appendix 13.

Authority to Commit Time

A Governor who seeks to have time available for any purpose—to think, to be with his family, to work on subjects he considers important rather than those considered important by others—must be careful to limit the number of persons who can make binding commitments of his time. When surveyed in 1976, the scheduling personnel in Governors' offices emphasized this point strongly. One commented:

> I think it is an absolute must that only *one person* handles the schedule. I have found in my years of experience that this and only this will avoid embarrassing confusion.

As a practical matter, most Governors do not schedule their own events and meetings because they do not have the records indicating their other commitments for the same date or other information on the competing demands for their time. As a result, many executive assistants and scheduling secretaries strongly urge their Governors never to accept an invitation for a specific date without checking with the scheduling secretary.

Following this advice is quite difficult, particularly when the person making a request is not asking for any specific time but is willing to schedule his activity to conform to the Governor's schedule. When confronted with a question such as "Can I come to see you one of these days and talk about . . . ?" a Governor may find it difficult to say no. Appointment secretaries are frequently confronted with people who say they have the Governor's agreement to schedule something when in fact all they have had is some temporizing response from the Governor. Scheduling secretaries learn quickly not to rely on reports of such conversations as true reflections of their Governors' wishes.

Some indication of how Governors limit the authority to commit their time was provided by a National Governors' Association survey which showed the following patterns:

PERSONS COMMITTING TIME	STATES
Only the Governor	3
Scheduling Secretary and Governor	17
Executive Assistant and Scheduling Secretary	6
Other (various)	7

In those cases where both the Governor and the scheduling secretary have the power to commit the Governor's time, the Governor usually does not make commitments without consulting with the scheduler, both for advice and to protect against the possibility that the time the Governor is trying to schedule has already been promised.

In managing the scheduling activity, it is important to remember that scheduling decisions cannot be neatly divorced from the Governor's political activities. In fact, the schedule often presents opportunities to improve the Governor's standing with local political leaders while accomplishing other objectives on trips out in the state or at meetings in his office.

One of the ways for a Governor and the scheduling secretary to use the schedule productively, particularly on trips, is to review the Governor's many roles in the context of each day's schedule. Those roles, as listed in chapter 1, are: head of the executive branch, legislative leader, head of his political party, national figure, family member and ceremonial chief.

For example, in his role as ceremonial chief, the Governor may be traveling to a smaller city to visit the nation's oldest veteran on his 110th birthday. In scheduling in that same location (and perhaps as part of the same event), consideration should be given to stopping by at the nearby state highway garage or state police post, having a cup of coffee with the mayor or local party leader, calling a major supporter on the phone, making a joint appearance with the local congressman (or letting him announce that his office will be the site of a "meet your Governor" session even if he cannot be there), visiting a local legislator (e.g., stopping by his store or law office), and doing something with the family while on the trip, such as bringing a younger child along.

Dealing with Scheduling Requests

Developing a system for handling scheduling requests is extremely important. The scheduling secretary plays a key role in making sure that requests which must be turned down are handled diplomatically. As an administrative secretary to a Governor in the Midwest put it:

> Appreciate that each request made of your Governor is the most important event the seeker has on his or her mind. They will not understand that there are 50 times that many requests flooding into the Governor's office (and probably won't care). The regret will have to be as gentle and as diplomatic as you can muster. Many will never understand, and you will have to learn to accept this.

To cope with the volume of invitations, most states have established standard procedures for dealing with scheduling. The process involves converting oral requests to written ones, particularly in the case of outside groups desiring to have the Governor speak at an event. One description of this process was obtained in the 1976 survey:

> In scheduling I found that one of the most important things to remember is to never commit the Governor on first contact, even if I know the date is available. Be very tactful and polite and promise to call them after visiting with the Governor and/or the chief of staff. In answering their request, if a letter has not been received by that time, I will always request one. It is very important to have these details in writing.

The handling of written requests varies from state to state. In some states, the scheduling office has authority to turn down requests. In others, a decision not to schedule is made by a scheduling committee or by the Governor and/or executive assistant in conjunction with the scheduling secretary.

Scheduling assistants generally keep both an appointments book and files relating to correspondence regarding particular dates. In some cases these are cross-classified by type of group, subject matter involved and/or location. Such cross-classifications make it easier to ensure that the Governor distributes his time reasonably among areas in the state and different types of groups.

A difficult question in scheduling is how to harmonize the desire of many organizations to schedule their programs months in advance with the Governor's need to reserve some flexibility for future commitments. If too much is scheduled in advance, problems will develop in meeting the schedule later.

Of the scheduling secretaries responding to the 1976 survey, about 80 percent reported that they have a limit on how far in advance they will schedule the Governor. These cutoff dates are somewhat flexible, depending upon the type of event. Typically, however, firm commitments of the Governor's time are not normally made for more than two months in advance, and some states schedule only three to four weeks in advance.

The problem of providing a timely response to a scheduling request for many months in the future while still maintaining flexibility can be handled in several ways. One way is to give tentative acceptances for major events, reserving the option to cancel later with reasonable notice. Another is to reply that the Governor would like to attend but can't commit his time so far in advance, and ask the group to resubmit the invitation later. Still another approach is to persuade the requesting group to schedule someone else to represent the Governor. Frequently the Governor's spouse can be a suitable substitute on a ceremonial occasion or to welcome a group to the state. In other cases, Governors' staff members, agency heads, and budget or planning directors will be acceptable representatives. When there is doubt as to whether a Governor will be able to attend an event, these types of substitutions provide a major advantage to him. When the time for the event arrives, there is no problem if he cannot attend because he was not scheduled to do so. However, if he does decide to attend, the group will be pleased to substitute him on the program for the official who would have represented him.

Meetings with Staff Members and Agency Heads

By their own estimate, Governors spend between 20 and 25 percent of their scheduled time in the management of state government. Most of this time is devoted to meetings in the Governor's office with agency heads, board or commission members, and staff members. A small portion is spent in field visits to state offices, institutions and other state facilities.

Commitments of the Governor's time for such meetings is handled by the same scheduling procedure, but usually on a less formal basis. The scheduling staff will generally set appointments for agency heads on the basis of verbal requests but will often ask if someone else (such as the executive assistant) can handle the matter. Not all agency heads are treated alike in this regard, with priority being given to those who have good rapport with the Governor and to directors of certain critical agencies.

The scheduling staff in many states is responsible for obtaining from the person responsible for the meeting (usually the person requesting it) a brief statement of the purpose of the meeting, those who will attend, and issues to be discussed. This information is quite helpful in briefing the Governor on the upcoming events of the day.

Scheduling Ground Rules

The problem of developing a Governor's schedule can be simplified considerably by the establishment of ground rules for what types of events will be scheduled. One scheduling secretary offered this advice:

> Establish ground rules from the very outset with your Governor, First Lady and staff. For example, if the Governor wants to be free on weekends, if only two evenings are to be scheduled, major events attended every other year, only two major speeches per week, etc.

It is important that the scheduling process take into account the Governor's need to have time for family purposes. In some states, the Governor's spouse sits in on scheduling meetings. Other arrangements, including regularly scheduled family time, may smooth relations among the Governor's family, the scheduling secretary, and the executive assistant on scheduling matters.

From the perspective of the scheduler, it is a matter of determining the work habits and preferences of the Governor and his family. It is also important, as one suggested, to learn whether the Governor is a "day person" or a "night person." Another appointments secretary described why it is vital to know how the Governor uses his time:

> If you don't know, find out as quickly as possible the work habits of your Governor. You will be unable to schedule his time without knowing how he uses it. Is he available and ready to start meetings on time, does he keep within the allotted time, or does he allow meetings to run one-half hour to 45 minutes late? It won't take more than a couple of out-of-sync meetings to throw the whole day off balance. Does he spend an inordinate amount of time on the telephone? You know he has a couple of phone calls to answer and schedule 20 minutes—one hour later he's answered those and placed two of his own, and you are now 40 minutes off schedule and his next appointment sits impatiently in the reception room. His meetings will now have to be compressed because the Governor has out-of-town speaking engagements and must leave the office within a few minutes.

From the Governor's perspective, this aspect of scheduling consists of deciding on personal time preferences and laying down the law to the scheduling staff. A number of former Governors stressed this point heavily. One advised new Governors as follows:

> . . . I think each Governor must make a very firm allocation of time both to himself and to his family. Most Governors do very badly in this respect and as a result do grave injustice to themselves and their families. Proper time in these areas provides the following:
>
>> *Rest.* Most bad decisions are made by Governors who are exhausted. It is almost universal that exhausted people do not respond well to pressure.

Time to oneself. I am a firm believer that this is necessary for contemplation and maintaining perspective both in terms of your responsibilities and yourself. It is very easy to lose your focus as Governor.

Family. Most Governors cheat their families and thereby themselves. . . .

Reflecting upon the demands on their time, Governors have suggested that scheduling ground rules need to be established in these categories:

Office time. It is easy to equate a blank on the Governor's schedule with the notion that he is not doing anything during that period. This is probably not the case; the Governor must have time for office work. A number of Governors insist on reserving a certain portion of the day, frequently a part of each morning, for office time. In addition to time for his own work, some Governors schedule office time for "drop in" visits by staff members and agency heads who have need for short conversations on pressing matters.

Vacations. The Governor's general preferences need to be known well in advance. If vacation time is not allowed for, the Governor will tend to find that he can take a vacation only by eliminating some events that have already been accepted.

Weekends. Many politically important events occur on weekends. It is important to decide early whether certain weekends will be blocked entirely for the Governor's personal use or whether certain days will be blocked (e.g., Sundays), but not others. Some Governors are willing to schedule considerable weekend time but try to take part of a day off during the week.

Evenings. Some Governors limit the number of evenings each week they will allow themselves to be scheduled. In other cases, such as when the Governor has young children, the early evening hours may be reserved for family use but the later evening hours may be available for scheduling.

Travel. The Governor's preferences on travel should be made clear because they will affect, for example, whether an evening meeting can be followed by an overnight stay and a morning meeting in the same location.

Frequency of events. Some Governors set ground rules on the number of major speeches, dinner events and similar commitments they will accept within a week.

Scheduling also becomes easier when the Governor and his scheduling staff agree on the types of events and visits which should routinely be scheduled, those which should routinely be declined, and those on which judgments need to be made on a case-by-case basis. The 1976 National Governors' Association survey included a long list of typical requests for a Governor's time. The responses are shown in appendix 13.

Active and Passive Scheduling

Because there is a tremendous influx of unsolicited invitations for the Governor, and because declining any invitation always has some negative consequences, there may be no pressure to generate new invitations. However, a case can be made that the schedule should be set by determining what the Governor wants to do to support and strengthen his political base, his objectives and his programs.

To determine the extent to which the scheduling staff seeks out invitations, the 1976 NGA survey of schedulers included the question: "Do you or others in the office seek out scheduled events for the Governor rather than just reacting to requests or events?" About two-thirds of the schedulers indicated that they react, while one-third indicated that they seek out events. Those who seek out events indicated a variety of means for doing so. When the Governor is scheduled to travel to a specific area of the state, the scheduling staff often will make arrangements for other appearances in that area. Examples given included meetings with state party leaders and local officials and making major announcements on program initiatives.

Breaking Scheduled Appointments

No matter how efficient the scheduling operation may be, there will be some instances in which the Governor will be unable to attend a scheduled event or meeting. Dealing with pain and disappointment in such circumstances will be considerably easier if the scheduling secretary has been honest initially. In doubtful cases, it may be better to guarantee some other state official (whose name would appear in the advance publicity) and then substitute the Governor, if possible.

The important rule in breaking scheduled commitments is to find a way to give the group in question as much of what they needed from the Governor as the circumstances will permit. A group that has scheduled the Governor to provide a brief welcoming comment to their convention doesn't need much; someone should be sent to fill the spot on the program with an official welcome to the state. A group planning to meet with the Governor over an issue can obviously be satisfied if they get the action they wanted the Governor to take. If the purpose of the Governor's visit was to indicate his support of some policy or person, a telegram from him will be helpful. Nothing will completely substitute for the Governor's actual presence, but these alternatives will usually keep his inability to appear from causing serious problems.

CHAPTER NINE

Dealing with the Mail and Public Contacts

An unanswered letter or a rude telephone response will probably never be forgiven. On the other hand, positive impressions can be made and even a sense of personal involvement can be created by the Governor by an effective office system which stresses, on the part of the entire staff, timely and sensitive answers to responsible inquiries.

— *a former Governor*

SUMMARY

Maintaining effective contact with the public is extremely important for a new Governor. The manner in which mail, telephone calls and other contacts with the public are handled will have a great deal to do with whether the Governor and his administration are perceived by the citizens in a positive or negative light.

It is possible for the Governor to reach personally up to a million people each year through the mail and other direct contacts. In addition to the political advantages, intensive contacts with the public can provide valuable information to Governors for decision making.

If it is not carefully handled, mail from the public can mount up and cause difficult problems throughout the Governor's term. To deal with the mail, the Governor should ensure that his office has established an effective system for routing different types of mail and answering it promptly. Mail can be divided into the following categories:

- *Personal mail of the Governor,* including both family correspondence and business mail of a personal and confidential nature, to be acted upon directly by the Governor or referred to a key staff member for preparation of a response;

- *Important business mail* from state and federal officials, associations, prominent citizens and others whose correspondence commands the attention of the Governor or a key aide;

- *Unorganized issue mail* from citizens who write independently to tell the Governor how they think he should handle certain issues or situations;

- *Organized issue mail,* the product of mail campaigns generated on a given issue by editorials or interest groups, which—like much of the unorganized issue mail—usually receives a standard form response approved by the Governor;

- *Case mail* from citizens who feel that the Governor can solve their problem, which usually requires substantial time and effort by a member of the Governor's staff or the state agency involved;

- *Invitations and other scheduling mail;* and

- *Miscellaneous mail.*

For mail that cannot be answered immediately because it requires time-consuming staff work or a policy decision, a referral system must be developed. The system should include (1) an initial acknowledgement with the promise of a swift reply, or a telephone response, which sometimes eliminates the need for a letter; and (2) a tracking system and performance standards for response time.

Whether the correspondence can be answered quickly or requires referral and staff work, whether it receives a form response or a carefully drafted letter of reply, any mail-handling system in the Governor's office should include:

- Strict review procedures for quality control;

- Clear guidelines as to which response letters the Governor should personally review and sign; and

- Careful control over the use of the Governor's signature when it is applied by an authorized staff member or signature machine, rather than the Governor personally.

Mail during the transition can be a special problem. While post-campaign mail is dealt with, mail in the Governor's office will tend to pile up. A new Governor should keep a close watch on the effectiveness of his new mail system during transition.

While many of the guidelines for handling mail can also be applied to telephone calls from the public, there are significant differences. A citizen who wouldn't expect a written reply to his letter for 10 days may be incensed if his call isn't returned the same day. Whereas a letter of response signed by the Governor may actually have been drafted by a staff member with the Governor's approval, a caller talks directly with the person who handles his problem; and considerable tact is required to convince many callers that a staff member is in a better position to help them than the Governor.

From the moment he takes office, a Governor is likely to be beseiged to lend the prestige of his name and office to many public and private causes through proclamations and endorsements. Early development of systematic guidelines for deciding when to approve and when to decline such requests will avoid difficult problems later.

Dealing with the Mail and Public Contacts

A Governor can reap sizeable rewards from good handling of citizen contacts in the form of improved communications and enhanced image with the electorate, but poor attention to citizen contacts can cost him dearly. All rhetoric about new management systems and responsive government will fall unconvincingly on the ears of a voter who wrote to the Governor last year about the poor condition of a local road and still has not received an answer.

A common debate in the Governor's office—as in a political campaign—concerns the balanced allocation of the Governor's time and effort among personal contacts with citizens, time with the press, and other activities. A strong argument can be made for maintaining considerable personal contact with the public. It can provide a sounding board and a source of support for the Governor's programs, and the political impact of public contact can be substantial.

For example, in a state of four million people, if the Governor successfully handles 200 pieces of mail a day and meets 20 individuals outside of normal state government contacts, he will have made over 300,000 contacts in a four-year term. Even assuming that 100,000 of these are duplicates, the impact is significant, particularly when it is recognized that a child's letter from the Governor will probably affect his parents, grandparents and neighbors. If 200,000 unduplicated contacts affect five people each, the Governor would, in four years, have reached personally a million people. In many cases, these would be individuals for whom personal contact may be more real than party loyalties or responses to campaign issues.

Not all Governors stress citizen contacts equally. Some place strong emphasis on events such as county and state fairs, city street fairs, picnics, athletic contests, and other activities where they can meet many people on a person-to-person basis. Others accord extremely high priority to the quality and speed of their responses to mail from constituents.

In addition to the political advantages, contacts with the public can provide valuable information to Governors for their decision making on state issues. Many people (including some Governors) believe that governments and those who lead them are too isolated from the people they serve. Many also believe that concerns of the average citizen often get lost in the rarified atmosphere of the state capitols.

One Governor expressed the need "to relax, think, and to talk to people who do not claim to be important. What little wisdom is left in the country is more apt to be found at the crossroads (not on a freeway, of course) or in the countryside than at the chamber of commerce or country club."

As the Governor's comment at the beginning of this chapter indicates, there is considerable risk in handling public contacts. Whatever is sent out to citizens on the Governor's letterhead will convey an image—good or bad—of the administration. And the warm image of the first family on a television program will disappear quickly for a father with children in tow who, on a visit to the state capitol, decides to drop in on the Governor's office only to be met by a haughty receptionist who says, by manner if not in words, that the Governor could not care less about him.

HANDLING THE MAIL

Early in the transition, procedures for dealing with the mail need to be established for the Governor's office. The new Governor need not participate directly in the design of routing forms and the filing system, but should be involved in setting the performance standards for the system and in defining what types of mail he wants to see personally. Those subjects are covered in this section. A suggested mail-handling system and sample forms for mail control can be found in appendix 14.

Types of Mail and Routing

Personal mail of the Governor (e.g., bills, family correspondence) and mail addressed "personal" to the Governor or marked "confidential" is usually routed unopened to the Governor or his personal secretary. When opened, some of this mail is found to fall into categories listed below and is put in the proper routing pattern. The remaining personal mail is acted upon by the Governor either by direct answer or by routing to a staff member for preparation of a response.

Important business mail is defined largely by the type of sender (e.g., other Governors, major state associations, prominent citizens, legislators, members of the Governor's administration). There does not appear to be any standard routing pattern among the states for this mail. In some states, it goes to the Governor directly after opening, and he decides how to route it or whether to answer it himself. In other states, it goes either to the Governor's executive assistant or personal secretary, who sends some of it to the Governor and assigns the remainder to various staff members before the Governor sees it. In some of the states that have staff members assigned to various functional areas (e.g., education), this mail is routed to them, and they decide what should be done with it.

Issue mail typically comes in two forms: (1) unorganized issue mail, in which citizens express their views on how a Governor ought to handle some major issue, and (2) organized mail campaigns, in which citizens inspired by editorials or interest groups write letters by the hundreds demanding support for a project or program.

In some of the smaller states, both unorganized and organized issue mail is routed to the Governor and handled like important business mail. In other states, the issue mail all goes into the correspondence or constituent services operation without being seen by the Governor. The most common practice appears to be to handle the organized issue mail through the use of a standard form letter which the Governor approves. The Governor then does not necessarily see each of the responses, but receives tabulations of the frequency of the mail taking particular positions on issues. In such a system, the organized issue mail would flow to the Governor with a proposed response already prepared by the staff. Some offices retain files on individual citizens by their areas of interest as indicated by past correspondence with the Governor's office.

Modern word processing and computer technology have permitted the development of sophisticated mail systems in some Governors' offices, easing the burden of responding to numerous pieces of issue mail. Memory typewriters allow individually addressed responses to be typed at high speed, replacing the use of form letters. The new Governor will not, during transition or the first 100 days, have time to become familiar personally with all of these systems, but he will want to be assured that members of his staff have considered their possibilities for both improving the quality of the office product and holding down staff costs.

Case mail involves citizens who are writing about a particular problem they are having with state (and sometimes local or federal) government. Typical writers include persons who (1) want particular roads fixed or traffic signals installed, (2) are having difficulties with welfare payments, (3) are confined in the state's correctional or mental health facilities, or (4) are concerned with applications for licenses or similar matters.

Case mail, by its nature, involves dealing with the state agency that has responsibility for the subject matter. In most states, referral to the department is automatic, and individualized follow-ups, such as a phone call to the person or a draft reply to be sent over the Governor's signature, are developed by the department. In certain states, someone in the Governor's office, or the ombudsman's office in the states that have one, assumes responsibility and works with the individual and the department rather than simply turning the case over to the department for appropriate action.

A special type of case mail comes from inmates of state correctional or mental institutions who write to complain about mistreatment, to seek pardons or paroles, or to protest their innocence. Such mail is often referred to the staff member who handles legal matters for the Governor, as well as to the pertinent probation and parole agency (if not the Governor). This permits some analysis of the volume and severity of potential problems at correctional and mental institutions and provides a dual check on the potential validity of the complaint.

Finally, some mail is received from mentally deranged persons who make threats, demand special privileges, purport to carry messages from God, or convey other types of troubled messages. These letters should be referred to the security staff, state police or local law enforcement agencies.

Scheduling mail seeks an appointment with the Governor, asks him to appear at an event, or otherwise involves commitments of his time. This mail is routed along with phone calls and visits on the same subject to the scheduling person.

Miscellaneous mail includes some mail that does not need to be answered (e.g., publications), as well as requests for such things as the Governor's picture and requests from school children for a description of what the Governor does or how he likes his job. In states that have one, the mail office handles these requests. In the other states, this duty falls to someone assigned other duties, such as the Governor's secretary or the press office.

Acknowledgements

Many types of incoming correspondence cannot be answered immediately because they involve such actions as consulting case records, developing a policy, or the return of an individual who is on vacation. Under these circumstances, some sort of acknowledgement is customarily sent. Sometimes, the acknowledgements advise the writer that his mail has been referred to a given department or to an individual in that department who will reply directly to him. In other cases, the acknowledgement letter will indicate that the Governor has asked a certain official to look into the situation discussed in the letter and report back to the Governor. In the latter case, the final substantive response would be prepared by the department for the Governor's signature. The choice depends in large part on how strongly the Governor feels about whether his signature must appear on responses to letters originally sent to him.

The decision on whether to use acknowledgements in all cases is a difficult one. The advantage of the acknowledgement is that it allows the Governor's office to respond quickly on even the most difficult subjects. The disadvantages are that acknowledgements double the number of letters that must be sent from the Governor's office and reduce the pressure on staff members to produce a substantive response on a timely basis.

A review of state practices indicates that no single pattern prevails in the use of acknowledgements. The states that acknowledge all correspondence are evenly split between those which have the final substantive reply prepared for the Governor's signature and those which have some other official sign the final reply. Among states which do not acknowledge, there is also roughly an equal split between those which have the final reply signed by the Governor and those which do not. Many states report that they use all these approaches, depending on the subject matter of the correspondence.

Response Times

Ideally, mail addressed to the Governor would be answered the same day it is received. Most Governors' offices cannot achieve anything close to that performance because much of their mail can be answered only after information is obtained from one or more state departments. However, one test that a new Governor can use for his mail system is whether it can do same-day or next-day responses to mail where the Governor's position has already been set and a letter stating that position has been previously approved.

A survey of the states in 1976 showed that response times were at least a week for most substantive types of incoming mail, but not normally more than 10 days. The longest average time reported was for mail concerning mental health patients and conditions in mental hospitals. Several states reported that responses to this type of mail consume up to 30 days.

Review Procedures

Under the most common procedures for dealing with the mail, the Governor, at some stage, personally reviews letters that will be sent to citizens over his signature. Letters that reflect new policies or important new statements about the reasons for policies would be reviewed personally and signed by the Governor. Sometimes they are reviewed in draft by the Governor but not reviewed again after final typing.

In situations which call for standard responses, the Governor would normally approve the standard response initially, but would not necessarily review such outgoing mail even though it would bear his signature. Examples of standard responses are congratulatory messages, routine responses to requests for the Governor's picture, and organized issue mail.

Where the Governor does not personally review individual responses in final form, two quality-control checks are normally needed. The first is simply a review of the letter received and the typed response to determine whether the quality of typing is acceptable, whether the proper standard response was used, etc. Such reviews are, in various states, performed by the head of the correspondence section, a special assistant, the Governor's secretary or another staff member. The second review—more difficult and nearly impossible to do perfectly—calls for screening outgoing correspondence to make sure that first names are used for persons whom the Governor knows personally. Usually, the Governor's personal secretary is in the best position to do such screening. Despite attempts to avoid the problem, a new Governor will often find that when he invited his closest and oldest friend to serve on an advisory committee, the letter went out over his signature with the salutation "Dear Mr. Smith" rather than "Dear John."

Guarding the Governor's Signature

The combination of answering the mail and the ceremonial and governmental aspects of a Governor's job will require his signature on a large number of documents. He will be asked to send autographed pictures to children, to contributors, to other state officials and to his staff. He may want his signature to appear on responses to all the mail that is addressed to him. By law, a Governor's signature is required on bills and veto messages, and on the commissions of countless state officials. His signature is also needed to approve certain forms of federal grants and to apply for others, and on extradition and pardon documents. Depending on state regulations, it may also be required on approvals for release of funds, out-of-state travel by state employees, certification of certain promotions, and approval of regulations of various departments. The Governor also signs countless copies of documents through which the state issues bonds and notes. Many Governors become adept at signing documents while conducting other office business without interruption.

In a small state, it is possible that a Governor could actually sign all of these documents. But in a large state, to sign everything would become a full-time job in itself.

Three systems exist to deal with this problem. The first is to delegate some of the document-signing responsibility to others, where permitted by state law. This is advisable when a Governor is not personally reviewing the materials involved (e.g., the payroll vouchers from his own office) and when he can delegate responsibility to someone he trusts. As a safeguard, it is wise to specify in writing to whom the authority is delegated and exactly the circumstances under which that person is authorized to affix the Governor's signature. Formal delegation of this responsibility is desirable only in circumstances where the legal basis for delegation is clear and where no public relations problems are created by having someone else affix the Governor's signature along with identifying initials.

The second approach is to allow one or more persons (usually the secretary) to create the Governor's signature manually. This is most frequently done on documents that have the Governor's personal touch—such as a letter he dictates but does not read, or a series of personal thank-you notes.

The third approach is a signature machine which can reproduce a Governor's signature in a way that is virtually indistinguishable from his personal handwriting. These machines can keep the Governor from becoming a clerk, but are also dangerous.

In the case of legal documents, a signature by a machine used by someone other than the Governor would probably not stand up if challenged. If a signature machine is used, considerable caution must be exercised in limiting access to it and in establishing conditions under which it may be used. Access may be limited to the Governor's secretary and his legal advisor or the aide in charge of mail and only for signing letters which the Governor has approved previously. Some Governors incorporate a code (putting a period after the middle initial for actual signatures and none for machine signatures, or forming one letter differently from their normal handwriting) so there is a ready answer to those who claim that the Governor approved something and that they have his signature to prove it. Another safeguard is tight control over access to the Governor's stationery so that persons not authorized to use the signature machine must break two barriers to create a letter from the Governor.

The Mail Problem during Transition

Everyone's good intentions notwithstanding, the mail will tend to pile up unanswered during transition and in the first few months after inauguration. The campaign staff will be busy handling congratulatory mail and sending thank-yous to contributors and campaign workers, and it will be hard to work on transition mail.

During this period, mail will begin to arrive which calls for substantive replies that no one is in a position to write easily. Suggestions about changes in state policy are difficult to handle when cabinet officers have not yet been appointed to deal with such issues. Letters about appointments to lower-level positions cannot be answered substantively until the Governor-elect has personnel-selection machinery in operation. Positions on the death penalty, abortion, federal spending, inflation and racism, as well as the third grader's question about "what Governors do," are all things that the Governor will want to develop responses to in time.

There is probably no solution to this temporary problem other than keeping it as temporary as possible. The Governor can see how bad it is if his secretary has set up a mail-control system, or simply takes a sample of a day's mail and checks two weeks later to see where it all is.

PHONE CONTACT PROCEDURE

With few exceptions, procedures for handling phone calls from the public in Governors' offices are basically the same as those used for the mail, in terms of who takes action and when referrals are used. The phone procedures may be much quicker, however, particularly in cases where detailed investigation of a complaint is not required. While tact is essential in framing written responses, a considerate and sensitive staff attitude is even more important when dealing directly with the citizen on the telephone.

Some states have guidelines requiring that phone calls to the Governor's office be returned during the day in which they are received. Although some people recommend that memos to the file be written on phone calls and personal visits to the Governors' office, most states do not follow this procedure consistently.

Frequently, the person making a phone call to the Governor has not thought through the details of his problem, and thus it may be more difficult to understand. While the correspondent is not likely to know or care what staff work went into the response from the Governor to his letter, dealing with a constituent phone call will usually involve asking the caller to talk to someone other than the Governor. Personnel in Governors' offices are concerned about this problem because, although doing the best job possible for the constituent frequently means having someone other than the Governor handle the call, the person calling may believe that he is entitled to the personal attention of the Governor and that the Governor will be in a better position to handle his problem.

CONSERVING TIME

A variety of techniques for conserving the Governor's time are discussed throughout this volume. In the area of public contacts, these include the use of tact in steering visitors or callers away from using the Governor's time when feasible alternatives are available. For example, rather than indicating that the Governor is totally unavailable, a good receptionist can indicate that the Governor is currently tied up and has several meetings scheduled, but might well be available if the visitor wants to take a chance on waiting. Then she can find out the purpose of the caller's visit and try to solve that problem while he is waiting.

Another effective suggestion for saving time stemmed from the 1976 survey of Governors' offices. One person handling public contacts suggested making telephone responses to certain types of correspondence. Generally, correspondence control systems are poorly equipped to handle longer, carefully written letters expressing views on a number of subjects. With such letters, various pieces may be farmed out to staff assistants and departments, and considerable time may be devoted to turning the resulting pieces into a coherent response. In such a situation, an alternative which the constituent may prefer is a call from someone on the Governor's staff to discuss the various problems cited in the letter. This approach also tends to avoid a long chain of correspondence, bouncing back and forth on the same subject, with the citizen reacting each time to a new issue or question suggested by the last letter and clogging the office mail system.

PROCLAMATIONS AND ENDORSEMENTS

Many citizens will wish to use the prestige and publicity associated with the Governor's office to enhance causes in which they are interested. The most common approach is to ask the Governor to issue a proclamation for any one of a variety of events or celebrations. These include charity drives; special days honoring individuals; special days, weeks or months honoring particular products, services or industries; and commemorations of new business openings. Recommending which of these to undertake and writing the text of the proclamations are frequently press office assignments. The key point on proclamations is to make sure that the Governor has some systematic way of deciding what to issue and what to avoid. Such standards ensure that a Governor will have fewer constituents angry with him personally because their proclamations were not issued.

A parallel problem arises with the use of the Governor's name on letterheads of charitable groups. This is clearly appropriate where the Governor solicits support from state employees, such as when he serves as the honorary chairman of a United Fund drive in the state capitol. The situation is more difficult when groups want to use the Governor's name to solicit outsiders. One approach is for the Governor to allow the use of his name in fund raising only for groups to which he belonged before taking office.

The same guidelines will be useful when the Governor is asked to lend his name to causes in other ways.

CHAPTER TEN

Dealing with the Press and Media

    The press, as I viewed it, was one of my strongest allies in informing the people about important issues. The press aided me greatly in getting my views accepted by the people and others in government.

— a former Governor

SUMMARY

The press can be an ally or an adversary, and probably will seem to be both. In reality, it will be both; and an understanding of the distinction is essential to achieving a good working relationship between the Governor and the newspapers, radio and television stations in the state.

Any Governor will want to earn favorable press coverage to build public support for his administration and his programs. The press, on the other hand, will see its proper role as informing the public of the facts, whether they are favorable or unfavorable to the Governor. When this happens to result in the kind of press coverage that benefits the Governor and his administration, the press will be his ally. Otherwise, it can be his adversary.

Because of this potential adversary relationship, it is easy for Governors and others in public office to become irritated with the press. Yet, a candid and open relationship with the press is the only way to achieve success in clearly portraying the administration to the public. Without that relationship, an administration that is successful in every other way will encounter serious problems.

It is important, therefore, for a new Governor and his key advisors to develop policies for dealing with the press in their new role. New Governors, of course, are already seasoned veterans in dealing with print media, radio and television in a campaign context. As a result, there is a tendency to underestimate the difficulty of communicating not only the Governor's ideas, but also the actions of the entire state government, once the new administration assumes office—and the responsibility that goes with it.

Governors who have been particularly successful with the media have been extremely accessible to the working press. Over half of the former Governors surveyed by the National Governors' Association in 1976 scheduled regular news conferences, usually weekly. Some held news conference more often during the legislative session. Others met with the press only when there was an important announcement to make or when an issue arose that demanded immediate response. A new Governor's press conferences—and how often he holds them—will be crucial in establishing his policies and his style in the minds of both the press and the public.

The press secretary should have daily access to the Governor and, perhaps equally important, should be familiar with the decision-making processes in the administration. In addition, he has the responsibility of representing the views of the press and the public to the Governor on critical decisions. Whether the press secretary will be a key policy advisor as well depends largely on his relationship with the Governor. In most states, the press secretary sometimes acts as spokesman for the administration; the extent to which he does so is likely to be determined by how deeply he is involved in policy matters and the Governor's own operating style.

A number of techniques can extend the Governor's reach beyond the statehouse press corps. Flying to major cities in the state to reach several newspaper and television markets in a single day and holding regular meetings with the editorial boards of the state's leading newspapers are two such techniques that are used by many Governors to broaden the scope of their press coverage. Some Governors also supply radio tapes and television film on newsworthy actions to outlying stations.

While the staff may resist ceremonial events, local press coverage of these occasions can be of substantial help in the new Governor's quest to stay in touch with the press and the electorate. Many Governors have found that only in their second or third terms could they afford to cut down on such appearances.

Dealing with the Press and Media

The right kind of media coverage can help convince the electorate that a Governor is doing a good job, that his programs should be supported, and that he should be reelected. It also can improve a Governor's ability to deal with the legislature and with personnel within state government, and thus improve his ability to govern. On the other hand, "bad press" can undermine a Governor's ability to lead and cost the opportunity for reelection.

Governors, like most leaders in both public life and private enterprise, wish to earn favorable press coverage. The problem, assuming such coverage has been earned, is how it can be achieved. By the time the election is over, the Governor-elect is usually well experienced in dealing with the press in a campaign context, but the scope and magnitude of the problems for which he is expected to have answers suddenly escalates. The mantle of responsibility for what goes on in state government quickly descends on him.

It is critical to the success of the new administration that the Governor-elect and his key advisors quickly develop policies for dealing with the press and media in this new context. As one step, virtually all Governors appoint a press secretary to handle their press and media relations. The role of the press secretary, his relationship to the Governor, and the function of the press office were discussed in detail in chapter 3, Organizing the New Governor's Office.

AN APPROACH TO MEDIA RELATIONS

There are definite limits to what a Governor and a press secretary can expect to achieve in press relations. They cannot create the image of an administration that is quick to identify and solve problems if the problems persist. The Governor cannot expect to convince the press to write about the openness of an administration that is not open, the responsiveness of an administration that does not respond, or the management skills of a Governor who does not manage well.

Nor can a press secretary portray the Governor and his administration as having particular objectives and goals if the Governor himself is not clear about what he wants to achieve. If a Governor wants to be remembered at the end of his term for having accomplished certain things, then those things must be identified early in the term so they can in fact be accomplished and so the Governor can be associated with their accomplishment. As one former Governor advised new Governors: "Develop a sound public information program to let the people know . . . two or three things you want to accomplish."

Attitude Toward the Press

It is easy for a Governor to become frustrated with the press. When bad news seems to sell more papers than good news; when reporters seem to believe that venal motives lurk behind every decision; when the most innocent of friendships is questioned as a conflict of interest; when reporters fail to detect the skill and wisdom that went into a policy, or seem incapable of understanding complex governmental issues; when allegations are reported on page one and factual denials on page 35; and when adverse editorial opinions seem to find their way into news stories—individual Governors have reacted with everything from fury to disappointment.

Notwithstanding the possible legitimacy of some complaints by public officials about the press, the uniform advice of press secretaries and former Governors surveyed by the National Governors' Association in 1976 was that an open and candid relationship with the press was essential to any successful state administration.

For example, one former Governor commented at length on his press relations which, in retrospect, he found to be among his most effective policies as Governor:

> My press relations were extraordinarily good. I have been asked by many how I managed to have such a "friendly" press. My short answer has been that we just did a good job, sticking loyally to the public interest, and this was what the press had every right to expect of me.
>
> But we did do some things the press liked. I was a strong advocate of open government. . . . The expression "government in the sunshine" was conceived by me and launched in our administration. We established the fixed routine of holding a wide-open press conference every Friday morning. This was the time that best suited the press. Everything said was transcribed (warts and all) and copies were delivered that afternoon. This minimized the note-taking and made for a little more relaxation. The reporter could pick out his "hard news" from his notes for his first story, then pick over other things for follow-up stories. A copy of each transcribed report was mailed to our list of all the state's editors and often served as material for editorial comment as well as just keeping the editorial departments current with what was going on.
>
> Not always, but often after the conclusion of one of these press conferences, I would ask the reporters to stick around for a "bull session" with me. In some of these, I launched a few trial balloons and benefited from answers I got from questions to them about both serious and nonserious matters.

The press, as I viewed it, was one of my strongest allies in informing the people about important issues. The press aided me greatly in getting my views accepted by the people and others in government.

I think any Governor who is fearful of the press is making a very serious mistake. If a Governor feels that the press is doing him harm, not good, his first impulse should be to check carefully and objectively what is printed. If he still feels that a wrong has been done to him, he should seek clarification or correction. He has much more to lose than to gain by seeking to hide, or by withdrawing into a shell. The biggest loss may be to limit seriously the Governor's capacity to pursue good government objectives.

Another former Governor commented:

The Governor . . . should . . . make it a primary and continuing task for himself and his staff to build and maintain a spirit and modus operandi which stresses cooperation with the press and the meeting of its legitimate continual needs for information and responses to inquiries. If the press senses a true spirit of cooperation and forthrightness on the part of the Governor and his office, then the Governor and his administration are far more likely to get a fair shake from the press when they need the press as a forum to convey to the public proposals, problems and accomplishments.

A Governor who is overly apprehensive or arrogant about what he sees as a hostile press and who largely ignores the press's legitimate news gathering needs until the Governor's hour of need does so at his own peril.

News media can sometimes be outrageously abusive, untruthful and arrogant, but the ignoring of the press's legitimate needs can only serve to aggravate those unfortunate instances and thereby encourage gross distortion of the proper perspective of the Governor and his administration.

Press Access to the Governor

As time permits, Governors generally follow the practice of granting interviews to virtually every reporter who insists on one. In some states, particularly the larger ones, the press secretary attempts to conserve the Governor's time by channeling as many interviews as possible into a group format, such as a press conference, or by arranging for the reporter to talk first with a staff member who can provide most or all of the information that is needed. However, there are times when a reporter will want to talk to the Governor personally and will not want to share the answers to his questions with other reporters at a news conference. On such occasions—for example, when an out-of-town reporter visits the capitol or when a reporter already has dug up considerable information for an exclusive story—it is usually advisable for the Governor to grant an individual interview.

Practices on news conferences vary considerably among the states. Half the Governors, according to the 1976 survey, have regularly scheduled news conferences, although in some states the regular schedule is frequently altered. Of those states reporting regular news conferences, the preponderance have them weekly. Twice monthly, twice weekly and daily press conferences are somewhat less popular. In some states, the news conference schedule changes when the legislature is in session. Of the press secretaries reporting no regularly scheduled news conferences, most said the Governor averaged at least two a month.

The arguments for frequent news conferences, as suggested by one press secretary, are that having them "(1) shows that the Governor is accessible, (2) allows him to keep what he feels to be the important issues in front of the people, and (3) prevents any one issue from being blown out of proportion since two or three days later there will be another news conference and other issues to discuss."

On the other hand, the arguments against frequent news conferences are that (1) there is no guarantee that there will be any topics worth discussing, (2) they take considerable time, and (3) it may be easier to highlight a particular issue when a news conference is called primarily to make a statement on that issue.

The survey of former Governors indicated that their opinions are also divided on the question of holding regularly scheduled news conferences. Forty-five percent of the former Governors are against regularly scheduled press conferences; 55 percent are for them. The frequency and format of press conferences depends a great deal on the size of the state, the size and aggressiveness of the state capitol press corps, and the Governor's personal style and rapport with the press.

From election day forward, the press will be looking for clues to the new Governor's goals and programs and his stand on various issues with more intensity than during the campaign. Consequently, he must prepare for press conferences, especially those early in his tenure, which are so critical to his image as Governor. In a press conference setting, considerable thought should go into exactly what the Governor wants to emphasize. The subject can then preferably be introduced in an opening statement, or on occasion members of the media can simply be alerted to the matters about which he will welcome questions.

Reaching Local Media

The Governor's access to local media markets will normally be through the statehouse press corps. Smaller daily papers and stations will be reached through wire services and syndicates, while most major city media will have their own representation in the state capitol. This arrangement is fine for most purposes, but does not capture all of the possibilities for exposure in local media markets outside the capital city.

What is generally missing in obtaining local coverage is some element that can be localized. For example, for evening news many stations would prefer to use their own reporters who are familiar to local viewers than to use material from a state capitol reporter. There are a number of ways to handle this situation without having the Governor out of the capitol. For radio, some states have a system by which they can feed taped material (including quotes from the Governor) to stations via telephone. Videotape and film can also be provided to TV stations that do not maintain cameramen in the state capitol. In addition, it is technically possible to provide audio and video of the Governor from the state capitol in dialogue with a reporter from an outlying city.

In some situations, Governors prefer to travel by air to reach the media markets of all major cities in their state. Using this approach, the Governor holds news conferences (generally at airports) throughout the state—all in one day. This can improve coverage considerably. The mere fact that the Governor views the subject as important enough to justify flying around the state to talk about it will heighten interest. Live interviews can be used in each media market, featuring questions of local interest as well as whatever the Governor may have come to discuss.

In many states, the development of good working relationships with weekly newspapers provides substantial exposure in smaller communities. Weekly papers are generally very responsive to press releases or to a "Governor's Column," in which the Governor reports on what he is trying to accomplish for the state. Other techniques for increasing exposure include:

- Picking slow news days for press releases and television appearances. An announcement of a small but interesting new program can make page one of metropolitan newspapers and get two minutes of prime-time TV news on a day when nothing is happening elsewhere. If, however, the Governor picks a day when a new Middle East conflict breaks out, a tornado strikes the state, or there is some other dramatic happening, the news may be buried on page 10 of the second section of any major newspaper.

- Going to the scene of crises such as floods, hurricanes or prison riots.

- Making sure that announcements of departmental programs and activities are released by the Governor rather than by the department head.

- Visiting frequently those cities that have local television but do not have television coverage at the state capitol. Such stations are usually happy to get the Governor on film.

- Utilizing the many ceremonial occasions which involve exposure, such as crowning queens, making awards and kicking off charity drives.

- Appearing in promotional tourism and trade advertisements.

- Working actively on national policy issues through the National Governors' Association. A number of Governors have found leadership of committees or subcommittees of NGA on matters of importance to the people of their states to be very beneficial in gaining coverage of those issues and their roles in dealing with them.

THE PRESS SECRETARY: ADVOCATE AND ADVISOR

In some administrations, the press secretary is a senior advisor to the Governor in his own right, and he is included in major meetings because his overall perspective is sought to aid in making the decision. In other states, the press secretary's advice is sought primarily on questions of press relations and how the press might treat particular policies or decisions.

As noted in chapter 3, one decision that the Governor, other top staff members and the press secretary must make is the extent to which the press secretary should be involved in substantive meetings on such subjects as the budget and legislative program. In the 1976 survey of press secretaries, opinions differed on the extent to which their role included participating in all major meetings. Some felt it was their role to report, not formulate, policy; others felt that they needed to be included in the decision-making process in order to reflect administration policies accurately and answer press questions about them.

Access to the Governor

There was one subject, however, about which the press secretaries surveyed indicated overwhelming agreement—their need for constant and quick access to the Governor. The comments of two were typical:

> It is important that a press secretary spend as much time as possible with the Governor himself in order to have a good grasp of the Governor's thinking at any given moment. This is especially important on both in- and out-of-state trips where the Governor could be in contact with members of the media.

> The most critical requirement for a press secretary to be able to function is that he report directly to the Governor and have total and free access to everything the Governor is involved in, whether governmental or political.

Along with the question of access, the Governor will need to make a decision early on the extent to which he will have the press secretary serve as a spokesman for the administration. In some states, where the press secretary is close to the decision-making process, he frequently speaks for the administration, issuing statements in his own name. In other administrations, the Governor personally, the executive assistant and the department heads make the public statements, with the press secretary confined largely to answering press questions and arranging for statements from others. The more common approach is somewhere between these two extremes, with the press secretary acting as spokesman on occasion, usually when it is impractical or inadvisable for some other official to do so.

Trying to Serve Two Masters

The press secretary's role, unlike that of any other member of the Governor's staff except the legislative assistant, involves the built-in conflict of trying to serve two constituencies. In the interest of good coverage and the public's right to information, the Governor wants the press secretary to serve the needs of the press. But the Governor also wants to avoid unfavorable press coverage insofar as possible and, on occasion, may not want to release information that the press would like to have. The press secretary must walk a tightwire deftly in order to serve his Governor and maintain the respect and confidence of the press at the same time. In providing advice to new Governors and their press secretaries, several press secretaries have commented on this point:

> The essential problem of news secretaries is that they are the victims of an inherent conflict between their two constituencies. The Governor would like to see the press secretary's role be essentially a public relations function, to publicize successfully the achievements of the administration. The working press, on the other hand, resent this function greatly. They see the press secretary as a source of news and as a spokesman for an administration which sometimes may fail, be embarrassed or make mistakes.
>
> The best advice I would offer is that the press secretary be an effective advocate of his two constituencies . . . to represent the media's attitude before the Governor and to argue the Governor's point of view effectively to the news media.

> The main characteristic of the person dealing with media for and with a Governor . . . is a combination of the ability to understand and live with the normal tension between the responsibility of the Governor's office and the responsibility of the media. If you don't understand what that means, there will be a communications problem at one end or the other, and probably both.

> There will be times when the Governor will wish the news media would go away and his press secretary join them. That, of course, is not going to happen.
>
> A Governor's press office that is doing a professional and creditable job would be working hard for both masters—the Governor and the press corps. Sometimes it seems an impossible and frustrating job, but there's no reason why it can't be done with a relative degree of success.

CHAPTER ELEVEN

The Budget: A Spending Plan and Policy Tool

> The major concern of every phase of state government turns on finding the money to accomplish the goal and then staying within the amount budgeted. This requires hours of attention, detailed knowledge, and tough decisions.
>
> — *a former Governor*

SUMMARY

The budget provides the basic structure for policy making in state government. During the transition, a new Governor must answer several critical questions with regard to his first budget, including:

• Should the new administration attempt to prepare a new budget or develop amendments to the predecessor's spending plan?

• How much initial budget preparation and review should be delegated to the Governor's staff?

• What kind of budget process suits the new administration best?

Whatever the approach, it is essential that a trusted member of the new Governor's staff set the budget process in motion between election day and inauguration.

To begin his involvement in the budget process, the new Governor should examine a fiscal overview or fiscal plan as soon as possible. This document summarizes anticipated revenues and expenditures for several years by major program categories. The Governor can use the fiscal plan as the basis for having his staff investigate the following questions:

• How good are the revenue estimates? What has been the track record in the past? Are there unanticipated balances or threatened deficits?

• Where are the "uncontrollable" spending increases occurring? Are there any surprises ahead, such as the need to repair neglected roads or finance unfunded pension liabilities?

• Can the Governor maintain a balanced budget without new taxes? Must major spending reductions or tax increases take place in the first term?

The new Governor will necessarily have a limited impact on the first budget. His longer-term influence on state priorities will be felt through the implementation of a budget process which focuses on issues important to the Governor.

Among the budget processes chosen by Governors have been:

• Incremental budgeting, in which spending proposals are evaluated against an accepted base, such as the spending level of the prior year;

• Zero-base budgeting (ZBB), in which budget decisions are made against a base of zero rather than last year's spending level;

• Planning-programming-budgeting (PPBS), in which programs are arrayed by functional categories rather than by agencies; and

• Combinations of two or more of these systems.

Whichever budget process the Governor feels most comfortable with, he should ensure that it:

• Sets out clear standards for agency budget submissions and highlights key options for gubernatorial decisions;

• Enables the Governor to set priorities for agency spending at *his* preferred level of detail;

• Encompasses capital budgeting, budgeting of federal funds, and non-general fund receipts;

• Permits budget adjustments when cutbacks or cost controls are necessary;

• Estimates the long-term fiscal consequences of short-term decisions; and

• Ensures that, when aggregated, the many individual budget decisions can be related to the Governor's goals.

The new Governor will also want to work with his legislative assistant and press secretary to discuss how best to use the budget message itself in articulating administration goals and the programs designed to achieve them. His handling of the budget will signal the degree to which the Governor wishes to be involved in the management of state government.

The Budget:
A Spending Plan
and Policy Tool

In government, as elsewhere, money represents power. If a Governor wants to use the power of his office to benefit the state's citizens and at the same time avoid squandering public resources, he must keep on top of the budget.

A new Governor may decide to take an active role in the budget-formulation process during his first few months in office, or wait to have his impact the following year. Whichever choice he makes, sooner or later he will have to come to grips with the budget process and adopt a fiscal plan by decision or default.

THE FISCAL PLAN

State situations and gubernatorial objectives differ so much that no single course of action, whether it be raising taxes and expanding programs or lowering taxes and curtailing services, can be said to be the "right" course for any particular Governor. But it can be said with certainty that a Governor who stumbles into a fiscal policy he doesn't feel comfortable with has made a mistake.

Public spending programs have a way of becoming cast in concrete once they are initiated. Even when this does not occur as a legal result of adopting a program, it is a common political result. While teachers throughout the state will salute the Governor who initiates a sharp increase in school aid in the first year of his term, that same Governor's popularity will be short-lived if he exhausts all his possibilities for funding increases in the first year and has nothing new to offer in the second. Likewise, new programs for construction of community colleges or institutions for the mentally retarded carry in their wake an inevitable expansion of operating costs once the facilities are opened.

It is not only good budgeting and planning practice, but also good politics for a Governor to know the fiscal consequences of all decisions before making them. Both the fiscal consequences and the period of fiscal concern span more than one year.

Although different administrations may wish to construct their plans differently, most begin with something similar to the following sample single-page plan for taxing and spending:

Sample Fiscal Overview, General Revenue Funds, Fiscal 1977-81
(In millions of dollars)

	\	Fiscal Year			
REVENUES	1977	1978	1979	1980	1981
Income tax	1,000	1,090	1,185	1,280	1,380
Sales tax	1,400	1,526	1,666	1,816	2,000
Other state sources	800	880	970	1,060	1,160
Federal aid	600	650	700	750	800
TOTAL REVENUES	3,800	4,146	4,521	4,906	5,340
EXPENDITURES					
Elementary and secondary education	1,100	1,205	1,310	1,420	1,530
Higher education	600	660	730	800	870
Welfare (including Medicaid)	1,400	1,500	1,605	1,710	1,815
Mental health	300	360	420	470	490
Corrections	100	105	110	115	120
Debt service	80	85	90	100	110
Other	250	275	300	330	360
TOTAL EXPENDITURES	3,830	4,190	4,565	4,945	5,295
Revenues-expenditures *	(30)	(44)	(44)	(39)	45
Beginning balance Surplus or (Deficit)	30	0	(44)	(88)	(127)
ENDING BALANCE	0	(44)	(88)	(127)	(82)

* See following discussion on budget-balancing approaches

No other numbers have more importance for the incoming Governor than the quarterly and yearly revenue estimates. Only if the state's revenue estimates are accurate can the fiscal overview actually guide the preparation and execution of the Governor's spending plans. If they are substantially off, a tremendous amount of political and operational damage will be inevitable.

The revenue assumptions used are traditionally prepared by either the department that collects taxes or the budget office, or some combination or duplication of the two. If more revenue is collected than had been anticipated, the Governor will be accused of "hiding funds," and will find that he has foregone expenditures or tax relief which he could have provided. The passage of Proposition 13 in California demonstrates the political danger of underestimating revenues and building up too large a balance.** If less money is taken in than estimated, end-of-year cutbacks will be extremely painful and damaging.

** In the California primary election on June 6, 1978, voters overwhelmingly approved an initiative to limit annual property taxes to one percent of market value, roll back assessments to 1975 levels, and confine increases in assessments to two percent a year. One of the proponents' arguments was that the state had not used its surplus to ease the citizens' tax burden. The measure, known as Proposition 13 because of its position on the ballot, caused nationwide repercussions. Other election results were interpreted as reflecting the same voter mood, and similar measures were put on the November general election ballot in several states.

In many states, the publication of revenue estimates has become a subject of heated dispute among Governors, treasurers, comptrollers, the legislature and even economists in universities and banks. A new Governor should inquire in a probing and detailed fashion as to the methods, assumptions and past accuracy of revenue estimates. Some states have developed sophisticated computer models to estimate state tax revenues. Estimates of federal reimbursements are also critical to the fiscal plan and should be required by the new Governor. As a rule of thumb, if net revenue has differed from the estimates by more than three percent, some changes should be made in the procedure.

The expenditures shown in a new Governor's fiscal overview should represent the first impressions of what he and his advisors think they would like to do. In the example, relatively substantial increases have been forecast in all fields of state endeavor. The overview, however, reflects tentative decisions to undertake major program expansion in mental health, while barely matching cost-of-living increases in fields such as welfare and corrections. At the same time, it shows expanded assistance to elementary, secondary and higher education at a rate well above the rate of inflation implicit in the revenue forecasts.

Useful as it is for financial planning, the fiscal overview also has value as a political planning tool. In the case of the example (and assuming, as is the case, that the state cannot run a substantial negative balance), the obvious choice is whether this Governor is interested in a relatively small tax increase. If he is not, he needs to make some changes in the amounts he plans to spend.

Obviously, a Governor cannot personally work out all of the assumptions which underlie such a fiscal plan. But he does need to provide broad policy guidance on questions such as the extent to which he wants to raise the level of welfare payments, or whether he wants major new and costly initiatives in school support, mental health, tax relief, or other areas.

When expenditures and revenues are far apart, the need for a tax increase becomes obvious if the Governor is to finance what he wants to do. In such a case, the fiscal overview should be used to forecast the year and magnitude of the tax increase (usually the earlier the better) and to ensure that a second tax increase will not be necessary during the term. In still other situations, the Governor may be looking for tax relief, and the overview may be used to understand what degree of holding the line on expenditures is necessary.

Whatever the policies involved, a Governor will find it is always better to have some sort of plan for dealing with the budget. A budget deficit and a need for a small tax increase are more palatable when they arise from a national recession that causes revenues to drop below expectations than when caused by the Governor's faulty fiscal planning. Granting tax relief in the first year of a term only to find that there must be a tax increase in the third year has to be the height of political folly for anyone who looks forward to reelection.

Having a fiscal overview will not prevent fiscal problems, nor will it remove the necessity for hard decisions down the road. What it will do is prevent a Governor from facing dilemmas of his own making.

DEALING WITH THE FIRST BUDGET

In practically all states, a new Governor assumes office after the budget is nearly completed. As a result, many new Governors do not have a significant impact on the budget submitted to the legislature for the following fiscal year. This means that the first 18 months of the administration (30 months in a state with a biennial budget) are spent attempting to operate within a budgetary framework set by the previous Governor. Furthermore, Governors with strong campaign commitments on taxing and spending will find it almost untenable to take a "hands off" attitude toward the first budget.

The first step will be to decide the extent to which the new administration's stamp should be put on the budget. This is as much a political question as a budgeting question, so its resolution should not be left to the budget staff alone. Regardless of the laws and schedules in effect, a Governor's public statements and budget changes can reflect one of three approaches:

• View the budget as the work of the previous Governor (good or bad), stress the lack of time to review and possibly change it, and plan to focus on the budget next year.

• Consider the basic outlines of the budget and the detailed allocations to each agency to be essentially the predecessor's work, but decide on "amendments" or changes to that budget in broad, policy-related areas. These might include the level of school aid and its distribution, the overall allocation to higher education, changes in the welfare payment level, new taxes or tax relief, and sponsorship of programs with which the new Governor became identified during the campaign.

• Undertake to make the entire budget the new administration's own by setting new budget totals for each agency, carrying out hearings or discussions with each of the agency heads, and in general, trying to compress into the time available all of the activities that would characterize the budget development process in the second year of the administration.

Getting an Early Start

Whatever the approach, a trusted member of the new Governor's staff must set the budget process in motion between election day and inauguration. This should be viewed as a full-time job, and one which must be begun early. The simplest approach is to make sure that a decision on whether to retain or hire a new budget director is made quickly so the Governor can obtain information about agency budget recommendations and his staff can attend budget hearings. If this cannot be done, finding a staff member or outside advisor with the time and inclination to do this work is critical if the Governor is to have an impact on the budget.

The budget represents the first real working contact between the Governor and his newly appointed cabinet members. This permits the Governor to set the tone for his relationship with them. As a practical matter, sessions dealing with the budget may be the major sources of substantive guidance from the Governor for individual cabinet members throughout the term. Working with cabinet members is essential to minimize the political problems associated with budget recommendations. A cabinet officer who feels he hasn't been consulted in the budget process makes a poor advocate before the legislature and special interest groups with whom he deals.

If the Governor is planning major budget changes, he must make sure he instructs his new appointees to begin their budget work immediately. This activity is desirable for the agency heads in any case, because it forces them to learn quickly the details of what their agency does and puts them in contact with the people who do it.

In his first dealings with the budgeting agency, the new Governor will want to remember that in many cases the budget agency is not operating solely on the basis of financial expertise, but rather is in the business of recommending policy. He will want to emphasize using the budget staff, and perhaps the planning staff, to get alternatives, not just a single recommendation.

Because estimates of revenue are critical to all other budget decisions, a Governor may seek the advice of an outside source of estimates as a supplement to his own staff. Or he may wish to make sure that when he considers estimated revenues, all critical assumptions are spelled out for him, and that the staff provides him with some "what would happen if" comments on their projections.

Wholesale revision of the first budget will be difficult because the agencies' submissions have been developed in accordance with formats and procedures established by the previous administration. In pondering budgetary decisions during the first 100 days, the new Governor will have the opportunity to consider whether data made available in the budget process are data which he really needs, and whether other information which he needs is missing. He will also want to consider whether improvements could be made in the way information is presented in the budget documents and budget message. These considerations will provide a basis for the budget procedure decisions of future years.

Delegating Budget Responsibilities

A new Governor without prior experience in government may underestimate the importance of the budgetary process. Budget making is about the only governmental process which imposes deadlines for a variety of major decisions. In deciding upon a budget, a Governor is dealing with questions such as how much of a raise to give his employees; whether to launch new programs and, if so, which ones; whether to discontinue old programs and, if so, which ones; how much money to give to school districts and under what conditions; whether to open new state institutions or close old ones; how much to give welfare recipients; what conditions to attach to eligibility for assistance; and other important issues.

Recognizing that budget decisions are fundamental and important, a new Governor must also recognize that a significant number of such decisions are tedious, complex, exceptionally dull and unimportant, both substantively and politically. If the Governor is not careful, the same budget process that results in a decision on building a new medical school or the magnitude of pay raises for state employees can also result in a budget director and an insurance commissioner arguing about whether an additional clerk typist is essential.

Given this situation, the Governor should decide how much of the budget decision making to delegate to others. He can delegate the entire exercise and require that appeals on budget conflicts be submitted to him, recognizing that accepting too many appeals effectively revokes the delegation. Or he can delegate nothing and make the rule that no budget total for any agency can be set by anyone other than the Governor. This means hearing out all budget controversies, from the size of welfare payments to a new clerk typist position. A middle ground does exist, and is most frequently taken by Governors, with the general budget strategy (e.g., lean year, fat year) and the major decisions being made by the Governor and the lesser decisions being made (subject to some appeal) by a budget director, finance commissioner or top gubernatorial aide, or some combination of those individuals.

In some cases, overall budget strategy—like political strategy—is the subject of relatively formal cabinet meetings or subcabinet discussions designed to test out various budget scenarios before setting agency targets.

A Governor's handling of the budget signals the degree to which he wishes to be personally involved in the management of state government. However, even if he does delegate substantial budget responsibilities, he should have enough interest in the process to make sure that it gives his agency heads an opportunity to be heard and that the resulting budget reflects his priorities.

THE BUDGET PROCESS

After delivering his first budget message, which will have been prepared under hectic and sometimes confusing conditions, the new Governor will want to plan the next budget process to reflect his personal priorities.

The budget schedule is set by starting with the budget submission date and working back through the steps necessary to produce a budget consistent with the state's laws and the Governor's spending priorities. If a budget is to be submitted on, say, January 15, there will need to be from 15 to 30 days between the making of the last budget decision and the submission date. This time is necessary for printing and for the calculation of summary tables.

To get all decisions made by about December 15, the Governor should expect to begin making a number of them by October 15. The extent to which the Governor personally makes these decisions and the types of information used to make them will, of course, determine how much time needs to be allotted for this stage of the budget process.

While the budget staff can do much analysis beforehand, some key parts of the process cannot proceed until the agencies have submitted their recommendations for spending and have provided information, such as estimated spending during the current fiscal year and program work loads, which is critical to analysis of those recommendations. That information is provided in the budget submission, which is typically required from the agencies in August, September or October.

In many states, the agency budget recommendations are public at the time of submission, or are made public by being included in the budget book. In these states, the Governor and his top staff will want to develop a policy with regard to agency submissions. If the Governor wants to take a public "budget-cutting" position, he may allow agencies to submit budgets without specifying targets in advance. On the other hand, if he wants to avoid the blame for cutting especially sensitive items out of agency budgets, he will want to set agency targets verbally ahead of time and hold cabinet members to them. In the case of agencies not under the Governor's control, such as education, there is little he can do to coordinate their recommendations in his final, published budget.

The process of developing a budget submission is time consuming for state agencies. Either the budget agency or the legislature, or both, frequently require that the budget be built from the bottom up and that it contain considerable detail on the proposed expenditures. Thus, in a large department such as mental health, the budget-preparation process would involve the development of planned expenditures in each major institution, the review of those proposals within the department, any needed revision of the institutional budget after the review, and the compilation of all institutional and other requests into a single mental health agency submission. If the budget agency requires that the submission contain an analysis of alternative levels of spending and/or indicate likely results from spending funds, the process will be even more time consuming for the agencies.

Generally, large agencies confronted with a budget-submission date in September will want to begin work as early as June. To make this work most useful, those agencies need to have the ground rules for the submissions, which are generally known as budget guidelines. These guidelines cover such matters as the formats to be used for reporting information, any assumptions to be used about inflation or employee compensation changes, any ceilings on the total amount of money that can be requested, the procedures for the portrayal of alternatives, and any priorities for program expansion being suggested by the Governor.

Much of what the Governor can accomplish in his review of the budget in the fall will be determined by the quality and coverage of the agency submissions that are developed in response to the budget guidelines issued in or around June. For this reason, the Governor needs to be involved in the process of establishing guidelines in the spring and early summer of the first year in office.

The Governor's Decisions on Budget Guidelines

Obviously, the detailed work of preparing the budget guidelines can be left to the budget staff. However, there are some decisions about the guidelines that the Governor will probably want to make, or at least will want to have the option to make.

Fiscal climate. Decision making in the fall about the budgets of individual agencies will be very difficult unless the budget guidelines have accurately reflected the fiscal climate in which final budget decisions are to be made. Once again, the accuracy of revenue projections is of paramount importance. For example, a Governor who will be emphasizing holding the line and making cuts in some programs to keep the total budget low should not be confronted with the need to review multiple proposals for unrealistic spending increases or to dash the expectations of those making such proposals. Conversely, a Governor who has substantial revenue growth will want to have full information on how effectively agencies could use additional funding.

To make sure that agency submissions are responsive to the fiscal situation of the state and the broad policy of the Governor on budget priorities, it will be necessary once again to review the state's fiscal position before the budget guidelines are issued. At that time, the Governor should review a current revision of the overview for (1) likely legislative action and amendments to the budget under review in the legislature, (2) changes in economic forecasts and thus revenues, and (3) changes affecting expenditures in future years. The budget staff should be able to provide a general briefing on these numbers, indicating the types of major added expenditures likely to be requested (e.g., across-the-board pay increases, increases in welfare payment rates, expanded school aid) and the increases in costs in major programs (e.g., Medicaid) likely to be beyond the control of the Governor.

As a result of the overview session, the Governor should be able to make tentative decisions on:

1. Whether to plan for changes in taxes, either increases or reductions;

2. Major areas of expenditure increase that he wants to consider as administration priorities; and

3. Any areas in which he desires a special effort to make reductions.

The overview session is also the place to make tentative decisions that will affect all of the agencies, such as a ceiling on new positions or decisions that all agencies should expand their ability to deal with citizen complaints.

The budget base. The fiscal overview decisions can feed directly into the most critical decision needed for constructing the budget guidelines. That decision concerns the totals against which individual agencies will develop their budgets. There are a number of mechanisms for setting the base, of which the most widely discussed recently has been zero-base budgeting.

Budgeting systems that allow agencies to request any amount they wish are rare. A much more common approach is to require agencies to build requests incrementally from some base, such as the spending level of the prior year. New spending is justified as an "increment" or increase and proposed cuts or "decrements" are reviewed using the base as a starting point. Persons who are basically comfortable with the current level or distribution of activity in state government will also find themselves comfortable with this *incremental approach* to budgeting.

The system that will most carefully raise to the Governor's attention the implicit priorities of his budget will be one that starts from a forecast of the costs of performing the same types and levels of state service for the fiscal year under consideration. That base level of "current services" will basically be:

1. The prior year's spending level, plus

2. Adjustments associated with uncontrollable changes in work load or activity, such as a projected increase in the welfare rolls or a decrease in enrollment which automatically affects the school aid formula, plus

3. Adjustments that are mandatory, such as increasing social security taxes, automatic adjustments built into some school aid formulas and the like, plus

4. Price-level adjustments that are not controlled by state government, such as increases in the costs of office supplies and paving materials, plus

5. Price-level adjustments under the control of the state but not under the control of agencies submitting budget requests. Examples are employee pay raises across the board and the charges of agencies providing motor pool, computer and other services.

Certain of the base-level assumptions (e.g., anticipated employee pay increases) can be set at zero to defer decisions on those matters, and the budget agency can crank uniform inflation increases into agency budgets after the level of activity has been decided upon.

With current services providing the base, the primary decision to make about guidelines is the type of justification the Governor will require for deciding upon increments above the base and cuts below it. It is not uncommon for agency heads to be asked to identify some of their low-priority programs in the base (e.g., if you had to cut into the base by five percent, what activities would be cut back?). It is very common for agencies to be permitted to try to justify increases in the base for new programs and expansion of existing ones.

Generally, the budget agency will want more detail on the impact of potential changes to the base than will the Governor. The Governor or his staff will, however, want to make sure that decisions coming to the Governor on changes from the base utilize information indicating the advantages and disadvantages of the change, as seen by both the line agency and the budget staff, and that information is provided on the political repercussions of the change.

As noted earlier, this type of incremental budgeting system is best suited for reviewers who are comfortable with the current levels of activity and costs of state government. A new Governor and his staff, and his newly appointed agency heads, may well not be in this position. Instead, they may even have campaigned on the issues of producing a better review of state spending and cutting the budget. They may be quite unwilling to presume the validity of the base.

The budgeting system that is designed to give no weight to whether an expenditure has been made in the past is a *zero-base budgeting system*. A zero-base system means that the base is not the prior year, or some percentage of the prior year's spending, but is literally zero. A zero-base system is designed so that initially the Governor would be making decisions, in effect, as though the state had no programs. Such a pure zero-base system, for example, forces the question, "Do we want to maintain mental hospitals at state expense?" "If so, how many?" An incremental budgeting system does not force such questions on the Governor.

In theory, zero-base systems, like other program-budgeting systems, segregate government activities into individual programs (e.g., maintain good fishing opportunities by stocking rivers and lakes with game fish). Within any program, "program packages" are created to reflect different levels of service and cost. For example, the packages for the hatchery/stocking function might summarize as follows:

PACKAGES	$ MILLIONS COST	OUTPUT FISH STOCKED
#1 Minimum Program	.3	3 million
#2 Intermediate Program	.7	8 million
#3 Current Level	1.0	12 million
#4 Current Level, plus new gamefish	1.3	14 million

Each of the individual packages would contain a summary of what is involved in the alternative and some attempt to measure output or effectiveness of the program. Packages can be ranked relative to other programs of the same agency (e.g., investments in fish compared to investments in parkland), and all packages can ultimately be ranked in relation to each other.

Jurisdictions that have experimented with zero-base budgeting have rapidly discovered that decision makers had little interest in starting at zero in the first year, and even less interest in asking questions pertaining to successive years. In practice, zero-base systems are not really zero based at all, but typically start with a base that is often a high percentage of current agency spending.

Where to set the base is a function of the fiscal situation, as well as the Governor's emphasis on cuts in old programs as distinct from new programs and the expansion of programs. In a relatively typical situation (no new taxes, enough revenue from existing taxes to finance some program expansion, and the Governor wants to make some program cuts if possible), setting alternative bases may best provide the Governor with the information he needs. In such a situation, the Governor might like to look at three levels:

1. What the budget would be and the consequence of operating at 90 percent or 95 percent of current service levels,

2. Current service levels, and

3. What the budget would fund at 105 percent or 110 percent of current service levels.

In most budgeting systems, setting a base is done to structure the advice of agency heads and the budget agency to the Governor's agency funding levels. However, in some budgeting systems the answer (the agency's target) is given in the guidelines rather than as a result of the process triggered by the guidelines. In such situations, the agencies budget against a single allocation. However, it is difficult for the Governor and the budget agency to prevent agency heads from advising the Governor that they believe that they should spend more. In practice, systems which tell agency heads to design budgets to previously fixed totals probably do not differ very much from ones that do not develop such totals until the budget review is complete.

Priority setting by agency heads. Budgeting systems differ in the extent to which they encourage heads of agencies to set priorities within their own agencies. These differences are most noticeable in cases where an agency head might be willing to give up an existing program or cut it back if he could have the savings to invest in some new program. Incremental budgeting systems, with their requirements of focusing review attention on new program proposals, tend to take any savings as given and require considerable justification of increases. Some argue that this discourages agency initiative in funding new programs out of the existing base. Alternative systems involve giving the agency head the capability, subject to the Governor's review, to substitute new for old programs within any given base. Most believe the latter approach is preferable.

Input information. The budgeting agency will normally want to review considerable information on the composition of proposed spending for particular programs. In the fish hatcheries case described earlier, for example, the budget-submission document would normally include information on the percentage of spending that would be for personal services, the amount for equipment, etc. Much of this information will not be of interest to the Governor. Generally, he will be more interested in the same thing as the citizen—what impact the expenditure will have on services received by citizens.

Output information. Budgeting systems differ in the extent to which they provide information on output in the budget submission materials and in the budget documents that go to the legislature. Some state budgets do not list any information purporting to show how programs work or what the expected benefits are. Other budget documents are devoted almost exclusively to planned output or effectiveness, with detailed financial tables relegated to an appendix.

Clearly there is no way to decide on an expenditure for a particular purpose by looking only at expenditure information. Whether there should be an increase of five percent in the manpower of the state police depends upon how the manpower would be used and what benefits that use might have for the individual citizen. Budgeting systems commonly require such information for proposed increases, though many of the incremental systems do not require the information for the base program.

Budgeting systems that place emphasis on output or results are often called "performance" budgets or program budgets. Their use requires that the work of state government be divided into a number of identifiable programs, each with its own objectives and methods of measuring achievement.

What Documents Should the Governor See?

Governors differ in the extent to which they wish to review detailed information about agency budgets. Some Governors preside over budget hearings involving each agency and read both the budget submissions and the review documents generated by the budget agency. Other Governors prefer to stay out of the day-to-day work of budgeting by giving considerable authority to their budget or finance directors to deal with individual agency heads. These Governors would normally read budget-related materials only when specific issues are referred to them as a result of disagreement between the budget and the line agencies. In the latter case, the Governor need not be interested in the design of the budget submissions, as he will not have to read them.

Some Governors change their involvement in the budget process over time, spending considerable time the first year learning the budget and putting the stamp of their priorities on it and then becoming less involved in successive years.

Whatever the level of the Governor's involvement, he will most certainly be making a number of key decisions relative to the budgets of individual agencies. The staff work for this can be arranged in a number of ways. The more formal systems provide issue papers to the Governor. In cases where such issues are likely to arise, the issue papers can be requested specifically as a part of the budget guidelines and become part of the agency budget submission. Then, after the budget agency has taken its position, the issue papers become the basis for the Governor's decision. The decision memorandum in appendix 8 is an example of such an issue paper.

Multiyear Format

As noted earlier, there are some very strong arguments for the Governor having available some projections of revenue and expenditure that represent his plan to manage the state fiscally for a period of years. Some states go beyond that private and personal plan into a more formal multiyear budget-projection and planning process for both operating costs (which is unusual) and capital outlays (which is more common).

Multiple-year projections are now used in budget submissions at the federal level and in a few states. Pennsylvania, for example, provides three-year projections in its budget for every program. Such projections are not plans, however. The total of the projected expenditures often exceeds the revenue available from existing taxes, leaving a decision to be made later on whether to raise taxes or cut projected expenditures.

Exempt Agencies

The statute which established the state's budgetary process will define what agencies are exempt from what portion of the Governor's budget-review process. The most common exemptions are the legislative and judicial branches. Normally, the budget agency will have the power to prescribe the *format* of the requests from these bodies, but often will not have the power to change the *amounts*. Even in circumstances where the Governor is not formally prohibited from altering the budget request of the legislative and judicial branches, Governors may refrain from doing so on the grounds either:

1. That they are separate branches and should have responsibility for their own budgets, or

2. That involvement by the Governor in their budgets would encourage extraordinary scrutiny and involvement in the budgets of the Governor's mansion and immediate office.

A more difficult question arises in connection with the offices of separately elected officials such as the lieutenant governor, attorney general, secretary of state, auditor, comptroller and treasurer. In some states, these statewide elected officials control major functions with large budgets. As elected officials, they have their own constituencies, often are of a different party from the Governor or a different wing of the same party, and have their own ties with the members of the state legislature.

The Governor often has the legal authority to include in his budget numbers for these officials that are different from what they have recommended.

Particularly when Governors traditionally have been reluctant to alter the budget requests of other elected officials, new Governors may find it difficult to get the cooperation of their staffs in participating meaningfully in a budget process that requires more of them than a simple documenting of requests. For example, they may be reluctant to provide recommendations on where their budget should be cut if cutting were necessary.

Practices and traditions vary among the states in dealing with budgets of elected officials. The issue needs to be faced explicitly early in an administration, probably in the context of budget guidelines.

Exempt Funds

State practices also vary on whether and how federal funds are subject to appropriation in a fashion similar to state funds.* Even where federal funds are not appropriated, the Governor can decide to review federally funded items along with the regular state budget items. This happens more or less automatically when federal funds are used to match state funds, as is the case in such major expenditure areas as Medicaid and welfare. In other cases, such as employment security and manpower (Comprehensive Employment and Training Act) programs, 100-percent federal funding is involved.

With 100-percent federal funding, the budget process does not really set the level of program activity, unless the Governor decides either to supplement federal funds with state funds or to turn back to the federal government some of its 100-percent money. Governors have increasingly questioned implementing new federal programs without firm assurance that the federal government will not impose additional matching requirements in later years, effectively forcing a state budget increase in order to save a politically popular program.

Another difficulty associated with review of these programs during the budget process, rather than in the federally mandated program cycles, is that the timing of review does not usually match the timing for final decisions on use of the funds. For example, a program may be administered on a cycle ending with allocation in January, which would be later than the state's budget review. The budget review would have to be based upon estimates of the funds to be allotted in January.

The Governor will find that he must deal with these budget processes because the uses of state and federal funds interact. For example, the level of funding for state-funded park maintenance workers should be related to the decision of how many public-service job slots will be allocated to the parks. Governors oriented toward "getting a handle" on federal

---

* See National Association of State Budget Officers, *Federal Funds Budgetary and Appropriation Practices in State Governments* (Lexington, Ky.: Council of State Governments, 1978).

programs operating in their states will probably want to make sure that their internal budget process (as distinct from the separate question of what is included in the budget document going to the legislature) includes all federal funds.

In many states, the formal budget process excludes revenue bond agencies such as state housing authorities, port commissions, toll highway authorities, industrial pollution bond authorities, college dormitory construction agencies and comparable bodies. Many of these organizations get no appropriated funds at all. Their costs, including their administrative costs, are paid out of the revenues generated by their activity. Such agencies, however, have the potential of exerting future impact on the general funds budget of the state and on the overall credit worthiness of the state, as several states have discovered when one or more of their revenue bonding agencies found that project revenues were insufficient to support debt-service costs. These authorities are frequently managed by independent boards with staggered terms and may resist an attempt by the Governor to include them in the budget process.

Still another potential for exemption from review (though not from inclusion in the Governor's budget) arises in the case of agencies and/or activities where the level of revenues controls the decision on how much to spend on the function or agency. Such situations arise when the total costs for a particular function or agency are set as the revenue from taxes or fees. Some state regulatory bodies operate on this basis, along with many state highway departments. Once a decision is made, for example, not to increase gasoline taxes and registration fees, budget review for the highway department becomes the allocation of resources within a given total rather than a process of determining the total to be made available.

The Format of Review Meetings

In a few states, it is the custom for the agency submissions to be presented to the Governor before the budget agency has had much chance to take a position. Sometimes, the agency head presents his budget at a public budget hearing, and the Governor and his staff members ask questions about it. In most states, however, while the Governor may get information copies of budget submissions, the primary meetings on the budget take place after the budget agency and the line agency have had some preliminary discussions and both have had the opportunity to take positions.

For those Governors who basically operate on an appeal basis from decisions of a finance or budget director, the format of budget review meetings will be set largely by the circumstances of the appeal. Appeal meetings will normally involve both the budget director and the head of the agency, each accompanied by staff members who can deal with whatever technical issues are at stake. The agency head makes a presentation of whatever he feels is unreasonable about the position of the budget agency, and the budget director defends his position. The Governor then either decides the issue or takes it under advisement in order to discuss it with advisors (which may include talking privately with one of the contending parties).

Where meetings with the Governor are the basic format by which all decisions on agency budgets are made, the meeting should be tailored to the decision-making style of the Governor. For example, some like to have such meetings include an initial briefing on the budget by either the agency head or the budget director. Other decision makers would rather rely upon written preliminary documents and confine the oral discussion to specific issues.

A perpetual problem in setting up budget meetings is deciding how large the meeting should be. Governors often find themselves more comfortable when meetings are small and limited to persons they have appointed as members of their own staff and in the line agencies and budget agency. On the other hand, confining budget meetings to such a small group frequently denies all concerned the sometimes useful detailed knowledge of senior career personnel from the line agencies and budget examiners from the budget agency.

One solution to this problem is to allow the budget director and agency head to bring anyone they want and to use this large meeting format for consideration of issues involving detailed knowledge, but not necessarily to the point of decision on all issues. The group can then be reduced to the Governor, the agency head and any trusted deputies, and those members of the budget staff and his personal staff whom the Governor wants to stay. The smaller group may be particularly appropriate for discussions of the political ramifications of various budget levels and for more delicate questions that may occur to the Governor in thinking about a program (e.g., personnel matters in the agency).

The Governor's decision-making style and relationships with agency heads (see following discussion) will also determine the extent to which he will permit either the agency head or budget staff to communicate with him about the budget in the absence of the other party. Some Governors, particularly those with legal backgrounds, see the budget-setting process as an advocacy proceeding with themselves cast in the role of a judge. In that mode, they discourage *ex parte* presentations—that is, statements by either the agency or budget agency without the presence of the other party. The theory is that this approach prevents either party from intentionally or unintentionally distorting the facts.

Other Governors are comfortable discussing the issues involved with the budget staff and reaching a decision after the agency personnel have left. The budget director may then be given the job of notifying the agency head of the Governor's decisions.

When Governors and Agencies Can't Agree

In states with strong executive budgeting, the Governor's budget request is the only budget request from executive agencies pending before the legislature, with the exception of requests from independent boards and elected officials. In this system, the Governor's agency heads would support the Governor's budget.

However, it doesn't quite work this way in practice, even in states with the strongest executive budget procedure. Members of the legislature and interest groups are frequently aware of what the agency's position was in the executive budget process and try to draw that position out in testimony. Agency heads have no interest in lying in such situations and need not be asked to do so. The type of guidance that can be given by agency heads can best be shown by the following illustration:

On Needing Additional Money

WRONG: We definitely need more money than the Governor's request allows; the Governor made a mistake in not giving it to us.

RIGHT: There is no question but what my agency could productively spend additional funds, but that is a position that I share with all of my fellow cabinet officers. We all recognize that our desires in total add up to more than you (the legislature) or the Governor would ever want to spend, and we recognize that you and the Governor are in a better position than we are to determine how our needs stack up against other needs.

On Taking the Heat for Something

WRONG: That item is missing from our budget because the budget agency took it out and I couldn't convince the Governor that they were wrong.

RIGHT: I won't try to kid you—this is something on which I would like to spend money. However, if you tell me that the total dollars available for this department are those shown in the budget request I will have to tell you that this item is not important enough to be funded, that other things are simply more important.

Having agency heads support the Governor's budget becomes more difficult in those states where, by law or tradition, the agency budget request goes directly to the legislature. Under such a system, in its most extreme form, the legislature starts budget review from some point other than the Governor's recommendations (e.g., legislative staff recommendations), and the Governor is simply one of many parties making comments to the legislature on the budget.

In strong executive budget states, various ways have been found to deal with a requirement for open submission of agency requests without turning the agency heads into advocates for totals different from those of the Governor. This is nearly achieved in those states where the guidelines for requests constrain the total that can be requested. Another approach is to have the formal agency request submitted after the total for a department has been decided upon.

Not all Governors strive for a strong role in the budget process. Where a tradition of strong legislative leadership in budget matters has developed, it may be possible to work out reasonable working relationships with the legislative budget leaders, leaving the Governor more time to concentrate on nonfiscal matters.

Management Relationships and the Budget

Many sections of this book deal with the problems that every Governor encounters in trying to manage the relationship between the staff and line officials. These tensions are particularly evident during the budget process. Situations will constantly arise in which the Governor is asked, in one way or another, to decide whether he wants to rely upon the agency head to decide priorities within his own agency. Following are three examples of situations where this is the issue:

Personnel. The extent to which the Governor or anyone on his staff should be able to tell the agency heads whom to hire and fire.

Administrative matters. The extent to which those in charge of central services (e.g., personnel, mail system, computers) can control the policies within departments over the objection of department heads.

Spending priorities. The extent to which the Governor or persons acting in his name can modify the internal priorities of the department head.

These issues are most easily understood if one starts with the relationship of the Governor and the agency head. The Governor's staff clearly should not be permitted to tell agency heads what to do if the Governor himself would not do so in the same circumstances.

The management model discussed in chapter 7 leaves room for the chief executive to adopt policies applicable to all departments where, by the nature of things, those objectives or constraints need to apply to all departments. For example, affirmative action or other general hiring goals (including patronage) may call for central rules. The model also permits the chief executive to become involved when individual decisions within the agency have repercussions on the welfare of the entire state. For example, a facility-closing decision that affected the administration's relations with particular legislators, or which altered the attitudes of residents of an area toward the entire administration, could give rise to chief executive involvement.

This corporate management model is by no means the only model available for government or private management. In the real world of government, management situations arise in which a Governor does not have that degree of confidence in certain agency heads. In such a circumstance, Governors look to staff members, such as personal staff and budget directors, to play a more aggressive role in individual agency management decisions than they would if the corporate management model were being used.

Because many major decisions in state government are made through the budget process, these management relationship questions tend to arise most often in the context of the budget. For example, in a discussion of the budget for parks, the budget agency will often raise specific and somewhat detailed issues as a basis for the Governor's final decision. Thus, the Governor may be drawn into a discussion of whether two additional secretaries are required in the central office. The Governor will probably be willing to sit through this discussion because it provides an indication of what types of expenditures are at stake in the discussion of overall levels and the reasonableness of the positions of the parties.

After the Governor has made his budget decisions, whether on an individual series of issues that together bridge the gap between the agency's position and the budget agency's or simply in terms of a total for the agency, the question remains whether or not the agency gets its two secretaries. This question will arise when the agency submits its budget detail in response to the revised budget level. Two quite different management styles can be applied to the final decisions. Governors should know the difference so that they may make a conscious choice among them, as this type of detail (which is important to the overall management style of the administration) is not normally raised formally with the Governor.

One point of view is that if the Governor has not explicitly decided on the secretaries, but has picked an appropriation level that conceptually excluded them, the secretaries are considered to be disapproved. The budget agency, in this view of management, should enforce the Governor's decision, and it would be inappropriate for the agency to try to go ahead despite the Governor's decision.

Another point of view argues that the Governor should be (and probably was) only interested in the two secretaries for the purpose of getting information on which to base a decision on the overall level of funding for the agency. From this perspective, the Governor was only setting the total resources to be requested for park operations during the fiscal year, not the detailed distribution of those resources within the operating department. That view would permit the park agency to hire the secretaries if it could do so within the budget total provided by the Governor. This latter view gives the director of the agency the capability, even within a budget total that assumed no new hiring, to swap positions.

A similar situation arises during the course of a fiscal year in which belt-tightening measures are required. The budget agency will tend to advocate across-the-board actions—such as freezing vacancies and postponing equipment purchases—designed to produce savings on a governmentwide basis. Unfortunately, these measures always produce strains within agencies that lead to exceptions. One test of the management style of an administration is whether the budget agency and the Governor will accept "deals" with agency heads whereby they are exempted from the particular freeze if they, in turn, will agree to produce the same savings by methods of their choosing.

CAPITAL BUDGETING AND BONDING

In some states, capital budgeting is separated from operations budgeting, both as a process and in the presentation of budget documents. In other places, the two processes are one and the same, with different presentations being used only to the extent that much capital in state government is in a different fund (e.g., a bond fund or road fund) from the state's general revenue fund. A few states have aggressively used their capital budgets to spur economic development in specific regions of the state.

For governments that use bonds to finance capital expenditures, the definition of capital items is difficult. Purchasers of general-obligation bonds are concerned with the overall ability of the issuer to pay debt service, but not generally with what is being financed by the bonds, so they tend not to impose discipline over definitions of what is "bondable." Thus, it is left to individual states to decide whether such things as furniture for a new building, books for a library, and renovation of an existing facility are capital items.

Capital planning has merit for all states and is particularly necessary in those states that issue substantial quantities of bonds to finance their capital needs. In the process of preparing legislative appropriations requests for projects to be financed through bonds, the Governor should make sure that someone has developed a forecast of the bond issues needed to fund the projects and has determined that the market will absorb that level of issuance without premiums on the interest rate or a downward adjustment in bond ratings.

In addition to this precaution, Governors often work to make sure that their bond ratings do not decrease and, when less than AAA, to increase them. This activity, if successful, will hold down the state's borrowing cost (the lower the rating the higher the interest necessary to attract buyers for the state's bonds) and prevent the embarrassment of having a rating lowered during the Governor's term—which often becomes a campaign issue. The rating services (Moody's and Standard and Poor's) use a variety of criteria, such as the wealth of citizens of the state and total state debt as a percentage of revenues, that are little influenced by a Governor in the short run. However, many state financial officials believe that it is appropriate, and useful, for some state official to visit rating agencies and investment bankers on Wall Street, either before each major bond issue or about every quarter. Generally, the state's bond counsel or investment advisor can arrange such sessions. The Governor's role in these sessions is to present briefly the fiscal posture of the state and make statements (e.g., how he is preventing spending from outrunning revenues) to reassure the financial community. A period of questions and answers generally follows.

If the Governor does not want to undertake these periodic missions to Wall Street, but does maintain an active bonding program, it may be useful for him to make sure the chief state budget officer and the treasurer or comptroller make the trips. While generally believed to be useful in maintaining or upgrading bond ratings, such trips usually are not successful if the Governor waits until the state's rating is reduced and then goes to Wall Street to seek a quick reversal of the rating decision.

WHEN FORECASTS MISS THE MARK

Because of unpredictable economic changes and human error, revenues and expenditures rarely turn out to be the same as those forecast. When there is a shortfall, most states have procedures requiring the Governor to curtail spending. Where expenditures fall below estimates and/or revenues begin to exceed estimates, the Governor is confronted with the problem of an unanticipated surplus, which will trigger a rash of spending requests from various interest groups. Because of the importance of these deviations from revenue and expenditure estimates, Governors generally like to be the first to know when revenues and expenditures during a current fiscal year are differing significantly from estimated levels. Some Governors simply rely upon their budget staff to inform them when major deviations begin to appear. Others have monthly reports on spending and revenues in relation to estimates so that they can spot trends.

Sometime in the course of a Governor's term, he is likely to face a situation in which significant reductions in spending are necessary. If the fiscal planning procedures recommended in this chapter are followed, it should be possible to avoid such situations during a current fiscal year—that is, instead of talking about cutting into spending of funds already appropriated, the Governor will be working to pare the budget request for the next year. This is much better than trying to cut within the context of an already enacted budget.

However, recession-induced failures in revenues, Proposition 13s and their equivalents, and a general desire to hold down spending when they first take office often cause Governors to look for ways to cut current-year spending. The most popular approaches include hiring freezes, equipment purchase freezes, and other across-the-board measures. These actions are generally dramatic in the eyes of the public and do save money, though at considerable expense in terms of the orderly operation of state government. In the long run, a preferable approach is to estimate the amounts that each cabinet officer should save, but give them some flexibility on how the savings should be made. This opens more possibilities (e.g., layoffs) that may be appropriate in particular departments.

To avoid concentrating cuts in agencies under the direct control of the Governor, Governors have (with mixed success) tried to lead independent agencies (e.g., state education agencies) to accept cuts comparable to those the Governor's agencies have been asked to make.

FISCAL IMPACT STATEMENTS

It is obvious that one should not adopt a course of action without knowing its major consequences. This practical principle is often violated by Governors and legislative bodies alike in making decisions with fiscal implications for state and local governments. Within the executive branch, this problem can often be cured by involving the budget agency in all decisions with fiscal implications, although the state budget agency will not normally focus on the local costs of state decisions, as distinct from the state government costs.

To deal with the comparable problem in the legislative process, some states have developed a "fiscal note" procedure, requiring a document to be prepared showing the fiscal consequences (for state and sometimes local governments) of legislation before the legislature votes on it. In many instances, the Governor's budget staff is responsible for the preparation of the fiscal notes or for review of the agencies' methods in preparing them. A Governor concerned about protecting the state's budgetary posture may find that requiring fiscal notes for bills that have some chance of passing can reduce the number of difficult or veto decisions that reach his desk later.

CHAPTER TWELVE

Approaches to Legislation

I cannot stress too strongly the importance of the Governor asserting leadership and control over the flow of proposals from his branch to the legislature.

— *a former Governor's legislative assistant*

SUMMARY

A new Governor's relationships with the legislature will have a far-reaching effect on the success of his administration. Not only will he need legislation to carry out many of his goals and appropriated funds to operate the state government, but his overall performance as Governor will be judged by many people on the basis of how successful he is with his legislative program.

While the Governor presents an annual legislative program in nearly all states, there are wide differences in how formally the program is presented. The new Governor's legislative approach is traditionally set out in his first three major speeches to the legislature, with the inaugural address outlining major themes and the state-of-the-state and budget messages presenting the details. The timing of these speeches will have a strong impact on decision-making activity during the transition period.

The process of developing the legislative program is begun in most states by reviewing proposals submitted by the agencies and combining them with key proposals developed by the Governor and his central staff. The Governor and his legislative assistant will want to specify guidelines for agency submissions and ensure that they are available well in advance of the legislative session, e.g., in September for a session beginning in January. Substantial review time provides other agencies with the opportunity to comment, as well as allowing for integration of the legislative program with the budget.

In about three-fourths of the states, the Governor's priority legislative program is distinguished in some fashion from the general category of bills which executive branch agencies would like to see enacted. The administration in about two-thirds of the states normally submits draft bills to implement each part of the Governor's legislative program. Sometimes these bills are submitted formally by the legislative leadership. In other cases, they are introduced on behalf of the administration by a cooperating legislator or "on request" by committee chairmen who may or may not endorse them.

After the program is submitted, ground rules on who should testify on behalf of administration bills must be developed and implemented. Agency directors normally handle most of this burden. In most states, the Governor will not testify, or will do so only in extraordinary circumstances. Immediate subordinates to the Governor—such as the legislative assistant, executive assistant or legal counsel—often testify on behalf of major bills.

Early in the transition, the new Governor will want to focus on a number of issues concerning relations with the legislature, such as:

• How announcements of actions affecting a legislator's district should be handled;

• What the role of the legislative leadership will be in formulating the Governor's programs;

• How legislators will be involved in bill signing and the attendant press coverage;

• How vetoes and forecasts of vetoes will be handled; and

• What ground rules will be set for special requests by legislators on behalf of constituents.

In all states but one, the Governor has the authority to veto legislation. Because the veto power is a major source of the Governor's influence in legislative matters, Governors are careful in the way in which they use it:

• All Governors use vetoes to express their views on constitutional issues;

• Many use the threat of a veto to signal their views on significant legislation; and

• Only a few will veto a bill if the legislature is certain to override the veto. Most will work instead toward a compromise with the legislative leadership.

Within a few months, the Governor will need to consider carefully his role in legislative elections, including primary elections in his own party. Many former Governors report that they became involved in party primaries, but a significant minority stayed out of primary fights. Another question to be considered is whether the Governor will attempt to exert an influence on the selection of his party's leaders in the legislature. Many Governors do, but others avoid any involvement in leadership selection.

Approaches to Legislation

The Governor-elect will find that his legislative relations problems begin the day after the election. Individual legislators will begin to lobby him and his staff on behalf of particular proposed appointees, bills and appropriations. From that day forward, legislative relations will be a vital part of the Governor's job.

The legislature is the key to the Governor's success in many areas. Correctly or incorrectly, the press corps and the public will judge the success of the Governor in part by how well he seems to get along with the legislature and whether he can get his programs enacted. Many of the things the Governor will want to accomplish in office will require legislation, and the continued operation of state government depends, of course, upon appropriations from the legislature.

The first legislative program is somewhat like the first budget. In both cases, the new Governor can, with the exception of some campaign promises, avoid trying to put together a major legislative program until the second year in office. Or he can move quickly to assert leadership through sponsorship of legislation. As crucial as legislative relations are, some Governors find that they do not get their legislative procedures fully implemented until the second year in office.

THREE MAJOR SPEECHES

The new Governor's approach to what he wants the legislature to accomplish is spelled out traditionally in three major speeches. The pace of decision making during the transition period is keyed in part by the timing of these speeches.

The Inaugural

The inaugural address is the first opportunity for the Governor to speak as Governor. For this reason, interest in the address focuses upon changes that may occur between the themes and rhetoric of the campaign and the Governor's position now that he is in office. Therefore, many inaugural addresses repeat campaign themes. By its nature, the inaugural is also something of an inspirational message for the administration team.

Specific financial and legislative proposals are normally not presented in the inaugural address. Many of those proposals simply cannot be finished by inauguration time, and many are customarily held for announcement in the state-of-the-state and budget messages.

Inauguration does provide an ideal time for announcing policies and procedures that go into effect immediately upon the new administration's assumption of governmental responsibility, such as new standards of ethics.

The State of the State

In practically all states, by law or tradition, the Governor addresses the first session of the legislature after he is elected to report on "the state of the state." In a few states, a reelected—or outgoing—Governor addresses the newly seated legislature to list the past term's accomplishments.

This speech is frequently used to convey the substance of the Governor's legislative proposals, ranging from the general to the very specific. Governors in some states combine this speech with budget proposals, but usually they are presented in a separate message.

A fairly standard approach to the state-of-the-state message is to cite some condition or problem of the state or its citizens—loss of confidence in government, economic underdevelopment, pollution, urban problems—to provide details of that condition, and follow with recommended legislative actions. In several states, notably Kansas, Michigan and Georgia, the state-of-the-state message is accompanied by an extensive set of goal statements for state government.

The Budget Message

The budget message is traditionally a presentation of the highlights of the Governor's budget recommendations. In some states, a complete budget message is printed and distributed along with the budget documents. This approach permits some flexibility in the message that is actually delivered, relieving the Governor of the need to cover all the points contained in the printed message.

The budget message normally contains a review of the financial condition of the state, any proposals for tax reductions or increases, and highlights of the expenditures being recommended. The budget is itself a request for appropriations legislation. In addition to requesting the enactment of his budget, the Governor may use the budget message to request legislation closely related to the budget, such as an employee pay plan or revisions in local aid formulas.

DEVELOPING THE LEGISLATIVE PROGRAM

Another of the early questions a new Governor faces is whether to have a formally identified "Governor's Legislative Program." Such a program has the advantage of putting the Governor in a position of leadership in the legislative session; he gets the credit (and blame) for the substance of legislation. Presumably, the legislation is sound and the Governor's support increases the chance that it will be enacted. If there are disadvantages, they are that it gives critics a ready target. And, in the event of a hostile legislature, having had his legislative proposals rejected can be damaging politically.

Officials in more than 90 percent of the states responding to a 1976 National Governors' Association survey reported that they have an identifiable Governor's legislative program. (See appendix 17.)

In about three-fourths of the states, the Governor's legislative package is distinguished from the total executive branch legislative program in some fashion. The Governor's program includes only bills in which he is taking a personal interest and to which he is willing to commit a certain amount of his prestige and political capital. The remainder of the executive branch program consists of bills which the agencies desire to see enacted for such purposes as improving administration of programs, authorizing new programs or activities that are not included in the Governor's package, or complying with new federal requirements.

The administration submits draft bills to implement each part of its legislative program in about two-thirds of the states. Sometimes these bills are submitted formally to the leadership. In other cases, they are introduced "by request" by a legislator, such as a committee chairman, who may or may not endorse the legislation. In still other cases, draft bills are simply provided to friendly legislators for introduction.

The choice of legislative sponsorship is particularly important in moving appropriations bills and key bills in a Governor's legislative program. Choosing key committee chairmen as sponsors and working with them before the administration's legislation is actually submitted can save hours of difficult lobbying later on.

In a number of cases, the Governor's legislative program includes bills that have previously been before the legislature. The Governor can endorse a particular concept as part of his legislative program in such cases, while using previously introduced legislation as the vehicle for the implementation of his recommendations. In other cases, persons working on a particular bill as part of the Governor's program may cooperate with the legislative bill drafting service in developing legislation that will satisfy the needs of both the Governor and the legislators interested in the same type of legislation.

When the Governor and his staff have been in office for some time, the development of a legislative program tends to be much easier. The program for a given year will consist of those bills that were supported in prior years but did not pass, new legislative initiatives arising from problems that have developed during the past year, a few of the many bills that will be proposed by state agencies, and possibly bills that reflect a new theme being pursued by the Governor. For a new Governor, with only a short time in which to act, preparing a legislative program can be more difficult, particularly because his new agency directors may not have had time to consider what legislation their agencies may require.

In addition to agency recommendations, a new Governor developing his first legislative program may draw upon suggestions from the following sources:

- The leadership of the Governor's party in the legislature;
- Campaign statements and position papers;
- Various interest groups; and
- Legislation booklets published by such bodies as the Advisory Commission on Intergovernmental Relations, Council of State Governments, National Conference of Commissioners on Uniform State Laws, and some federal agencies.

Most Governors have adopted a system for reviewing agency legislative proposals. These review processes help to identify bills for the Governor's program. They also are designed to ensure that no agency requests legislation that conflicts with the Governor's priorities or his budget and legislative program, that the objections of one agency to the legislative proposals of another are heard and considered, and that reasonably well-drafted bills and explanatory notes are available prior to the introduction of the legislation. The importance of such a review system was stressed by the former Governor's aide whose quotation begins this chapter. He went on to say that preliminary review:

> (a) reduces the time legislatures have to spend resolving executive agency differences because they can be resolved before bills are introduced; (b) assures consistency with the Governor's legislative and administrative objectives; (c) establishes at the very outset the Governor's leadership in his own administration; and (d) reduces the number of vetoes that may be necessary to stop a bad piece of legislation.

Another former aide observed:

> The Governor and his staff should keep a look out for "housekeeping bills" that come up from the departments. There are two dangers: one, that it ends up providing too many bills for the administration floor leaders to handle and, two, many Governors have suffered from a "little old housekeeping bill" that had some bombshell provision that did not become apparent until it hit the legislative floor.

As conducted by most states, the legislative program review begins with the central staff (budget agency or Governor's legislative assistant) sending each agency a schedule for submission of legislative recommendations, along with procedural requirements such as the submission of draft bills and explanatory comments. After the first year in office, there is considerable advantage in having the submissions well in advance of the legislative session (e.g., in September for a session in January). Agencies generally know what form they want their legislative programs to take by the fall before the session. Substantial review time provides other agencies the opportunity to comment, as well as permitting integration of the legislative program with the budget.

Simplified procedures are called for in cases where a gubernatorial policy decision is clearly necessary. For example, decisions on whether to have a land-use planning bill or whether to initiate state regulation of auto repair can be made before the complex process of drafting such legislation is begun.

An example of one state's procedures for legislative issue development and analysis and coordination of state agencies' legislative activities is shown in appendix 18.

PRESENTING THE LEGISLATIVE PROGRAM

As noted earlier, much of the Governor's legislative program is presented in the state-of-the-state message and, to a lesser degree, in the budget message. Some Governors also use special messages to the legislature as a device for recommending legislation and for emphasizing particular problems. In the fall of 1976, about half the Governors reported that they had submitted at least one special message to the last regular session of their legislature. Governors in some states submit special messages in writing and do not appear before the legislature, while others deliver all such messages in person. (See appendix 17.)

Agency directors normally serve as the primary defenders of the Governor's program at legislative committee hearings. However, certain bills, such as those dealing with ethics, election laws and freedom of information, may not fall within the jurisdiction of state agencies reporting to the Governor. In such cases, the responsibility for testimony may be assigned to an agency director, a central staff member such as the planning or budget director, or a member of the Governor's staff.

The question of when, if ever, a Governor and members of his immediate staff should testify is of considerable concern in many administrations. At the federal level, the tradition is that the President may not be called to testify by Congress. Furthermore, some authorities believe that the President should not be permitted to use the hearings as a forum even if he so desires. At the federal level, staff members who head certain major offices which are part of the Executive Office of the President (such as the Chairman of the Council of Economic Advisers and the Director of the Office of Management and Budget) are expected to testify whenever they are called by a committee and to seek the opportunity to testify from time to time. However, the immediate staff of the President has normally not volunteered to testify and has generally refused strong invitations to testify except under the most unusual conditions.

In considering ground rules on who should testify, the Governor should take a consistent position. A Governor who sends his executive assistant as a witness for one bill will have no basis for denying his presence when it is requested by another committee.

The prevailing practice among states, according to the 1976 survey, is for the Governor to provide a staff member to testify upon request, but rarely to testify himself. (For details, see appendix 17.)

GETTING LEGISLATION PASSED

Governors generally seek to maintain close contact with members of the legislature. Most maintain "open door" policies for legislators; that is, the Governor will always see any legislator, and no major efforts are made to divert them to staff members. Only one state responding to the 1976 survey indicated that there are some circumstances where individual legislators are not able to see the Governor even if they insist on it. The former Governors responding to the survey all agreed with the suggestion that the new Governor should maintain an open-door policy for legislators.

However, as a practical matter, the Governor's schedule will lead many legislators to deal directly with the liaison staff or the executive assistant, especially on days when the legislature is in session. Legislators are sufficiently familiar with the workings of state government to recognize that they are better off discussing some subjects with the staff rather than the Governor.

More than two-thirds of the states have traditional formats for meetings between the Governor and legislators. The most common of these are dinners at the Governor's mansion for legislators, a reception at the mansion at the time the legislative session opens, breakfast meetings with the legislative leadership, weekly luncheons or office meetings with the leadership of the Governor's party during the legislative session, and social gatherings near the end of the session.

Early Decisions

Early in the first term, the new Governor's actions in legislative relations will probably set a precedent for the remainder of his term. The key questions on which he will need to focus include:

- Announcements of actions affecting particular parts of the state and the role, if any, of legislators from the affected areas. If the announcement of local projects is to be shared with legislators (who generally find the practice a useful way of getting local publicity), the Governor must decide whether that privilege is to be extended only to legislators from the Governor's political party, and if so, whether all members of the party have the privilege or only those with a record of supporting the Governor's programs in the legislature.

- Procedures for signing bills. Will formal mechanisms for bill signing be established with press coverage and participation by legislators? If so, to what extent will this activity be bipartisan?

- Legislative relations. What ground rules will be set for handling special requests by legislators on behalf of constitutents for things like special tours of the Governor's mansion and pictures of the Governor?

- The role of legislators in formulating the Governor's legislative program. Will the Governor's legislative assistant and/or department heads be encouraged to consult with legislative leaders in the formulation of a program and other decisions, or will consultations of this type be limited to discussions approved by the Governor after he has reached tentative decisions?

State traditions vary on the extent to which legislators are consulted before the introduction of a legislative program and/or budget. One former Governor's aide has commented:

> I would stress the importance of attempting to involve legislative leaders in the legislative program. This is a sore spot with some legislators who want to know early in the game something about the program. But most important is to make sure that they are alerted or given a briefing on the program and budget the day or night before public announcement. It is even courteous to invite legislative leaders of the opposite party to have a briefing before public announcement of the budget or particular programs.

The Veto Power

In all states but North Carolina, the passage of a bill by the legislature is followed by a period during which the Governor decides whether to sign or veto it, or in some states whether to exercise such options as the amendatory veto, item veto or item-reduction power.

One sensitive question is whether the Governor should commit himself in advance to sign or veto a particular measure. The question often arises in a press conference when a reporter asks something like: "Governor, you have indicated that the bill has some features to which you object strongly. Does that mean it will be vetoed if it reaches your desk in its present form?" In answering that question, the Governor must weigh the value of putting public pressure on the legislature against the risk of alienating some legislators who resent what they see as public interference in their process.

Another problem with announcing an intention to veto in advance is that it may increase the probability of legislators voting for the bill. Such a vote on a popular but questionable measure can give a legislator the best of both worlds—a "yes" vote on the measure and, assuming the veto is sustained, avoidance of enactment.

There is little agreement among the Governors on exactly when the veto power should be used, beyond agreement that it should be used on legislation that the Governor believes is unconstitutional.

The most aggressive use of the veto—one used by few Governors—would occur if the Governor were to see his role as fundamentally that of a legislator who had the power to use the veto as a kind of super-no vote, vetoing all bills he would oppose if he were in the legislature.

Under a somewhat less aggressive approach, a Governor would follow the presumption that all bills he would oppose if he were a legislator should be vetoed, but he would not veto some of them because of the possible political consequences. Legislative assistants responding to the survey were about evenly divided as to whether their Governors would follow that policy.

A third and more restrained view, which was supported by more than three-fourths of the legislative assistants who responded, holds that once a bill has passed both houses, the Governor should sign it unless he has very strong objections to it. Bills with technical errors are likely to be an exception, of course. Vetoes of such bills are sometimes actually requested by their sponsors so they can be passed again in proper form.

The narrowest view that can be taken of the veto power is that it should be used solely on grounds of constitutionality or of balancing the budget, without the Governor's injecting any views, no matter how strongly held, about the merits of the legislation. Governors reject this narrow concept of their power, according to the survey.

Another frequent problem for some Governors—but not all, since overriding a Governor's veto is very unusual in some states—is what to do when they oppose a bill, but a veto would be politically unpopular and would not kill the legislation because it would be passed over the veto. Responses to the survey indicated that nine out of 10 Governors either definitely or probably would veto the bill anyway.

Once a bill has been presented to the Governor for signature or veto, some procedure is required to provide advice to the Governor for his decision. In some states, this procedure is quite formal, involving a short note from the staff member who runs the procedure (normally the legislative assistant or legal counsel) to all potentially affected agencies soliciting their recommendations. These views are combined with the views of affected interest groups (which normally do not have to be solicited), an analysis of the bill, and advice from members of the Governor's staff, as well as the bill itself, into a bill file which goes to the Governor. In other states, the procedure is much less formal, although the substance is similar. For example, about one-third of the states make the agencies responsible for identifying legislation that has been passed and initiating comment. About the same number of states do not require agency responses, but assume that if an agency does not comment, it does not object to the bill. Only two states reported no formalized procedures for dealing with enrolled bills.

When a tentative decision is made on signing or vetoing legislation, almost all Governors make it a point to notify any agency directors whose recommendations are different from the tentative decision. Procedures vary from state to state and from bill to bill within a state, but the clearly prevailing process is to give the agency director the opportunity to make his case to the Governor if he has not already done so in person. A few Governors may use public hearings in this situation.

All but one of the responding legislative assistants indicated that they notify the affected legislators of a tentative decision to veto a bill. This notification is considered a courtesy to the legislators involved and can also uncover new arguments for signing the legislation.

Results of the 1976 NGA survey on the Governor and the veto are tabulated in appendix 17.

It should be emphasized that constitutional (and occasionally statutory) provisions set rigorous deadlines and procedures for vetoes. Failure to meet these requirements has led in several states to lengthy litigation and the nullification of vetoes. The new Governor's process for handling veto problems should take these constraints into account.

THE LEGISLATIVE APPROPRIATIONS PROCESS

The appropriations bill or bills which encompass the Governor's budget recommendations, as modified by the legislature, present a special problem for the legislative aide. First, the appropriations process typically occurs piecemeal, and any given action by an appropriations subcommittee may produce a "ripple" effect by requiring modifications in order to balance the budget. The budget agency is generally assigned to monitor this sort of thing and keep the Governor and legislative advisor informed so that appropriate offsetting actions may be taken.

Second, the tax program must be matched to the appropriations process, a balancing act that often leads to major stalemates between administration and legislature. This also requires continual involvement of the budget staff in the legislative process.

Finally, the appropriations process provides many opportunities for legislative "log rolling" which in turn presents the Governor with a number of decisions about item vetoes of legislators' pet projects.

These factors, among others, combine to make the appropriations bill or bills a major part of the legislative aide's work load and should be planned for accordingly.

SPECIAL SESSIONS

It is common for the Governor to have the power to call special sessions of the state legislature. In some cases, the session is confined narrowly to the subject of the Governor's call; in others, more flexibility exists. The Governor's problem is to determine when to call a special session and to what degree to limit the subject matter covered by the call.

One point of view is that legislative sessions represent a hazard to the Governor and the people of a state and that anything the Governor can do to avoid them makes a major contribution to the public good. On the other hand, the Governor may wish to use the vehicle of a special session to force the legislature to deal with one or more issues that might have been deliberately avoided or accidentally lost in a regular session. In addition, situations do arise in which legislative action is truly needed before the next regular session is scheduled.

While no general advice can be provided on the calling of special sessions, experience in many states indicates that when decisions on special sessions are made on the basis of "pushing the legislature around or embarrassing its members," the decisions frequently backfire. In general, reaching agreement with the legislative leadership on the need for a special session and the topics to be included can protect all parties concerned.

THE GOVERNOR AND LEGISLATIVE ELECTIONS

The nature and extent of a Governor's involvement in elections to the state legislature and in the selection of legislative leadership has been a politically sensitive question for many Governors.

Primaries in the Governor's Party

It can be argued that the Governor must be active in contested primaries within his own party in order to make sure that the party fields strong candidates, to support his own faction or wing of the party, to unseat legislators who wear his party's label but do not support his programs, and to fulfill the role of party leader. On the other hand, it can be argued that the Governor should never be active in his party's legislative primaries because his involvement would interfere with the right of local party members to choose their district's candidates, because such action is not conducive to party unity under the Governor's leadership, and because the person he supports may lose and he may, therefore, be confronted with legislators of his own party against whom he campaigned.

A majority of legislative assistants responding to the 1976 survey on this point indicated that their Governors did become involved in party primaries for legislative seats in selected cases. However, about one-fourth said their Governors took a hands-off view toward party primaries.

General Elections

While a case can be made against participating in primary elections, the same considerations do not necessarily apply to the Governor's involvement in general elections. Few, if any, Governors would want to be in the position of not having lifted a finger for a candidate of their party in a legislative election.

The choice which a Governor faces is how deeply to become involved. The Governor may want to hold his involvement to a minimum, thereby reducing the chances of alienating legislators of the opposite party, avoiding an image of being partisan and combative, and encouraging an image of being Governor of all the people. Or, he may cherish the idea of getting rid of certain legislators from the opposite party, obtaining or retaining control of the legislature by his party, and solidifying his influence with his party's members of the legislature by having them indebted to him for help in their campaigns.

The 1976 survey of Governors' legislative assistants suggests that the Governors were about equally divided between these opposing views of the proper approach:

- Some involvement by the Governor, such as endorsing candidates of his own party, is appropriate, but a major campaign effort is not.
- As the leader of his party, the Governor is obligated to campaign as much and as hard as his schedule will permit.

Governors are, of course, involved in legislative races in ways other than campaigning directly for individual candidates. Particularly in a year when legislative elections are being held but the Governor is not running, the Governor can be of assistance in raising money for candidates. He can also provide candidates with technical assistance from his staff and with help from his political supporters. When both the Governor and legislators are running, they can develop common campaign themes and endorse each other.

LEADERSHIP SELECTION

Governors obviously have considerable interest in who is selected to be the party's leaders in the legislature. In many states, Governors exert an influence on the leadership selection process, but the process is often so subtle that it is difficult to pinpoint. In other states or other circumstances, Governors avoid any involvement in leadership selection.

To examine different views on this issue, the NGA survey asked legislative assistants to indicate which of a group of statements "most closely resembles your Governor's *public* position on the selection of legislative leadership." The responses were as follows:

> The selection of leadership is strictly an internal matter of governance for the legislature. The Governor should play absolutely no role in the process. (25 states)

> Because the selection of legislative leaders in the Governor's own party will have an effect on management of the state, the Governor should be consulted, should feel free to express his opinions, and those opinions should be accorded some weight. (6 states)

> Leadership selection is critical to a successful administration. The Governor can and should play a very active role. (no states)

It is important to note that the answers above relate to public positions on leadership selection. As one experienced watcher of state politics commented after reading the results of this survey:

> I . . . find it very difficult to accept . . . that a Governor plays no role in the selection of legislative leaders. The Governor's ability to communicate, albeit on a very personal basis, with key legislators to make his preference and annoyances clear, cannot be avoided. It is probably safe to say that a Governor will make no public endorsement or comment on a struggle for legislative leadership. It is probably also safe to say that it is rare that a Governor will let someone else perform this function for him, even on a discreet basis. I think it is unlikely that the Governor actually remains neutral in most situations.

LEGAL ASPECTS OF LEGISLATIVE-EXECUTIVE RELATIONS

From the perspective of a single state, it is easy to overlook the possibility that individual struggles between the Governor and the legislature may raise broader legal questions that involve the interpretation of comparable provisions in the federal and various state constitutions. Governors and their legal and legislative advisors should be alert to the possible constitutional implications of situations that raise these types of issues:

- The ability of a legislative body or any committee or official thereof to make appointments to any body exercising executive functions;

- Membership by legislators on boards or in other positions that involve executive action;

- Legislative veto of administrative actions; and

- Delegation by the legislature of its power to act as a general body to any component (e.g., a committee) of the legislature.

These issues are explored in greater depth in the National Governors' Association publication, *Legal Advice for the Governor,* Governor's Office Series report no. 4 (Washington, D.C., November 1976).

CHAPTER THIRTEEN

State-Federal Relations

The central federal relations problem for states is the fact that when members of the congressional delegation say they represent a state, they mean the mix of constituencies, interests, issues and individuals which combined to elect them to office. Generally, they do not include the policy and operational concerns of the state government in the list of interests they represent. The differentiation between the state and the state government is not intentional; rather, it is a natural consequence of the members' national or local perspective.

— *a Governor's representative in Washington*

SUMMARY

The new Governor will face important state-federal issues in the transition period and early in his term because federal regulations and funds affect many elements of state government operations. Some of the state-federal activities that must be dealt with include:

• *Designation of responsibility for federal programs.* The Governor may designate which state agency is to have administrative and financial control of particular federal programs. These options should be analyzed in detail to determine the implications of designating one agency over another.

• *Approval of grant applications and state plans.* The Governor frequently must review or approve a federal grant application before the federal agency involved will authorize funds. In other programs, the Governor must approve the required state program plans before federal funds are released. The new Governor should be reluctant to approve plans presented by agencies at the last minute. He often will want his staff to explore ways to restructure the state's implementation of certain federal programs before approving a proposed plan.

• *Supporting or opposing federal legislation and regulations.* The Governor will receive numerous requests from the National Governors' Association, state agencies and other groups to take a position on federal legislation and regulations, and perhaps to testify at congressional hearings.

• *Compliance issues and audits.* Previous administrations will have committed the state to grant conditions in order to receive federal funds. The new Governor will frequently be confronted with contentions from federal agencies that the state is not in compliance or is using federal funds incorrectly. He should ask his staff to question these claims carefully because federal regulations may have been unclear or temporary. He also may be able to amend the prior administration's program plan to conform more closely to his own priorities.

A Governor has a variety of mechanisms and processes with which to address these and other state-federal issues:

• *The National Governors' Association* enables Governors to speak with a strong, collective voice in the development of national policy. Through the NGA, Governors work closely with the Administration and Congress on the resolution of crucial state-federal issues. The offices of NGA, individual states and associations of state officials are located in the Hall of the States near the U.S. Capitol.

• *Washington offices,* which are maintained by nearly 30 states, can provide a variety of services. They include analyzing key state-federal issues, monitoring the flow of federal dollars to the state, maintaining contact with members of Congress and Administration officials, and representing state officials at Washington meetings.

• *The state-federal relations staff* in the Governor's immediate office can complete staff work on the Governor's positions on national issues, establish liaison with the state's congressional delegation, and coordinate state agency positions on federal legislation or regulations. The state-federal relations staff can be located in the Governor's office, the planning or budget agency, or divided among several locations.

• *Other groupings of Governors* include regional Governors' associations, regional commissions, and organizations created through interstate compacts.

• *The state's congressional delegation* may have partisan differences with the Governor, but it shares with him a common objective to maximize federal support and resolve state-federal issues in a manner favorable to the state. Congressional offices have the proximity and resources to provide great assistance on state-federal issues.

The impact of the state's relations with the federal government on the success of a state administration and the importance of major national policy issues to the state's citizens argue for an active role for the Governor in state-federal relations.

State-Federal Relations

The new Governor will be impressed continually by the direct relationship between the accomplishments and activities of his administration and the federal influence on state government. Many program choices open to Governors are constrained by federal laws and regulations, and much of the money spent by states and their political subdivisions comes from the federal government.

During federal fiscal year 1978, federal outlays to state and local government amounted to almost $80.3 billion, or about $365 for every man, woman and child in the United States. This sum represents about one-fourth of total state and local government spending during the period. Although federal aid has not been growing faster than state and local revenues for the last few years, the period from 1950 to 1976 saw the share of total state and local spending paid for by the federal government jump from 10 percent to 25 percent.

These figures still understate the impact that federal assistance has on state spending patterns, however. Many programs that involve state as well as federal revenues are directed in significant ways by the federal government. Examples are such matching grant programs as Medicaid, public assistance and transportation. Federal requirements for state performance in such areas as equal employment opportunity, pollution control, and occupational health and safety also affect state operations and costs even when no federal grants are involved.

THE NEW GOVERNOR'S STATE-FEDERAL AGENDA

The first months in office will inevitably include resolution of various federal program issues or problems. The new Governor and his staff are confronted frequently with situations in which the mid-level staff in a line agency indicates that the Governor "must" take a certain action or be faced with some dire outcome such as the loss of federal funds in particular programs. Two general principles to keep in mind are: (1) a federal request for "state action" directed to a lower-level state line agency official is frequently posed differently than if it were directed to the Governor, and (2) federal recommendations and sanctions emanating from informal conversations often differ from formal written positions. Answers to the necessary preliminary questions will influence the Governor's response to these initial "crises."

The major types of state-federal issues likely to be confronted early in a new Governor's term are discussed in the following sections.

Designations for Federal Programs

The Governor in most cases has the authority to designate the state agency to administer a particular federal program and the agency to receive the primary use of federal funds under that program. These designations may include the placement of new federal assistance programs and requests from state agency heads that they assume or give up responsibility for certain programs. Such requests may be attempts to acquire control of contested programs before the new administration fully understands the issues involved. It is important that these designations be carefully examined to ascertain the range of options available and the likely implications of each.

The fundamental point to remember is that when the statute authorizing a particular grant program does not prescribe a particular state agency or organizational form for administration, the Governor—subject to whatever state legislation is involved—has considerable flexibility in making the assignments.

Grant Applications and State Plans

In a number of programs, the federal agency will not provide funds to a state agency until the grant application has been signed or reviewed by the Governor. In other programs, the Governor's approval is required on state program plans before assistance is allocated. Typically, such documents are completed at the last moment and require the Governor's immediate signature.

The first procedural step that a new Governor will want to consider is to remind all appointed agency heads to avoid placing him in situations in which he must either accept a grant application or state plan without changing a comma or be held responsible for cutting off the flow of federal aid to the state. Agency heads must relay this procedure to all program chiefs within their agencies. A process for early review of plans and applications may enable the Governor to utilize federal programs to meet his goals.

The Governor's flexibility is dependent on the program. A program such as public assistance offers little flexibility in processing plans and applications. But the Governor's impact can be substantial in setting priorities which have major policy impact. In the case of social services (Title XX) funds and the location of facilities for sewage treatment, for example, the new Governor will want to determine quickly the range of possible policy decisions.

The following questions illustrate the type of information that is important in the Governor's review of state plans and applications for federal assistance:

- Does the plan contemplate the use of all federal funds that are available to the state? If not, why not?
- Can the federal funds being applied for be substituted for state funds to operate existing programs rather than funding new program activity? If substitution could be made, but isn't recommended, why not?
- Were any of the projects or activities to be supported rejected for state funding by either the prior Governor or the legislature? If so, what are the political, legal and substantive consequences of moving ahead with federal funds?
- How does the application or plan reflect the kinds of changing priorities and emphases articulated in the campaign, as distinct from continuing the policies of the former Governor?
- How does the application or plan relate to other state programs and dollars in meeting administration goals and priorities?
- Have all the agencies that might have a position on the activities or be claimants for funds been consulted in the preparation of the document, and are there agencies that do not agree with the proposed allocation of resources?
- Have interest groups and local governments concerned with the activity been consulted in the preparation of the document? Do their views different from what the Governor is being asked to approve?

Federal Legislation and Regulations

Governors will be asked frequently to use their influence to support or oppose federal legislation and regulations. The requests will come from a variety of sources, including the National Governors' Association, regional Governors'associations and fellow Governors, state agency personnel, and individual citizens and interest groups. The Governor's ability to evaluate these requests depends on an understanding of the legislation or regulation and of the political consequences of alternative actions.

It is important to remember that taking no position at all is an option, and frequently an attractive one. For a variety of reasons, a Governor may have a position on major (and even minor) national issues and may want to articulate that policy, but in many cases he is not obliged to do so.

Compliance Issues and Audits

In accepting federal grants, prior administrations will have committed the state government to a number of grant conditions. These include across-the-board requirements such as equal employment opportunity, adherence to the Davis-Bacon Act (requiring payment of the prevailing wage level for workers on federally supported construction projects), and merit system standards. In addition, individual commitments will have been made to federal agencies in connection with specific grants. At any point in time, it is likely that the Governor will discover that some state agencies are "under the gun" from federal agencies for failing to comply completely with some of the cross-cutting requirements or, in the eyes of the federal officials involved, failing to keep the commitments made when the grant was approved. In addition, federal auditors may be making claims against the state based upon previous uses of federal program funds which they allege to be "incorrect."

There is no uniform prescription for dealing with these problems. It should be remembered that claims against state agencies for "improper actions" may not indicate serious management problems in the agencies. Federal regulations may have been misinterpreted or perhaps were only temporarily applicable. On the other hand, when a federal agency indicates that its counterpart state agency is not performing well, a new Governor may be able to use the information available from the federal officials—assuming that it is correct—and the expertise of his own staff to make improvements in the agency.

A Governor also may be able to change a state plan in midstream. For example, a Governor who is inaugurated in January does not have to decide whether to continue the prior administration's plan until the next plan year starts (say in October) but in most programs can seek to amend the plan.

In addition, the Governor can seek the assistance of members of the state's congressional delegation in responding to administrative or policy problems with federal agencies if the agencies are not responsive. However, going directly to the congressional delegation before administrative remedies have been reasonably well exhausted within federal agencies tends to build up resentments that can hurt later on. You may win on a specific case but have continuing difficulty in the future as the overruled federal agency proceeds to do everything "by the book."

STATE-FEDERAL MECHANISMS

There are a variety of staff agencies and processes that can be used by new Governors in coming to grips with federal program management and federal policy issues.

The National Governors' Association

The National Governors' Association devotes substantial attention to providing policy research and technical services for Governors. Its primary mission in Washington, D.C., is to address the problems and opportunities associated with state-federal relations. NGA produces a weekly newsletter and a variety of information and action reports on pending federal issues of importance to Governors. Through its committee and subcommittee structure, it provides Governors with the opportunity to be directly involved in the formulation of national policy in areas of their particular interest. At its semiannual meetings, NGA takes positions on a wide range of state-federal issues, pursuant to voting by the Governors themselves. The association's Executive Committee can adopt positions on issues and specific legislation not covered at the meetings.

Because its membership includes Governors of all the states and its internal processes are democratic, NGA deals most effectively with issues on which Governors agree or can hammer out agreement rather than with issues which divide the Governors along regional or political lines. NGA normally provides leadership on such issues as the level of funding for grant programs to state governments, the distribution of federal assistance among state and local governments, the strings attached to federal assistance, and federal laws and regulations that tend to increase the costs of doing business for states. As the Governors' policy instrument, NGA also works closely with the Administration and Congress to formulate and implement new national policy on welfare reform, community development, water management, disaster assistance, energy impact assistance, and many other key state-federal policy issues.

The new Governor will discover that by taking a major role in the NGA committee and subcommittee structure and representing NGA at congressional hearings and in meetings with top federal officials, he will have a substantial impact on the resolution of key state-federal issues and will perform a valuable service to the Governors collectively.

In addition, there are extensive resources which the new Governor may take advantage of in the Hall of the States, located near the U.S. Capitol in Washington. Developed by the National Governors' Association in 1976, the Hall of the States contains the offices of more than 50 individual states or associations of state officials. Its library, computer, printing and meeting facilities are available to all Governors.

The Washington Office

The Washington office represents the Governor—and in several cases, individual state agencies and/or the legislature—in the nation's capital. Nearly 30 states, as well as Puerto Rico, maintain offices in Washington, most of which are located in the Hall of the States. These offices vary considerably in size and mission. For some states, the Washington office is a relatively small operation, staffed by one, two or three persons and emphasizing grantsmanship for state agencies. Other states maintain relatively large staffs—up to 15 persons—that focus intensively on the legislative process, as well as liaison with the congressional delegation and specific home-state problems.

Depending partly on the size and capability of its staff, a state may direct its Washington office to perform any one or more of the following functions:

- Serving as a one-stop information office on state-federal issues, programs and regulations;
- Obtaining specific information on particular federal programs for the Governor and other state officials, preparing comprehensive analyses of federal policy issues and status reports on federal initiatives in both the legislative and executive branches, and briefing the Governor as appropriate on developments of state concern in Washington;
- Arranging appointments for state officials with federal officials;
- Serving as the state's representative at selected meetings in Washington;
- Preparing congressional testimony for the Governor or other state officials;
- Providing full-time liaison with the state's congressional delegation and supplying members and their staffs with information and state policy positions on issues;
- Providing official interpretations of state policy and responding to questions from members of the executive branch, as well as Congress;
- Monitoring the flow and flexibility of federal dollars to the state and its local governments;
- Participating in legislative strategy and policy-development meetings of the National Governors' Association;
- Participating in meetings of the Governor's senior staff;
- Serving as a "door opener" and catalyst for semiprivate interests that are negotiating with state and federal officials; and
- Acting as the general eyes and ears and troubleshooter for the state in Washington.

By virtue of their location, Washington offices have both handicaps and advantages in providing assistance to Governors on state-federal issues. Their Washington location makes it difficult for the staff members in these offices to be directly involved in the day-to-day administration of their state government in general and state-federal programs in particular. However, people in the Washington offices are usually in a stronger position to understand the nuances of actions by the Administration and Congress and to assess the state-federal implications of positions being urged by the Governor. Washington also is a much better location for working out compromises that are acceptable to a variety of states and other interests.

The State-Federal Relations Staff

Intergovernmental or state-federal relations staffs have been established in many states to meet the myriad state-federal responsibilities facing the Governor. Their duties frequently include:

- Maintaining liaison with the state's congressional delegation, particularly in states lacking a Washington office;
- Providing staff work to establish and disseminate the Governor's position on federal issues;
- Providing a point of coordination or control for agency personnel wishing to take a position on proposed federal legislation or regulations under Office of Management and Budget (OMB) circulars;
- Administering the state clearinghouse for the review of proposed federal projects and actions under OMB Circular A-95;
- Helping agencies, along with the Washington office, to decide whether to seek federal grants and performing a grantsmanship function;
- Reporting federal assistance received in, or by, the state;
- Staffing the Governor's preparation for meetings of the National Governors' Association and regional groupings of Governors;
- Providing staff work for the Governor and representing him on such organizations as regional commissions and boards of multistate entities; and
- Becoming involved in casework regarding state problems referred by members of the congressional delegation and federal problems requiring action.

In some states, the state-federal relations staff, or at least a part of it, is located in the immediate office of the Governor. In other states, state-federal functions will be found in the central planning or budgeting agency. Some states place part of the functions in a department of community affairs. The most common pattern, however, is to divide the state-federal responsibility among several offices.

The size and impact of the state-federal relations staff in a Governor's office is also influenced by the extent to which other staff aides exercise intergovernmental responsibilities. For example, a Governor's staff member specializing in energy and environmental issues may take a major role in dealing with federal as well as state policies in those fields.

When state-federal functions are divided between the Governor's immediate office and another staff agency within state government, the Governor's office usually handles those with the highest political sensitivity. These functions include taking positions on major federal issues, maintaining relations with the state's congressional delegation, and resolving interagency disputes over federal issues.

The more routine state-federal activities that involve heavy commitments of staff time are often located outside the Governor's office. They include the A-95 clearinghouse, A-85 regulation review, grantsmanship, state plan reviews and monitoring the flow of federal funds.

Arguments for placing state-federal functions in the Governor's immediate office include:

- The Governor's staff is in a better position to resolve disputes among agencies than a staff member from one of the agencies.

- Being on the Governor's staff increases the capacity of the state-federal relations personnel to command attention from federal and other state officials.

- The federal relations function is a key element of the Governor's overall leadership role and deserves high organizational status.

- In some states, the Governor views a move to national office as his most likely next political step and wants to devote special attention to handling national issues well.

Arguments against placing state-federal functions in the Governor's immediate office include:

- The Governor is actively trying, for political, budget or management reasons, to keep his immediate office small, and state-federal relations can readily be moved to an agency.

- The Governor's immediate office is generally not a good place to handle such routine functions as the A-95 clearinghouse.

- The Governor's span of control cannot be effective unless the number of functions in the immediate office is limited.

Governors frequently find both sets of arguments to be persuasive, as evidenced by the number of states where the responsibility for state-federal relations is divided between the Governor's own office and some other agency of state government.

Planning, Budget and Line Agencies

Even when few intergovernmental functions are lodged there, state planning agencies usually contribute substantially to the Governor's decision making in dealing with federal programs. The planning agency itself is generally supported to some degree by federal funds and is occasionally used as an "incubator" for new federal programs when they are first begun, as happened in some states with such programs as the Comprehensive Employment and Training Act, Law Enforcement Assistance, and Special Programs for the Aging. The planning agency also is generally involved with assisting agencies, through such techniques as population projections, in developing and reviewing their federal program plans. New Governors seeking second opinions on federal issues when they are not totally satisfied with the recommendations of a line agency will often call upon the state planning agency.

Like planning agencies, state budget agencies vary substantially in their size and approach to federal programs. Some budget agencies have intergovernmental relations staffs that work closely with federal funding issues in the budget process, and also perform a number of the intergovernmental functions listed above. Like the planning agency, the budget agency (where the two are not combined) is a potential source of second opinions for a new Governor. The budget agency is usually the best equipped staff agency to perform major analyses involving all agencies, such as the level and expenditure of federal funds in the state.

In addition, it should be noted that a number of state legislatures now appropriate the federal funds received or anticipated by the state. In some states, this development has led the state budget agency to establish mechanisms to track federal funds in order to assure better budget control and more complete budget submittals.

Most contacts between federal and state officials involve line agencies in such fields as health, social services and transportation. Many of these contacts are routine reporting, inspecting and verifying activities rather than policy-formulation activities.

Line agency officials in state government also make contact with their counterparts in other states through executive branch associations. These associations typically arrange meetings of state personnel, disseminate information about state and federal activities, and seek to influence federal legislation and regulations. If they adopt positions that are inconsistent with those of their Governors, they may undermine the Governors' efforts on state-federal issues. This problem has occurred on occasion in the past, but the National Governors' Association voted in 1975 to mandate consistency between the positions of NGA and the associations, as well as closer interaction.* The associations represent another forum and set of staff resources through which Governors, working closely with line agency officials, can influence national policy.

Key line agency officials can, in effect, be used as staff by the Governor in dealing with federal policy affecting their areas of interest. Depending on the competence of the personnel involved, a new Governor may choose to rely heavily upon agency directors, rather than his immediate staff, for assistance in dealing with federal issues.

Other Groupings of Governors

Governors have developed other groupings that provide alliances and staff support for a variety of federally related activities.

Governors are organized in ways that vary from region to region. In some cases these groupings are oriented to particular regional issues such as education or economic development, and in others they are used for multiple issues of interest. In addition, most Governors participate in regional commissions funded under Title V of the Public Works and Economic Development Act or in the Appalachian Regional Commission.

---

* See Kenneth C. Olson, *The Proliferation of State Executive Branch Associations* (Washington, D.C.: National Governors' Conference [now Association], August 1975).

Many Governors belong to organizations such as water development and port authorities that are created through interstate compacts.*

There also are associations of both Democratic and Republican Governors.

The Congressional Delegation

Regardless of political differences that may exist, the congressional delegation represents a major source of potential assistance to the Governor seeking to deal with state-federal issues. Both experience and logic suggest that members of the delegation have considerable interest in helping the Governor ensure that state-federal issues are resolved in ways favorable to the state. When a federal regulation is changed, when a grant program is amended to provide more money to the state, when a federal project is attracted to the state, the credit can inure to members of the delegation as well as to the Governor.

Members of the delegation also have a staff capacity to become deeply involved in broad state-federal issues, in addition to the problems of individual state agencies with their federal counterparts. This fact further emphasizes the need for the Governor's state-federal relations staff to establish effective working relationships with the delegation staff.

Early in the term, the new Governor and his staff should consider techniques for strengthening relations with the delegation. These efforts might include organizing breakfasts with the delegation when the Governor is in Washington or inviting the delegation to the capitol to meet with the Governor and state legislative leadership. Although political differences may complicate relations between the Governor and the delegation, there is a common desire to improve the state's standing, and congressional seniority is an important resource which new Governors should consider.

POWER POINTS IN STATE-FEDERAL RELATIONS

An important basis for the Governor's federal relations activities is his power of appointment and removal of key department heads. The Governor should exercise his authority to give clear guidance to agency heads regarding which federal policies to support, which to change, and how to use particular grant funds.

This approach is of little help to Governors dealing with state-federal problems in line agencies, such as state education agencies, which the Governor does not directly control. The Governor's primary mechanisms in these cases are the state budgeting process and federal rules that give the Governor a role in grant administration.

All state budgets include matching funds required to obtain federal

---

* Major regional and interstate organizations which offer opportunities for gubernatorial participation are described by Leonard U. Wilson in *State Strategies for Multistate Organizations* (Washington, D.C.: Council of State Planning Agencies, 1977).

funds in programs with matching requirements. The budget review process is an opportunity for the Governor to establish or modify agency plans for the utilization of federal funds. The allocation issues—how funds should be allocated among state agencies reporting to the Governor, other state agencies and elected officials, and local governments—are sometimes complex. They arise in such programs as traffic safety, law enforcement, manpower and social services.

While powers and procedures vary among states, Governors generally can authorize agencies to spend federal funds not anticipated when the budget was adopted by the legislature. They often also control the mechanisms used by state agencies to spend grant funds for establishment of positions, allotment/apportionment of funds, and lease of office space.

In the sign-off procedures described earlier, a number of federal agencies have made gubernatorial approval a condition for federal assistance. In addition, agencies reporting to the Governor can review proposed federal grants from state agencies and local governments through the A-95 process. Some states also have statutes requiring all line agencies to obtain the approval of the Governor or an agency responsible to him before applying for any federal grant.

LEVEL OF INVOLVEMENT

During the transition and first six months in office, a number of important subjects will clamor for the Governor's attention. Appointing the cabinet, preparing the state-of-the-state message and first legislative program, developing a budget or amending a prior one, and tackling administrative and policy changes are just a few of the major challenges.

The importance of state-federal relations issues in this period will depend in part on how difficult and time consuming these other challenges are. The pervasive influence of federal policies and programs on the states, however, means that the approach adopted to state-federal relations in the early months of the administration will directly affect the success or failure of the administration in its later stages. A persuasive argument can be made that the new Governor should immediately assign state-federal issues to a top-level transition staff member, quickly establish the mechanisms to obtain expert advice, and designate state-federal relations as an area of high priority for his administration.

If the patterns of existing Governors can be used as a guide, there is no single "correct" level of involvement by Governors in state-federal relations. Some Governors make it a practice not to become personally involved in state-federal relations except through activities of the National Governors' Association or in the case of a major dispute with a federal agency. Other Governors assume an active posture on state-federal issues and allocate a significant portion of their time to them.

There are several arguments for active involvement by the Governor in state-federal relations. Governors seeking to change state policies in energy production or consumption, environmental management, social services and other key policy areas often must deal with a major federal relations component. For example, when the federal government owns a substantial percentage of all land, as is the case in many western states, state land-use policies will be heavily affected by the federal government. Moreover, the Governor's involvement in state-federal issues can assist the state by attracting more federal funds and using them more effectively. An increase in federal dollars will free state dollars for other activities. Finally, some state-federal issues, such as amending programs to benefit a particular state, are popular issues within the state, and effective work on them will be well received.

Despite these advantages, active involvement in state-federal issues can detract from the time available to address state issues and to administer the state government. This is particularly true in the case of those issues which do not seem to have an immediate effect on state programs, such as antitrust legislation. In addition, some Governors may feel that the state's interests are adequately represented by the combined involvement of state agencies and the congressional delegation.

Regardless of the decisions made on the organization and staffing of state-federal relations and the personal involvement of the Governor in these matters, the issues involved will have a major impact on the success of the administration and will therefore require early and careful attention from a newly elected Governor and his staff.

CHAPTER FOURTEEN

Approaches to Reorganization

> An unresponsive bureaucracy and a state government structure reluctant to change are most frustrating to a Governor striving to implement his policies. Although resistant to accommodation, merger or abolition, governmental reorganization often is a prerequisite of effective public services.
>
> — *a former Governor*

SUMMARY

Once a Governor comes to grips with managing state government, reorganization is usually a high priority. A 1978 National Governors' Association survey found that more than one-third of the Governors favored major reorganization of their state governments.

Reorganizations in some states will require constitutional amendments and/or statutory changes. Many states have enacted reorganization procedures under which the Governor sends the legislature a reorganization plan which becomes law unless either house votes against it within a certain time period.

One approach to reorganization is the establishment of a public reorganization task force. Such task forces help build public support for reorganization but, in some instances, may not share all of the Governor's interests and priorities. A more cautious approach is for the Governor to work selectively with key individuals to develop reorganization options. Staff expertise on reorganization may be obtained from private consulting firms, the Governor's immediate office, planning and budget offices, and the National Governors' Association. Making sure that agency officials, legislators and affected groups have a chance to contribute will help the Governor assess the effects of reorganization options and will add to public support for any reorganization proposal.

Major reorganization actions most frequently considered to increase the Governor's executive authority and management capacity include: (1) expanding the Governor's appointment power; (2) reducing the number of statewide officials chosen by popular election; (3) eliminating fixed terms of office for cabinet officers; (4) ensuring that appointees serve at the pleasure of the Governor; and (5) eliminating situations where boards and commissions operate state agencies.

The Governor will generally have more difficulty in rearranging the functions of line agencies than of staff agencies. A cabinet of between 10 and 20 members facilitates gubernatorial management of line agencies. If states have a large number of agencies, they can be merged into larger departments, such as a multimodal transportation department encompassing many small agencies.

In considering reorganization of staff support agencies, new Governors should bear in mind that:

- Some shifting of staff responsibilities will probably be inevitable during the first year;
- After completing the first budget and legislative program, the new Governor will probably want to consider new policy-making processes for subsequent years;
- The disruptions in work and reporting relationships that result from reorganizing staff functions are more easily overcome when the administration is new; and
- Although the honeymoon period is of varying length, legislatures are generally more supportive of executive reorganization early in the term.

While the operating procedures of state government differ markedly, the location of staff support agencies will have a direct bearing on how policy is made. Combining budget and planning functions has become increasingly popular. Points to consider regarding this alternative include:

- Because the budget and planning staffs perform key functions for the Governor, a combination of the two maximizes the Governor's direct control over his administration;
- If they are relatively weak agencies, merger may strengthen them; and
- Conversely, if the Governor wants to emphasize an issue area not receiving attention in a combined budget and planning agency, he may want to separate it from the agency.

If state government reorganization is not practical, the Governor can consider other approaches, such as (1) designating "lead" agencies to ensure coordination of activities involving several agencies; (2) designating super secretaries, usually on his immediate staff, to supervise groups of agencies; (3) instructing his assistants for agency liaison to monitor interagency progress in achieving objectives; or (4) appointing subcabinets.

Approaches to Reorganization

During transition, the Governor-elect is in the difficult position of knowing that he will probably want to make some changes in the organization of state government, but not knowing yet what those changes will be. At the same time, he is recruiting to fill vacancies within the existing state organization chart. If he does not fill the vacancies, little will be accomplished in the departments.

One solution to this problem is for the candidates for Governor to start the reorganization process during the campaign by initiating the staff work and task forces required to put a reorganization package together. But, because reorganization is not the most pressing order of business in a campaign, this is rarely done.

THE REORGANIZATION DECISION

Once Governors are elected, however, reorganization is frequently an important priority for them. One-third of the Governors surveyed by the National Governors' Association in 1978 considered their state governments clearly in need of reorganization. Between 1974 and 1977, the survey showed, 23 states undertook substantial reorganizations. Results of an NGA survey of state reorganization procedures, along with reorganization activities since 1974, are available from NGA's Center for Policy Research.

However, most Governors find themselves early in the first term without specific ideas on governmental reorganization. A Governor in this situation who feels he is likely to want to make major organizational changes needs to be careful to advise new appointees of the possibilities of reorganizations affecting them.

Authority for Reorganization

Some state organizational patterns are prescribed in state constitutions, particularly the offices and functions of elected officials. Some state constitutions go further and prescribe departments or set limits on the total number of departments. Of course, where organizational patterns are set by the constitution, the normal process for constitutional amendment would have to be followed to change them.

Most state organizations are established by statutes. Reorganization normally means simply passing a bill that eliminates the legislation creating the old structure and enacts the new.

Some states and the federal government have adopted procedures that facilitate reorganization. In most of these cases, the Governor can send a reorganization plan to the legislature, and it becomes law within a stipulated period (usually 60 days) unless either house votes against it.

Governors contemplating reorganization in states where they do not have this power may wish to consider seeking to acquire it first.

Early Steps to Consider

New Governors seeking broad-based aid or support for reorganization generally may choose between two approaches.

The first is to appoint a citizens' commission or group of business leaders to explore the potential for reorganization and to make recommendations. This approach has the advantage of building consensus on the reorganization and the disadvantage of being beyond the Governor's control. It also tends to excite large groups of state government employees and special interest groups to become more concerned about organization as it applies to them than about the day-to-day business of state government.

The other approach is to have all work on reorganization proceed quietly until the Governor decides what he wants to do and begins the process of consultation with affected individuals and groups. Proceeding without publicity has the disadvantage of not involving many people who could be helpful in the process, but it can be less disruptive of the functioning of government.

A number of consulting firms claim expertise in this area, and some have demonstrated their skill in working with state government. Alternatively, reorganization staff work can be done in state planning and budgeting offices, or under the supervision of a Governor's staff member using a task force drawn from various state agencies. The National Governors' Association can also provide help in comparing reorganization alternatives in other states.

Choosing the approach to staff work on reorganization is a crucial decision the Governor must make when the process begins. In states undertaking reorganization projects, according to the NGA survey, the Governor's immediate office completed the staff work in seven; the state planning office in three; the budget office in three; and a combination of planning, budget and Governor's staff in five. Other sources of staff work mentioned included the department of administration, state legislative staff, and reorganization commissions.

Once the initial staff work is done, getting the comments of agency heads before announcements are made is essential to understanding details and predicting reaction.

A Caution on Reorganization

Reorganization is not an end in itself, nor is it an automatic cure for the problems of coordinating state programs. It may be true that, in a given state, vocational education programs are not well coordinated from high school to junior colleges, or that social services provided through the welfare system overlap and even conflict with those provided through the mental health system. Merger of functions does not necessarily solve the problem in either case, and it may just transfer the problem from the Governor's desk to the desk of a new super secretary.

While no panacea for all the ills of state government, reorganization efforts have been quite popular with Governors and legislatures over the past 20 years. Some Governors, including one who ran for President, have cited reorganization as one of their major accomplishments in office. office.

STRENGTHENING EXECUTIVE CONTROL

The Governor's control of state government clearly is affected by the number of appointments available to him. A state civil service system which limits the Governor's appointment power, together with requirements for election of various state officers (frequently producing officials not of the Governor's party), will limit severely the Governor's power to make policy and manage government.

The argument for separate election of other state officials is, in many cases, that it provides a kind of check on the power of the Governor. Among the arguments against separate election are that it:

- Creates a "long ballot," making it difficult for the voter to understand who the many candidates are and what they stand for;

- Prevents the Governor from having the control he needs to be accountable to the people for the operation of the executive branch of state government; and

- Discourages cooperation among the officers involved, in that they are often of opposite parties and not part of any team.

Any reorganization proposal involving the elimination of an elective office would require a constitutional amendment, which is why such proposals are often considered separately from reorganizations involving only statutory change. While removal of an elected official's position requires a constitutional amendment, changing the functions of such an official may require only a statute, unless the constitution prescribes those functions in great detail.

Giving the Governor greater authority to place persons of his own choosing in charge of major state activities will also strengthen his ability to manage the executive branch. This can be done in several ways, including:

- Eliminating fixed terms of office for appointees, so that they merely serve at the pleasure of the Governor;

- If fixed terms cannot be eliminated, reducing them so that the Governor can decide more often whether to renew appointments; and

- Strengthening the power of the Governor to remove persons from office. For example, in some cases the Governor can only remove for such causes as commission of a felony and malfeasance. If this is changed to permit the Governor to remove a person from office simply because he has not satisfactorily conducted that office, it will strengthen the Governor's authority considerably.

Removing state agencies from the control of boards or commissions would also enhance the Governor's executive power. Major departments in a number of states are guided by board or commission members whose terms are fixed and extend beyond the Governor's term of office. Although the powers of these boards vary from state to state, they exercise considerable control exclusive of the Governor. Boards and commissions, whether supervising a department or acting in an advisory capacity, often are a target of reorganization efforts.

The pattern in state reorganizations over the past 20 years has been to move in the direction of having major state functions (e.g., welfare and transportation) managed by a single individual rather than by a board, although many of the older boards still appear on organization charts as advisory bodies. In some cases, compromises have been made that retain the board or commission structure, but increase the power of the Governor by, for example, having the Governor rather than the board select the operating head of the department.

A common pattern among states is for functions involving education to be organized in a board or commission form, such as a board of education for elementary and secondary education and a board of regents for higher education. It is also common for regulatory bodies and professional licensing agencies to be headed by boards or commissions. In addition, federal legislation has encouraged the role of boards and commissions in certain programs such as manpower and support of the arts.

REORGANIZATION OF LINE AGENCIES

The Governor generally has more flexibility in assigning and reassigning staff functions among his immediate staff and the planning and budgeting agencies than he does in changing the functions of line departments. However, a number of methods have been devised to reorganize such major line functions as transportation, welfare and mental health.

Many observers believe that the number of cabinet members should not exceed the number that might reasonably be controlled and supervised by the Governor himself—a number variously estimated between 10 and 15. Most states have significantly more agencies, however. Moving to a smaller number of persons reporting to the Governor can be handled in one of two ways:

1. Completely merging agencies to form the new organization, or

2. Creating super secretaries who have the responsibility of supervising a group of agencies without merging the agencies themselves.

The first approach is implemented variously in different states but tends toward the following:

- A department of transportation, merging separate functions dealing with highways, aeronautics, mass transportation, transportation planning, and in some states, auto licensing, highway safety and regulation of rail and motor carriers.

- A department of social services, combining welfare and social service programs, vocational rehabilitation and programs for the aged, and which can include health and correctional programs if separate law enforcement and health departments are not desired.

- A department of health, combining mental health, public health and comprehensive health planning, and sometimes encompassing the Medicaid program. The alternative is to administer Medicaid with welfare.

- A natural resources-environment department, combining park management, fish and game, environmental protection, mineral regulation, and—sometimes—agriculture functions. A frequent variant is to organize the environmental protection component separately.

- A law enforcement agency, including the administration of the federal law enforcement assistance program and the administration of any state police and corrections functions.

- An umbrella business regulatory agency, covering regulation of financial institutions (savings and loans, banks, credit unions) and insurance, as well as licensing of professions.

- An umbrella support service agency, combining such functions as personnel, printing, data processing, building maintenance, space allocation, construction, accounting and sometimes tax collection.

Obviously, within the concept of a small number of large agencies, a variety of permutations and combinations of agencies are possible.

Where existing departments are not to be merged, but super secretaries are to be appointed, roughly the same allocation of functions is followed. In that case, the greatest problem is maintaining the power of the super secretaries, who have limited statutory authority as compared to department heads. Solving this problem is made easier if the super secretaries are appointed before the cabinet officers and, in turn, have a hand in appointing them.

In contemplating reorganization by consolidating existing departments, a new Governor may find it is important that the person who would likely become the head of the consolidated group be appointed to head one of the departments to be merged and that other appointees in that group be individuals who would be willing to facilitate reorganization, rather than fight it.

ORGANIZATIONAL OPTIONS FOR STAFF SUPPORT

In the first 100 days of an administration, the Governor will have little opportunity to determine organizational locations for staff functions. Instead, the problem will be one of finding adequate capacity, wherever it is, to meet the Governor's immediate need for staff work. Most Governors will have been in office for some time before they develop the outlines of a preferred organization of staff functions in state government, particularly when they want to initiate a thorough review of reorganization options.

However, if a new Governor uses the period between the end of the first 100 days and the end of the first year in office as the time to consider reorganization of staff as well as line functions of state government, there are a number of factors to be considered.

1. Reorganization generally involves a certain amount of disruption of activities as new reporting relationships are developed, offices are moved, and procedures are changed. From the perspective of a full term, the sooner these front-end costs are incurred, the more likely they are to be forgotten by the next election, and the longer the period will be during which the Governor can reap the benefits of the reorganized structure.

2. Although the magnitude and duration of the "honeymoon" period varies from situation to situation, legislative bodies generally give Governors more leeway in organizing their staff functions early in their term.

3. A certain amount of shifting of staff responsibilities is inevitable during the first year, whether reorganization is an objective of the new administration or not. Even though the personnel selected by the new administration are likely to have different skills and interests, the organizational patterns which they inherit will tend to reflect those of the prior administration.

4. The new Governor will likely be interested in different processes (e.g., new budget processes) for arriving at major policies. During the first 100 days, the staff support organization probably will fail in some respects to meet the Governor's particular needs.

The following discussion considers different approaches to organizing the staff functions of state government.

Alternative Central Staff Locations

One way to view different patterns of state organization for such staff functions as intergovernmental relations, personnel, planning and budgeting is in terms of the extent to which these functions are found in line agencies rather than in the immediate office of the Governor. As with many organizational matters, some of the distinctions become obscured in the real operating procedures of state governments. Nonetheless, observation of many state governments suggests that the differences in formal organization, which are discussed in the following sections, do make a difference in how policy is made.

"Executive Office of the Governor." In this model, intergovernmental relations, budgeting, planning and other activities that support the policy-making functions of the chief executive are all in agencies that do not report to the head of any of the cabinet departments. At the federal level, agencies that are organized in this fashion within the Executive Office of the President include the White House Office, the Domestic Policy Staff, the National Security Council, the Office of Management and Budget, and the Council of Economic Advisers.

In this form of organization, the staff functions are separated from support or housekeeping functions such as data processing and building maintenance. Personnel functions are often handled by separate departments which are either independent or grouped with other support functions. Some personnel policy capability (e.g., for labor negotiations and pay-level decisions) may be separated from day-to-day personnel responsibilities and lodged in the executive office.

Department of administration. Another common approach is for many central staff functions such as budgeting and, to a lesser extent, planning to be organized in a department which also houses all or a major part of the support functions. Under some common patterns, budgeting is housed with accounting in a department of finance, or budgeting and accounting (and sometimes planning as well) are housed in a department of administration.

This form of organization is designed to put more power in the hands of a single person—the director of administration—than the models that have budget and/or planning functions as separate parts of the executive office of the Governor. The director of administration is given substantial control over such things as office space and computer utilization (and sometimes personnel), while also having the staff capability to advise the Governor and his staff on policy matters.

Other departments. Still another approach is to use existing line agencies for certain staff functions that affect many different departments.

The most common arrangements of this type involve one or more of the following assignments:

- Location of state-local liaison responsibilities in a department of local or community affairs;
- Administration of state support of substate district and local planning by a department of local or community affairs;
- Placing responsibility for state planning in a department of local affairs, with the economic development function either included or located in a department of commerce, or placing state planning within a department that has both local affairs and commerce functions; and
- Having all staff work on personnel matters done by a department of personnel.

Budget functions, which clearly involve the review of competing demands for various functions, are not normally found in line departments other than a department of finance or administration.

Advantages and disadvantages of various locations. The primary argument against putting a staff function such as planning or budgeting into an operating department is that the department will find itself attempting to coordinate the activities of organizationally equal departments. For example, having the planning agency in a department of economic development or community affairs would give the director of that department responsibility for dealing with the planning processes of the department of highways or transportation. Some experts see problems with this form of horizontal coordination. They argue that the director of one department does not have the stature within the organization to perform this coordinating role with other departments.

A second problem associated with housing central staff in line departments is the potential difficulties it creates for the central staff in dealing with the remainder of the department. For example, while a central planning staff could develop a general state planning process, it might have difficulty in imposing that process on activities that are carried out in various functional areas in the same department, not to mention the difficulties associated with imposing the process on other departments. Obviously, the approach which the head of the department takes toward having a central staff function located in his agency will have a great deal to do with whether or not it creates a problem.

A third argument against placing central staff functions in particular line departments is the difficulty in coordinating those functions with others (such as budgeting) that are found in administrative service departments or in the Governor's office.

A somewhat different set of arguments applies when central staff functions are located with support functions in a department of administration or equivalent. This approach does not generally present the problem of one cabinet officer trying to coordinate the activities of another. The department head's authority over administrative services, together with the cross-cutting nature of staff activities such as budgeting, intergovernmental relations or planning, generally results in little difficulty in getting other department heads to cooperate.

Location of staff functions in an administrative department does present the other two problems associated with location in line agencies—namely, difficulties in reviewing one's own department (e.g., as both a budget submitter and reviewer) and possible coordination difficulties, as in circumstances where the budget function is in a department of administration but intergovernmental and planning responsibilities are elsewhere.

Concentration of staff responsibilities in planning and/or budget agencies whose directors report as staff directly to the Governor is very common. The primary advantage of this pattern is its clear distinction between staff and line functions. Problems associated with other central staff arrangements, such as the suspicion of favoring one department over another and the difficulty of reviewing major budgets and functional plans emanating from within their own agency, are generally absent.

Before considering the impact of individual personalities on organizational choice, the following generalizations about the location of central staff functions may provide some general guidance:

1. Organizing central staff functions in line departments such as economic development or community affairs is not generally the most useful alternative to the Governor.

2. Concentrating central staff functions under the control of a director of administration or finance will tend to create a stronger role for a single department head than will, for example, having separate directors of budget, planning and administration.

Whether this result is desirable or not depends upon how involved the Governor wants to be in the day-to-day administration of state government. A Governor who prefers to devote a considerable percentage of his time to such subjects as budgeting and interagency coordination may not be comfortable with having this much responsibility in a single individual outside of his immediate staff. On the other hand, a Governor whose interests lie in broad policy questions may see considerable merit in an organizational arrangement designed to ensure that day-to-day management will be handled by someone other than himself.

3. Having capability for central staff functions separated from both line departments and support service activities (such as a department of administration) will provide benefits available from no other arrangement. These benefits will include: (a) independent budget review of all line and support agencies, rather than having some of them, in effect, review themselves; (b) increased capability for competing ideas to arrive in the Governor's office from multiple sources (which some Governors will view as a problem, not a solution); and (c) somewhat greater flexibility in the use of staff to respond to shifts in the Governor's own interests.

The Impact of Personnel

In many states and in many circumstances, including those illustrated below, the preferences, strengths and capabilities of individuals in key positions have caused the actual distribution of responsibility and power to differ from that shown on organizational charts without any changes in formal powers.

1. Where a staff function, such as planning, is lodged in an existing line department headed by an individual whom the Governor considers to be a close advisor, getting cooperation from other departments becomes nearly as easy for the department as for an independent budget and/or planning agency.

2. Where a staff agency head (such as a budget and/or planning director) is particularly close to the Governor and is a strong personality relative to the heads of separately organized support services such as accounting, building maintenance and data processing, the staff agency head may become the de facto director of administration with major control over the operation of the support functions.

3. Where there is a particularly strong person in the immediate office of the Governor who is interested in day-to-day management, many of those functions will shift to the Governor's office—supported by the staff of the planning and/or budget agencies.

4. Where a Governor has a department of administration with planning and/or budget functions, but wants to play more of a role in day-to-day administration than this form of organization implies, he frequently develops direct reporting relationships with the heads of budget and/or planning divisions.

While much can be said for attempting to define permanent state government organizational patterns, the availability of personnel for particular posts tends to influence both informal organization and decisions about formal organizational changes. No particular organizational pattern can be prescribed as "optimal." Selecting an organizational pattern is less a scientific quest for the right answer than a matter of finding the approach that works and staying with it.

COMBINED PLANNING AND BUDGETING AGENCIES

State governments are constantly reorganizing. Many of these reorganizations reflect trends in federal programs, state programs and underlying problems. In such cases, the tendency is for many states to be making similar changes at about the same time. Creating agencies to deal with environmental problems and putting highway departments into multimodal departments of transportation are examples of this type of reorganization. In other areas, such as organizational location of the planning and budget functions, no consistent pattern appears, although the functions are combined in more states now than was the case 10 years ago. Six alternative locations for the planning and budgeting functions, two of which combine them, are shown in appendix 16.

Consideration of the merits of combining planning and budgeting functions (or of taking apart those combinations that new Governors may find in existence in their states) is made more difficult by the many different patterns of activities found among state planning agencies. Some agencies consider their primary mission to be support for the policy making of the Governor and derive much of their work load on special assignments from him. Some, whether combined with budget agencies or not, are heavily involved in the budget process through capital budgeting, development of program effectiveness measures, impact or program analysis, and actual preparation of budget review documents. Some are heavily into promoting economic development and/or urban policy, while others concentrate on land use and physical construction programs (e.g., highways and parks). Some tend to view planning of future state government activities as paramount, while others see in planning the potential for leading decisions of private enterprise and local government as well as state government. These priorities are found in varying combinations in individual states.

In addition, the efficacy of a combined planning and budgeting staff also depends upon the orientation of the budgeting staff and the desire and ability of the Governor to change that orientation. As noted earlier, some state budget staffs consider their functions to be primarily oriented to analysis of the cost implications of existing policies and day-to-day financial administration. Others consider themselves to be the primary support for all of the Governor's policy-management functions.

For a new Governor, the problem is further complicated by the fact that the budget and planning staffs may well be undergoing substantial changes in orientation already because of his own preferences and the leadership of the persons he has put in charge of those staffs.

There is no universally correct answer as to which organizational arrangements will best serve the purposes of a particular Governor, given the staff capabilities available in the planning and budget offices which he inherits.

In cases where the jurisdiction and interests of separate planning and budgeting offices overlap, there is still no obvious answer as to how to organize them. Some Governors place a premium on "tidy" organization and are concerned whenever they note overlapping jurisdiction. They would be likely to combine the competing offices. Other Governors fear that depending upon a few sources of advice will isolate them from information they need and are willing to pay some price in order to assure themselves of competing staff agencies offering different advice. Part of the appetite for such competing advice should depend upon whether it is available elsewhere, such as from members of the staff of the immediate office of the Governor.

Recognizing that the appropriate location of the planning and budgeting offices has been the subject of considerable controversy in most states, and almost any statement on the subject is likely to arouse disagreement somewhere, the following are probably reasonable generalizations for the consideration of a new Governor and his staff:

1. A decision on organizational location frequently is influenced by questions of political control. A few planning and/or budget functions will be found in state agencies that are not under the direct control of the Governor (e.g., independent elected officials and commissions with staggered terms). Because both functions basically provide staff support to the chief executive, new Governors tend to want to control them and to favor reorganizations that will produce this control.

2. Part of the organizational decision must depend upon the competing aspirations of the agencies now involved and their current capabilities, as well as the Governor's view of the divisions of labor that would result from change. For example, some budget staffs have little interest in budget preparation beyond the current and next fiscal year. In such a setting, a long-range planning effort by the planning staff might complement the activities of the budget staff without the need for merger of the two. Conversely, when the budget staff uses long-term projections for budgeting and management purposes and the planning staff wants to deal in the same types of projections, a stronger case for merger can be made.

3. When the Governor detects weaknesses in both planning and budgeting staffs that are, in effect, complementary, merger may be necessary. An example would be a budget staff that was not policy oriented enough and a planning staff that was not sufficiently down to earth.

4. Conversely, when a Governor seeks to emphasize a function that appears to have been submerged in a combined planning and budgeting staff, separation of the two may be appropriate. For example, a Governor with strong interests in "futures" projects and directions of state economic growth might feel uncomfortable with a combined planning and budget agency that was heavily oriented away from traditional planning concepts.

Some of the advantages of merged planning and budgeting staffs can be achieved without total merger of the two functions through internal organization of planning and budget staffs. Some states, for example, have combined planning and budgeting into a single staff agency; others have created separate divisions for planning and budgeting within a department of administration. This move shifts responsibility for coordination of the two staffs from the Governor to the head of the combined agency, but can give the Governor separate planning and budgeting staffs to deal with should he choose to do so.

SEPARATE PLANNING AND BUDGETING OFFICES

In situations where planning and budgeting are to be established (or retained) as separate functions, Governors have found a variety of satisfactory arrangements for having the work of the two staffs complement each other.

For example, some states have used the planning staff to complement the activities of a narrowly focused budget staff. In this context, the planning staff can be used to provide staff work on major issues interacting with the budget (e.g., welfare payment levels, tax policy), establish program categories and goals and objectives for programs, and participate in the budget review.

Other states use the budget staff heavily for issues that are frequently the responsibility of the planning staff in other states. For example, many planning staffs do the work for state government reorganization, but some budget staffs will be found to have this responsibility.

Regardless of the organizational form chosen, the new Governor should recognize that the planning and budget staffs both represent a large percentage of the staff capacity available to him. Unlike the immediate staff of the Governor, these staffs are likely to have considerable experience in dealing with the state and federal programs involved and with key middle managers in state agencies. They are also likely to be familiar with some of the political problems involved and the past history of many issues. Given these capabilities, finding some arrangement to make sure that this staff capacity is oriented toward the Governor's current interests is vital to a successful administration.

OTHER COORDINATING MECHANISMS

Consolidating a number of small agencies into fewer large agencies is certainly not the only way for a Governor to ensure that two agencies will work together closely when their functions are related. Other common mechanisms include:

• Using agency liaison assistants from the Governor's office to take leadership in getting agencies to work together;

• Designating one agency head as "lead" for a group of agencies working on a common subject;

• Appointing agency heads to task forces oriented toward particular issues; and

• Appointing "subcabinets" composed of related agencies in such fields as economic development and health.

CHAPTER FIFTEEN

Ethics and Standards of Conduct

    Dedicate yourself to give your full time and attention to the job of being a knowledgeable, honest, forthright public servant. Leave a heritage of being an individual who tried his best to be a good Governor. Establish a reputation for being an honorable person.

— a former Governor

Remember you serve, not rule.

— a former Governor

SUMMARY

The immediate establishment of high ethical standards and strict enforcement of them is of critical importance to any new administration. Major areas on which to focus include state procurement, contractual services, regulatory decisions and the Governor's own finances.

State government is big business; it buys millions of dollars worth of goods and services each year. The financial success of many businesses and individuals is directly affected by the state's purchasing power. State officials exercising this power can favor some contractors over others by changing the timing of the procurement, altering specifications to fit a certain product, or disqualifying various bidders and contractors through quality decisions. Specific cases of abuse may include:

- Direct bribes, where money or items of value are exchanged for favorable decisions;

- Indirect bribes, where money, gifts or travel are offered by suppliers who are rewarded later by contracts or favorable decisions; and

- Minor conflicts of interest, where an official receives items of value because of his position, which are generally considered too minor to directly influence decisions.

To help prevent direct bribes the Governor can (1) declare that improprieties by purchasing officials and agency heads will not be tolerated and that prosecution will be certain; (2) make special efforts to recruit individuals of impeccable background for sensitive positions; (3) use strictly competitive bidding in as many areas as possible; and (4) establish special review procedures for any extraordinary cases, such as single bidder response or the award of professional contracts.

The new Governor should immediately identify what policies exist for preventing indirect gifts to employees and minor conflicts of interest. Policies should clearly prohibit unethical conduct under the penalty of dismissal. The policy may strictly prohibit any transfer of value regardless of size.

Corruption may also occur in state regulation of industries. Many policy decisions made by regulatory agencies have a major financial effect on the industries within their jurisdiction. The temptation to influence illegally the official who sets truck limits or approves rate increase proposals is great. Efforts directed at eliminating purchasing improprieties should also apply to regulators. Even more difficult to police is the conduct of regional officials such as food or health inspectors. The Governor must again express strict ethical policies, perhaps rotate inspectors, and protect businesses which report unethical conduct by state officials.

State officials often have confidential information which, if leaked, could result in profit for certain individuals. A statute prohibiting the disclosure of information for profit may be useful, as would periodic reviews of land acquisitions.

It is usually difficult for state employees to steal state money because of complicated accounting procedures. State property can be more easily stolen, however, and the Governor should encourage agency directors to take an immediate inventory of all property within their jurisdiction and make sure that inventory controls are effective.

To avoid any difficult situations with regard to his own finances, the Governor should consider (1) not participating in any quasi-judicial decisions of the awards of any contracts or selection of engineers; (2) placing all assets which could possibly be connected with a conflict of interest in a blind trust; and (3) making all personal financial records available to the public.

There is sometimes confusion regarding the benefits the Governor should receive as a public person and costs he should bear as a private citizen. The new Governor should become acquainted with state restrictions on the use of state cars and planes, expenses for modifications to the executive residence or acquisition of personal property, and the family contribution for food or liquor. These policies should be examined early, modified if necessary, and clearly and consistently followed.

Ethics and Standards of Conduct

A new Governor faces the reality that the public will hold him accountable for the conduct of state employees. No matter how remote from the Governor personally, no matter how unrelated to the Governor's policies, corruption anywhere in state government will reflect adversely on him and his office. Setting a high ethical tone early obviates the difficulties inherent in raising ethical standards later.

It is probably unreasonable to expect that all illegal or unethical conduct in government can be prevented, but a Governor can:

- Articulate a high standard of conduct;

- Set a high standard by his own conduct and that of his top appointees;

- Establish appropriate standards of ethics for all state employees, with enforcement mechanisms; and

- Encourage vigorously the prosecution of any violators.

To cope successfully with the danger of corruption in state government, a Governor will need to understand its most common forms and ways of dealing with them.

Unethical Purchasing Practices

States have immense buying power. They purchase food, clothing, bedding and personal items for inmates and mental patients; buy or rent computers and data processing equipment, office equipment and supplies, and vehicles; purchase construction materials; let construction contracts; rent office space; and hire consultants, architects and engineers.

The people who control this purchasing power can greatly affect the profits of the firms and individuals who sell to the state. In the case of competitively bid items, they can favor particular suppliers by the timing of the procurement, by gearing specifications to particular product lines, and by making "quality" decisions about certain product lines that qualify some bidders and disqualify others. In purchases that are not normally subject to competitive bidding, such as certain professional services, the ability of the purchaser to favor one firm or individual over another is almost unlimited.

Over time, firms seeking to do business with the state tend to develop a common view of the purchasing practices that prevail in the state government. Some of them will feel that they have little choice (other than abandoning the business) but to work within the existing system, regardless of how ethical or unethical it may be. These conditions can lead to a variety of corrupt or unethical relationships between purchasing officials and suppliers, which ultimately penalize the taxpayers and sour the moral climate of governmental activity, including:

- Direct bribes—the exchange of money or other items of value for favorable governmental decisions.

- Indirect bribes—gifts to the purchasing official in the form of entertainment, travel, meals, liquor and other items of value which, while they may be viewed by some as accepted supplier conduct, lead to a relationship that fosters decisions favoring the supplier.

- "Minor" conflicts of interest—things of value which may accrue to the purchasing official by virtue of his position, such as an occasional free lunch or a box of cheese for the office at Christmas.

Outright bribes can be eliminated by preventing them from being useful for the supplier and increasing the perceived odds of getting caught. Some steps to produce these results are:

- A clear declaration from the Governor to the central purchasing agency, and to heads of agencies involved in purchasing decisions, that he will not tolerate any improprieties, will prosecute any violator, and will hold each department head accountable for developing written procedures, in concert with the central purchasing agency, to prevent any irregularities in purchasing operations.

- Special efforts in the selection of state purchasing officials to ensure that they are competent and honest people.

- Purchasing procedures which utilize competitive bidding whenever possible. Two useful questions are: "When isn't competitive bidding practicable and feasible?" and "Why not?"

- Special procedures within the purchasing operation for review of situations which suggest problems, or situations where considerable individual discretion is involved, such as identical bids or single bidder responses.

- Selection boards with frequently changing membership for procurements where intangibles are a major factor, as in professional contracts.

- And, a mechanism by which suppliers may report irregular practices directly to the Governor or someone designated by him.

In those states where these actions are not fully covered by law or executive order, the most effective tool in preventing indirect bribes and dealing with minor conflicts of interest would be the establishment of a clear policy that provides for outright dismissal as one of the penalties for violation.

The strongest possible policy is to prohibit all transfers of anything of value from suppliers to anyone in a position to influence purchasing decisions. This approach prohibits the acceptance of even a cup of coffee. Less stringent standards may permit such practices as a vendor paying expenses for a visit to his production facility or free lunches where business is transacted.

Corruption in Regulatory Functions

The economic power of the state's regulatory agencies, in terms of real dollars and cents, generally exceeds the state's economic power as a buyer. Thus the potential for corruption in this area can be even greater than in direct purchasing.

Policy-setting regulatory decisions, such as those prescribing the allowable costs for a regulated utility or establishing air pollution standards or truck weight limits, represent great opportunities for attempted bribery of high-level officials within an administration. Generally, the same policies which apply to purchasing should apply to regulatory functions.

A much more difficult problem arises in applying these general policies to individual state employees, working away from a central office and thus largely free of supervision, in circumstances where the economic impact to a business of an adverse decision can be many times greater than any special consideration the state employee might seek. Examples of state activities that present potential problems are:

- Inspection of restaurants, milk producers, meat and poultry operations, and other food production facilities;

- Enforcement of occupational health and safety regulations;

- Inspections of work in progress in highway and public building construction;

- Environmental protection and pollution control inspections; and

- Safety inspections and weight regulation enforcement in trucking.

The strategy for preventing corruption in these circumstances involves having clear policies and objective inspection standards, rotating inspectors, and making clear that the Governor is determined to prevent corrupt practices and will protect businesses from retaliation if they report violations.

Taking Unfair Advantage of Employees

Supervisors are always in a position to encourage favors from their employees, such as taking the boss to lunch or buying him elaborate gifts and giving parties. If this problem is a significant one, it can be addressed by a law or executive order prohibiting gifts to superiors. Some people may consider this approach unnecessarily harsh, however.

Using Inside Information

State employees possess a variety of inside information that can be of value to those outside government or to themselves. Examples are advance knowledge of regulatory decisions, planned purchases of highway rights-of-way or parkland, and interchange locations, as well as information about competitors' economic situations in regulated industries.

A statute which prohibits an employee from disclosing inside information for profit is a key to preventing such practices. Some internal investigatory mechanism to spot-check land acquisitions and the chain of title prior to acquisition is also a good policy.

Stealing State Property

Governmental fiscal procedures are so complex and involve so many parties that stealing cash from government is difficult. Stealing property of value is another matter. Regulations on property control are frequently loose, and practices which condone some degree of theft may have developed over the years, particularly in decentralized state institutions.

There is, of course, the petty pilferage which converts office supplies into school supplies, and personal use of the office copying machine is not uncommon. More serious abuses occur with personal use of long-distance phone privileges, state cars and expense accounts, and with the theft of items such as state-owned batteries and tires. These practices, which afflict business as well as government, are sometimes hard to prevent.

A new Governor would be well advised to instruct all new cabinet officers to make an immediate inventory of personal property that is supposedly in their possession, for the purpose of correcting the records as they assume control. This should also be done in the Governor's mansion. The Governor also should take all necessary steps to assure that the state's personal property inventory system is as reliable as possible and that it is properly supervised, that temptation for state employees to make unauthorized use of state property is reduced to a minimum, and that there is an independent procedure for spot-checking or cross-checking inventory records that would be likely to uncover improprieties.

Unique Problems for the Governor

Even Governors who take care to set a tone of honesty and ethical conduct in their administrations sometimes have difficulty avoiding the appearance of questionable actions. To avoid potentially difficult circumstances, the following steps should be considered:

- Adopt a conscious and announced policy of not intervening in any pending quasi-judicial situation and of never being personally involved or consulted in the selection of contractors, architects and consulting engineers; and

- Place all assets that could give rise to conflict-of-interest questions in a blind trust for the duration of the term.

Many Governors also regularly release details of personal finances, including income tax returns.

Another area where carefully developed procedures are important is policy toward certain expenditures by the Governor and his family. It is useful to make early decisions on such matters as:

- The extent to which the state should pay for modifications in the structure and interior decoration of the mansion or for such things as outdoor play equipment, stereo and TV equipment, and special china;

- Whether the state's payment of food costs extends to all mansion occupants at all times, or whether there should be some family contribution to the state for food, or even separately purchased family food;

- Whether gifts of food and liquor will be accepted for mansion use; and

- Whether transportation provided by the state for the Governor and his family should be used for campaign trips by the Governor on his own behalf or for other candidates, or other travel that is not related to state business.

These decisions should be made quickly so that the Governor can determine from the outset whether he wishes to retain traditional state support for some costs or develop new procedures.

CHAPTER SIXTEEN

The Governor and His Family

My wife and I, with our children, frankly discussed this phase of our lives together soon after we started into the Governorship. We then agreed that this was going to be a limited experience that we would fully enjoy but that would surely have an end. The time would come when the applause would stop for us, and others would be having their turns in the spotlight—their challenges to build their own steps of progress. And we decided that when that time came, we would find strength and joy in our knowledge and satisfaction from the work we had done in that great office, that we would have the grace to accept the change happily and readjust our lives accordingly. We thoroughly enjoyed every hour of our Governorship, and when it ended and the applause stopped we accepted this too as a natural and desirable condition of life.

— a former Governor

SUMMARY

While the Governor-elect is faced with new professional challenges, he and his family will undergo an equally demanding personal transition. Former Governors have commented that the long hours are a particularly difficult aspect of being Governor. If the Governor wishes to maintain any kind of personal life, he must schedule his time and ensure that free time is not eroded by his staff.

The privacy available to the Governor and his family, however, will generally be limited. Adjustments must be made to the lack of anonymity at public gatherings.

Another concern for the first family will be security precautions, which are handled by the state police or highway patrol in most states. Unless security is clearly provided for by statute, the new Governor will need to make several early decisions on the type of security he and his family will require. A security system should not be so extensive as to isolate the Governor, nor will he want to accept the major invasion of privacy which an excessive system would impose. The Governor should consider a number of questions in designing a security system, including:

- Will the Governor's office receive 24-hour protection? What type of clearance system will be used? What resources will the security force have to restrain an intruder?

- What type of personal security should be used outside the office?

- Should the Governor's family be accompanied by a security agent at all times or only at public events?

The management of the Governor's household should be considered soon after election to determine how it will be used for social occasions, personal and business commitments. Because the role of the Governor's spouse has changed and some Governors have chosen not to live in the mansion, the traditional operation of the mansion may need to be revised by the Governor and spouse.

The executive residence will be easier to manage than a normal home in some respects because a household staff is usually provided by the state. The staff must be supervised, however, and social use of the mansion must be managed by the first family. An effort should be made to visit with the outgoing Governor and first family to determine which staff members might be retained, how the mansion can be organized, what decorating changes need to be made, and other general information.

Guidance on separating family expenses from state expenses should be sought. Staffing decisions must also be made on a mansion manager and perhaps a social secretary. If there is a state historical society involved with the house, early contact should be initiated.

The social secretary or the Governor's spouse should obtain the traditional annual social calendar which indicates obligatory social occasions involving the mansion and first family. These events will be supplemented with various dinners for legislators, campaign kickoffs, casual staff meetings, and other entertainment and business functions.

The mansion can serve many other purposes, such as holding a large open house for groups and individuals that may feel neglected during the Governor's hectic first year. For any function, guest lists must be double- and triple-checked to ensure that no one is overlooked and there is a rational explanation for who is invited and who is not.

The Governor's spouse may choose from a variety of roles. A spouse may make available time to the Governor's office and participate in ceremonial functions. Another option is to utilize the prestige of the office for charitable activities. Spouses in a number of states have chosen to share in the business of running government and often act as special policy and political advisors. Many spouses will have active personal careers to which they will continue to devote their energies. Whatever role is assumed, the Governor's spouse has considerable opportunity to make important contributions to the state.

The Governor and His Family

The transition period and the continuing management of state government provide an enormous challenge for the new Governor. Unfortunately, this challenge comes at a time when the Governor and his family are in the midst of other major transitions, including adjusting to new roles and a new home.

TIME AND PRIVACY

As noted in the discussion of the typical Governor's day in chapter 1 and in the discussion of scheduling in chapter 8, the Governor will find it difficult to maintain any kind of personal life unless he makes sure that it, too, is scheduled and that the schedule is maintained.

The extent to which a Governor will be willing and able to devote long hours to his job will depend upon his family circumstances and his ability to function for extended periods with little rest or relaxation. Thus, there can be no magical formula for handling personal scheduling. Whatever his scheduling approach, a Governor will want to avoid letting members of his staff consider the time he has set aside for personal and family use as "free" time which they can utilize.

The Governor will be recognized almost everywhere he goes, as will some members of his family. This makes it difficult to maintain any normal family life outside of the home.

Being in the limelight can also create a "withdrawal" problem later, when the Governor becomes a former Governor; the first family will benefit by recognizing election to public office as a unique but finite experience.

SECURITY

Part of the loss of privacy for a Governor and his family stems from the need in most states for relatively heavy security for the Governor, his immediate family and the mansion.

In most states, security is handled by the state police or highway patrol and is budgeted in that agency rather than in the Governor's office.

The head of the security detail normally reports directly to the Governor. In states with fairly elaborate security machinery, the security officers may perform some of the tasks that were handled by the advance staff during the campaign, such as arranging transportation and meals.

Unless a Governor serves in a state in which his personal security arrangements are prescribed by statute, he will make many decisions about security for himself and his family—and he must make them early.

Obviously, no personal security system can be perfect. The resources required for complete security and the isolation such a system would impose are probably unacceptable to most Governors. Personal security systems do, however, provide some deterrent to aggressive action against a Governor and protect him against physical violence in angry crowd situations.

The extent to which a Governor may want to trade personal and family privacy for improved security is a uniquely personal choice. The following questions indicate the types of problems to be discussed with the agency responsible for protecting the Governor and his family.

The Office

- Is the office protected day and night and accessible only to persons who are being watched during their visit (except while in the Governor's presence), or who (particularly in the case of cleaning and maintenance personnel) are known to security personnel and in some way checked out by them?

- Are physical arrangements and the availability of security personnel sufficient to deal with a person who seeks to see the Governor and, being turned down, decides to force his way in?

- When a group demonstrates outside the office and the demonstration turns sour, can sufficient force be mobilized to protect the Governor and state property?

Personal Security

- Is the Governor ever outside his residence or office without being accompanied by at least one trained security officer who is armed?

- When he is traveling by car, is his security officer in radio contact?

- In a crowd situation, such as at a banquet or a parade, is a security officer in a position to provide adequate protection for the Governor? Does he have instructions as to the actions he should take in the event of an emergency?

Government Operations

Another aspect of security involves governmental operations which, for one reason or another, a Governor doesn't want to be public. Even the most open government will have occasion for secrecy, such as decisions soon to be announced publicly or discussions with subordinates about the competence of individuals. The simplest security system may seem inadequate to some and paranoid to others. Some simple procedures include:

- Having someone make sure that the office wastepaper is destroyed without being read (e.g., using shredders or the equivalent);

- Having occasional electronic sweeps of key offices;

- Obtaining assurance that phone conversations are as secure as possible; and

- Deciding whether the Governor wishes to have certain telephone conversations monitored by a secretary and, if not, using phone equipment that blocks out other listeners when a line is in use.

For security reasons, if for no other, some gubernatorial aides believe that Governors should never drive cars.

The First Family

The three questions in the above section on office security can also be applied to the residence. In addition, this question should be asked: Do the Governor's spouse and minor children ever appear in public places without the presence of a security officer:

- When the event is publicly announced and may be attended by any interested citizen?

- Where the participants are all known, such as at school events or luncheons?

- Where the participants are not known, but where someone intending harm could not predict the event (e.g., shopping)?

SOME HOUSEHOLD NOTES

Many of the traditions that have developed around the social and ceremonial functions of the office of the Governor and the Governor's mansion have been predicated on the notion that the Governor would be male, married to someone who would act in the capacity of "first lady," and living in the mansion. Unmarried Governors have, in the past, used close female relatives in the first lady's role.

While Governors and their spouses in a majority of states still fit this pattern, an increasing number do not. For example, in 1978 two Governors were women, several Governors declined to live in the mansion, and a number chose not to follow all the social traditions associated with the office of Governor and/or the mansion.

It is reasonable to expect that many of the traditions described in this section will continue to change as a result of such factors as:

- The increasing percentage of women in key roles in state legislatures, appointive state offices and local government, suggesting that if normal career paths to the Governorship are followed, the number of women Governors will increase;

- The increasing proportion of the population that is divorced, widowed or separated, and the increasing acceptance of this status by the electorate; and

- The increasing emphasis by society on roles for women other than spouse.

Managing the Mansion

Most states provide a Governor's mansion and staff, and they often view the mansion as a facility to be used by the public as well as by the immediate family of the Governor. Some mansions, like the White House, are designed to enable public use and private family use to proceed without interrupting each other. Many, however, are not so designed, and some areas (e.g., hallways and kitchens) must serve both the family portions and the public areas of the mansion.

Managing the household is made easier by the fact that gardening, cooking, cleaning and maintenance are normally taken care of by the state. The job is harder than keeping a private home, however, because the staff must be supervised, questions resolved on the use of the mansion for other purposes, and state social functions given at least general guidance, if not specific direction.

Between election and inauguration the Governor will be busy deciding how large an immediate staff he will have, how it will be organized, and what it will cost. Careful thought should also be given to the mansion. The outgoing family may offer advice on questions such as which staff members to retain and what interior decorating changes might be made. Focusing upon these questions early will be helpful to the family. If additional funds are needed from the legislature, the Governor can request them when the budget is submitted. Care should be exercised in making these decisions because the family will have to live with them for the entire term.

One sensitive question is how to segregate family costs from the costs paid by the state. It is important that the staff be aware of the dual functions served by the mansion as a residence for the first family and a focal point of state business.

Two staffing decisions concern the possible appointment of a mansion manager and a social secretary. Someone must take active charge during preparations for major social events in the mansion, both of the mansion staff and of activities such as menu selection. This may be done by a member of the household, by one of the regular mansion staff members, or by another full- or part-time staff member.

The second staffing decision is whether to have a social secretary to handle requests for use of the mansion, to schedule personal time, and to develop invitation lists. Again, this responsibility may fall to a member of the household, the mansion staff, or another staff member.

The state may have a commission or some other agency charged with the preservation of the mansion. If so, it is well for the Governor or spouse to meet with this group early to work out matters such as furnishings, when the mansion will be open to the public, and events to be held there.

The family will want to learn the history of the mansion and the traditions of furnishings provided by the state in order to discuss them with guests as well as for their own information.

Social Functions

New occupants of the mansion may be able to obtain the social schedule from the preceding year. This schedule will include traditional events such as the Governor's prayer breakfast and annual receptions for members of the legislature. The mansion manager will need to consider whether these traditional functions are to be changed in any way.

Beyond these functions, a number of events will probably prove to be necessary, including:

- Inevitable casual meetings in the evening or early morning with the Governor's immediate staff. These close associates of the Governor should recognize that they are basically invading the family's privacy. The kitchen staff should be alerted to provide a reasonable flow of coffee and drink mixes for self-service.

- Breakfast, lunch or dinner meetings, usually planned with little notice, during a legislative session to allow the Governor to meet informally with members of the legislature on particular issues.

- Business breakfast, lunch and dinner meetings, usually planned with reasonable notice, for special groups such as editors of newspapers, labor leaders, business leaders and cabinet members.

- Visits of relatives and family friends and, in some cases, house guests such as key political supporters and visiting dignitaries.

The mansion can effectively combine business and entertainment at functions such as:

- A lunch or evening function in connection with the opening of the state fair;

- A dinner for major contributors;

- Christmas or other holiday parties for the immediate staff of the Governor, the cabinet, or both;

- Kickoff dinners or lunches for major charity campaigns within state government; and

- Receptions in honor of outstanding state citizens, ranging from athletic teams and recipients of special awards to retiring state employees or departing staff members.

These functions all serve useful governmental purposes. During the campaign, many people will have developed the feeling that they know the first family on a personal basis. As the Governor works through the frantic first half year in office, most of these people will have only limited contact with him and may begin to feel neglected. Opening the mansion for a relatively large party will help to overcome this feeling.

A number of the Governor's working contacts will believe that they "should" know the family personally and see them fairly frequently. Members of the press corps, legislators, the Governor's immediate staff and the heads of agencies may have this feeling. Having a few social functions for these groups may be much easier than maintaining consistent contact with them during normal working hours.

Guest Lists

The development of guest lists for mansion functions is extremely important. The Governor will probably be very careful in daily affairs to avoid distinctions that make some people feel less important than others. The same care should be taken in issuing invitations to the mansion.

All kinds of problems can develop when two legislators from the same party and with the same relationship to the Governor find that one of them has received an invitation to the mansion and the other has not.

Lists should be double- and triple-checked for accuracy and updated frequently. If all members of the Governor's immediate staff are to be invited, it is important to make sure that staff members hired in the past two weeks are included. When legislators are invited, someone on the Governor's legislative staff should make sure that there is some basis for the list (e.g., all committee chairmen and their spouses).

THE GOVERNOR'S SPOUSE

As in the campaign, some activities for the Governor's spouse are generally viewed as essential. These include joint appearances with the Governor at social affairs, entertaining with the Governor, and occasional traditional entertaining without the chief executive.

There is, of course, no law or tradition that says a Governor's spouse must adhere to any particular pattern. She or he can take the view, as some Governors' spouses do, that being married to a Governor is little different from being the spouse of a lawyer or other professional. Thus, the spouse may choose to concentrate on raising children, practicing law, teaching, writing or participating in various organizations.

There are other choices. Even if Governors' spouses do not have a driving interest in some area of government, they can help the Governor by offering some of their time. The demand for the Governor's time will always exceed the supply and, in many cases, the spouse will be a good substitute. This approach will give the first family media exposure and will please whatever group is involved.

Events in which a spouse can participate are numerous, including:

- Ribbon cuttings and digging the first spadeful of earth for state or private buildings, such as a new industry locating in the state;

- Christening the first car produced by a new auto plant, toaster from a new production line, or other symbol of state industry;

- Distributing state checks for the first tax refund of the year, employee merit awards, scholarships, lottery prizes, and grants to mental health centers, hospitals, children's homes and school districts; and

- Welcoming people to the state or the state capitol at conventions of trade associations, labor unions or fraternal groups.

All these activities serve both governmental and political purposes. A spouse can also strengthen charitable or other favorite activities by utilizing the prestige of office.

The Governor's spouse also has the option of sharing in the business of administering the state government by serving as a special advisor on policy and operations or making a contribution in governmental areas of personal interest, such as the arts, reading skills, mental health, child abuse or aging.

A first lady brings a number of assets to this kind of work in addition to her personal strengths. She has the capacity to command the attention of the news media and to obtain quick responses from state officials. She can influence legislators, cabinet officers and the Governor's staff on many matters. And she has the ear of the Governor and often his support for the projects which she may choose.

All these assets can be utilized by husbands of Governors as well as wives.

Appendixes

The following appendixes supplement the text and parallel the handbook chapters. Topics addressed include transition, personnel and office organization, gubernatorial staff support, policy development, management, mail and scheduling, executive-legislative relations and reorganization, as well as general information about state government organization.

Information contained in the appendixes was derived from a variety of sources. These include surveys conducted in 1978 by the National Governors' Association Center for Policy Research on planning, budgeting, reorganization, and organization and operation of the Governor's office. In response to the 1978 questionnaires, planning directors, budget directors and Governors' executive assistants throughout the country described decision-making procedures, sources of gubernatorial staff support and reorganization experiences, and provided other information which was used in developing both text and appendix material. Additional appendixes are based on surveys distributed by NGA to Governors and their staffs in 1976 and incorporated into previous materials for new Governors.

Actual procedures used in Governors' offices relating to scheduling, transition, correspondence control, policy development, legislative relations, and general management were the basis for a number of appendixes. Sample decision memoranda, budget issue papers, transition timetables, scheduling procedures and other techniques were adapted from memos, practices and recommendations from a number of Governors and their key staff assistants.

The following appendixes, therefore, are designed to provide the new Governors with a variety of techniques, procedures and systems currently used by Governors and their staffs to manage and direct state government.

APPENDIX 1

A Transition Timetable

This suggested timetable outlines typical transition actions for a hypothetical state. For the most part, it is a synthesis of techniques tried and found workable by new Governors in the past.

While the timetable may be usable as it stands in many cases, it may need to be modified to conform to statutory schedules or tradition in some states. For example, the timetable calls for some transition planning on the part of the new Governor before he knows the election results. Although this is desirable in all cases, it may not be realistic in situations where the election is so close that all resources must be devoted to the campaign. Also, the timetable presumes that the new Governor has until March to present the budget or that he must file proposed amendments to his predecessor's budget in March. In reality, these requirements vary from state to state.

The timetable is divided into sections dealing with specific time periods. Within each section will be found schedule suggestions for both the new Governor and the outgoing Governor.

Before the Election

The Candidate

During the campaign, the candidate should appoint someone to assume responsibility for transition planning. In order to avoid having transition work cut into the campaign efforts, this would normally be someone who was not heavily involved in the campaign itself. The person responsible for transition planning should undertake at least these steps:

1. Read *A Handbook for New Governors* published by the National Governors' Association.
2. Become familiar with the state statutes governing transition.
3. Discuss past transitions briefly with former Governors and their aides and, if practicable, the current Governor and/or his aides.
4. Develop a preliminary transition schedule covering the period between election and inauguration and a few of the key events, such as the state-of-the-state message and budget submission, which follow inauguration. This schedule should include major appointments, transition briefings, inauguration planning, and the windup of campaign-related activities.
5. Develop a preliminary transition plan for what staff will be used, where it will be housed, and how the effort will be financed.
6. Begin to collect ideas about key appointments of the new administration. A candidate who feels that he has a reasonably good chance to be elected should appoint someone to establish a set of files indicating major appointments and including letters and suggestions of potential appointees.

The Incumbent Governor

If the incumbent is himself a candidate, it is unlikely that he will do anything by way of planning for transition before the election. If he is not a candidate, he may wish to consider having briefings for the candidates on such subjects as the state's financial situation and major state problems. Briefings would cover many of the same subjects suggested for issue papers in the post-election period.

The incumbent Governor can also plan for the transition period by having papers prepared for his successor on the state's fiscal situation, budget questions, and other issues likely to confront him. Further, plans for the steps to be taken for the orderly leaving of office can be made.

Between Election and Inauguration

The Governor-elect

The Governor-elect and his staff will be undertaking a number of transition activities

239

at the same time during this period. The list below attempts to list first those things that should be done as early as possible:

1. Appoint an individual or committee to handle inauguration arrangements, preferably someone not involved in transition work which will require all staff likely to be available.

2. Arrange to disassemble the campaign, again using people who will not be involved in transition and who are not expected to have roles in the new administration, or people whose new responsibilities can begin later in the term.

3. Review and approve plans for the transition office—who will work there, in what roles, where they will be placed physically, and how the bills will be paid.

4. Establish procedures for handling mail associated with appointments, taking care to separate correspondence concerning key appointments, such as department heads, from correspondence from persons seeking lower-level jobs (and those seeking higher-level jobs who may be qualified only for lower-level ones).

5. Establish procedures for handling all other mail.

6. Contact the outgoing Governor and agree in principle to work for a smooth transition. Check on major points such as whether he is designating a transition coordinator.

7. Take a vacation.

8. Read *A Handbook for New Governors* and have staff members do the same.

9. Attend the National Governors' Association Seminar for New Governors, for which current Governors serve as faculty.

10. Make as many designations of persons to assume roles in the immediate office of the Governor as possible, placing particular emphasis on the persons responsible for the mail and the office manager. Encourage them to meet with their counterparts in the outgoing Governor's office.

11. Meet with the outgoing Governor to arrange for transition and to be briefed on his view of the office of Governor and the state's problems.

12. Begin making key appointments outside of the immediate office of the Governor, working first on whomever will handle the budget function and agencies likely to have major problems affecting the budget and legislative program, such as transportation, social services (welfare), mental health, and education (if appointed by the Governor).

13. Establish procedures for the development of the budget and legislative program and begin to implement those procedures by reading materials and attending briefings provided by the outgoing administration.

14. Start work on the inaugural address.

15. Meet with the scheduling coordinator and establish a tentative schedule through March. It is recommended that this schedule be very light on speeches and events in view of the need to work on transition and the new budget and legislative program.

16. Consider appointments to all positions that must be filled in some fashion at inauguration, opting for acting directors of agencies where the positions cannot be filled on inauguration day.

17. Complete work on the staffing plan for the immediate office of the Governor. And, checking against the budget, establish salaries, reporting relationships, functions and office space allocation. Assign someone to arrange the logistics of the physical move from the transition office.

18. When enough appointees have been designated to make the meeting worthwhile, have a meeting of top staff and appointees to agency head positions to discuss such subjects as confirmation strategy, press relations, budget, general expectations of agency heads, working with the immediate office of the Governor, etc.

The Outgoing Governor

The outgoing Governor should find that there is comparatively little that he personally has to do in connection with transition. For example, there is no need to supervise transition in the sense of reviewing every issue paper to go to the new Governor. The new Governor and his staff may prefer to work with agency directors and the budget office directly. In any case, the outgoing Governor's role is more one of making staff capabilities available to the new team than of actually working with that team himself. The major obligations of the outgoing Governor and staff are as follows:

1. Offer assistance to the new Governor. While contacting the outgoing Governor is included on the checklist for the new Governor, transition probably starts better if assistance is volunteered by the outgoing Governor than if the new Governor is forced to ask for assistance.

2. Consider whether to establish a single point of contact for transition matters, and designate someone if this approach is chosen.

3. Advise staff members and agency directors that the transition is to be a cooperative one, and that they should expect to provide time for discussions with their successors when they are designated and with the new Governor, if requested.

4. Direct the budget staff to prepare a fiscal overview and budget issue papers and make them available to the new Governor.

5. Develop a crisis management paper.

6. Assign responsibility for the preparation of issue papers for issues that are not linked to the budget.

7. Decide on what transition assistance is to be provided with respect to office space, and communicate the decision to the new Governor.

8. Decide on a records retention and disposition policy, preferably after discussions between staffs of the outgoing and incoming Governors, and implement that policy.

9. Arrange for discussions on changing occupancy of the Governor's mansion.

10. Have the scheduling coordinator prepare a schedule of customary events (e.g., Governor's reception for legislators, Governor's Day at State Fair) for the new Governor.

11. Periodically check personally with the new Governor to ascertain that he is satisfied with the staff work he is getting from the administration.

Post-Inauguration
The New Governor

The duties of the new Governor are discussed in detail in the text. Key duties associated with winding up the transition effort include closing out the transition office, thanking the prior Governor for transition assistance, receiving the reports from any transition task forces, holding some sort of seminar for the new agency directors, and completing work on the budget and legislative program.

APPENDIX 2
Critical Dates in Gubernatorial Transition

State	Term of office	Date of next election	Expected inaugural date	Legislature Convenes†
Alabama	4	1982	Jan., 1st Mon. after 2nd Tues.	Feb., 1st Tues. (a)
Alaska	4	1982	Dec., 1st Mon.	Jan., 2nd Mon. (b)
Arizona	4	1982	Jan., 1st Mon.	Jan., 2nd Mon.
Arkansas	2	1980	Jan. 9	Jan., 2nd Mon.
California	4	1982	1st Mon. after Jan. 1	Dec., 1st Mon.
Colorado	4	1982	Jan., 2nd Tues.	Jan., Wed. after 1st Tues.
Connecticut	4	1982	Jan., 1st Wed. after 1st Mon.	Odd: Jan., Wed. after 1st M⋯ Even: Feb., Wed. after 1st M⋯
Delaware	4	1980	Jan., 3rd Tues.	Jan., 2nd Tues.
Florida	4	1982	Jan., 1st Tues. after 1st Mon.	Apr., Tues. after 1st Mon.
Georgia	4	1982	Next session of General Assembly after election	Jan., 2nd Mon.
Hawaii	4	1982	Dec., 1st Mon.	Jan., 3rd Wed.
Idaho	4	1982	Jan., 1st Mon.	Jan., Mon. on or near 9th d⋯
Illinois	4	1980	Jan., 2nd Mon.	Jan., 2nd Wed.
Indiana	4	1980	Jan., 2nd Mon.	Jan., 2nd Mon.
Iowa	4	1982	Jan., 2nd Mon.	Jan., 2nd Mon.
Kansas	4	1982	Jan., 2nd Mon.	Jan., 2nd Mon.
Kentucky	4	1979	5th Tues. after election	Jan., Tuesday after 1st Mon⋯
Louisiana	4	1980	Mar., 2nd Mon.	Apr., 3rd Mon.
Maine	4	1982	Jan., 1st Wed. after 1st Tues.	Jan., 1st Wed. after 1st Tue⋯
Maryland	4	1982	Jan., 3rd Wed.	Jan., 2nd Wed.
Massachusetts	4	1982	Jan., Thurs. after 1st Wed.	Jan., 1st Wed.
Michigan	4	1982	Jan. 1	Jan., 2nd Wed.
Minnesota	4	1982	Jan., 1st Tues. after 1st Mon.	Jan., Tues. after 1st Mon.
Mississippi	4	1979	1st Tues. after certification of election or as soon thereafter as possible	Jan., Tues. after 1st Mon.
Missouri	4	1980	Jan., 2nd Mon.	Jan., Wed. after 1st Mon.
Montana	4	1980	Jan., 1st Mon.	Jan., 1st Mon.
Nebraska	4	1982	Jan., 1st Thurs. after 1st Tues.	Jan., 1st Wed. after 1st Mor⋯
Nevada	4	1982	Jan., 1st Mon.	Jan., 3rd Mon.
New Hampshire	2	1980	Jan. 1st Thurs.	Jan., 1st Wed. after 1st Tue⋯
New Jersey	4	1981	Jan., 3rd Tues.	Jan., 2nd Tues.
New Mexico	4	1982	Jan. 1	Jan., 3rd Tues.

Limitations on length of session	Years sessions are held	Deadline for agencies or departments to submit budget estimates	Date budget to be submitted to legislature
30 L in 105 C	Annual	Feb. 1	By 5th day of regular business session
None	Annual	Oct. 1	3rd legislative day of session
None	Annual	Sept. 1, each year	By 5th day of regular session
60 C (c)	Odd (c)	Sept. 1, even years	Date of convening of session
None	Even (d)	Specific date for each agency set by Dept. of Finance	Jan. 10
None	Annual (e)	Aug. 1-15	10th day of Jan. session
(f)	Annual (e)	Sept. 1	Odd: 1st session day after Feb. 3 (if change in Gov., 1st session day after Feb. 14); Even: Wed. after 1st Mon. in Feb.
June 30	Annual (g)	Sept. 15; schools, Oct. 15	By Feb. 1
60 C (c)	Annual	Nov. 1	45 days before regular session
40 L	Annual (g)	Sept. 1	By 5th day of session
60 L (c)	Annual (g)	July 31, even years	Odd: 3rd Wed. in Jan.; 20 days in advance to legislative members
None	Annual	Aug. 15	By 5th day of session
None	Annual (g)	Specific date for each agency set by Bureau of the Budget	Mar., 1st Wed.
Odd: 61 L or Apr. 30 Even: 30 L or March 15	Annual	Sept. 1 even years (flexible)	Within 1st 2 weeks after session convenes
None	Annual (g)	Sept. 1	By Feb. 1
Odd: None Even: 90 C (c)	Annual (g)	Oct. 1 before odd-year sessions Sept. 15 before even-year sessions	Odd: Within 3 wks. after session convenes Even: Within 2 days after session convenes
60 L	Even	Specific date set by admin. action but no later than Nov. 15 of odd years	As Governor desires
60 L in 85 C	Annual (e)	Dec. 20	By 1st day of regular session. New Governor-elect: 5-day grace period
None	Annual	Sept. 1, even years	By close of 2nd week of regular session. Governor-elect (1st term): By close of 6th wk. of regular session
90 C (c)	Annual	Sept. 1	Jan., 3rd Wed.
None	Annual	Set by admin. action	Within 3 wks. after legislature convenes
None	Annual (g)	Set by admin. action	10th session day
120 L	Odd	Oct. 1, even years	Odd: Within 3 wks. from 1st Mon. in Jan.
(c, h)	Annual	Aug. 1 before convening of legislature	Dec. 15
Odd: June 30 Even: May 15	Annual	Oct. 1	By 30th day
90 L	Odd	Sept. 1, even years	1st day of session
Odd: 90 L (c) Even: 60 L (c)	Annual (g)	By Sept. 15	By 30th day of regular session
60 C (i)	Odd	Sept. 1	By 10th day of session
(i)	Odd	Oct. 1 in even years	Odd: Feb. 15
None	Annual (g)	Oct. 1	3rd Tues. after opening of session
Odd: 60 C Even: 30 C	Annual (e)	Sept. 1	By 25th day of regular session

State	Term of office	Date of next election	Expected inaugural date	Legislature Convenes†
New York	4	1982	Jan. 1	Jan., Wed. after 1st Mon.
North Carolina	4	1980	Jan. 1	Jan., Wed. after 2nd Mon.
North Dakota	4	1980	Early Jan. to coincide with opening of legis. session	Jan., 1st Tues. after 3rd day
Ohio	4	1982	Jan., 2nd Mon.	Jan., 1st Mon. (j)
Oklahoma	4	1982	Jan., 2nd Mon.	Jan., Tues. after 1st Mon.
Oregon	4	1982	Jan., 2nd Mon.	Jan., 2nd Mon.
Pennsylvania	4	1982	Jan., 3rd Tues.	Jan., 1st Tues.
Rhode Island	2	1980	Jan., 1st Tues.	Jan., 1st Tues.
South Carolina	4	1982	Jan., 1st Wed. following 2nd Tues.	Jan., 2nd Tues.
South Dakota	4	1982	Either 1st Mon. in Jan. or within 20 days thereafter	Jan., Odd: Tues. after 3rd M Even: Tues. after 1st M
Tennessee	4	1982	Jan. 15	Jan., 1st Tues.
Texas	4	1982	1st Tues. after convening of legis. or as soon thereafter as possible	Jan., 2nd Tues.
Utah	4	1980	Jan., 1st Working Day	Jan., 2nd Mon.
Vermont	2	1980	Jan., 1st Thurs.	Jan., Wed. after 1st Mon.
Virginia	4	1981	Jan., Sat. after 2nd Wed.	Jan., 2nd Wed.
Washington	4	1980	Jan., 2nd Wed. unless otherwise provided by law.	Jan., 2nd Mon.
West Virginia	4	1980	Jan., 1st Mon. after 2nd Wed.	Jan., 2nd Tues.
Wisconsin	4	1982	Jan., 1st Mon.	Jan., 1st Tues. after Jan. 8 (
Wyoming	4	1982	Jan., 1st Mon.	Jan., Even: 4th Tues. Odd: 2nd Tues.

SOURCE: The Council of State Governments. *The Book of the States, 1978-79* (Lexington, Ky., 1978), pp. 34-35, 116, 142-45, and telephone survey, September 1978.

FOOTNOTES: APPENDIX 2

†All states elect new legislatures in November of even-numbered years except Kentucky, Louisiana, Mississippi, New Jersey, and Virginia. Alabama, Louisiana, Maryland, and Mississippi elect all legislators at the same time to four-year terms.
Key: L—legislative day; C—calendar day; N—natural day.
(a) During the quadrennial election year, sessions convene on the second Tuesday in January.
(b) Except in January immediately following the quadrennial general election, the session convenes on the third Monday.
(c) Session may be extended for an indefinite period by vote of members in both houses. Arkansas: $2/3$ vote (this extension can permit the legislature to meet in even years); Florida: $3/5$ vote; Hawaii: petition of $2/3$ membership for not more than 15 days; Kansas: $2/3$ vote elected members; Maryland: $3/5$ vote for 30 additional days; Mississippi: $2/3$ vote of those present may extend for 30 C days (no limit on extensions); Nebraska: $4/5$ vote; Virginia: $2/3$ vote for up to 30 days; West Virginia: $2/3$ vote.
(d) Regular sessions begin on the first Monday in December of each even-numbered year (following the general election) and continue until November 30 of the next even-numbered year. It may recess from time to time and may be recalled into regular session.
(e) Second session is basically limited to budget and fiscal matters. Maine: in addition, legislation in the Governor's call, study committee legislation, and initiated measures. New Mexico: legislature may consider bills vetoed by the Governor at the preceding session. Utah: legislature may consider nonbudget matters after $2/3$ vote of each house.

Limitations on length of session	Years sessions are held	Deadline for agencies or departments to submit budget estimates	Date budget to be submitted to legislature
None	Annual (g)	Early September	2nd Tues. following 1st day of annual session (by Feb. 1 in years following gubernatorial election)
None	Odd	Sept. 1, even years	1st wk. of session
80 N	Odd	Even: July 15 (may extend by 45 days)	Dec. 1 prior to session
None	Annual	Nov. 1 (Dec. 1 when new Governor elected)	Odd: Within 4 wks. of convening unless change in Governor—then Mar. 15
90 L	Annual (g)	Sept. 1	Immediately after convening of regular session; incoming Governor—following inaugural
None	Odd	Sept. 1, even years	Dec. 1, even years
None	Annual (g)	Nov. 1	As soon after organization of legislature as possible
60 L (i)	Annual (g)	Oct. 1	24th day of session
None	Annual (g)	Sept. 15 or discretion of board	Jan., 2nd Tues.
Odd: 45 L Even: 30 L	Annual	Sept. 1	Dec. 1
90 L (i)	Odd (k)	Oct. 1	Odd: During organizational session Even: During 1st 15 C days after convening
140 C	Odd	Date set by budget director and legislative board	By 7th day of session
Odd: 60 C Even: 20 C	Annual (e)	Sept. 25	3 days after start of regular sessions, 1 day after start of budget session
None (i)	Odd (l)	Sept. 1, even years	Jan., 3rd Tues.
Odd: 30 C (c) Even: 60 C (c)	Annual (g)	Aug. 1, odd years	Odd: Within 5 days of convening of regular session
60 C	Odd	Date set by Governor	Dec. 20 prior to session
60 C (c, m)	Annual	Aug. 15	1st day of session, except for 1st year of new Governor, then 1 month after convening of session
None	Annual (g)	Dates set by sec'y, Dept. of Administration	By last Tues. in Jan. in odd years
Odd: 40 L Even: 20 L	Annual (e)	Aug. 15	Jan. 1

(f) Odd years: not later than first Wednesday after first Monday in June; even years: not later than first Wednesday after first Monday in May.
(g) The legislature meets in two annual sessions, each adjourning sine die. Bills carry over from first to second session.
(h) The first session of a new legislature, every other even year at the beginning of the gubernatorial term, is limited to 125 C days; other years, 90 C days.
(i) Indirect restrictions only since legislators' pay, per diem, or daily allowance stops, but session may continue. Nevada: no limit on allowances; New Hampshire: constitutional limit on expenses of 90 days or July 1, whichever occurs first, 15 days salary and expenses for special sessions; Tennessee: constitutional limit on per diem and travel allowance only, excluding organizational session.
(j) Day after if first Monday falls on a legal holiday.
(k) Legislature convenes for 15 days in January to organize and introduce bills. It reconvenes the fourth Tuesday in February.
(l) The legisture may and in practice has divided the session to meet in even years also.
(m) Governor must extend until general appropriation is passed.
(n) The legislature, by joint resolution, establishes the calendar dates of session activity for the remainder of the biennium at the beginning of the odd-numbered year. This date may be subject to changes.

APPENDIX 3

State Provisions for Gubernatorial Transition

State	Legislation pertaining to transition	Appropriations available to Governor-elect	Governor-elect participation in preparing state budget for coming fiscal year	Gov.-elect hires staff to assist during transition	State personnel made available to assist Gov.-elect	Office space avail. to Gov.-elect	Provisions for acquainting Gov.-elect staff with office procedures & routine office functions	Provisions for transfer of info. (records, files, etc.)
Alabama	No	No	No	D-No state funds avail.	D	D	D	No
Alaska	No	*	Can make alterations	*	No	*	D	D
Arizona	No	No	No	D-No state funds avail.	No	No	D	D
Arkansas	No	*	*	*	D	*	D	D
California	*	*	*	*	*	*	*	*
Colorado	*	$10,000 minimum	*	*	*	*	No	No
Connecticut	*	$25,000	*	*	No	D	D	D
Delaware	*	$15,000	Recommends adjustments	*	*	*	D	D
Florida	*	*	*	*	D	*	D	D
Georgia	*	$50,000 maximum	*	*	*	*	No	*
Hawaii	*	$50,000	*	*	*	*	*	*
Idaho	*	*	Can submit amendments	*	No	*	D	No
Illinois	*	$50,000	*	*	D	*	D	D
Indiana	*	*	No	*	D	*	D	*
Iowa	*	$10,000	*	*	D	No	D	No
Kansas	No	No	*	D-No state funds avail.	*	D	D	No
Kentucky	*	*	*	Normally not, but statutorily permissible	*	*	*	*
Louisiana	No	*	*	*	No	No	D	*
Maine	*	*	*	*	*	*	D	D
Maryland	*	$45,000 maximum	*	*	*	*	*	*
Massachusetts	No	*	No	*	*	*	D	D
	*	*	*	No	No	*	D	D

246

State								
Montana	*				*	*	*	D
Nebraska	No	$25,000			No	D	*	D
Nevada	*	*$30,000	Can make alterations		*	*	*	D
New Hampshire	*		Can revise		*	*	*	No
New Jersey	*		*	Budget	*	*	*	D
New Mexico	*		No		*	*	*	D
New York	No	$25,000	*		D	D	*	D
North Carolina	*	N.A.	*		D	D	*	D
North Dakota	*		D		*	*	*	*
Ohio	*		No		D	*	*	*
Oklahoma	*	$30,000	*		*	*	*	*
Oregon	No	D	D	D–state funds may or may not be available	D	D	*	D
Pennsylvania	*	$100,000 maximum	D		D	D	*	*
Rhode Island	No	No	Can recommend adjustments to legis.		No	D	*	D
South Carolina	No	*	Can recommend adjustments to legis.		D	D	*	*
South Dakota	No	*$10,000	*		*	*	*	D
Tennessee	*	D	D		*	*	*	*
Texas	No	D-up to outgoing Gov.	No		D	*	D	*
Utah	No	D-up to outgoing Gov. & Gov.-elect	*		*	*	*	D
Vermont	No	$12,000	*		*	*	*	*
Virginia	No	*$25,000	D		D	D	*	D
Washington	*	*	No		*	D	*	D
W. Va.	No	*	*		D	D	*	D
Wisconsin	*	*	*		*	D	*	*
Wyoming	No	No	No		No	No	*	No

Source: The Council of State Governments; based on statutory and constitutional search and telephone survey, September 1978.

* = Yes.
D = Discretionary.

APPENDIX 4

Model Gubernatorial Transition Act

Every election year is apt to bring with it changes in Governors. While this has relatively little effect on day-to-day operations of state government agencies, it has a marked and sudden effect on the way in which the work of the Governor's office is carried out. Every new Governor, therefore, is concerned with arrangements to smooth the transition from one administration to the next.

A number of devices have been used to assist the newly elected Governor in the transition period: funds to hire staff and rent office space, provision of office space in the state capitol complex, assignment of state personnel, transfer of records from the outgoing administration, briefing of staff on routine office procedures and participation in budget preparation for the coming fiscal year.

These practices in gubernatorial transition have been developed largely without statutory authority, though at least 13 States do have such legislation. Subjects covered in it include one or more of the following appropriations: office space and staff; availablity of records and information; budget review including matters of revision, recommendations, preparation, hearings and submittal dates.

A 1968 Council of State Governments' report entitled *Gubernatorial Transition in the States* indicated that no State had a statute providing comprehensive assistance to a newly elected Governor.

The following proposal, based largely upon a New Jersey law, Chapter 15 of Title 52, does provide for comprehensive assistance for the Governor-elect.

The suggested measure identifies the need that requires legislation promoting the orderly transfer of the executive power in connection with the inauguration of a new Governor. It authorizes expenditures by the Governor-elect for office space, staff members and supplies. In addition, situations for limiting expenditures and suspending the Act are set out. The proposal assigns to the outgoing Governor duties in assisting the Governor-elect and provides the Governor-elect with assistance in revising the budget drafted by the outgoing Governor. The measure also authorizes funds to implement the purposes of the Act.

Suggested Legislation

(Title, enacting clause, etc.)

1   Section 1. [*Definition.*] "Governor-elect" means the person who is
2   the apparent successful candidate for the office of Governor, as as-
3   certained by the Secretary of State following the general election.

SOURCE: Council of State Governments, *1972 Suggested State Legislation* (Lexington, Ky., October 1971), pp. 41-44.

Section 2. [*Declaration of Purpose.*] The [Legislature] declares it to be the purpose of this Act to promote the orderly transfer of the executive power in connection with the expiration of the term of office of a Governor and the inauguration of a new Governor. The interest of the State requires that such transitions be accomplished so as to assure continuity in the conduct of the affairs of the state government. Any disruption occasioned by the transfer of the executive power could produce results detrimental to the safety and well-being of the State and its people. Accordingly, it is the intent of the [Legislature] that appropriate actions be authorized and taken to avoid or minimize any disruption. In addition to the specific provisions contained in this Act directed toward that purpose, it is the intent of the [Legislature] that all officers of the state government so conduct the affairs of the state government for which they exercise responsibility and authority as (1) to be mindful of problems occasioned by transitions in the office of Governor, (2) to take appropriate lawful steps to avoid or minimize disruptions that might be occasioned by the transfer of the executive power, and (3) otherwise to promote orderly transitions in the office of Governor.

Section 3. [*Expenditures Authorized; Limitations.*]

(a) The director of the [purchasing division] is authorized to provide, upon request, to each Governor-elect, for use in connection with his preparation for the assumption of official duties as Governor, necessary services and facilities, including:

(1) suitable office space appropriately equipped with furniture, furnishings, office machines and equipment, and office supplies as determined by the director of the [purchasing division] after consultation with the Governor-elect, within the state capitol complex.

(2) payment of the compensation of members of office staffs designated by the Governor-elect at rates determined by him; *provided,* that any employee of any agency of any branch of the state government may be detailed to such staffs on a reimbursable or non-reimbursable basis; and while so detailed such employee shall be responsible only to the Governor-elect for the performance of his duties; *provided further,* that any employee so detailed shall continue to receive the compensation provided pursuant to law for his regular employment, and shall retain the rights and privileges of such employment without interruption. Notwithstanding any other law, persons receiving compensation as members of office staffs under this subsection, other than those detailed from agencies, shall not be held or considered to be employees of the state government [except for purposes of the public employees' retirement system];

(3) payment of expenses for the procurement of services of experts or consultants or organizations thereof for the Governor-elect may be authorized at rates not to exceed [$100.00 per diem for individuals];

(4) payment of travel expenses and subsistence allowances, including rental by the state government of hired motor vehicles, found necessary by the Governor-elect, as authorized for persons employed intermittently or for persons serving without compensation, as may be appropriate;

(5) communication services found necessary by the Governor-elect;

(6) payment of expenses for necessary printing and binding;

(7) each Governor-elect shall be entitled to conveyance of all mail matter, including airmail, sent by him in connection with his preparations for the assumption of official duties as Governor.

(b) The director of the [purchasing division] shall expend no funds for the provision of services and facilities under this Act in connection with any obligations incurred by the Governor-elect before the day following the date of the general elections.

(c) In the case where the Governor-elect is the incumbent Governor, there shall be no expenditures of funds for the provision of services and facilities to such incumbent under this Act, and any funds appropriated for such purposes shall be returned to the general funds of the treasury.

Section 4. [*Duties of Outgoing Governor.*] It shall be incumbent upon the outgoing Governor to:

(1) provide channels enabling the Governor-elect to:

(i) inform career civil servants of his program goals and new polices; and

(ii) effect communication channels with the administration of government. The Governor-elect may obtain information from the Governor's administration by circulating questionnaires or by other means. Information sought may include any questions which will effect the intent of the [Legislature] in enacting this legislation, as expressed in Section 2 of this Act. Such contacts may also include inquiries designed to elicit descriptions of programs, recommendations and justifications for elimination, curtailment or expansion of services, projections of future developments or needs within program areas, recommendations for administrative changes, comments upon anticipated federal developments which might have program or budgetary implications for state programs and elaboration of procedural details; and

(2) direct that all official documents, vital information and procedural manuals shall be given to the Governor-elect.

Section 5. [*Budgetary Information to Be Given Governor-elect.*] If the Governor under whose supervision the budget report has been prepared will be succeeded in office in [January] next following, then:

(1) the [budget officer] shall make available to the Governor-elect so much as he requests of the information upon which the Governor's budget report is based, and upon completion of the Governor's budget

report shall supply the Governor-elect with a copy thereof. The [budget officer] shall also make available to him all facilities reasonably necessary to permit him to review and familiarize himself with the Governor's budget report;

(2) after a review of the Governor's budget, the Governor-elect may prepare revisions and additions thereto. The [budget officer] shall assist, upon request, in the preparation of such revisions or additions;

(3) the [budget officer] shall have as many copies of the revised budget report printed as the Governor-elect requests;

(4) not later than the convening of the next [Legislature], the [budget officer] shall compile a summary of the revised budget report containing the revenue and expenditure recommendations of the Governor-elect and not later than [February] shall transmit a copy of the revised budget report to each member of the [Legislature]; and

(5) upon request, the [budget officer] shall distribute copies of the revised budget report to public libraries, schools and state officials. The [budget officer] shall make copies of the revised budget report available to the general public at a reasonable charge for each copy.

Section 6. [*Appropriation of Funds.*] There are authorized to be appropriated to the director of the [purchasing division] all funds necessary for carrying out the purposes of this Act but not to exceed [$50,000.00] for any one gubernatorial transition to remain available during the fiscal year in which the transition occurs [and the next succeeding fiscal year]. The Governor shall include in the budget transmitted to the [Legislature], for each fiscal year in which his regular term of office will expire, a proposed appropriation for carrying out the purposes of this Act.

Section 7. [*Short Title.*] This Act may be cited as the Gubernatorial Transition Act.

Section 8. [*Effective Date.*] This Act shall take effect....

APPENDIX 5

How Executive Assistants View Their Roles

	Agree Strongly	Agree	No Opinion	Disagree	Disagree Strongly
The most useful thing I do is save the Governor's time.	11	17	2	5	1
I am a facilitator or coordinator of policy rather than a policy maker.	6	21	0	8	0
I spend considerable time encouraging agreement among people who really don't need to see the Governor.	11	23	1	1	0
Since the Governor's schedule represents many key decisions, I play a major role in schedule decisions.	7	17	4	5	0
The Governor prefers that agency heads refer questions to me to determine whether he needs to be involved, rather than contacting him directly.	9	16	2	7	0
My influence on office staff members' decisions is not unlike my influence on decisions of agency heads who report to the Governor.	2	16	5	11	2
I am criticized frequently in the press as the source or cause of bad decisions.	0	2	7	19	7
The press tends to overestimate my policy-making role.	0	9	13	11	2
Although I am close to the Governor, our relationship is a business rather than a personal one.	1	12	2	15	5
The decisions we make obviously affect the Governor politically, but beyond that I leave his political problems to others.	2	8	4	16	6
My political role is as important as my administrative or policy role.	7	14	2	13	0
My role is to provide the Governor with impartial and independent advice.	13	16	3	3	0
I often serve as a sounding board or devil's advocate for the Governor.	11	24	0	0	0
Since I serve as a "surrogate" for the Governor, I must be constantly aware of his thinking on issues.	20	12	1	2	0

SOURCE: Responses by Governors' executive assistants in 36 states to a 1976 NGA survey.

APPENDIX 6

How Agency Liaison Officers View Their Roles

	Agree	No Opinion	Disagree
The major reason for having this position is that the Governor needs someone to work with agencies where he cannot remove the agency head.	8	3	12
Although the Governor can legally remove many agency heads with whom he must deal, it is easier for him to work through me than to fire the agency head.	14	1	8
The agency head is generally capable, but one or two weaknesses make it important to monitor him to assure that the Governor's policies are all honored.	18	3	2
When I disagree with the head of the most important agency with which I deal, we both feel free to take the issue to the Governor.	14	2	7
When I disagree with the head of the most important agency with which I deal, we both feel free to take the issue to some decision maker other than the Governor.	8	—	14
Even when the Governor appoints one of his closest supporters as an agency head, that person will still tend to be captured by the bureaucracy of that agency.	19	1	2
Part of my job is to explain the Governor's position to the agency head.	11	2	10
Part of my job is to explain the agency head's position to the Governor.	21	—	1
When conflicts arise between agencies that are my responsibility and agencies that are the responsibility of others on the Governor's staff, they are more likely to be resolved by us than by the agencies.	14	2	7
Correspondence addressed to the Governor concerning agency matters is rarely forwarded to the agency directly; except on minor matters, it generally comes to me first.	21	1	1
Some of the people I find most useful are civil servants in second- and third-level positions in the agency.	5	5	13

SOURCE: Responses by agency liaison officers in 23 states to a 1976 NGA survey.

APPENDIX 7

Gubernatorial Staff Support by Planning and Budget Offices

The planning and budget offices are important sources of staff support for the Governor. They may be particularly helpful to the new Governor, who is seeking readily available and competent assistance but is still recruiting his immediate office staff and acquainting himself with the many state agencies and their potential services. In a 1978 survey, the National Governors' Association asked Governors' executive assistants whether the planning and budget offices in their state provide eight typical services that are vital to the Governor's programs. The table below is based on responses from 31 states.

Service Provided	Planning Office No. of States	Budget Office No. of States
Develops management options not requiring legislative action	20	26
Develops policy options not requiring legislative action	23	25
Reviews federal legislation, rules, regulations and guidelines	26	20
Responds to gubernatorial correspondence, including information requests	25	26
Develops gubernatorial legislative program	20	18
Lobbies for gubernatorial legislative programs	13	17
Develops or monitors gubernatorial management systems such as Management by Objectives	9	20
Performs "troubleshooting" functions such as solving problems in other agencies	19	23

NOTE: In the same 1978 survey, the executive assistants were asked whom the planning and budget officials in their state report to for each of the eight typical services that they perform. The most frequent response in each category was that they report directly to the Governor; the second most frequent response was that they report to the Governor's executive assistant.

APPENDIX 8

Policy Development

The process of defining, proposing and implementing policy will be systematized and strengthened continually during the Governor's term of office. Many Governors have implemented relatively formal procedures for developing and reviewing policy. This appendix presents examples of four typical policy development procedures and techniques. The first example, which shows how a formal policy process can be instituted to ensure a consistent policy thrust throughout the state executive branch, is adapted from an actual Governor's memo to his department and agency directors.

M E M O R A N D U M

FROM: The Governor
TO: Heads of Line Departments and Staff Agencies
SUBJECT: Policy Review Process

As you are aware, during the last budget cycle we began experimentation with a program-oriented budgeting process. This experience was so useful that we are moving into a more rigorous program budgeting system under my direction with the joint staff support of the budgeting and planning offices.

We also need a system for reviewing prospective agency actions and/or new policies which take place or are formulated outside of the annual budget process. During the regular course of managing state agencies, or working with citizen boards, issues arise which require specific action or adoption of policy in which the Governor's office should be routinely consulted prior to the action. Such consultation now takes place through a variety of relatively informal mechanisms, such as short telephone or personal conversations, letters, memos or meetings, which do not always permit adequate analysis of the action or policy at hand.

I have decided, therefore, to implement a more formal system for reviewing key policy issues and major agency actions which meet certain criteria described below. I want to emphasize that the intent of requiring review of these actions is to enhance the accountability of this administration to the legislature and to the public. It will not be permitted to delay making decisions, but rather will help make better ones. The essence of the review process is that the viewpoints of and impacts on parties who might be significantly affected by a given agency action or policy are assessed in some organized fashion. This will give my office the opportunity to weigh the proposed action against the general goals and objectives of this administration and our statewide perspective.

Basically, each agency head must decide if certain actions contemplated are of such significance that comments should be sought from my office prior to taking action. As a general guideline, I do not want to review routine administrative matters. The types of policy issues or actions which I do want to review are those which meet one or more of the following criteria.

Memo to Heads of Departments/Agencies
page 2

1. Policies or actions which may affect the interest or operating programs of one or more agencies other than the agency initiating the action or proposing the policy. This would include such things as proposals to move programs or functions from one agency to another, proposals from one agency to utilize facilities or land controlled by another, such as a request for the department of transportation to take state parkland for a right of way, and proposals to centralize or obtain central clearance for support services such as printing.

2. Policies or actions which may change an agency's substate regional field structure and/or location of offices providing services to the public, which may affect the interests of a community or neighborhood in which a facility is proposed to be located, or which may change the pattern of delivery of one agency's services which must be coordinated with those of other agencies. Examples of this type include changes in location of district field offices, proposals to colocate or not to colocate related services, proposals to develop community group homes for target groups, etc.

3. Policies or actions which may affect the interests, prerogatives, or statutory responsibilities of locally elected officials or local governments. Examples here include changes in methods of consultation with local officials regarding service delivery patterns and realignment of substate planning area boundaries.

4. Policies or actions which purport to be the official position of the state and/or an agency with regard to proposed federal legislation, regulations, guidelines, construction projects or programs. In addition to obvious examples, this criterion would cover such things as agency reaction to proposed federal land management regulations or policy and designations of wilderness areas.

5. Policies or actions which establish or change the level of benefits, reimbursement rates, user fees, allocation formulae or project screening criteria affecting providers, beneficiaries or recipient jurisdictions. Examples would include such things as proposed changes in the priority formula for ranking water and sewer grants, adjusting reimbursement rates for health care providers in the Medicaid program, and changes in shares of federal funds in "pass-through" programs.

As a general rule, your proposed actions should be submitted in writing, with enough preplanning and lead time so that the review is worthwhile. The initiating agency, in cooperation with appropriate other parties including other affected agencies, should prepare a short issue paper which will become the basis of the review. The issue paper should be concise, specify the issue, relate the pertinent facts, outline the alternatives and their consequences (both current and future), and make a recommendation. I have asked my staff, the state planning office and the state budget office to review these proposed actions to make sure that the affected parties agree on the issue, the facts, the alternatives and the description of the consequences of the alternatives.

One final point. If an agency head plans to meet with me to discuss such issues, adequate time should be allowed between my receipt of the issue paper and the time of the meeting. Except in genuine emergency situations, this time interval should be at least three days.

Cabinet Subgroups

The following example illustrates how the Governor in one state has organized formal cabinet subgroups to consider pressing issues and problems and to propose specific policy actions. This approach may be particularly useful in states which have no constitutional or statutory cabinet structure, or states where the number of department heads in the Governor's cabinet is too large to deal effectively with emerging issues. The subcabinet approach, as well as the policy process outlined in the preceding memo, can also be extremely workable in preparation of the Governor's legislative program. See appendix 18 for an example of how the subcabinet technique can be adapted to legislative issue development.

<u>M E M O R A N D U M</u>

TO: All Members of the Governor's Cabinet

FROM: The Governor

SUBJECT: Rearrangement of Cabinet Subgroups for Policy Development

In order to facilitate this year's policy development and review process, and in an effort to ensure that all cabinet-level agencies are provided with adequate access to the forums in which decisions affecting their responsibilities and operations are made, I am directing that certain rearrangements be instituted in the present structure of the cabinet subgroups.

I am convinced that the cabinet subgroup system which we have been utilizing is a valuable and beneficial means to achieve cooperation and coordination among the various agencies of state government. On the whole, I have been pleased with the commitment which has been made to the cabinet subgroup process. I am concerned, however, that at times those agencies which might have an interest in a particular issue being considered by a subgroup but which are not normally recognized as members of that subgroup may be limited in their ability to input into the decision-making process.

Therefore, in order to ensure proper access by state agencies to the deliberations of the various subgroups, I am rearranging their membership according to the following criteria: (1) Each subgroup shall be composed of <u>both primary and auxiliary member</u> agencies. (2) The commissioner, coordinator, director or secretary of each agency shall maintain the major input and attendance at the meetings of those subgroups on which his or her agency is designated as a primary member. (3) Appropriate <u>division heads or designated alternates</u> may represent the agency on subgroups where the agency is designated as an auxiliary member. (4) All subgroup members (primary and auxiliary) when in attendance at subgroup meetings, shall have an equal vote in deciding issues before the subgroup. For the purpose of conducting business, however, a quorum shall be constituted by the presence of a majority of the primary members of the subgroup.

Under this arrangement of subgroup composition, auxiliary members have the option of participating in subgroup discussions only during times when issues of particular concern to their agency are being dealt with. This should not, however, limit the continual participation of

Memo to Governor's Cabinet
page 2

auxiliary members at all subgroup meetings if they should choose to do so. Primary subgroup members on the other hand are expected to participate at all meetings.

With the foregoing in mind, therefore, I am directing that the membership of the cabinet subgroups be composed as follows:

I. EXECUTIVE MANAGEMENT CABINET SUBGROUP

-Primary Members-

Bureau of Administration
Bureau of Finance and Management
Office of the Governor
Bureau of Personnel
State Planning Bureau

II. ECONOMIC AFFAIRS CABINET SUBGROUP

-Primary Members-

Department of Agriculture
Department of Commerce and Consumer Affairs
Department of Economic and Tourism Development
Office of Energy Policy
Bureau of Finance and Management
State Planning Bureau
Department of Revenue
Department of Transportation

-Auxiliary Members-

Bureau of Administration
State Economic Opportunity Office
Department of Education and Cultural Affairs
Department of Labor
Department of Military and Veterans Affairs
Department of Natural Resource Development
State Planning Bureau

III. HUMAN RESOURCES CABINET SUBGROUP

-Primary Members-

State Economic Opportunity Office
Department of Education and Cultural Affairs
Department of Health
Office of Indian Affairs
Department of Labor
Department of Public Safety
Department of Social Services
Department of Vocational Rehabilitation

-Auxiliary Members-

Department of Commerce and Consumer Affairs
Bureau of Finance and Management
Department of Military and Veterans Affairs
Bureau of Personnel
State Planning Bureau

Memo to Governor's Cabinet
page 3

IV. NATURAL RESOURCES CABINET SUBGROUP

-Primary Members-

Department of Environmental Protection
Department of Game, Fish and Parks
Department of Natural Resources Development
State Planning Bureau
Department of School and Public Lands

-Auxiliary Members-

Department of Agriculture
Office of Energy Policy
Bureau of Finance and Management
Department of Transportation

Additionally, I am requesting that all subgroups adhere to certain procedures which I believe will facilitate the management of subgroup affairs and reinforce their effectiveness. First, subgroups, in consideration of the various issues before them, should be strongly decision oriented. I depend heavily upon the subgroups to collectively provide me with action recommendations on a number of matters. If, therefore, subgroups serve more as debating societies than decision-making forums, much of their value is lost from my perspective. It is my intention that the subgroups recognize themselves as being primarily crisis oriented. This is not to preclude, however, the use of the subgroup mechanism for general policy discussions as time will allow.

Furthermore, to provide for efficient administration of subgroup business, I should like all subgroups to adhere to the following operating criteria: (1) Formal operating procedures including the use of necessary parliamentary measures such as motions, amendments, etc. (2) Reliance upon the State Planning Bureau to provide the central/coordinating staff function including the preparation of minutes and agendas. This is important -- agendas must be circulated in advance of all meetings and minutes published and circulated afterward. (3) Designation by each subgroup member of agency staff personnel to work in conjunction with State Planning Bureau staff on specific issues before each subgroup. (4) Subgroup meetings should be held at least once a month or more frequently as the work load requires.

I ask that you provide my office with copies of each meeting agenda and the minutes of your subgroup meetings. Minutes should be written as soon after subgroup meetings as possible and distributed to agency members and my office in a timely fashion. I also ask the chairperson of each subgroup to periodically brief my executive assistant on the subgroup's activities and work.

Finally, I am directing that the methods and procedures outlined in this memorandum be put into effect immediately -- that is, at the next scheduled meeting of each of the subgroups. However, if you have any questions or comments concerning the membership and operation of the subgroups, please do not hesitate to bring them to my attention. I would be glad to visit with you about any concerns you might have in this regard.

Thank you for your continued cooperation.

cc: Executive Assistant
    Office of the Governor

Decision Memorandum

The policy development process, and in fact all functions of the Governor's office requiring executive decisions, can be facilitated by various decision-making tools and techniques. A decision-making procedure which conserves time, condenses important material clearly, and presents the Governor with several viable and recommended policy alternatives will be of considerable value to the chief executive. The following example, drawn from one state budget director's decision memorandum to his Governor, effectively fulfills these criteria.

MEMORANDUM FOR THE GOVERNOR

FROM: Budget Director

SUBJECT: City Street Improvement Program

      The Department of Transportation (DOT) is seeking to announce publicly a $250 million, five-year program which would do the following:

- Continue to increase DOT control over projects on both the state and nonstate road systems in the city; and

- Fund projects using reallocation of "city agreements" dollars in the first fiscal year and a new series A authorization thereafter.

      In reviewing the proposed program, you should address the following major issues:

I. Does the program have transport merit?
   (This is an informational issue.)

II. a) Should you commit the state to the full program in view of its multiyear nature?
    b) Should you "bond the gift" of federal reimbursement?

III. To what extent should the state accept greater responsibility both on and off the state system for accomplishment of work?

IV. Should this initiative be given priority over other possible new initiatives?

Your broad program options are:

1. Approve five-year, $250 million program (DOT recommendation);

2. Approve two-year program of roughly $100 million;

3. Approve one-year program of $50 million; or

4. Disapprove program leaving regular fiscal 1979 program of $25 million; study further the impact possible as part of the fiscal 1980 budget review.

Memo for the Governor
page 2

The Bureau of the Budget (BOB) recommends either option 4 or 3 due largely to the uncertainty of costs and funding in future years. The bureau acknowledges in the following issues that the program has merit but also points out problems with costs, funding and precedent.

ISSUE I -- Does the program have transport merit?

It is acknowledged that the program has considerable transport merit. There is some disagreement between DOT and BOB as to the degree of achievement in each of the improvement categories:

Capacity. Through intersection channelization, signalization and parking removal, extra turn lanes, and in some areas, extra through lanes will be provided. The bureau's review shows that improvement depends to a significant degree on the removal of parking. There is considerable uncertainty whether parking removal can be implemented successfully.

Environmental Quality. To the degree capacity improvements allow cars to move more efficiently, emissions will be reduced.

Bus Transport. Bus transportation will be made more attractive by providing exclusive bus lanes and signal overrides. Although exclusive bus lanes have enjoyed much success elsewhere in the country, the traffic signal override is considered by federal officials as unproven and experimental. Also included are bus shelters and bus turnouts.

Other Benefits. Safety will be enhanced, as well as the rideability and overall appearance of the street system. The program will also provide jobs.

ISSUE II (a) -- Should we commit the state to the full program in view of its multiyear nature and reliance upon additional bond authorization?

The proposed funding for the program would be through existing program categories in fiscal 1979 and with new bond authorization thereafter.

Fiscal 1979 funding. Undertaking this program will mean dropping some work already announced in the fiscal 1979 program. The following table shows how the fiscal 1979 portion of the program will be funded:

Program Category	Published Road Program	New Allocation Road Program ($ millions)	This Proposal	Total
$200 million Series A Federal Aid	200.0	175.0	25.0	200.0
City Agreements	32.6	7.6	25.0	32.6
Supplemental Freeways	167.7	167.7		167.7
Road Fund	390.7	406.0		406.0
TOTAL	791.0	756.3	50.0	806.3

The projects to be dropped are from the regular Road Fund category pushed out by the projects from the $200 million Series A Federal-Aid category.

Memo for the Governor
page 3

Fiscal 1980-83 funding. A new Series A Bond authorization could be required as early as fiscal 1980. The authorization would be needed as follows:

	($ millions)					
Fiscal Year	79	80	81	82	83	TOTAL
Existing Funds	50					282
New Authorization		53	57	59	63	

Fiscal years 1980-83 above include a six percent inflation rate which increases the cost of the program by $32 million.

The cost of the program is still higher when you consider the following:

- $219 million in debt service over the life of the bonds.
- Precedent. This program will increase pressures for similar initiatives in other areas, especially in the suburbs, as the logical extension of the program.
- Operations. The program will require 100 new man-years annually. DOT will take over construction supervision from the city.
- Capital investment needs. To the degree the program removes or restricts parking on the street system, it will create pressures for off-street parking facilities.
- Cost to the city. The city will have the added burden of enforcing parking restrictions.

Your alternatives are:

1. _____ Approve the five-year, $282 million package. DOT argues the state would commit this amount regardless of the program over the period. (DOT recommendation.)

2. _____ Approve two years, keeping within the existing bonding authorization.

3. _____ Approve only the fiscal 1979 portion now, leaving a decision on fiscal 1980 to be made during budget review in the context of the year's total Series A program. (BOB recommendation.)

ISSUE II (b) -- Should you "bond the gift" of federal reimbursement?

The anticipated bonding for the program would enable the state to use 25-year debt to provide extra current cash to the Road Fund. The bureau is opposed to this method of finance on grounds that:

- It trades off short-term cash for long-term debt. The net cash inflow in this case would be approximately $71 million over the five-year program, but there would remain $340 million in debt to be paid in future years.
- The added cash in the Road Fund clouds the underlying problem (i.e., falling revenues, rising costs) and therefore leads the state to possibly more commitments, further aggravating the long-term burden.

Memo for the Governor
page 4

Your alternatives are:

1. _____ Approve the bonding for current federal reimbursement. (DOT recommendation.)

2. _____ Approve the bonding with the stipulation that current federal reimbursement be earmarked for the Series A Interest and Retirement Fund.

3. _____ Approve the bonding, leaving federal reimbursement on a deferred basis as is currently the practice on supplemental freeway bonds.

The bureau recommends alternative 2 or 3.

(The decision memorandum would follow the same format -- posing the question, listing concisely the major considerations for and against it, and presenting the policy alternatives with recommendations -- for issues III and IV.)

Issue Analysis

During the budget and policy-making processes, issues and policy alternatives must be fully analyzed before a decision memorandum can be prepared for the Governor. Particularly in the budget process and in legislative program development, issues can be analyzed in detail according to an accepted format. The following issue analysis paper, taken from an actual state document, is an example of a formalized method of analyzing broad policy and budget questions.

AGENCY: Department of Industry, Labor and Human Relations
PROGRAM: DILHR Commission

A. Issue: What changes should be made in the management structure of the Department of Industry, Labor and Human Relations (DILHR) to promote more efficient administration of the agency and more effective performance of its quasi-judicial functions?

B. Recommendations:

1. A new office of department secretary should be established, the secretary to be appointed by the Governor, with the consent of the Senate.

2. The quasi-judicial functions of the current commissioners should be handled by a newly created Labor and Industry Review Commission whose members would not be distracted from their adjudicative responsibilities because of the administrative burdens of the daily management of a major state agency.

3. The new commission should consist of three full-time members, who will be appointed by the Governor with the consent of the Senate for staggered six-year terms.

4. The Governor may elect to appoint the incumbent DILHR commissioners to complete their existing terms in the new Labor and Industry Review Commission.

5. The department will be administered by a secretary, deputy secretary and executive assistant, the latter two positions to serve at the secretary's pleasure.

C. Problem Definition: The Department of Industry, Labor and Human Relations is governed by a three-person commission. When the Industrial Commission was formed, its mission was primarily quasi-judicial and the three members of the commission concentrated on this task. At the time, the department had a staff of 30 persons and an annual budget of $75,000. The commission was not required to manage and develop policy for a complex and multifaceted agency.

This has changed. The Industry, Labor and Human Relations Commission now has quasi-judicial responsibilities of increased complexity and work load and is also responsible for administering six major programs. The department's annual budget is now $51.0 million (84% federal funds) and its staff numbers 2,561.

The efforts by a three-member commission to administer an agency as complex as DILHR have led to a number of problems. Those who make agency decisions, policies and rules are the same people who hear appeals from those policies and decisions. The lack of responsibility within the agency has frustrated the effective functioning of a major state agency. The results are both clear and unacceptable: damaged morale on the part of the agency's employees and diminished service to the citizens of our state.

D. Analysis of Need: Past commissions have tried with only marginal success to address the above management problems. A 1974 study by the Department of Administration concluded that several changes should be made for the agency to operate most effectively. It recommended that the quasi-judicial function be separated from the rule and policy-making activity and that administrative accountability and leadership be specified.

The department's overall direction, public image and morale have suffered because the commission still has not reached a satisfactory delineation of its policy and administrative responsibilities. While an attorney general's opinion concluded that under ss. 15.06(4) the commission chairman shall personally direct the agency's administrative activities subject to the policies of the commission, the distinction between administration and policy is not always clear. The current interpretation by two of DILHR's commissioners is that the chairman's role is limited to chairing formal meetings and that all three commissioners have equal responsibility and status in departmental operations. As a result, the commission has been obliged to spend a great deal of time focusing its attention on details of administration rather than considering basic policy questions about the programs and direction of the department.

As a result, the commission has been less able to deal with its quasi-judicial functions than its members would like. The commissioners admit that they devote inadequate time to claims review and are dissatisfied that they must use "short-cut" techniques to accommodate the heavy review work load.

In conclusion, major problems in the Department of Industry, Labor and Human Relations' governing structure significantly impair its policy, administrative and quasi-judicial operations. The most urgent is with the administrative structure: a definite need exists to pinpoint decision-making accountability and responsibility, and to separate case review from administration and policy making.

E. Patterns in Other States: Iowa, Minnesota, Illinois, Michigan and California were surveyed to learn how they organized the administrative and quasi-judicial responsibilities of their industry and labor departments. The information shows us the thinking of other state governments. While not always strictly comparable, the organizational differences, similarities and trends are summarized below.

All the labor and industry departments have review or appeal bodies for employment security and workers' compensation, attached either to the department or to individual divisions. Employment security boards are usually part-time; workers' compensation, full-time. The boards generally consist of three gubernatorially appointed members with staggered terms.

Appeal boards are attached to state labor departments for administrative purposes only. Their staffs are generally small—at least a secretary. Their legal counsel is usually provided by departmental attorneys or by attorneys general. Hearing officers remain in the labor department.

In all five states, the labor and industry departments are headed by a single director who serves at the Governor's pleasure and has at least a deputy and a chief assistant. These three positions are unclassified.

F. Analysis of Alternatives: Many possible alternatives address the problems noted in DILHR. These could involve minor to radical changes and could involve shifts in the structure and responsibilities of other state departments. The alternatives discussed below are limited to options affecting DILHR's administrative structure and quasi-judicial performance.

The issue as posed here has two direct components. First, what should be the administrative management structure of DILHR? Second, what organization should perform DILHR's quasi-judicial activities? Each component has its own array of alternatives.

1. OPTIONAL ADMINISTRATIVE STRUCTURES
   a. DILHR Policy Board

This option retains intact the department's current administrative structure but replaces the present DILHR commission with a nonjudicial, independent, part-time policy board and a secretary who implements and administers the board's policies. This option locates the policy-making process in a single group which has no direct responsibility for administration.

Such a board would be open to the same conflicts that weaken the energies of the present commission and impede its prompt response to major policy questions.

Also, it would be difficult to keep board members adequately informed on departmental developments and on the effects of their policy decisions within the agency.

This alternative further blurs accountability for administrative management of a major state department.

b. DILHR Secretary

This option creates an Office of the Secretary to make policy and administer the agency.

A single governing executive would give DILHR the benefit of coordinated programs and decisive direction expected of administrative departments. It would establish single-point responsibility, foster coordination, encourage integrated direction of its various divisions, and facilitate administrative accountability.

This option most directly addresses the policy and administrative problems which have prevented DILHR from realizing its full potential as a major administrative agency. While this alternative would resolve DILHR's administrative problems, it does not address the appropriate form for the agency's claim review operation.

2. OPTIONAL QUASI-JUDICIAL ARRANGEMENTS

Claims review responsibility was lodged in the Industrial Commission to shift the disputed workers' disability claims from an overburdened circuit court system. The options discussed below continue the tradition of administratively reviewing claims as a valid state objective.

a. Secretary Responsible

The commission would be abolished as a device for reviewing claims with those responsibilities delegated to the secretary of the department. This would reduce the costs of claims review by limiting the number of decision makers from three to one. This would facilitate decision making because only one person need be involved and would avoid split decisions on controversial reviews.

The secretary could delegate the review function to someone within the agency, perhaps a chief legal counsel. Or, a single commissioner could be attached to the secretary to review claims.

This option would provide significant policy flexibility during the review process. The secretary could modify basic policy when the circumstances of particular disputes merited such adjustments.

However, this option fails to officially separate policy making from quasi-judicial activities. The individual responsible for policy making would still be responsible for claims appeals; thus, claimants might not receive as impartial a review of their claims as possible. It could also overburden a secretary or single commissioner because of the large claims review work load. Finally, the delegation of review responsibility to the secretary would not be in the state's tradition of three-member quasi-judicial commissions.

b. Attach Review Commission to DILHR

A second option would abolish the existing DILHR Commission and replace it with a new review commission attached to DILHR for administrative purposes only. This option keeps all labor and industry-related matters in the same agency, thus simplifying record keeping and case tracking. It complements existing multifunding source cost models, avoids duplication, and reduces the paperwork and administrative overhead of a separately attached commission.

The new review commission would be able to reduce expeditiously the current commission review backlog because of the minimal start-up time, physical proximity to case files, and ready access to DILHR's legal and secretarial support services. Existing staff review attorneys could be attached to the review commission without creating additional administrative overhead costs.

The drawbacks to this option are as follows: (1) it costs more to operate a separate three-member review body than to have an agency secretary or single commissioner responsible for claims review; and (2) creating another three-member body perpetuates the practice of using three people to handle adjudication when it can be argued that only one person is necessary.

Despite these disadvantages, this option recognizes and affirms administrative law and organizational trends in this state. It is consistent with sound management and legal principles and is a reasonable and practical resolution to the problems noted above.

G. Implementation Timetable and Related Costs: Within three months of the passage of the budget bill, but no later than January 1, 1978, the existing DILHR Commission will be abolished and a new Office of DILHR Secretary will be created. The Office of the Secretary will consist of a secretary (unclassified, executive salary group 7) appointed by the Governor with the Senate's consent, a deputy and executive assistant (both unclassified) to serve at the secretary's pleasure, and an administrative secretary from the classified civil service.

A new three-member Labor and Industry Review Commission will be established to review contested employment-related claims. It will be attached to DILHR for administrative purposes only, under ss. 15.03 of the state code. The commissioners will be full-time (executive salary group 5; chairman, salary group 6) and appointed by the Governor with the consent of the Senate for staggered six-year terms, as provided in ss. 15.06 of the state code. The Governor may appoint the incumbent DILHR commissioners to complete their existing terms in the new Labor and Industry Review Commission.

The new DILHR Secretary should take whatever administrative steps necessary to prepare office space and furnishings for the new commission. The secretary should transfer the Commission Review Section (six attorneys and four legal typists; all classified positions) from the Bureau of Legal Affairs, Job Service Division, to the new Labor and Industry Review Commission, as well as the related property, records and nonfederal moneys.

No additional positions are required to implement these changes, as illustrated by the following:

Abolish

1 Commissioner
1 Commissioner
1 Chairman
1 Assistant to chairman
1 Legislative liaison
1 Legal advisor
3 Administrative secretaries
5 Attorneys (GPR)
TOTAL: 9.5

Transfer

6 Commission review attorneys (FED)
4 Legal typists (FED)
TOTAL: 10

Recreate

1 Department secretary
1 Deputy secretary
1 Executive assistant
1 Administrative secretary
1 Commissioner
1 Commissioner
1 Chairman
1 Administrative secretary
1 Review attorney (GPR)
TOTAL: 9

APPENDIX 9

How State Planning Offices Spend Their Time

States utilize the planning office and its staff in myriad ways. Some state planning offices may devote well over 50 percent of their functional staff time to land-use planning, while in other states time may be fairly evenly divided among a number of planning functions. Separate from these general planning functions are a diverse assortment of management and planning responsibilities. The two tables below are based on a 1978 survey conducted by the National Governors' Association. The first table lists planning functions ranked according to the number of state planning offices devoting more than 20 percent of their staff time to the function. Figures reflect responses from 41 states, the District of Columbia, American Samoa, Guam and Puerto Rico.

Planning Function	Number of State Planning Offices Devoting		
	Over 20%	11-20%	1-10%
	Of Total Staff Time to That Function		
Economic Resources and Development Planning	12	9	21
Land-Use Planning	5	15	19
Government Management Planning	5	3	25
Natural Resources and Environmental Planning	4	11	24
Financial Planning, such as revenue forecasting, tax policy, bonding and budgeting	3	7	22
Manpower Planning	3	2	23
Energy Planning	3	2	26
Transportation Planning	1	3	25
Law Enforcement Planning	1	0	15
Development Project Planning	0	7	24
Other Human Resources Planning	0	7	26
Capital Investment Planning	0	6	26
Health Planning	0	2	22
Other	7	7	9

The second table lists typical planning responsibilities ranked by the number of state offices that devote more than 20 percent of their staff time to the task. Figures are based on responses from planning offices in 44 states, the District of Columbia, American Samoa, Guam and Puerto Rico.

Planning Responsibility	Number of State Planning Offices Devoting		
	Over 20%	11-20%	1-10%
	Of Total Staff Time to That Responsibility		
Managing and administering state and federal programs	8	17	18
Developing portions of the budget, including the capital budget	6	13	29
Developing policy or management options not requiring legislative action	5	13	27
Coordinating plans and policies including A-95 review	5	15	27
Developing and implementing functional plans	5	10	16
Undertaking tasks related to local, substate and regional issues	5	10	30
Developing and maintaining information systems for planning use	3	6	31
Developing or lobbying for gubernatorial legislative programs	2	4	25
Developing or monitoring management information systems such as Management by Objectives	1	3	24
Responding to gubernatorial correspondence, including information requests	0	7	37
Engaging in activities related to federal and multistate issues	0	6	37
Other	3	1	7

APPENDIX 10

State Agencies Designated to Handle Federal Planning Programs

A number of federal programs require states to perform various forms of functional planning in order to obtain federal financial assistance. The state agency responsible for these planning functions is usually designated by the Governor. The major federal programs with such planning requirements are listed in the table below.

Federal Domestic Assistance Catalog Number	Program	Agency with Primary Responsibility	% of States	Agency with Subcontracted Functions	% of States
NA	A-95 Clearinghouse	Planning Office	61	Planning Office	8
		Budget Office	16	Budget Office	6
		Community Affairs	12	Natural Resources	2
14.203	HUD Section 701	Planning Office	59	Community Affairs	8
		Community Affairs	24	Planning Office	6
		Economic Development	8	Budget Office	4
11.305	EDA Section 302	Planning Office	51	Community Affairs	6
		Economic Development	26	Budget Office	2
		Community Affairs	8	Economic Development	2
11.308	EDA Section 304	Economic Development	38	Economic Development	4
		Planning Office	28	Planning Office	2
		Governor's Office	16	Community Affairs	2
11.418	Coastal Zone Planning 305	Planning Office	22	Planning Office	4
		Natural Resources	12	Natural Resources	4
		Environment	6	Coastal Commission	2
11.419	Coastal Zone Planning 306	Planning Office	16	Planning Office	4
		Natural Resources	12	Natural Resources	4
		Coastal Commission	6	Coastal Commission	2
NA	State Science, Engineering and Technology	Planning Office	41	Universities	6
		Governor's Office	16	Planning Office	4
		Economic Development	10	Budget Office	2
15.400-15.402	Outdoor Recreation Planning	Natural Resources	39	Planning Office	4
		Parks Agency	33	Parks Agency	4
		Environment	10	Natural Resources	2
16.500-16.503	Law Enforcement Assistance	Criminal Justice	82	Planning Office	4
		Public Safety	4	Criminal Justice	2
		Local Affairs	2	Public Safety	2
17.232	CETA Planning	Labor	37	Manpower	8
		Manpower	20	Planning Office	4
		Human Resources	12	Local Affairs	2
65.001	Water Resource Planning	Natural Resources	43	Environment	4
		Water Resources	29	Water Resources	2
		Environment	18	Agriculture	2
66.426	Water Quality Planning 208	Environment	43	Planning Office	10
		Natural Resources	20	Environment	4
		Health	12	Water Resources	4
66.418	Wastewater Treatment Plants	Environment	43	Planning Office	4
		Health	24	Environment	4
		Natural Resources	16	Health	2
28.001; 38.001; 48.001; 52.001; 63.001; 75.001; 76.001	Title V Regional Commissions	Governor's Office	22	Economic Development	10
		Economic Development	22		
		Planning Office	12		
28.001	Appalachian Regional Commission	Economic Development	14	Economic Development	2
		Planning Office	6		
		Governor's Office	2		

SOURCE: Responses by officials in 44 states, the District of Columbia, American Samoa, Guam and Puerto Rico to a 1978 NGA survey requesting information on placement of responsibility for a variety of federal programs requiring states to perform functional planning. There are secondary designations where the agency with primary responsibility has subcontracted a portion of the task to another agency.

APPENDIX 11

Sample Policy Statement

STATEWIDE KINDERGARTEN

To implement a quality statewide kindergarten program which will ensure that every five-year-old child in Georgia has the opportunity to develop the knowledge, skills, and language necessary to maximize subsequent achievement in school.

Children who reach the age of five during the next few years will be completing their education in the last decade of this century and will be living and working in the 21st century. Life styles then are expected to be even more complex and technical than they are now. Young adults will need as much skill and knowledge as possible to deal effectively with the daily decisions they will face.

Citizens are expected to be much more mobile in the 21st century than they are today, moving frequently from state to state, even country to country. Georgia's young adults will be competing in a national labor market, including competition with individuals from other states within their own home state. We need to provide our young people every advantage feasible to meet the challenges they will face at the turn of the century.

The children in 45 other states have an opportunity for an extra year of public education -- statewide kindergarten. All states, with the exception of Mississippi, Alabama, New Hampshire, and North Dakota, are currently providing partial funding for the implementation of a statewide kindergarten program. Most of our children are not afforded this opportunity. Kindergarten is doubly important in Georgia since we have a higher proportion of low income families than most states, and most children from lower income families lack developmental skills to profit fully from their schooling. Our children need a quality kindergarten experience to keep pace with children elsewhere.

Kindergarten Advantages

The value of kindergarten is better understood in light of research which has been conducted over the past decade. Approximately one-half of a child's intellectual ability is developed by the time he or she reaches the age of four. An additional one-fifth of the child's full ability is developed between ages four and six. Therefore, a child must be reached as early as possible to maximize learning potential.

If a child is not provided adequate opportunity by the age of six, permanent deficiencies are likely to result. Efforts to overcome these deficiencies at a later age are extremely costly and are rarely successful. Only a quality program for younger children will make a difference.

SOURCE: *Governor's Policy Statement*, 1977 edition, George Busbee, Governor (Atlanta: Georgia Office of Planning and Budget, 1977), pp. 17-20.

Programs which largely result in "baby-sitting" provide little improved capacity for children to learn.

Statewide kindergarten in Georgia will provide additional benefits. First, it would equalize the opportunity for all children to participate. The only children who receive the benefits of kindergarten now are those from the poorer families, those from the wealthier families, those within school systems having programs for all five-year-olds, and those who have the severest need.

Second, kindergarten is a cost-effective investment in that it reduces both retentions in the first grade and delayed retentions in the second and third grades. These retentions are currently costing the taxpayers of Georgia over $12 million annually. The implementation of kindergarten will reduce the need for remedial programs, another savings to the taxpayers. High quality kindergartens, along with effective elementary and secondary programs, also will reduce the need for expensive social services programs. These programs largely serve school dropouts; not for a few years of the individual's life, but throughout it.

Finally, statewide kindergarten will have a secondary economic benefit. Firms establishing new factories and offices tend to view locations more favorably which have sound educational programs, and the availability of kindergarten is a significant factor.

A Full Program

Georgians have been anticipating a statewide kindergarten program for several years. In 1972, the General Assembly took the first step in this direction with passage of the Adequate Program for Education in Georgia (APEG) Act. Responding to this action, an increasing number of colleges and universities have established training programs for Early Childhood teachers. Currently, over 5,000 individuals in Georgia are trained to teach kindergarten.

Yet, less than 15 percent of our five-year-olds are now served by the State-sponsored program. The principal obstacle to full implementation of a statewide program is the unavailability of funding. A fully-funded one-half day kindergarten program will cost in excess of $30 million annually. A continuing commitment of this magnitude cannot be initiated in a single year, or even over two years. The full program will require a gradual phasing in over at least five years as additional revenues become available.

Additional reasons why this program must be phased in are the preparation time and leadership personnel needed by local school systems. Although an adequate supply of certified kindergarten teachers is available, local school systems would not be able to absorb the new personnel, locate sufficient classrooms, or design and implement high quality programs within one or two years. Although the APEG Act authorizes the allotment of leadership personnel for kindergartens, funds have not yet been appropriated for this purpose.

GOVERNOR'S ACTION PROGRAM

Expansion of Statewide Kindergarten Program. The Governor proposes the aggressive expansion of the Statewide Kindergarten Program in fiscal year 1978. Accordingly, he is recommending that the appropriation for this program be increased by $5.39 million to make State-funded kindergarten available to approximately 25 percent of all five-year-olds in the State. To ensure that the kindergarten program is properly developed and implemented, the Governor further recommends that $120,000 of the appropriation for kindergartens be used for leadership personnel.

Full Implementation of Kindergarten Program. To achieve full implementation of a statewide kindergarten program by the school year 1981-82, the Governor will sponsor legislation to amend the Adequate Program for Education in Georgia Act by specifying the following implementation schedule:

- Fiscal year 1978 - 25 percent of five-year-olds.
- Fiscal year 1979 - 45 percent of five-year-olds.
- Fiscal year 1980 - 65 percent of five-year-olds.
- Fiscal year 1981 - 85 percent of five-year-olds.
- Fiscal year 1982 - all five-year-olds.

In the remaining fiscal years of his administration, the Governor will make every effort to comply with this schedule.

Quality of Kindergarten Program. To ensure that the developing kindergarten program is of the highest possible quality, the Governor has requested the following actions by the State Board of Education:

- Requiring that each local school system submit an annual plan for assessing developmental needs of prospective kindergarten students and for selecting students having the greatest developmental needs for placement in kindergarten until such time that all five-year-olds within the system are served. This plan would not be required from those local school systems which have a Comprehensive Plan previously approved by the State Board.
- Requiring that by July 1, 1978, all teachers of five-year-old students in Georgia hold a kindergarten teaching certificate.
- Adopting by July 1, 1977, standards for the effective guidance and development of statewide kindergarten; and by September 1, 1977, a State plan for the implementation of kindergarten statewide.

APPENDIX 12
Administrative Organization

As the following table indicates, cabinet government at the state level is authorized and convened in a variety of ways. Similarly, depending on their state's constitutional and statutory provisions, traditions and their own personal styles, individual Governors will manage and utilize their cabinets differently. Charts on the following two pages illustrate two common types of state executive branch organization.

STATE CABINET SYSTEMS

State	Authorization for cabinet systems	Criteria for cabinet membership	Number of members (excluding gov.)	Frequency of cabinet meetings	Open cabinet meetings
Alabama	Tradition	Gov. determines (a)	24	Gov.'s discretion	Meeting results public
Alaska	Governor	Gov. determines (b)	15	Semimonthly	No
Arizona	...	...	...	...	...
Arkansas	Statute	Gov. determines	17	Gov.'s discretion	Yes (c)
California	None	(d)	9	Weekly	No
Colorado	Statute	Statute	16	Gov.'s discretion	Yes
Connecticut	...	...	...	...	...
Delaware	Statute	Statute	11	N.R.	Yes
Florida	Constitution	Constitution	6	Semimonthly	Yes
Georgia	None	(d)	28	Monthly	No
Hawaii	Statute	(e)	16	As required	No
Idaho	None	Dept. head	18	As required	Yes
Illinois	Admin. order	(f)	29	Monthly (g)	Full cabinet, yes; subcabinets, no
Indiana	N.R.	N.R.	6	Semiweekly	No
Iowa	...	...	...	...	...
Kansas	Governor	Gov. determines	17	Weekly	No
Kentucky	Statute	Statute	9	Semimonthly	No
Louisiana	Statute	Statute	21	(h)	Yes
Maine	Gov.'s directive	Gov.'s directive	29	Monthly (i)	Full cabinet, yes (i)
Maryland	Statute	Statute	16	Monthly	No
Massachusetts	Statute	Statute (j)	13	Weekly	(k)
Michigan	Governor	Governor	17	Full cabinet, semiannual; subcabinets, every 5-6 wks.	No
Minnesota	...	...	...	...	...
Mississippi	Gov.'s directive	Gov.'s directive	9	Semiweekly	No
Missouri	Statute	Dept. directors/gov.	15	(h)	Open to press
Montana	Governor	Appt. to office (l)	20	3-4 times a year	Yes
Nebraska	...	...	...	...	...
Nevada	...	...	...	...	...
New Hampshire	...	...	...	...	...
New Jersey	Governor	Dept. heads (m)	19	Monthly or as needed	No
New Mexico	Executive order	Gov. determines	13	Monthly (full & subcabinets)	Yes
New York	...	...	...	N.R.	...
North Carolina	(n)	(n)	18 (Exec. Cabinet)	As required	Yes
North Dakota	...	...	...	...	...
Ohio	Statute	Statute	N.R.	Weekly	No
Oklahoma	Gov.'s directive	Governor	(o)	Monthly	Yes
Oregon	None	N/R	10	Daily	No
Pennsylvania	Statute	Statute (j)	21	4-5 times annually	Yes
Rhode Island	None	N.R.	17	Every 4-6 weeks	No
South Carolina	...	...	...	...	...
South Dakota	Governor	Dept. heads (j)	23	(p)	No
Tennessee	Statute	Statute	27	Monthly or at gov.'s discretion	No
Texas	...	...	...	...	...
Utah	Tradition	Tradition	8	Weekly	Yes
Vermont	Governor	Gov. determines	6	Weekly	No
Virginia	Statute	Appt. to office/Gov.	6	Semiweekly & as needed	No
Washington	Admin. order	Gov. determines	17	Weekly	N.R.
West Virginia	...	...	...	...	...
Wisconsin	...	...	...	...	...
Wyoming	...	...	...	...	...

N.R.—No response.
(a) The governor selects his cabinet from appointed department heads.
(b) The governor traditionally selects the 15 commissioners who are department heads within the executive branch.
(c) Portions of the meetings or entire meetings may be closed.
(d) Reported as not applicable.
(e) Although there is no official designation of cabinet members, all single executives of principal departments are under the supervision of the governor.
(f) Full cabinet: directors of code departments and single-headed agencies. Subcabinet: members selected from agencies with expertise in the functional areas covered by each subcabinet.
(g) Subcabinet meetings are held more frequently, if needed.
(h) Cabinet system recently established.
(i) In addition, Maine's Cabinet Management Committee meets twice a month (not open to the public).
(j) Additional members selected by the governor.
(k) Alternate weeks are open meetings; other weeks are reserved for executive sessions.
(l) Executive agency directors and cabinet-rank officials within the executive office.
(m) Whose positions have been established by the state constitution or by statute.
(n) The Council of States is established by the constitution. Members, in addition to the governor and lieutenant governor, are all the heads of operating departments elected by statewide ballot. The Governor's Cabinet has no legal basis. Members, in addition to the governor and his executive assistant, are the heads of operating departments appointed by the governor. The Executive Cabinet, established by executive order, is made up of all members of the Council of States and the Governor's Cabinet.
(o) Organized into five minicabinets.
(p) Weekly when the state legislature is in session; semimonthly during the rest of the year.

SOURCE: Council of State Governments, *The Book of the States, 1978-79*, vol. 22 (Lexington, Ky., 1978), p. 129.

Kentucky Executive Branch

(An example of a state with a formal, statutory cabinet system of government.)

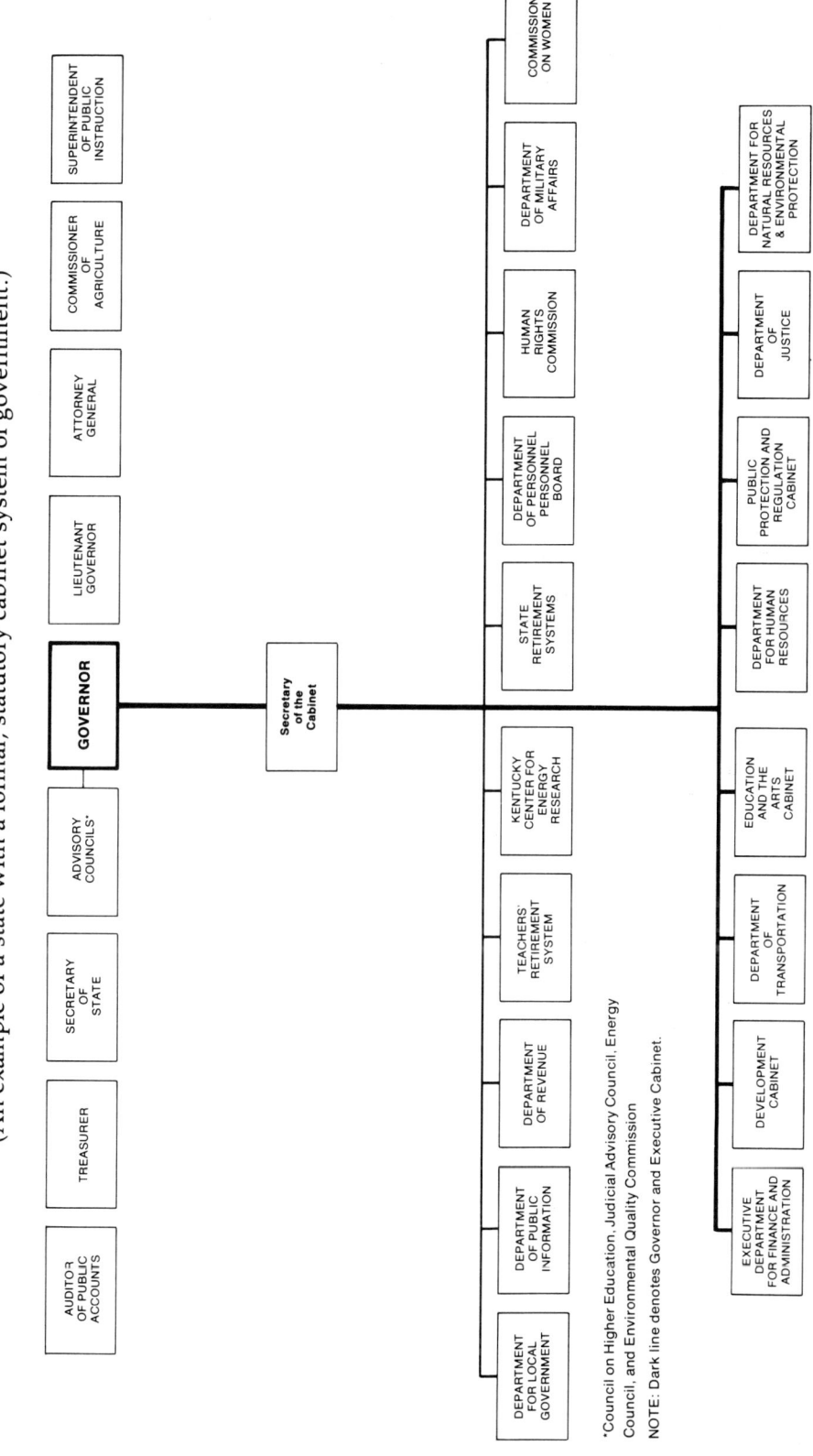

*Council on Higher Education, Judicial Advisory Council, Energy Council, and Environmental Quality Commission

NOTE: Dark line denotes Governor and Executive Cabinet.

South Dakota Executive Branch

(Typical of several states which have a constitutional limit of 20 to 25 cabinet departments. This structure results in alternative uses of cabinet and subcabinet groups.)

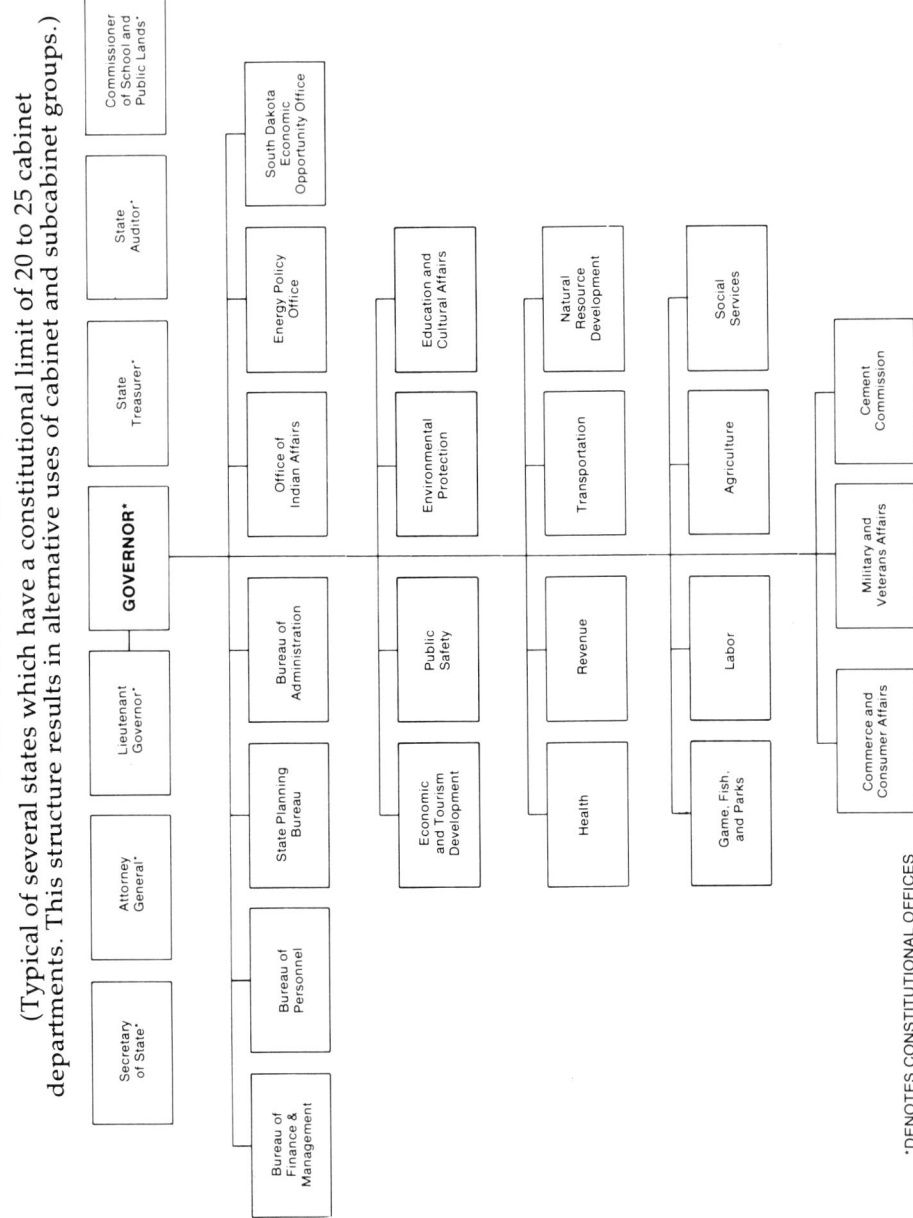

*DENOTES CONSTITUTIONAL OFFICES

APPENDIX 13

Scheduling

How well a Governor manages his time in the face of incredible demands on it will have a large impact on the future success of his administration. Thus, decisions on scheduling policy and procedures are among the most urgent that a new Governor will have to make. The material in this appendix is intended to assist new Governors and their staffs in dealing with this most vexing problem.

The first table, based on responses to a 1976 National Governors' Association survey of Governors and their schedulers, indicates the percentage of the average Governor's working time that is devoted to various major functions. The second table, based on responses to the same 1976 survey, provides guidance as to how experienced Governors would respond to typical requests for their time. The proposed scheduling procedure that follows the tables is adapted from a system, outlined in a memorandum from an executive assistant to his Governor, which has worked successfully in practice. Samples of basic scheduling forms are included at the end of this appendix.

Of course, actual scheduling procedures and forms will differ as Governors and their schedulers adapt them to the needs of their individual states.

HOW GOVERNORS SPEND THEIR TIME

Activity	Column A Schedulers' estimates	Column B Governors' estimates
	(percentage of total work time)	
Managing state government	29	27
Working with the legislature	16	18
Meeting the general public	14	—
Ceremonial functions	14	13
Working with the press and media	9	7
Working with the federal government	7	7
Working with local governments	7	7
Political activities	6	8
Recruiting and appointing	6	8
Miscellaneous activities	16	9

NOTE: Percentages in Column A are based on responses from those handling the Governor's schedule in 40 states; percentages in Column B are based on responses from Governors of 16 states. Totals do not add to 100 percent, but are averages of the respondents' estimates of the portion of a Governor's work time devoted to a particular activity.

GOVERNORS' RESPONSES TO TYPICAL SCHEDULING REQUESTS

Event or Request	Number of States Where Governor Would Accept		
	Generally	Sometimes	Rarely
State fair opening	25	5	7
County fair opening	6	14	16
Highway ribbon cutting	10	18	10
100th anniversary ceremonies for community of 5,000 people	7	16	15
Request by legislator for meeting with group of constituents visiting state capitol with no special business to conduct	26	10	2
Request by freshman legislator to see Governor with no subject specified	31	4	3
Request by more senior legislator (e.g., committee chairman) to see Governor with no subject specified	36	2	1
Request by legislative leader of opposition party to see Governor with no subject specified	35	2	2
Address annual meeting of state chamber of commerce	22	15	1
Address annual meeting of association of homebuilders	10	26	3
Address annual AFL-CIO statewide meeting	30	7	1
Individual citizen with no prior contact with Governor and no organization affiliation wishing to talk to Governor about abortion	2	7	30
Head of small teachers organization wishing to talk to Governor about increased school aid	8	20	11
Head of school administrators association (statewide) wishing to talk to Governor about increased school aid	8	20	11
Group wanting to complain about a department head	5	14	17

NOTE: Responses do not all add to same total because not all respondents answered all questions.

MEMORANDUM

TO: The Governor

SUBJECT: Proposed Scheduling Procedures

Responsibilities

The receptionist in the outer office refers phone requests for meetings with the Governor to the executive (and scheduling) secretary; greets persons wishing to see the Governor; advises the executive secretary of callers who arrive without an appointment; advises the executive secretary of the arrival of scheduled appointments and makes sure they are comfortable if there is a wait.

The executive secretary is responsible for the management of the Governor's daily and advance schedules. She controls, subject to rules indicated below, the movement of people and paper into the Governor's office. She notifies staff members when the Governor is available to see them, escorts people into and out of the office from the outer office, and helps the Governor return phone calls while keeping as close as possible to the schedule. She makes sure (occasionally using backup help) that the Governor has appropriate briefing material before each meeting. She is responsible for all future scheduled activities; she is the keeper of the schedule book, the person who handles all invitations, etc.

The Daily Schedule

Preparation of the daily schedule is the responsibility of the executive secretary. A sample of the daily schedule is attached. The daily schedule shows beginning and ending times for meetings, the persons involved in each appointment (except in the case of large delegations), and the purpose of the meeting.

Every activity on the Governor's schedule should include the name of the staff person responsible for the meeting. This responsibility includes preparing or acquiring the meeting brief (see below) and performing any follow-up on the meeting which the Governor may determine to be necessary.

The daily schedule shall be distributed to the staff by the executive secretary not later than 3:00 p.m. of the preceding day. Copies will go to the Governor, executive assistant, press secretary, reception desk, and other staff members who request copies, and the press.

The Meeting Brief

The staff person or line agency head responsible for a meeting involving the Governor should prepare or acquire a meeting brief. The executive secretary will collect these briefs before the day of the meeting and hold them for attachment to the Governor's copy of the schedule for the proper day. Late briefs that are submitted on the day of the meeting shall go directly to the executive secretary who will give them to the Governor. To keep the system simple, it will be permissible to substitute an oral briefing by the responsible staff member immediately before the meeting, provided that the schedule provides time for it. If the purpose of the meeting is to reach a major decision on governmental policy or management, the Governor must be provided with a more thorough issue analysis.

Schedule Requests

The treatment of schedule requests will vary.

Members of the immediate staff have the privilege of walking into the Governor's office at any time without statement of purpose and without schedule clearance. Except when they are trying to schedule some group, they need not follow regular scheduling procedures. The executive secretary should control their access only to assure that they do not all converge on the Governor at once or while he is making phone calls, but never to challenge their right of access. No paperwork is needed to schedule them.

Another group is the "mandatories" -- those people that the Governor will have to see if they cannot solve their problems in other ways. This group includes staff agency heads, heads of line agencies, legislators, newspaper editors, key party officials, members of the congressional delegation, heads of major interest groups, etc.

The key point in dealing with mandatories is to encourage them to define the reason that they want to see the Governor. This is critical to solving the problem without wasting the Governor's time, to deciding whether a staff member should be present at the meeting, and to providing the Governor with materials that will prepare him for the meeting. Except when the subject is so simple that even a letter would waste everyone's time, every effort should be made to get a written statement of the purpose of the meeting. The executive secretary needs to recognize that the Governor will often be willing to see mandatories on a confidential subject, yet should remind them that it is in their interest to indicate the subject matter in advance of a meeting.

The third category, or "nonmandatories," includes virtually everyone not in the staff or mandatory categories; i.e., constituents, community leaders, businessmen, school children, Girl Scouts, etc. Scheduling requests from this group should always be in writing, especially when such meetings are to be outside the office, so that lines of staff responsibility are clearly established and misunderstandings can be avoided.

Written scheduling requests should indicate the persons attending the meeting, its location, the purpose and extent of the Governor's participation (such as a speech) and details on arrangements (whether a meal will be provided or appropriate dress).

The Advance Schedule

Once a week (preferably Monday morning) the executive secretary will issue the Governor's advance schedule, which receives the same distribution as the daily schedule. The advance schedule will contain all the Governor's future commitments; normally, schedule commitments should not be made more than three months in advance.

The advance schedule indicates when the Governor will be away from the capital, so that staff members can adjust their plans around his and suggest other activities and events that the Governor might schedule for the same trip. The advance schedule also provides a good view of how busy the Governor will be on a particular day.

Memo to the Governor
page 3

Dealing with Scheduling Requests

The executive secretary should meet regularly with the Governor twice a week to discuss his schedule. At that time, the executive secretary should present all proposed additions to previously approved schedules, as well as a comparable list of invitations proposed for rejection with the Governor's approval. The executive assistant should attend these meetings, and the press secretary should be invited to attend whenever possible.

Between the biweekly scheduling meetings, the executive secretary usually will not be able to commit the Governor's time. However, she can handle the situation with mandatories by telling them that she has tentatively scheduled them for a particular time but will have to wait for the scheduling meeting to make sure that the appointment doesn't conflict with the Governor's own plans for that day. This procedure should not be used for nonmandatories or events outside the office. Urgent requests for "same day" appointments must be handled on an ad hoc basis. Between scheduling meetings, the executive assistant -- using discretion on whether checking with the Governor is necessary -- has the authority to commit the Governor's time. No one else can.

Scheduling Rules

The Governor, in consultation with the executive secretary, executive assistant, and the press secretary, should set some scheduling rules which will guide them in making recommendations to the Governor at the scheduling meetings. This should help keep scheduling meetings to 15 minutes. A format designed to be filled out by the Governor for decisions on general scheduling rules is provided below.

1. Never schedule anything in the evening that lasts past ____ p.m.

2. Never schedule anything in the morning that starts before ____ a.m.

3. Always leave for recreational/personal use the following days and times:

Day	Time	
_____	_____ to	_____
_____	_____ to	_____
_____	_____ to	_____

4. Never schedule activities on more than ____ Sundays and ____ Saturdays per month.

5. No more than ____ activities after 6:30 p.m. in a week/month.

6. No more than ____ speeches requiring preparation in a week/month.

7. Allow ____ minutes between scheduled arrival in the office and the first meeting.

8. Allow ____ minutes per day for phone calls, unscheduled visits with immediate staff and in-box.

9. Others.

Memo to the Governor
page 4

Active Scheduling

The Governor is generally welcome anywhere in the state at any time. This is the premise of active scheduling. If the scheduling exercise consists of sorting invitations into piles marked yes and no, the Governor will never control his schedule. Instead he will be operating at the whim and caprice of his staff, agency heads, and program chairmen of various groups and totally missing the many persons whom he must seek out.

An active schedule should first be built around themes of the administration. If employment is to be a theme, the Governor needs to be doing substantive and media events that relate to that theme.

SAMPLE

THE GOVERNOR'S DAILY SCHEDULE

Wednesday, June 7, 1978

Time	Activity	Notes
8:00	Arrive office	
8:15	Scheduled Meeting: Sarah, Tom	Dispose of Scheduling requests (Sarah)
8:45	Taping Session: Bill Jones, UPI Kathy	Taping of State Development Issues (Kathy)
9:15	Briefing: Higher Education Tuition Ted Smith and staff	Background Information (Ted)
10:30	Office work time	
11:15	Leave for drop-in Mental Health Center	Announce Opening New Wing, Luncheon speech (Joan)
1:30	Return office	
1:45	Bill signing: Speaker Thompson and delegation, Joan and media	Sign new criminal code bill (Joan)
2:00	Drop-in: Representative Edwards, Senator Phillips and delegation	Present petition on coal slurry development (Warren)
2:10	Decision meeting: Policy relative to Governor's position on beltway implementation; Jim Brown, Commissioners X and Y	Decide state position on proposed policy resolution (Warren)
3:15	Return phone calls and staff time	
4:00	Briefing: Proposed procedure changes, building board; board members and Ted Smith	No decision required policy meeting to follow (Ted)
4:30	Review Governor's office budget (John)	Decision expected (John)
5:00	Leave for drop-in, state Home Builders at Hotel Plaza, nothing formal, no speech	(highway patrol)
5:30	Leave Hotel Plaza for residence	(highway patrol)
5:45	Return residence	(highway patrol)

SAMPLE

THE GOVERNOR'S ADVANCE SCHEDULE
As of May 19, 1978

Monday, August 21		See daily schedule
Tuesday, August 22	9:00 a.m.	Depart for Falls City
	9:30 a.m.	Groundbreaking, Smith Park
	12:00 noon	Lunch with Tribune editorial staff
	5:00 p.m.	Drop-in, Homebuilders Convention
August 23	8:00 a.m.	Depart for Chicago, Regional Governors' Meeting
	6:30 p.m.	Dinner with friends, Chicago
August 24-25		In office
August 26-30		Vacation, out of office
August 31	6:00 p.m.	Opening remarks, annual meeting, State Education Association
September 14-17		Regional Governors' Conference, Indianapolis
September 24		State Democratic Convention
September 27-29		National Governors' Association, Washington, D.C.

Appointment Request Form

PHOENIX, ARIZONA

Date:_____
Taken by:_____
　　　　　　Initial

REQUEST FOR APPOINTMENT WITH GOVERNOR CASTRO:

Date Requested_____　　Time:_____

Name_____　　Telephone_____

City_____

Subject Matter:_____
_____

Referred to:_____

Appointment Request Form

DATE: _____

REQUEST FOR APPOINTMENT WITH GOVERNOR EDWARDS

FOR: _____

_____ PHONE: _____

REQUEST FROM: _____ PHONE: _____

RE: _____

_____

_____

DATE & TIME: _____ YES _____ NO _____

ALTERNATE: _____ YES _____ NO _____

CALL RECEIVED BY: _____

Preliminary Request

_____ _____
CITY   DATE OF FUNCTION

_____
FUNCTION AND DETAILS

_____
WHERE

_____
DETAILS

CONTACT:

_____   PHONE: (O)_____
NAME

_____   (H)_____
ADDRESS

_____
CITY

REMARKS:
      TIME   DAY   MONTH   YES_____NO_____

Telephone Request for Appearance

TELEPHONE INVITATION TO GOVERNOR CASTRO

DATE_____

TIME OF DAY:_____ DURATION OF EVENT_____

TYPE OF EVENT_____No. Attending_____
      (Name)

CITY_____LOCATION IN CITY_____

INVITATION EXTENDED BY:_____

Address_____Telephone_____

  ACCEPT_____   DECLINE_____

If accepted:

LV. PHOENIX _____ARRIVE_____

DEPART_____ARRIVE BACK IN PHOENIX_____

MODE OF TRANSPORTATION: Auto_____ PLANE_____ Other_____

DRESS: Formal_____ Informal_____

Will Mrs. Castro accompany the Governor? Yes_____ No_____

GOVERNOR WILL BE MET BY_____AT_____

WILL REPRESENTATIVE OF GOVERNOR BE ACCEPTABLE? Yes_____ No_____

Ifso, Name of Representative_____

 Address_____Telephone_____

WILL GOVERNOR DELIVER SPEECH? Yes_____ No_____

 If so, how long & when_____

CC:

Speaking Engagement Form

SPEAKING ENGAGEMENT

DATE: _____ DAY: _____ TIME: _____

ORGANIZATION: _____

WHERE TO BE HELD--ADDRESS & DIRECTIONS:

_____

_____

DINING: ( ) YES   ( ) NO   TIME: _____

PRESIDENT: _____

MAILING ADDRESS: _____ OFFICE PHONE: _____

_____ HOME PHONE: _____

_____

CONTACT: _____ OFFICE PHONE: _____

ADDRESS: _____ HOME PHONE: _____

_____

DETAILS: (Business Suit, casual or formal   (Phone # where Governor can
         wear goes here)   be reached goes here)

REMARKS:

    (# of persons expected
    Agenda and all other pertinant data goes here)

APPENDIX 14

Managing the Mail

The following sample memorandum, drawn largely from an actual memo to a Governor from one of his key staff assistants, illustrates a mail control system that has worked in practice. It is intended to guide new Governors and their staffs in tailoring a system to their own states' needs. Suggested formats for a simple daily mail log, monthly correspondence report, and correspondence routing slip are included at the end of this appendix.

M E M O R A N D U M

TO: The Governor
SUBJECT: Proposed Mail Control System

The essence of this proposed system is that all incoming mail addressed to the Governor is logged in at a single point and assigned to individual staff members. If the mail leaves the office for some intermediate action, such as the preparation of a response by a department, it is logged out and later back in. When final action -- such as sending the Governor's response -- is taken, the log is cleared. The system will have a tickler file for responses that are unreasonably slow and a summary report capability file so that the Governor will know how fast the mail is being answered in terms of both the type of mail and the individual staff member involved. The system will not be applied to mail addressed to persons other than the Governor, but individual staff members can choose to join the system if they desire.

Opening and Sorting

A staff aide for correspondence will open the mail and sort it using these ground rules:

- Publications without a personalized cover letter will not be logged and will be routed to the person who would be most interested in them. Publications transmitted by a personalized cover letter will be treated as normal mail.

- All invitations will go to the scheduler.

- All requests for information about the state, state flags, seals and the like will go to the travel council. Staff will check the way in which these are now handled (e.g., does the Governor get some credit for having sent the materials when the incoming is addressed to him?) and see if the council will also handle sending pictures that do not need special endorsements. Within one week, staff will determine whether the logging system should be applied to these requests and whether the travel council should handle additional mail components such as children's letters.

- All mail that the Governor is likely to want to see before a response is prepared; all mail addressed to the Governor from heads of state agencies; all legislative mail addressed to the Governor; all mail from the congressional delegation (but not their staff members) addressed to the Governor; and all mail that the correspondence aide cannot decide what to do with will go to the executive assistant.

- The Governor will receive directly all truly personal mail, which is mail not related to the management of state government.

Memo to the Governor
page 2

- All mail from any federal official or regarding federal issues will go to the federal-state relations aide unless it falls into one of the classifications above.
- All case mail (including mail dealing with the application of general principles to particular individuals, such as prisoner letters, mental health cases, requests to fix particular roads, complaints about the actions of individual state employees, and the like) will go to the constituent services aide.
- All mail asking about personal characteristics and/or opinions of the Governor or dealing with press matters will be sent to the press aide. Mail with an out-of-state return address will not be logged unless it obviously comes from a source which the Governor would clearly want to respond to.
- Mail requesting proclamations, birthday greetings, autographed baseballs and the like will go to the press office and will be logged if it has an in-state return address.

Log

The correspondence aide will complete a log sheet for each day's mail following the format attached. The log sheets will be kept in a file by the reception desk, which will have the advantage that whoever is working that desk can answer any caller wondering what happened to his correspondence.

When the mail is opened, the correspondence aide will enter the date, the person to whom the correspondence was referred, the sender's name and the subject matter or purpose of the letter. These sheets will normally be handwritten though the sample attached is typed for legibility. The correspondence aide also will assign a suspense date based upon a judgment of the difficulty in responding and the following standard times:

Type of Mail	Working Days
Simple requests for available materials or mail which can be answered with form letters	5
Invitations, requests for meetings	5
Case mail	10
Substantive mail not suitable for form response (e.g., mail urging the Governor to support a particular position)	7
Pro forma responses (e.g., thank you notes)	4

(These standard times are taken from a survey of Governors' offices.)

Action by Staff

The staff member will receive mail for action with no markings other than the date-received stamp. (This means that if the staff member wants to know the suspense date -- which he or she doesn't need to know -- checking with the correspondence aide would be required. Given the standard times listed above a staff member should estimate the suspense date correctly.) For mail that is not referred to a department, the staff member merely prepares whatever reply is necessary. That reply, after signature by the appropriate staff person or the Governor, goes back to the correspondence aide with the envelope. If the originating staff member is going to make copies for any purpose, add two copies of the outgoing and one of the incoming. If no copies are being made for the originating staff member, the correspondence aide will handle copying. The action may also be cleared in ways other than correspondence. If the

Memo to the Governor
page 3

matter is handled by phone or personal contact or a decision is made that no action is required, the staff member merely notes this on the original correspondence and returns it to the correspondence aide. If the aide doubts that the noted action really solved the problem, the correspondence is routed to the executive assistant for approval. If the executive assistant agrees that the action is closed, it is returned to the aide. If not, the matter is reviewed with the staff member involved.

If the matter is to be referred to a department, the staff member involved can exercise one of three options:

- Refer the correspondence to a department with no record and no copy, relying on the overall system to signal when something is overdue. This system is feasible only if the staff member has faith in his ability to recall which department would have been given the letter based upon the short log entry and if the department does not lose the correspondence;
- Refer to the department, keeping one's own records of what was referred to whom when; or
- Refer to department through the correspondence aide. This method has these advantages: (1) there will be a central record of where correspondence is, (2) the correspondence aide will not bother the staff member about deadlines when something is pending in a department, and (3) the aide can follow up with departments or remind the staff member when follow-up is due. The disadvantanges are: (1) the extra routing takes a little longer, and (2) some staff members will want to maintain direct contact with the departments rather than have a more impersonal system. Unless this option is chosen the "Refer to" and "Return to" columns on the mail log will remain blank.

Regardless of the method used to refer to departments, when the proposed response or other information arrives from the department the staff member involved is still responsible for clearing the action by the procedures indicated for those actions that do not require referrals.

Intra-Office Assignments

It will sometimes be the case, particularly with material routed initially to the executive assistant, that some other staff member will be assigned action. When this is the case, the executive assistant (and others) can route through the correspondence secretary, which switches responsibility, or route directly and retain responsibility.

Filing

Two copies of each response will be maintained. One, with the incoming letter, will be filed by subject matter. The other will be circulated in the reading file and filed chronologically.

Reminders

The system is designed to make reminders simple. The correspondence aide should make entries for separate staff members on separate sheets. On the same day each week she should send a copy of all sheets that have overdue actions on them to the staff member involved. The Governor and the executive assistant can determine how the mail flow is going at any time simply by looking at the log book and reduce the need for formal reporting. Initially, however, a formal report should be tried at the end of the first and second months after the initiation of the system. The format for that report is attached. It is compiled simply by counting entries in the log.

Sample Mail Control Forms

DAILY MAIL LOG

Date	Assigned To	Sender	Purpose/Subject	Referred To	Returned To	Ack.?	Suspense	Cleared
10/29	Sarah	R.A. Williams	Late Refund Check	Tax Comm. 11/1	Sarah 11/6	No	11/12	11/7
10/29	"	W.R. Smith	Poor treatment in state hospital			No	11/12	11/5

MONTHLY LOGGED CORRESPONDENCE REPORT
as of (date) _____

Staff Member	Recv.	Items This Month Cleared	In Hand	Today's Overdue	In Hand Month Ago	Overdue Month Ago
Exec. Asst.	200	45		17	40	15

OFFICE OF THE GOVERNOR
ROUTING SLIP

TO: _____

FROM: _____

DATE: _____

DATE COMPLETED ACTION NEEDED _____

_____ For your information

_____ For your comments and return

_____ Please return, with information on which we may base a reply

_____ Reply directly to origin. Return original and copy of reply to this office

_____ Prepare response for Governor's signature

_____ Take action as you deem appropriate

COMMENTS: _____

APPENDIX 15
Budget Agency Functions

	Revenue Estimating (Primary)	Revenue Estimating (Secondary)	Fiscal Research	Fiscal Notes	Organization & Management Analysis	Accounting (Primary)	Accounting (Secondary)	Pre-Audit	Data Processing (Primary)	Data Processing (Secondary)	Legislative Review	Planning	Program Policy/ Issue Analysis	Program Evaluation	Federal/State Relations	Debt Management	Cash Management	Economic Analysis	Other
Alabama																			
Alaska			X	X	X						X		X	X					
American Samoa					X														
Arizona	X		X								X		X		CDE			X	
Arkansas	X		X	X							X	C	X	X	ABCDE			X	X
California	X		X	X		X			X		X		X	X	A	X(1)		X	
Colorado	X		X	X							X	CP	X	X	ABCDE			X	X(2)
Connecticut																			
Delaware			X		X	X									B				
Dist. of Col.																			
Florida	X(3)		X	X(4)	X						X	P	X	X				X	
Georgia	X		X	X(5)	X			X(6)			X	P	X	X	ABC			X	
Guam		X(7)	X	X	X						X	P	X	X	ABC E			X	X(8)
Hawaii	X	X(9)	X	X	X						X	P	X	X	D	X	FG		
Idaho	X		X	X							X		X	X	ABC			X	
Illinois	X		X	X	X						X	FCP	X	X	BCDE	X	X	X	
Indiana	X		X	X							X	P			AC				
Iowa	X		X		X	X			X	X	X		X	X	ABD			X	

Budget Agency Functions (continued)

	Revenue Estimating (Primary)	Revenue Estimating (Secondary)	Fiscal Research	Fiscal Notes	Organization & Management Analysis	Accounting (Primary)	Accounting (Secondary)	Pre-Audit	Data Processing (Primary)	Data Processing (Secondary)	Legislative Review	Planning	Program Policy/Issue Analysis	Program Evaluation	Federal/State Relations	Debt Management	Cash Management	Economic Analysis	Other
Kansas	X		X	X	X						X	P	X	X	A(10)			X	
Kentucky		X(11)	X	X	X							P	X	X	ACD	X	G		
Louisiana	X		X		X	X								X	AC		F	X	
Maine		X(12)	X		X						X				AD				
Maryland		X(13)	X		X				X(14)				X	X					
Massachusetts	X(15)		X								X		X	X	A	X			
Michigan																			
Minnesota	M		M	X	M	M					M			X	ABM	M	GM	M	
Mississippi	X	X	X	X	X								X	X	A				
Missouri	X		X		X						X	LCP	X	X	CDE			X	
Montana	X(16)	X(17)	X	X	X				X		X	FP	X	X	AC			X	
Nebraska		X(18)	X	X	X						X		X	X	Review only				
Nevada	X		X					X			X					X			
New Hampshire	X		X		X							P	X						X(19)
New Jersey	X	X(20)	X	X	X	X		X				P	X	X	CD		FG		X(21)
New Mexico	X		X					X			X	P						X	X(22)
New York	X		X		X			X		X	X	P	X	X					X(23)
North Carolina		X(24)	X		X	X		X			X	P	X	X	BCDE			X	
North Dakota	X		X			X		X				LP	X	X	CE				
Ohio	X		X		X						X		X	X	C	X	X	X	

294

State										Federal/state relations					Cash mgmt
Oklahoma	X									X		X		X	
Oregon		X	X	X						X		X		X	G
Pennsylvania	X(25)	X								X	C	X		X	
Puerto Rico			X			X				X	P	X		X	
Rhode Island	X		X	X	X					X			AC	X(26)	G X(27)
South Carolina	X	X	X		X		X	X					A	X	
South Dakota	X	X	X(28)	X						X(29)	CP	X		X	
Tennessee	X		X				X			X			A		
Texas	X(30)	X								X	LCP	X	ABC	X	
TTPI*															
Utah	X	X			X										
Vermont	X	X	X				X			X		X		X	
Virginia		X								X	CP	X	A	X	X(31)
Virgin Islands	X	X(32)								X	CP	X	C		X(33)
Washington	X(34)	X	X			X				X	CP	X	ABCD		
West Virginia															
Wisconsin	X	X(35)	X	X	X			X	X	X	CP	X	ABCD	X	F
Wyoming	X(36)	X		X	X								C		

SOURCE: National Association of State Budget Officers, *Budgetary Processes in the States* (Washington, D.C.: December 1977), p. 4.

NOTE: In revenue estimating, accounting, and data processing columns, secondary designation means the budget agency is involved in the activity, but another agency has primary responsibility.

CODES: *Planning—*
L — Local
F — Functional
C — Comprehensive state
P — Policy planning
M — Performed by Dept. of Finance (Minnesota) by a unit other than the Budget Division

Federal/state relations—
A — Approval of agency grant applications
B — Planning assistance for and monitoring of grant applications
C — A-95
D — Information on grant awards: 1082 reports, etc.
E — Assistance to agencies and local government on obtaining grants, or information on grant program

Cash management—
F — Receipt and disbursement of cash on a continuing basis
G — Determining, on a continuing basis, amounts to be kept in demand or time deposits, or invested in short- or long-term securities

*Trust Territory of the Pacific Islands

295

Budget Agency Functions (continued)

FOOTNOTES

1. California—Maintaining a central warning system.
2. Colorado—Approval of fund transfers.
3. Florida—Executed through Revenue Estimating Committee comprised of representatives from Division of Budget, Legislature, Comptroller, Depts. of Revenue, Business Regulation and Motor Vehicle and Highway Safety.
4. Florida—Upon request of Governor, Legislature or other.
5. Georgia—Responsibility is joint with the State Auditor's office and Office of Planning and Budget.
6. Georgia—Agency requests equipment purchases, certain contracts and certain personnel actions (have impact on agency's personnel cost).
7. Guam—Dept. of Revenue and Taxation and Dept. of Commerce.
8. Hawaii—Local auditing of territorial programs within the Executive Branch.
9. Hawaii—Dept. of Taxation is responsible for tax revenue estimates working in conjunction with the Governor's Advisory Committee on Tax Revenue Estimates.
10. Kansas—Recommendations on agency grant applications.
11. Kentucky—Department of Revenue.
12. Maine—Agency Collecting Revenue.
13. Maryland—Board of Revenue Estimates.
14. Maryland—One of six large centers.
15. Massachusetts—Responsibility of the Budget Bureau with the aid and counsel of the Department of Corporation and Taxation.
16. Montana—General Fund only.
17. Montana—Dept. of Revenue.
18. Nebraska—Revenue Dept. makes projections with only review function served by Budget Division.
19. New Hampshire—Management supervision; all state agencies.
20. New Jersey—Division of Taxation.
21. New Jersey—Program objective monitoring = monitor programs and their objectives to determine progress in reaching objectives.
22. New Mexico—Review contracts for professional services; review out-of-state travel requests; propose and administer salary plans for exempt employees (political appointments); serve as revenue sharing liaison; draft general appropriations act; prepare capital budgets and plans; budget adjustments.
23. New York—Management assistance and coordination—conducts management surveys; studies specific interdepartmental and intergovernmental problem areas; and develops statewide information systems, organization models and methods, and cost-reduction/productivity-increase plans; state-local relations—monitors the fiscal affairs of New York City and other major urban centers; employee relations and compensation—works closely with state Office of Employee Relations to recommend and evaluate policy on matters affecting the state's relationships with its employees and their representatives and participates in collective negotiations; reviews and recommends policy on public employees retirement plans of the state and its subdivisions; analyzes the provisions and impact of negotiated agreements and other policies affecting terms and conditions of state employment; and administers statewide functions relating to employee compensation.
24. North Carolina—Governor—Advisory Budget Commission—General Assembly.
25. Pennsylvania—Dept. of Revenue.
26. Rhode Island—Recommend bond sale including amount by project and term.
27. Rhode Island—Negotiations of hospital rates. Engineering review of capital projects.
28. South Dakota—Only at the request of legislators.
29. South Dakota—All departments review bills introduced which apply to them.
30. Texas—Comptroller of Public Accounts.
31. Virginia—Development, storage, retrieval and dissemination of data on the social, economic, physical and governmental aspects of the state to provide relevant and reliable information for use in state government and by other governmental bodies.
32. Virgin Islands—Approval of personnel action, approval of fund transfers.
33. Virgin Islands—Coordination of state energy policy.
34. Washington—Dept. of Revenue is responsible for primary revenue estimating for most major taxes; however, this agency has responsibility for all the estimates used for the budget.
35. Wisconsin—By statute, responsible for revenue estimating; however, the Dept. of Revenue provides assistance.
36. Wyoming—State Auditor.

APPENDIX 16

Alternative Planning and Budget Office Locations

The following charts, developed by the National Governors' Association on the basis of the experiences of Governors and their planning and budget officers, illustrate alternative models for organization of the planning and budget functions.

OPTION A: Planning and Budget Combined as a Staff Agency Reporting Directly to the Governor

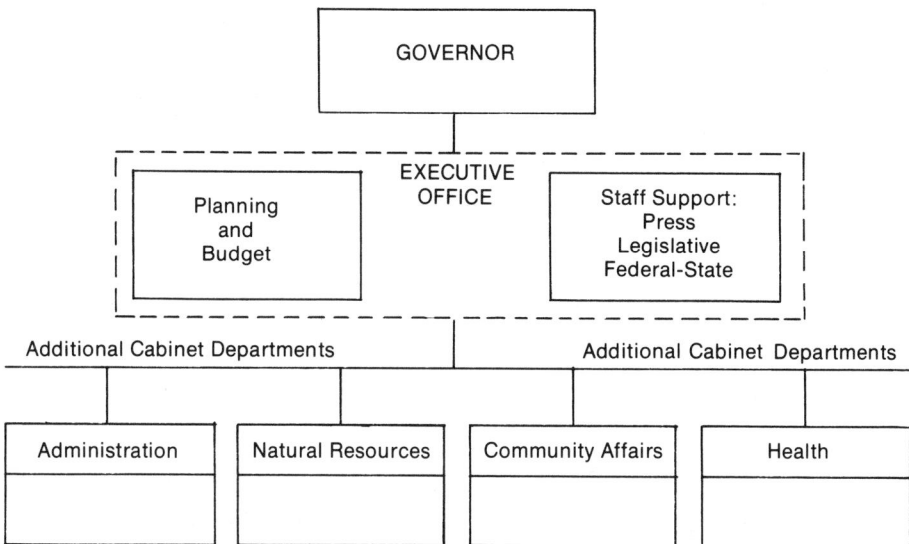

OPTION B: Planning and Budget Combined in an Agency Housing Functions Such as Administration and/or Finance

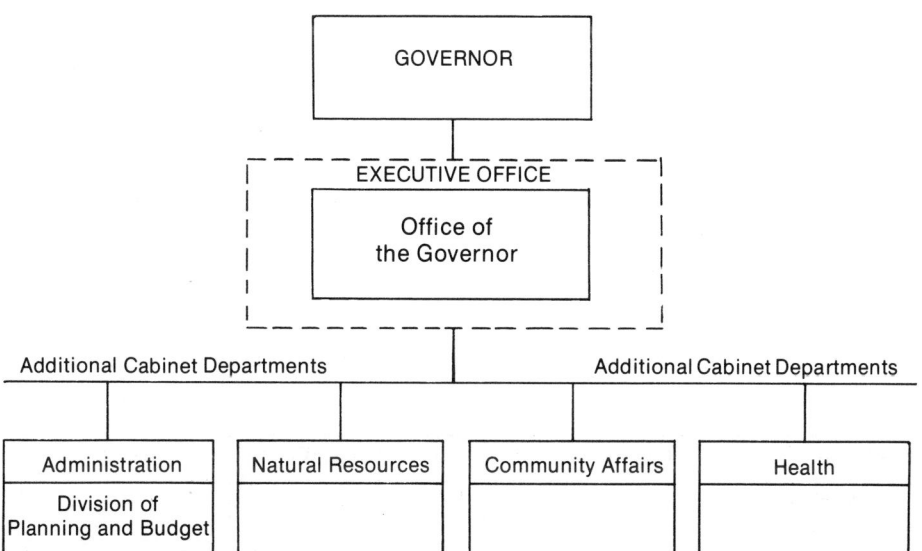

OPTION C: Planning and Budget as Separate Staff Agencies Reporting Directly to the Governor

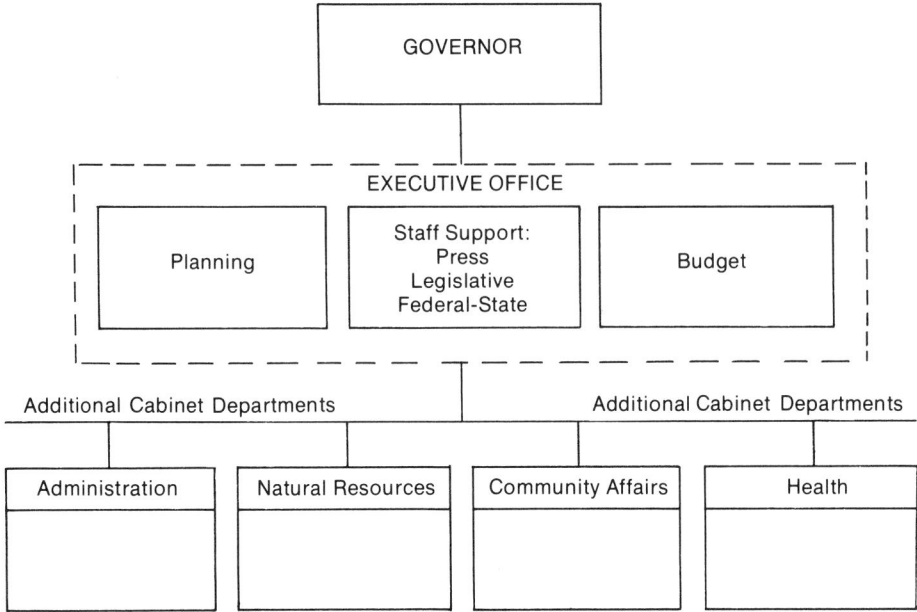

OPTION D: Planning as a Staff Agency Reporting Directly to the Governor and Budget Housed in Administration and/or Finance

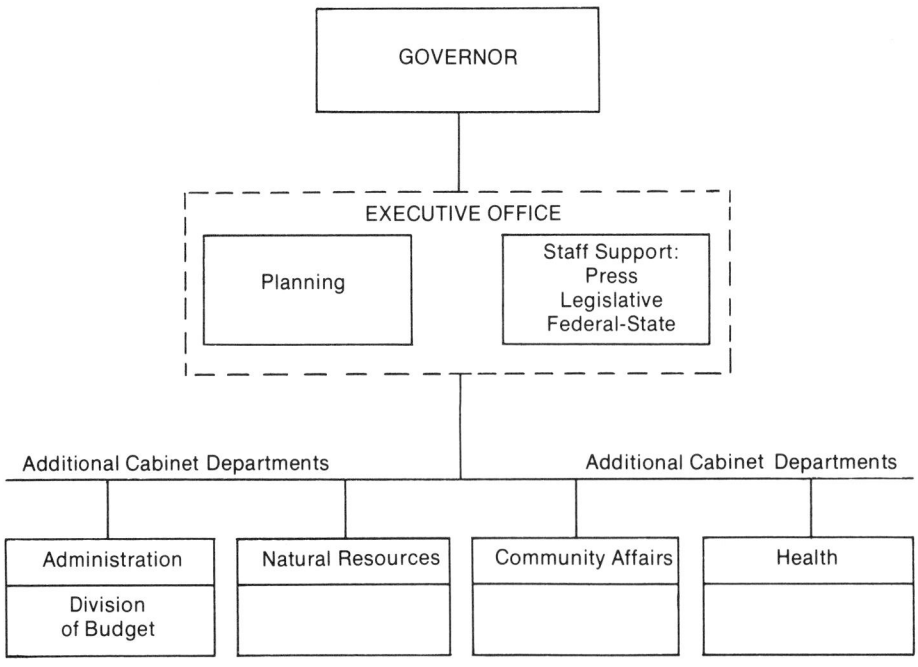

OPTION E: Planning Reporting Through a Line Agency and Budgeting a Separate Staff Agency

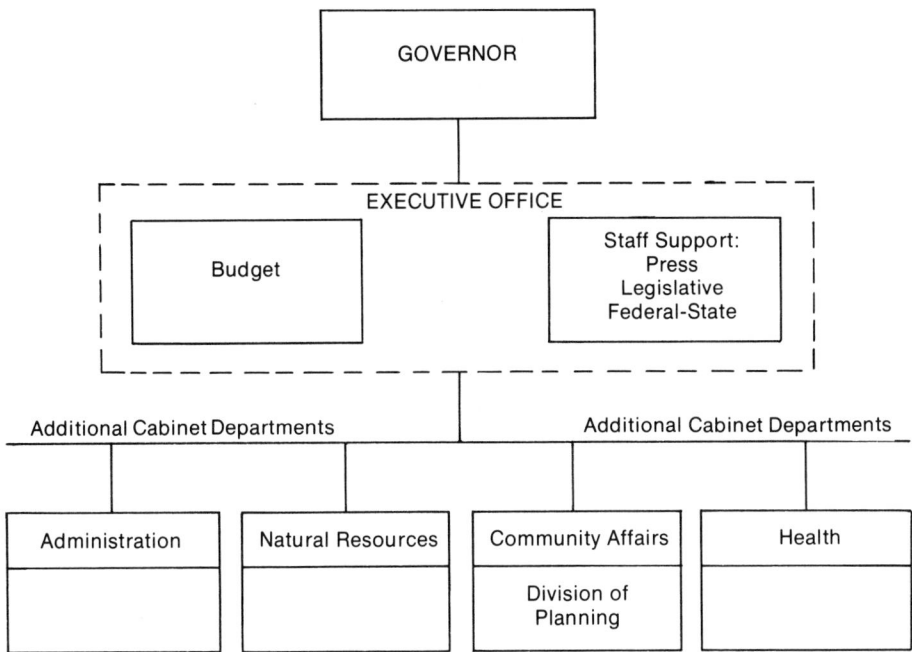

OPTION F: Planning Reporting Through a Line Agency and Budgeting Housed in Administration and/or Finance

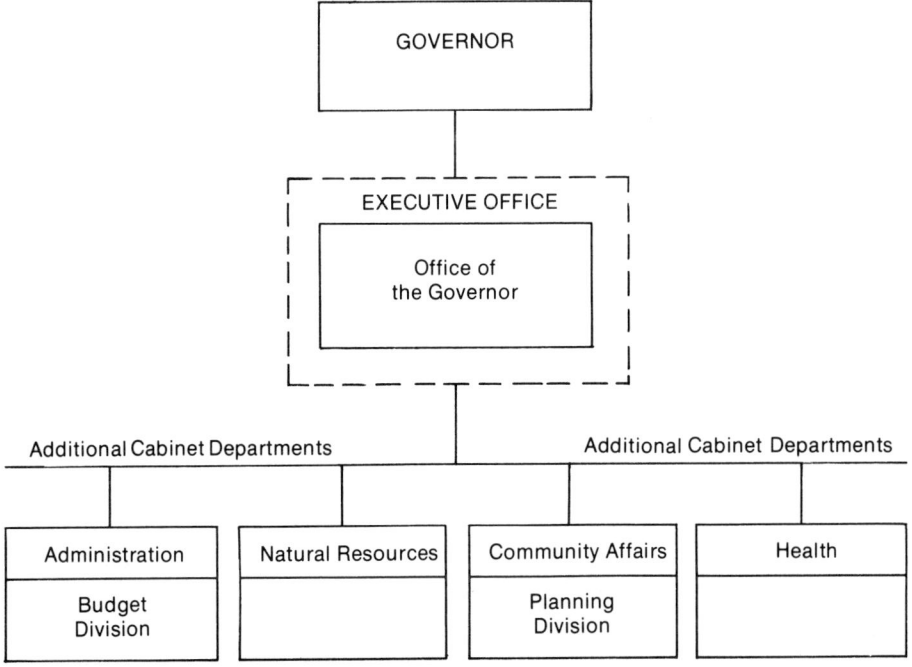

APPENDIX 17

The Governor and the Legislature

Governors may take differing approaches in their relationships with the legislature. In addition to the mechanics of developing and presenting a legislative program, a new Governor must make early decisions on lobbying, dealing with individual legislators, use of staff assistants in legislative relations, and veto policy. The following three tables, based on a 1976 survey by the National Governors' Association, give some indication of how Governors exercise their legislative role. Source for the tables is Thad L. Beyle, "The Governor as Chief Legislator," in *State Government* 51:1 (Winter 1978), pp. 2-10. While responses to the survey were received from 37 states, not all responded to each item. Therefore, the figures in the tables are based on the actual number of responses received for that particular item.

The Governor's Legislative Program

	No. of states	Percent
DEVELOPING THE PROGRAM		
Have a somewhat formalized procedure by which each agency is asked to submit recommendations, which are then reviewed and the agencies advised of what is approved for submission.	22	60
Have a more informal procedure by which agency heads check with legislative liaison or the Governor on what is appropriate to submit.	12	35
Have no procedure at all. Agencies generally make their own decisions.	2	5
IDENTIFYING THE GOVERNOR'S PROGRAM		
A list of bills recommended for enactment by the Governor.	29	90
Distinguish between the Governor's program and the departments' or agencies' programs.	28	78
A prepared summary of the Governor's legislative recommendations.	27	84
Submit draft bills to implement every item in the Governor's legislative program.	20	56
No list of bills, but extracts from messages and press conferences indicating legislation recommended by the Governor.	8	22
Do not use a concept of "Governor's legislative program" as such, although the Governor does from time to time take positions on legislation.	6	17
PRESENTING THE GOVERNOR'S PROGRAM		
Governor presents state of the state message.	36	(35 in person)
Governor presents budget message.	35	(23 in person)
Governor presents other messages (energy, transportation, economy, etc.)	21	(13 in person)

The Governor and the Veto

GOVERNOR'S VETO PHILOSOPHY

	Agree	Disagree
A decision to sign or veto should be based solely on grounds of constitutionality or balancing the budget and the Governor should not interpose his or her feelings or position on the question.	0	32
The considerations that go into the decision to sign or veto legislation should be the same as those that go into a decision on whether to propose a particular bill. All "bad" bills (ones for which the Governor would not vote were he a legislator) should be vetoed.	3	27
In considering whether to veto legislation, the presumption should be that all "bad" bills (as defined above) should be vetoed. However, this presumption should not lead to vetoes in all cases, as political consequences of vetoes need to be taken into account.	14	15
A decision to sign or veto is not the same decision as one a legislator would make to support a particular bill. The presumptions should be that a bill which has passed both houses should be signed unless the Governor has a very strong objection to it.	23	8
Hard case veto: If the administration were confronted with cost-increasing legislation that was very popular (e.g., a tax-relief bill), but which the Governor opposed, although he was certain that the veto would be overridden, would he veto the bill?	Yes—7 Probably yes—21 Probably no—3 No—0	

GOVERNOR'S VETO PROCEDURE

	Yes	Percent
Governor or staff requests comments on legislation from agencies.	34	94
Legislative liaison/staff examines legislation and makes recommendation.	33	94
Legislative liaison/staff requests comments on legislation from affected parties or interest groups.	31	86
Governor routinely receives opinions from attorney general.	16	44
Governor assumes that unless the affected agencies object, they concur in his signing the bill.	12	39
Governor puts the burden of identifying the legislation and initiating comment on the agencies.	9	30
No formalized procedure; each bill handled separately.	4	15

GOVERNOR'S VETO NOTIFICATION PROCEDURE

	Yes	Generally	Sometimes	No
Notifies the affected legislators of intentions.	29	3	3	1
Notifies the affected agency of intentions, if the agency head would have problems with the decision.	30	3	1	2
Is there an appeals process for the agency?	18	...	...	12
Is there ever a public hearing?	2	1 (when written)	1	29

The Governor and Lobbying

LEGISLATIVE ACTIVITIES OF GOVERNOR'S LEGISLATIVE ASSISTANT/STAFF

	Often	Sometimes	Never
Lobby with individual members	31	4	1
Discuss legislative calendar with leadership	22	12	1
Recruit witnesses to testify before committees	16	16	3
Encourage agencies and interest groups to lobby	15	14	6
Provide questions for friendly legislators	13	20	2
Prepare floor speeches	2	19	13

LOBBYING

	Yes	No
Does legislative liaison have floor privileges when legislature is in session?	21	14
Do you have rules regarding lobbying by state agency heads or other state staff?	20	15

Nature of rules:

Must clear positions in advance with Governor's office.	4 states
Traditionally staff & agency heads don't oppose Governor's bills or "linger" near the legislative chamber.	2 states
They are discouraged from these activities but expected to be on call for testimony.	2 states
Registration and reports are required where legislative liaison is not included in job description.	2 states

STATE'S TRADITION ON GOVERNOR/STAFF TESTIFYING BEFORE LEGISLATIVE COMMITTEE

	Will testify upon request	Rarely	Generally no, but depends	Does not testify	Would refuse strong request to appear
Governor	7	2	2	15	2
Executive assistant/chief of staff	27	1	1	2	. . .
Legal counsel	24	1	1	1	. . .
Press or news secretary	10	1	1	16	. . .
Legislative assistant	22	2	2	3	. . .

POLICY FOR DEALING WITH INDIVIDUAL LEGISLATORS

	Yes	Percent
Governor has an open door for legislators. He will always see them; no major efforts are undertaken to divert them to staff members.	27	75
Significant attempts are sometimes taken to handle legislators who wish to see the Governor by having staff members handle their problem, but if a legislator does not find these satisfactory he always has the option of talking to the Governor.	6	17
Combination of 1 and 2 above.	2	6
There are some circumstances where individual legislators will not get to see the Governor even if they insist on it.	1	3

APPENDIX 18
Legislative Program and Procedures

For most new Governors, one of the most difficult challenges is the development of a legislative program and the adoption of a process for dealing with legislators and legislation. The techniques involved vary from state to state, according to constitutional and statutory requirements, legislative-executive traditions, the Governor's style and political strength, and the personalities involved. Although many of the basic principles are the same, there is no method that will work equally well in all states. Nevertheless, the system adopted by one veteran Governor—which is outlined in the following two memos—may be instructive. It utilizes the cabinet subgroup method outlined in a memo by the same Governor in appendix 8.

MEMORANDUM

September 7, 1977

TO: All Members of the Governor's Cabinet

FROM: The Governor

SUBJECT: 1978 Legislative Issue Development Process

This will serve as a follow-up to my memorandum of August 26th [see Cabinet Subgroups, appendix 8] concerning the Policy Development and Issue Identification Process for the 1978 Legislative Session. I ask that the following procedures and schedule be adhered to by all cabinet subgroups as you progress in the consideration of legislative issues.

Allow me to underscore an important point. It is imperative that we have an understanding that no legislative proposals are to be introduced in the 1978 session without my approval. This holds true in all cases -- there will be no exceptions. This was the case last year and in previous years, but with this being the last legislative session of my administration it takes on increased importance.

I will designate the members of this year's Legislative Task Force in the next couple of days. My executive assistant will notify the designated cabinet members so they may begin their work in conjunction with the subgroup activity. As in previous years, my executive assistant will once again serve as the Chairman of the Legislative Task Force.

General Guidelines

1. Beginning now, all subgroups should meet weekly to consider action issues and draft legislation.

2. To the degree possible, all subgroup sessions should be decision oriented. Since we are operating under a restrictive time frame this year, we cannot afford the luxury of prolonged debate on a myriad of issues.

3. Formal parliamentary operating procedures must be utilized at all subgroup sessions.

4. The State Planning Bureau will be responsible for coordination of subgroup activities and preparation of agendas; however, due to time and work-load constraints, each subgroup should make its own arrangements for the preparation of minutes of subgroup sessions.

Memo to Cabinet Members
page 2

5. Periodic meetings of subgroup chairmen and representatives of the Office of the Governor, State Planning Bureau and Bureau of Finance and Management should be held. These meetings should occur approximately every two weeks. The planning bureau will be responsible for calling these sessions.

6. Actions taken on proposed issues by any subgroup should be reported to John Smith in the State Planning Bureau. He has the responsibility of keeping the Governor's office briefed on all outside information.

Schedule of Target Dates

1. September 6 to September 20. Identification and development of action issues. (All agencies.)

2. September 16. Deadline for submission of legislative proposals/ideas having budgetary impacts. (All agencies and the Bureau of Finance and Management.)

3. September 21. All day cabinet meeting and report to the cabinet on progress of legislative process, including identification of legislative themes and preliminary overview of the state's financial condition. (Bureau of Finance and Management, State Planning Bureau, Professor Burns and cabinet subgroups.)

4. October 3. Deadline for preparation of draft legislation for consideration by cabinet subgroups. (All agencies.)

5. October 14. Deadline for draft legislation to clear cabinet subgroups. Subgroups should recommend either: (a) no action/disapproval of proposal; (b) develop as departmental issue; or (c) develop for inclusion in administration's legislative package. (All agencies and cabinet subgroups.)

6. October 15 to October 17. Legislative Task Force completes review of subgroup recommendations. (All day schedule on all three days. Detailed information will be forthcoming from my executive assistant.)

7. November 1. Legislative Task Force completes review of subgroup recommendations and reports to Governor.

8. November 2 to November 18. Subgroups meet to consider referrals from Legislative Task Force. Finalize legislation. (All subgroups.)

9. December 1. Final Legislative Task Force Report to the Governor.

10. GOVERNOR MAKES FINAL DECISION ON 1978 LEGISLATIVE PROGRAM.

Although this schedule does not require subgroup consideration of draft legislation until October, it should be remembered that these are deadline dates. To avoid a pile-up of the work load during October, subgroups should consider and act on draft legislation as soon as possible following its preparation by the lead agency on the issue. Subgroup recommendations on draft legislative proposals should be forwarded to the State Planning Bureau for transmittal to the Legislative Task Force.

Memo to Cabinet Members
page 3

You will note that this entire process has been condensed and "speeded up" compared to past legislative sessions -- in past years, we have at times been making final decisions on legislative proposals even after the actual start of the session. Hopefully, this will not occur this year, and hopefully we will all be able to stick to this schedule. Additionally, all during this scheduled process, my personal staff and I intend to work with the Democratic legislative leadership to get their input in the development of issues. We want to then be able to take our suggestions for legislative proposals and budgetary items to the entire Democratic caucus. Thus, another very important reason for adhering to the schedule is to give us time in the month of December to work with legislators in the sponsorship of bills.

Thank you for your assistance and cooperation in this matter.

cc: Lieutenant Governor
    Executive Assistant to the Governor

M E M O R A N D U M

January 20, 1978

TO: All Members of the Governor's Cabinet
FROM: The Governor
SUBJECT: Legislative Analysis and Procedures

At the January 12th cabinet meeting we discussed procedures executive branch agencies should follow during this legislative session. Out of the meeting came two general statements to guide your activities.

1. Unless I indicate specifically to the contrary, each agency is free to pursue those policies, positions and programs in the legislature that relate to that agency. The bottom line is to work for the passage of proposed legislation in the best interest of your agency and to work for the defeat of that which is not. This is obviously to be done within the context of the policy position I have previously outlined.

2. Agencies must notify the Governor's office of the position and actions they are taking on bills.

This approach will require more communication and coordination between our offices than in recent years if this branch is to adopt a consistent position. The responsibility of notifying my office rests with you. If the policies of the agencies do not correspond, or if our party's legislators take differing positions, I'll attempt to bring the people together to resolve potential conflicts or to arrive at a common understanding of the divergent positions that will be pursued. I reserve the right to make the final determination on the position of the executive branch, but I assure you that, within the time constraints imposed by the session, everyone with an interest in the discussion will be afforded an opportunity to present and defend their points of view before I make a final determination.

The Legislative Task Force will continue throughout the session as a focal point for the resolution of divergent opinion in the executive branch, and as a source of advice and counsel on resolution of differences that might be advocated by our party's legislators, and the executive branch agencies. It will also review activities of the executive branch with respect to enacting bills that I have identified as major pieces of legislation. The purpose of the LTF is to make recommendations to me, and I'll act on these recommendations only after meeting with the affected agencies.

I will attempt to be available each week-day morning at 10:30 a.m. in the Governor's office meeting room to discuss with agencies the recommendations the LTF has made that impact on the agencies. My staff will notify you if an item affecting your agency has been slated for discussion. You will be provided a copy of the recommendation made by the LTF. This 10:30 time slot won't be limited to those items only. You may also use this time to discuss any related legislative matters. If you anticipate coming over to meet with me at that time, please try to let my executive assistant know the day before and tell him what matter you want to discuss. However, even if you cannot anticipate this in advance, feel free to pop in unannounced. This meeting is your forum and I encourage you to use it. I hope we can use these meetings to resolve problems before they get out of hand.

I want to reemphasize the importance of your keeping me informed of your activities. Please send me any handouts, written presentations for committees or floor action, or any other written documentation you develop that would be of benefit to me.

My staff has organized an information system, so we will have background and comments on bills. This information will be retained with the specific piece of legislation so at a glance I can determine the agency positions and read your comments. To insure agency comments on each bill, I have a form that impacted agencies are to complete. The purpose is to provide me with information on the impact that this bill will have, to identify early conflicts between agencies or between agencies and our party's legislators, and to flag bills where the other party's sponsors may be vulnerable to attack. This last one requires political analysis that only cabinet members and their close staff can effectively provide. To insure that the agency view is represented and the political analysis completed, I am requiring that the head of the agency review and sign the form before it is returned.

The form, which accompanies this memo, is self-explanatory, but please note a few items:

A. Information at the top of the form will be filled in by my staff, the rest by you and your agency. The agency contact person should be one that I or members of my staff can contact for additional information. This may be you or someone else in your agency. (You will still have to sign off on each form.)

B. The summary is not to be merely a restatement of what it says on its face. I want to know the real effect of it, what it does and how. What impact it will have on the current organization, structure and functions of state or local government should be stated. This is information that only those of you directly involved in the administration of these programs can provide, so I will rely heavily on this information through the session and again on bills that are passed and come to my desk for action.

C. We are aiming for a turnover of two working days. This may press some agencies, but we have no control over the mechanism or procedures of this session and have to be ready to respond at any time. We will log these summary sheets when they are sent out, so if they are not returned in a timely manner my staff will notify you. This will just help as a reminder to you during this hectic session.

D. You are to retain the second page (yellow copy) for your files. If your agency position shifts on a bill after the first review, complete a blank form with your updated analysis and return it to my office staff. If you intend to take an active position on a bill, but you have not received a form from my office, fill out a blank form and send it over.

These forms are to be all-purpose ones to allow you to continue administering your agency and dealing with the legislature in your own manner. If this paper shuffle causes you significant problems, let me know. To speed delivery of information, try to have the forms hand delivered to my office staff. Because of the confidentiality, all forms are to be transmitted in envelopes.

I fully expect that you will be subject to repeated criticism when actively pursuing policies and programs with the legislature. This criticism is inevitable, but I want each of you to know that I will stand by you when your actions are proper. We need not, and will not, apologize for doing what we believe to be right.

Memo to Cabinet Members
page 3

If you don't have time to notify me of your actions ahead of time, proceed with the assurance that I realize that prior notification is not always possible. However, I do expect to be notified after the fact in these instances. I trust you will always use your best judgment and common sense in these matters, and I can ask no more.

This is to be an open process, and I've attempted to impose only minimum restraints and procedures on you. Where problems arise or you need advice, contact me. I'll make every effort to meet with you, but when that is not possible (which regrettably is too often during the session) I rely on my executive assistant to bring these matters to my attention so I can aid in resolving problems or offering advice.

As a final note, current legislative rules require that agency bills be introduced on the sixth legislative day. To avoid needless controversy, every effort should be made to comply with this requirement. I have been advised that department bills must be noted as such -- so please remind your sponsors of this.

Thank you and good luck!

Sample Legislative Form

Send white copy back   Confidential -- cabinet members and key staff only
to Governor's office   RETURN WITHIN TWO WORKING DAYS
Keep yellow copy for   OFFICE OF THE GOVERNOR
department files   LEGISLATION REVIEW AND ANALYSIS

DATE _____

BILL _____   SPONSORS _____

REVIEWING AGENCY _____ REVIEWING AGENCY _____
****

Agency contact person _____ Phone _____

SUMMARY OF THE BILL (1. Background 2. Problem being addressed 3. How does bill solve the problem) Feel free to attach additional information.

ANTICIPATED POSITION OF THE AGENCY (mark the appropriate spaces):

____ Proposal developed by this agency
____ Support, actively work for passage
____ Support, without active involvement
____ Support, with amendments the agency will propose
____ Neutral
____ Oppose, unless significantly amended
____ Oppose, without active involvement
____ Oppose actively
____ Undecided at this point
____ Other _____

AGENCY COMMENTS AND RECOMMENDATIONS (mark the appropriate spaces):
____ If passed in the present form, a gubernatorial veto should be considered
____ Raises potential constitutional problems or questions
____ If passed, may have significant budgetary implications
____ If passed, major problems may result in the administration of this
____ Not properly drafted, numerous technical problems
____ If passed, would mandate additional staff not in the budget
____ Appears to be an "anti-administration" bill
____ If passed, would serve "special interests" (namely, _____)
____ No apparent need for the bill
____ Agency desires active gubernatorial support of the agency position
____ Makes needed revisions in the statutes
____ If passed, would aid in the proper administration of state government
____ If passed, could be carried out with existing personnel and budgets
____ Needed to meet federal requirements
____ If passed, would jeopardize federal monies
____ Requires two-thirds vote for passage (either emergency or an appropriation)

LIST COMMENTS, ARGUMENTS FOR AND/OR AGAINST THIS BILL

IF ANOTHER AGENCY COULD MORE APPROPRIATELY COMMENT ON THIS BILL, TO WHAT AGENCY WOULD YOU SUGGEST THIS BILL BE REFERRED? _____

PROPOSED AMENDMENTS ATTACHED: _____ yes   _____ no

APPROVED BY _____ DATE _____

Sample Legislative Form

ALASKA
1977 LEGISLATIVE PROPOSAL
REQUEST FORM

AGENCY REQUESTING: Department of _____

Division of _____

Staff Contact _____

SUBJECT OF
PROPOSED BILL: _____
_____
_____

BRIEF SUMMARY: _____
_____
_____

(Attach a more detailed explanation if you can.)

ESTIMATED FISCAL
IMPACT: _____

OTHER STATE AGENCIES
CONSULTED: _____
_____

CONSTITUENT GROUPS:

    Those Opposed: _____
_____

    Those in favor: _____
_____

    Those yet to be
    contacted: _____

Has this or a substantially similar bill been introduced in the Legislature in the past? Yes_____ No_____ Bill No._____.

PREFERRED HOUSE OF INTRODUCTION: _____

RATE THE BILL'S IMPORTANCE TO DEPARTMENT: _____

DRAFT ATTACHED: Yes_____ No_____

APPROVAL BY COMMISSIONER: _____

DATE: _____

Selected Bibliography

Interest in state Governors and their roles within the American federal system has increased in recent years. The studies, monographs and reports cited in the following bibliography also indicate that a broader perspective of analysis is evolving in recognition of the growth in the capacity and scope of state governments and of the expanding role of Governors.

In order to provide new Governors, their staffs, and others interested in the Governor and his office with a guide to the available literature, this bibliography was assembled by Stephen Bernheim, Thad L. Beyle and Charles H. Williams of the University of North Carolina at Chapel Hill. It was derived chiefly from an earlier work by Thad Beyle and J. Oliver Williams, *The American Governor in Behavioral Perspective;* Larry Sabato's recent book on the modern Governorship, *Goodbye to Good-Time Charlie: The American Governor Transformed, 1950-1975;* files of the National Governors' Association; and a review of recent publications by practitioners and scholars.

Selected Bibliography

Abernathy, Byron R. "The Governor's Removal Power." In Joseph F. Zimmerman, ed., *Subnational Politics: Readings in State and Local Government*. 2nd ed. New York: Holt, Rinehart and Winston, 1970.

———. *Some Persisting Questions Concerning the Constitutional State Executive*. Governmental Research Series no. 23. Lawrence: University of Kansas, 1960.

Ahlberg, Clark D., and Moynihan, Daniel P. "Changing Governors—and Policies." *Public Administration Review* 20 (Autumn 1960), pp. 195-205.

Alexander, Herbert E., and McKeough, Kevin L. *Financing Campaigns for Governor: New Jersey, 1965*. Study no. 16. Princeton: Citizens' Research Foundation, 1966.

Allen, David J. *New Governor in Indiana: The Challenge of Executive Power*. Bloomington: Indiana University, Institute of Public Administration, 1965.

Anderson, William, et al. *Government in the Fifty States*. New York: Holt, Rinehart and Winston, 1960.

Anton, Thomas J. *The Politics of State Expenditure in Illinois*. Urbana: University of Illinois Press, 1966.

Backman, Ada E. "The Item Veto Power of the Executive." *Temple Law Quarterly* 31 (Fall 1957), pp. 27-34.

Baldwin, Thomas F., and Newton, Lowell. "State Government and Broadcast News: A Survey of Facilities, Services and Attitudes." *Journal of Broadcasting* 12 (Spring 1968), pp. 145-154.

Bane, Frank. "The Job of Being a Governor." *State Government* 31 (Summer 1958), pp. 184-189.

Barone, Michael, et al. *The Almanac of American Politics 1976: The Senators, The Representatives, The Governors—Their Records, States, and Districts*. New York: Dutton, 1975.

Battle, John S. "Work of the Governor's Office." Proceedings of the Sixty-Fourth Annual Meeting of the Virginia State Bar Association, 1954, pp. 230-237.

Bell, James R., and Ashley, T. J. *Executives in California Government*. Belmont, Calif.: Dickinson Publishing Co., 1967.

Bell, James R., and Darrah, Earl L. *State Executive Reorganization*. 1961 Legislative Problems no. 3. Berkeley: Bureau of Public Administration, University of California, 1961.

Belluch, Bernard. *Franklin D. Roosevelt as Governor of New York*. New York: Columbia University Press, 1955.

Berman, David R. *State and Local Politics*. Boston: Holbrook Press, 1975.

Bernick, Emil Lee. "The Role of the Governor in the Legislative Process: A Comparative State Analysis." Ph.D. dissertation, Department of Political Science, University of Oklahoma, 1976.

Bernstein, Melvin H. "Political Leadership in California: A Study of Four Governors." Ph.D. dissertation, Department of Political Science, University of California, Los Angeles, 1970.

Beyle, Thad L. "The Governor as Chief Legislator." *State Government* 51:1 (Winter 1978), pp. 2-10.

———. "The Governor's Formal Powers: A View from the Governor's Chair." *Public Administration Review* 28 (November/December 1968), pp. 540-545.

———. "The North Carolina Governorship: An Agenda." *NCInsight* 1:4 (Autumn 1978), Raleigh: North Carolina Center for Public Policy Research, p. 4.

———. "State Executives." Richard H. Leach, ed., *Compacts of Antiquity: State Constitutions*. Atlanta: Southern Newspaper Publishers Association Foundation, 1969, pp. 27-34.

Beyle, Thad L., and Wickman, John E. "Gubernatorial Transition in a One-Party Setting." *Public Administration Review* 30 (January/February 1970), pp. 10-17.

Beyle, Thad L., and Williams, J. Oliver. *The American Governor in Behavioral Perspective*. New York: Harper & Row, 1972.

Black, Earl. *Southern Governors and Civil Rights: Racial Segregation as a Campaign Issue in the Second Reconstruction*. Cambridge: Harvard University Press, 1976.

———. "Southern Governors and Political Change: Campaign Stances on Racial Segregation and Economic Development, 1950-1969." *Journal of Politics* 33:3 (August 1971), pp. 703-734.

———. "Southern Governors and the Negro: Race as a Campaign Issue since 1954." Ph.D. dissertation, Department of Government, Harvard University, 1968.

Botner, Stanley B. "Gubernatorial Succession—Question in Several States." *University of Missouri Business and Government Review* 6 (March-April 1965), pp. 24-30.

Bradley, Leonard Keelon, Jr. "Gubernatorial Transition in Tennessee: The 1970-1971 Experience." Master's thesis, Department of Political Science, University of Tennessee, Knoxville, 1973.

Brooks, Glenn. "The Business of Being Governor." *State Government* 31 (Summer 1958), pp. 145-149.

———. *When Governors Convene: The Governors' Conference and National Politics*. Baltimore: Johns Hopkins Press, 1961.

Buechner, John C. *State Government in the Twentieth Century*. Boston: Houghton Mifflin, 1967.

Burke, Timothy P. "The Partial Veto Power: Legislation by the Governor." *Washington Law Review* 49 (February 1974), pp. 603-616.

Burns, Robert V. "The Politics of State Executive Branch Reorganization with Special Emphasis on the Role of Staff: The South Dakota Case." Ph.D. dissertation, Department of Political Science, University of Missouri-Columbia, 1975.

Carleton, William G. "The Southern Politician 1900 and 1950." *Journal of Politics* 13 (May 1951), pp. 215-231.

Carley, David L. "Legal and Extra-Legal Powers of Wisconsin Governors in Legislative Relations." *Wisconsin Law Review*. January/February 1962, pp. 3-64; 280-341.

Carone, Patrick A. "The Governor as a Legislator in West Virginia." Ph.D. dissertation, Department of Political Science, Duke University, 1969.

Carter, Dale E. "When Governors Change: Symbolic Output and Political Support." Institute of Governmental Affairs Research Report no. 5. Davis, Calif.: Institute of Governmental Affairs, University of California, 1968.

Chase, Karen A. *Reorganization of State Government: A Selective Bibliography*. Berkeley: Institute of Governmental Studies, University of California, 1968.

Cheatham, Richard. "An Overview of Contemporary Gubernatorial Inaugurals." *Southern Speech Communication Journal* 40 (1975), pp. 191-203.

Coffman, Tom. *Catch a Wave: A Case Study of Hawaii's New Politics*. Honolulu: University Press of Hawaii, 1977.

Committee for Economic Development. *Modernizing State Government*. New York: Committee for Economic Development, 1967, pp. 45-61.

Connery, Robert, and Benjamin, Gerald, eds. *Governing New York State: The Rockefeller Years*. New York: Academy of Political Science, 1974.

Connor, J. E., and Morgan, R. E. "Governor and the Executive Establishment." *Academy of Political Science Proceedings* (January 1967), pp. 173-182.

Cornwell, Elmer E., Jr., et al. "Professional Staff for Governors' Offices Subject of Questionnaires." *Bulletin of the Bureau of Government Research*. University of Rhode Island, September 1968, pp. 1-2.

Council of State Governments. "Bibliography: Seminar for New Governors-Elect." Lexington, Ky., November 1970, pp. 1-5.

———. *The Book of the States*. Chicago and Lexington, Ky., published biennially.

———. *Budgeting by the States*. Lexington, Ky., 1967.

———. *Central Management in the States*. Lexington, Ky., 1970.

———. *The Governors of the States, 1900-1974*. Lexington, Ky., 1974, compiled by Samuel R. Solomon.

———. *The Governors: The Office and Its Powers*. Lexington, Ky., 1972.

———. *Gubernatorial Transition in the States*. Lexington, Ky., 1974.

———. *Issues in Gubernatorial Succession*. Chicago, 1969.

———. *National Governors' Conference, 1908-1968*. Chicago, 1968.

———. *Reorganizing State Government: A Report on Administrative Management in the States and a Review of Recent Trends in Reorganization*. Chicago, 1950.

———. *Selected Bibliography on State Government: 1959-1972.* Lexington, Ky., 1972, p. 237.

———. "Trends of State Government: As Indicated by the Governors' Messages." *State Government* (published annually in the spring or summer issue).

Council of State Planning Agencies. *The State Planning Series.* Edited by David K. Hartley and Dwight E. Jensen. 16 vols. Washington, D.C., 1977.

Cowart, Andrew T. "Electoral Choice in the American States: Incumbency Effects, Partisan Forces, and Divergent Partisan Majorities." *American Political Science Review* 67 (September 1973) pp. 835-853.

Cox, James L. "Executive Reorganization in Delaware." *State Government* 43 (Summer 1970), pp. 184-190.

Crittenden, John. "Dimensions of Modernization in the American States." *American Political Science Review* 61 (December 1967).

Darrah, Earl L., and **Poland, Orville.** *Fifty State Governments: A Comparison of State Executive Organization Charts.* Berkeley: Bureau of Public Administration, University of California, 1961.

Dennis, James M. "State Executive Branch Reorganization: The Case of Florida." Ph.D. dissertation, Department of Political Science, University of Florida, 1974.

Derthick, Martha. *Between State and Nation: Regional Organizations of the United States.* Washington, D.C.: Brookings Institution, 1974.

Di Salle, Michael V. *The Power of Life or Death.* New York: Random House, 1965.

Dolliver, James. "State Planning and the Governor's Office." *State Planning Issues.* Lexington, Ky.: Council of State Governments, May 1973, pp. 39-40.

Dometrius, Nelson C. "Measuring Gubernatorial Power." *Journal of Politics,* forthcoming.

Douglas, Charles G., III. "Gubernatorial Veto Power in New Hampshire." *New Hampshire Bar Journal* 15 (1973) pp. 9-18.

Dye, Thomas R. "Executive Power and Public Policy in the States." *Western Political Quarterly* 27 (December 1969), pp. 926-939.

———. *Politics in States and Communities.* 3rd ed. Englewood Cliffs, N.J.: Prentice-Hall, 1977.

Egger, Rowland. "The Governorship of Virginia, 1776 and 1976." *University of Virginia Newsletter* 52 (August 1976), pp. 41-44.

Eley, Lynn W. *The Executive Reorganization Plan: A Survey of State Experience.* Berkeley: Institute of Governmental Studies, University of California, 1967.

Eli, Jack C. "A Study of Political Attitudes and Voting Behavior in the 1970 Tennessee Gubernatorial Election." Ph.D. dissertation, Department of Speech, Southern Illinois University, 1971.

Engleman, Jerald L. "Emergency Powers of the Governor in North Dakota." *North Dakota Law Review* 50 (Fall 1973), pp. 101-116.

Eulau, Heinz, and **Koff, David.** "Occupational Mobility and Political Career." *Western Political Quarterly* 15 (September 1962), pp. 507-521.

Fannin, Paul, et al. *The Office of Governor in Arizona.* Phoenix: Bureau of Government Research, Arizona State University, 1964.

Farber, Daniel. "Executive Privilege at the State Level." *University of Illinois Law Forum* (1974), pp. 631-648.

Favoriti, Richard E. "Executive Orders—Has Illinois a Strong Governor Concept?" *Loyola University Law Journal* 7 (Spring 1976), pp. 295-311.

Flinn, Thomas. "Governor and Legislature: A Case Study in Political Decision-Making." Ph.D. dissertation, Department of Political Science, University of Minnesota, 1957.

———. *The Governor and the Minnesota Budget.* Inter-University Case Program no. 60. New York and Indianapolis: Bobbs-Merrill, 1961.

Fox, Douglas M. *The Politics of City and State Bureaucracy.* Pacific Palisades, Calif.: Goodyear Publishing Co., 1974.

Gale, Frederick K. "A Study of the Relationships Among the Indiana State Board of Education, the State Superintendent of Public Instruction, and the Governor." Ed.D. dissertation, Department of Education, Ball State University, 1970.

Gantt, Fred, Jr. *The Chief Executive in Texas: A Study in Gubernatorial Leadership.* Austin: University of Texas Press, 1964.

———. "The Governor's Veto in Texas: An Absolute Negative?" *Public Affairs Comment* 15:2 (March 1969). Austin: Institute of Public Affairs, University of Texas.

Gately, James J. *A Register of the Governors of the States of the United States of America, 1776-1974.* Collingswood, N.J.: Gateford Publications, 1974.

Gere, Edwin A. "Patterns of Federal-Regional Interstate Cooperation in New England." Ph.D. dissertation, Department of Political Science, State University of New York, 1968.

Gibson, Lorenzo T. "The Role of Governor in the Legislative Process: A Comparative Study of the Governor of Maryland and the Governor of Virginia." Ph.D. dissertation, Department of Political Science, University of Virginia, 1968.

Gleason, Eugene J., Jr., and Zimmerman, Joseph F. "Executive Dominance in New York State." Paper presented to the Northeastern Political Science Association, Saratoga Springs, N.Y., November 9, 1974.

Gove, Samuel K. "Why Strong Governors?" *National Civic Review* 53 (March 1964), pp. 131-136.

Graves, W. Brocke. *American Intergovernmental Relations: Their Origins, Historical Development and Current Status.* New York: Scribner's, 1964.

Gray, Virginia. "Innovation in the States: A Diffusion Study." *American Political Science Review* 67 (December 1973), pp. 1174-1185.

Grupp, Fred W., Jr. "Variations in Elite Perceptions of American States as Referents for Public Policy Making." *American Political Science Review* 69 (September 1975), pp. 850-858.

"Gubernatorial Executive Orders as Devices for Administrative Direction and Control." *Iowa Law Review* 50 (Fall 1964), pp. 78-98.

Guida, Joseph F. "Prisoner or Keeper?—The Management Styles of Two Virginia Governors." Undergraduate honors thesis, University of Virginia, Charlottesville, 1976.

Haider, Donald. *When Governments Come to Washington: Governors, Mayors and Intergovernmental Lobbying.* New York: Free Press, 1974.

Hain, Paul L., and Smith, Terry B. "Congress: New Training Ground for Governors?" *State Government* 48:2 (Spring 1975), pp. 114-115.

Hale, George E. "A Field Interview Study of the Effect of Executive Leadership Style on the State Budgetary Process in Delaware During the Peterson and Tribbett Administrations." Ph.D. dissertation, Department of Political Science, Syracuse University, 1975.

Halevy, Balfour J. *A Selective Bibliography on State Constitutional Revision.* New York: National Municipal League, 1963.

Harvard, William C., ed. *The Changing Politics of the South.* Baton Rouge: Louisiana State University Press, 1972.

Havel, James T. "The Executive Veto in Kansas." *Bulletin of Governmental Research Center.* Lawrence: University of Kansas, March 15, 1969, pp. 1-3.

Herman, William R. *The National Economy and the Governors.* Washington, D.C.: National Governors' Conference Center for Policy Research and Analysis, Report no. 3, August 1975.

Herndon, James, et al. *A Selected Bibliography of Materials in State Government and Politics.* Lexington: Bureau of Government Research, University of Kentucky, 1963.

Hevesi, Alan G. *Legislative Politics In New York State: A Comparative Analysis.* New York: Praeger, 1975. See especially chapter 7, "The Governor as Lawmaker," pp. 81-128.

Hirst, David W. *Woodrow Wilson: Reform Governor. A Documentary Narrative.* New York: N. J. Van Nostrand Reinhold, 1965.

Hodges, Luther H. *Businessman in the Statehouse: Six Years as Governor of North Carolina.* Chapel Hill: University of North Carolina Press, 1962.

Hoopes, Roy. *What a State Governor Does.* New York: John Day, 1973.

Howard, S. Kenneth. *Changing State Budgeting.* Lexington, Ky.: Council of State Governments, 1973.

Hy, Ronald. "An Inquiry into Policy Values in the States of the United States: A Content Analysis of the American Governors, 1943 to 1971." Ph.D. dissertation, Department of Political Science, Miami University, 1972.

Hyman, Drew W. "Citizen's Advocacy and Political Responsiveness in a Polycentric Political System: A Study of the Governor's Branch Offices in Pennsylvania." Ph.D. dissertation, Department of Political Science, University of California, Los Angeles, 1975.

Inlander, David W. "Dilemma in Springfield: The Scope and Limitations of the Governor's Amendatory Veto Power in Illinois." *Loyola University Law Journal* 5 (Summer 1974), pp. 394-411.

Iowa, State of. *The Governor's Office.* Office of the Governor, Des Moines, 1968.

Ivy, Glenn H. "An Organization Structure for Gubernatorial Leadership in Texas State Government." Ph.D. dissertation, Department of Political Science, University of Texas, 1970.

Jauchius, Rollin D. "Gubernatorial Roles: An Assessment by Five Ohio Governors." Ph.D. dissertation, Department of Political Science, Ohio State University, 1971.

Jewell, Malcolm E. "State Decision-Making: The Governor Revisited." In Aaron Wildavsky and Nelson Polsby, eds., *American Governmental Institutions*. Chicago: Rand McNally, 1968, pp. 545-565.

———. "Voting Turnout in State Gubernatorial Primaries." *Western Political Quarterly* 30:2 (June 1977), pp. 236-255.

Johnson, James A. R. "Volunteers in State Programs." *State Government* (Spring 1974), pp. 67-70.

Kallenbach, Joseph E. *The American Chief Executive: The Presidency and the Governorship*. New York: Harper & Row, 1966.

Kallenbach, Joseph E., and Kallenbach, J. S. *American State Governors 1776-1976*. Dobbs Ferry, N. Y.: Oceana Press, 1977.

Key, V. O., Jr. *American State Politics: An Introduction*. New York: Knopf, 1957.

Kidman, Peter N. "Gubernatorial Transition in West Virginia." Ph.D. dissertation, Department of Political Science, University of West Virginia, 1972.

———. "Gubernatorial Transition in West Virginia." Paper delivered at the West Virginia Political Science Association Meeting, October 1972.

Kress, Guenther. "When Governors Change: The Case of Medi-Cal." Davis: Institute of Governmental Affairs, University of California, Research Report no. 4, 1971.

Lipson, Leslie. *The American Governor: From Figurehead to Leader*. New York: Greenwood Press, 1968.

Lockard, Duane. *The New Jersey Governor: A Study in Political Power*. New York: Van Nostrand Reinhold, 1964.

———. *The Politics of State and Local Government*. New York: Macmillan, 1963.

Lockard, Duane, ed. "A Mini-Symposium—The Strong Governorship: Status and Problems." *Public Administration Review* 36:1 (January/February 1976), pp. 90-98.

Locke, Russell A. "State Executive Positions and Political Careers." Ph.D. dissertation, Department of Political Science, Tulane University, 1972.

Lucey, Patrick J. "Wisconsin's Productivity Policy." *Public Administration Review* 32:6 (November/December 1972), pp. 795-799.

Maher, Theodore J. "Power to the States: Mobilizing Public Technology." *State Government*. Spring 1972, pp. 124-134.

Maine, State of. *The Governor's Office: A Manual of Operations*. Office of the Governor, Augusta, 1974.

Martin, James W. *An Executive Office of the Governor for Kentucky*. Lexington: College of Business and Economics, University of Kentucky, 1972.

———. *Staffing the Office of the Governor*. Lexington, Ky.: Council of State Governments, 1971.

McCall, Tom. "Oregon: Come Visit but Don't Stay." *State Government*. Summer 1973. Special issue on land use.

McCally, Sarah P. "The Governor and His Legislative Party." *American Political Science Review* 60 (December 1966), pp. 923-942.

McGown, Wayne F. "Gubernatorial Transition in Wisconsin." *State Government* 44 (Spring 1971), pp. 103-106.

McNatt, Hugh B. "Constitutional Law—Incumbency Prohibition—Is Georgia In Step with the Times?" *Mercer Law Review* 22 (Winter 1971), pp. 473-479.

Mercer, Gordon E. "The Southern State Executive: A Study of Political, Social and Psychological Characteristics." Ph.D. dissertation, Department of Political Science, University of Florida, 1971.

Michaelson, Ronald D. "An Analysis of the Chief Executive: How the Governor Uses His Time." *State Government*, Summer 1972, pp. 153-160.

———. "The Illinois Executive and Urban Problems." In The Illinois Assembly on the Office of Governor. *The State and the Urban Crisis*. Urbana: Institute of Government and Public Affairs, University of Illinois, 1970, pp. 27-35.

———. "The Politics of Gubernatorial Endorsements in Cook County, Illinois: An Empirical Analysis." Ph.D. dissertation, Department of Political Science, Southern Illinois University, 1970.

Mileur, Jerome M. "The Politics of State Administrative Reorganization Studies." *Bulletin of the Bureau of Government Research*. University of Massachusetts, December 1967, pp. 1-4.

Miller, Edward J. "Executive Legislative Relations in Maryland: The Governor as Chief Legislator." Ph.D. dissertation, Department of Political Science, University of Pittsburgh, 1973.

———. "The Governor and Legislation: The Initiation of Central Clearance in Maryland." *State Government*, Spring 1974, pp. 94-95.

Morehouse, Sarah McCally. "The Governor as Political Leader." In Herbert Jacob and Kenneth Vines, eds., *Politics in the American States: A Comparative Analysis.* 3rd ed. Boston: Little, Brown & Co., 1976, pp. 196-241.

———. "The State Political Party and the Policy-Making Process." *American Political Science Review* 67 (March 1973), pp. 55-72.

Morey, Roy D. *Politics and Legislation: The Office of Governor in Arizona.* Arizona Government Studies no. 3. Tucson: University of Arizona, Institute of Government Research, 1965.

Mosher, Frederick C. "Limitations and Problems of PPBS in the States." *Public Administration Review* 29 (March/April 1969), pp. 160-167.

Muchmore, Lynn. "The Governor and the Planner." *State Planning Issues* 1:1 (Spring 1976), pp. 1-4.

National Governors' Association. *Charting New Directions: The Governors' State of the State Messages 1978.* Washington, D.C., February 1978.

———. *Governors of the American States, Commonwealths & Territories 1978: Biographical Sketches and Portraits.* Washington, D.C., February 1978. Editions previous to 1977 published for the National Governors' Conference by the Council of State Governments, Lexington, Ky.

———. *1978 Directory of Staff Assistants to the Governors.* Washington, D.C., 1978. Published annually.

National Governors' Conference (now National Governors' Association). *The American Governors: Their Backgrounds, Occupations, and Experience.* Washington, D.C., June 1975. Previous editions published by the Council of State Governments, Lexington, Ky.

———. *Constraint and Concern: The Governors' State of the State Messages.* Washington, D.C., February 1976.

———. *The Critical Hundred Days: A Handbook for the New Governor.* Washington, D.C., 1975.

———. *Federal Roadblocks to Efficient State Government,* vol. 1, and vol. 2, *Agenda for Intergovernmental Reform.* Washington, D.C., 1977.

———. *The Governors' Contribution to the Quest for National Energy Policy and Program.* Washington, D.C., 1975.

———. *The Governor's Office.* 10 vols. Washington, D.C., 1976.

———. *Innovations in State Government: Messages from the Governors.* Washington, D.C., June 1974.

———. *Making Hard Choices: The Governors' State of the State Messages.* Washington, D.C., February 1977.

———. *Meet the Governors.* Excerpted from the 65th Annual Meeting of the National Governors' Conference, Lake Tahoe, Nevada, June 4, 1973. Lexington, Ky., 1973.

———. *On Being Governor.* Governor's Office Series no. 1. Washington, D.C., 1976.

———. *Proceedings of the National Governors' Conference 1976.* Sixty-eighth Annual Meeting, Hershey, Pa., July 4-6, 1976. Washington, D.C., 1976. Proceedings of previous annual meetings published for the National Governors'Conference by the Council of State Governments, Lexington, Ky. and Chicago, Ill.

———. *States' Responsibilities to Local Governments: An Action Agenda.* Washington, D.C., 1975.

Nunn, Robert W. "Oregon's Display Lighting Ban and the Governor's Emergency Powers." *Oregon Law Review* 54 (1973), pp. 669-675.

Olsen, Raymond T. "The American Governor: Executive Management for System Change." *State Government,* Winter 1971, pp. 26-30.

Olson, David J. "Citizen Grievance Letters as a Gubernatorial Control Device in Wisconsin." *Journal of Politics* 31 (August 1969), pp. 741-755.

Olson, Kenneth C. *The Proliferation of State Executive Branch Associations.* Washington, D.C.: National Governors' Conference, August 1975. Adapted from reports submitted by the author to National Governors' Conference meetings, February and June 1975.

———. *The States, Governors and Policy Management.* Washington, D.C.: National Governors' Conference Center for Policy Research and Analysis, Report no. 2, July 1975.

———. "The States, Governors and Policy Management: Changing the Equilibrium of the Federal System." *Public Administration Review* 35 (December 1975), special issue on policy management, pp. 764-770.

Ransone, Coleman B., Jr. "The American Governor in the 1970s." *Public Administration Review* 30 (January 1970), pp. 1-44.

———. *The Office of Governor in the United States.* University, Ala.: University of Alabama Press, 1956.

———. "Political Leadership in the Governor's Office." *Journal of Politics* 26 (February 1964), pp. 197-220.

———. "Scholarly Revolt in Dullsville: New Approaches to the Study of State Government." *Public Administration Review* 26 (December 1966), pp. 343-352.

Rich, Bennett M. "The Governor as Administrative Head." In John P. Wheeler, Jr., ed., *Salient Issues of Constitutional Reform*. State Constitutional Studies Project, series 1, no. 2. New York: National Municipal League, 1961, pp. 98-114.

———. "The Governor as Policy Leader." In John P. Wheeler, Jr., ed., *Salient Issues of Constitutional Reform*. State Constitutional Studies Project, series 1, no. 2. New York: National Municipal League, 1961, pp. 80-97.

———. *State Constitutions: The Governor*. State Constitutional Studies Project, series 2, no. 3. New York: National Municipal League, 1960.

Ries, John C. *Executives in the American Political System*. Belmont, Calif.: Dickenson Publishing Co., 1969.

Ringham, Stuart R. "The Governor-Elect to Governor: Transition in the American States." Ph.D. dissertation, Department of Political Science, University of Iowa, 1972.

Roberts, Nancy. *The Governor*. New York: Charlotte, McNally and Lofflin, 1972.

Roeder, Richard B. "Energy in the Executive." *Montana Law Review* 33 (Winter 1972), pp. 1-13.

Rose, Douglas D. "National and Local Forces in State Politics: The Implication of Multi-Level Policy Analysis." *American Political Science Review* 67 (December 1973), pp. 1162-1173.

Sabato, Larry. *Aftermath of 'Armageddon': An Analysis of the 1973 Virginia Gubernatorial Election*. Charlottesville: Institute of Government, University of Virginia, 1975.

———. *Goodbye to Good-Time Charlie: The American Governor Transformed, 1950-1975*. Lexington, Mass.: Lexington Books, 1978.

Sanford, Terry. *But What About the People?* New York: Harper & Row, 1966.

———. *Storm Over the States*. New York: McGraw-Hill, 1967.

Schlesinger, Joseph A. *Ambition and Politics: Political Careers in the U.S.* Chicago: Rand McNally, 1966.

———. "The Governor's Place in American Politics." *Public Administration Review* 30 (January/February 1970), pp. 2-10.

———. *How They Became Governor: A Study of Comparative State Politics, 1870-1950*. East Lansing: Michigan State University Press, 1957.

———. "The Politics of the Executive." In Herbert Jacob and Kenneth N. Vines, eds., *Politics in the American States: A Comparative Analysis*. 2nd ed. Boston: Little, Brown & Co., 1971, pp. 210-237.

Schultze, William A. "On the Governors' Powers." In James A. Reidal, ed., *New Perspectives in State and Local Politics*. Waltham, Mass.: Xerox College Publishing, 1971, pp. 247-266.

Silverman, Jason. "Governor William Gilpin and the Southerners." *The Social Science Journal* 14:1 (January 1977), pp. 127-139.

Smith, Hulett C. "West Virginia's Constitution and the Governor." *West Virginia Law Review* 71 (April-June 1969), pp. 253-259.

Solomon, Samuel R. "The Governor as Legislator." *National Municipal Review* 40 (November 1951), pp. 515-520.

———. "Governors, 1950-1960." *National Civic Review* 49 (September 1960), pp. 410-416.

———. "Governors, 1960-1970." *National Civic Review* 60:3 (March 1971), pp. 126-146.

———. "United States Governors, 1940-1950." *National Municipal Review* 41 (April 1952), pp. 190-197.

Sprengel, Donald P. *Gubernatorial Staffs: Functional and Political Profiles*. Iowa City: Institute of Public Affairs, University of Iowa, 1969.

———. "Legislative Perceptions of Gubernatorial Power in North Carolina." Ph.D. dissertation, Department of Political Science, University of North Carolina, Chapel Hill, 1966.

Stewart, John C. *Governors of Alabama*. Baltimore: Pelican Press, 1975.

Stratton, William G. "A Former Governor Views the Office." In Joseph F. Zimmerman, ed., *Subnational Politics: Readings in State and Local Government*. 2nd ed. New York: Holt, Rinehart and Winston, 1970.

Sullivan, Gerald E. "Incremental Budget-Making in the American States: A Test of the Anton Model." *Journal of Politics* 34 (1972), pp. 639-647.

Swinerton, E. Nelson. "Ambition and American State Executives." *Midwest Journal of Political Science* 12 (November 1968), pp. 538-549.

Tarver, Gene F. "A Comparative Study of Gubernatorial Roles in Four Southern States." Ph.D. dissertation, Department of Political Science, University of Kentucky, n.d.

Trickey, David F. "Constitutional and Statutory Bases of Governors' Emergency Powers." *Michigan Law Review* 64 (December 1965), pp. 290-307.

Tropp, Peter. "Governors' and Mayors' Offices: The Role of the Staff." *National Civic Review* 63:5 (May 1974), pp. 242-249.

Turett, J. Stephen. "The Vulnerability of American Governors, 1900-1969." *Midwest Journal of Political Science* 15 (February 1971), pp. 108-132.

Vaughn, James M. "Constitutional Law—The Governor's Item Veto Power." *Missouri Law Review* 39 (Winter 1974), pp. 105-110.

Victorson, Morton J. "Gubernatorial Election 1972: A Perspective from West Virginia Political History." Paper delivered at the West Virginia Political Science Association Meeting, October 1972.

Walker, Harvey. *Executive-Legislative Relations*. Constitutional Studies Project. New York: National Municipal League, 1959.

Walker, Jack L. "The Diffusion of Innovations Among the American States." *American Political Science Review* 63 (September 1969), pp. 880-889.

Way, Almon L., Jr. "The Role of the Governor in the State Legislative Process: A Case Study of South Carolina." Ph.D. dissertation, Department of Political Science, University of South Carolina, 1974.

Welsh, Matthew E. "The Role of the Governor in the 1970s." *Public Administration Review* 30 (January/February 1970), pp. 24-26.

Wendelsdorf, Scott T. "Constitutional Law—The Power of a Governor to Proclaim Martial Law and Use State Military Forces to Suppress Campus Demonstrations." *Kentucky Law Journal* 59 (1970-1971), pp. 547-572.

Williams, Charles H. "The 'Gatekeeper' Function on the Governor's Staff." *Western Political Quarterly*, forthcoming.

Williams, G. Mennen. *A Governor's Notes*. Ann Arbor: Institute of Public Administration, University of Michigan, 1961.

Williams, John R. "Nebraska Governors and Education—1905-1915 and 1955-1965." Ph.D. dissertation, Department of Education, University of Nebraska, 1970.

Williamson, Homer E. "Legislative-Executive Relations in Minnesota." Ph.D. dissertation, Department of Political Science, University of Minnesota, 1971.

Wisconsin, State of. "The Executive Office Transition." Madison: Office of the Governor, November 1970.

Wood, Robert C. "The Metropolitan Governor: Three Case Inquiries into the Substance of State Executive Management." Ph.D. dissertation, Harvard University, Department of Government, 1949.

Wright, Deil S. "Executive Leadership in State Administration: Interplay of Gubernatorial, Legislative and Administrative Power." *Midwest Journal of Political Science* 11 (February 1967), pp. 1-26.

———. *Understanding Intergovernmental Relations: Public Policy and Participant Perspectives in Local, State, and National Governments*. North Scituate, Mass.: Duxbury Press, 1978.

Wyner, Alan J. "The Governor as Political Leader and Chief Executive." Paper delivered at the National Conference on Government, National Municipal League, Boston, November 1965.

———. "Governor-Salesman: Restrictions on Executives Have Caused Many to Focus on Industrial Promotion and Good Publicity." *National Civic Review* 56 (February 1967), pp. 81-86.

———. "The Governor's Office: 14 Offices as Seen by Participant Observers." Ph.D. dissertation, Department of Political Science, Ohio State University, 1968.

———. "Gubernatorial Relations with Legislators and Administrators." *State Government* 41 (Summer 1968), pp. 199-203.

———. "Staffing the Governor's Office." *Public Administration Review* 30 (January/February 1970), pp. 17-24.

Zimmerman, James L. "The Office of Governor of New York: Its Development Under Nelson A. Rockefeller." Master's thesis, Baruch College of the City University of New York, 1972.